CONTENTS

Acknowledgements

To all of those who contributed time, attention, and energy to this project, we offer our heartfelt appreciation.

We are especially grateful for the capable and tremendously helpful input from our editor and publisher at the Book Publishing Company, Cynthia and Bob Holzapfel, and Gwynelle Dismukes and the other editors who helped with the production, Warren Jefferson for the cover design, and Barb Bloomfield for food styling.

Deepest appreciation to our cherished advisers and those who shared with us many hours of valuable insight: Michael Klaper, MD; Registered Dietitians Dr. Janice Joneja, Shelley Case, Janet Krenz, Jan Patenaude, Brenda Davis, and Lisa Monteiro.

Special thanks to those who helped with research: Syd Baumel; Dr. Gurdev and Dr. Karen Parmar; Jonathan Bean; Chanchal Cabrera; Dr. Paul Appleby; Dr. Stephen Walsh; Dr. Zoue Lloyd-Wright; Dr. John Livesay; John Davis; and Meghan Fitzpatrick.

Warm acknowledgement to those who gave of their time and energy to sample recipes, give feedback and suggestions, and support this project in a variety of ways: Michael Stepaniak; Daniel Aronson; Dennis Palmer; Laughing Rivers Sangha and The Community of Mindful Living in Pittsburgh; Barb Bloomfield; Bhora Derry; Bob Sidebotham; Patrick, Lalita, and Samera Hamill-Maeyer; Kurtis Conlinn; Valerie McIntyre; Alan Carpenter; Marj Rodwell; Gerry Kilgannon; Casper Bych; Jan Bulman; Pam Lucke; Sam Jeong; Soban Jeong; Nygal Brownson; Andrea Welling; Lizanne Foster; Joseph Forest; Laura Bruno; Ethan J. DeMitchell; Melanie Joy; Nancy Lanctot; and Susan Solomon.

Sincere gratitude to those who provided samples of their outstanding products for development and testing of our recipes: Bob's Red Mill and Dennis Gilliam; Ener-G-Foods and Jerry Colburn; Enjoy Life Foods and Bert Cohen; Omega Nutrition and Robert Gaffney; Grainworks and Doreen and Dwayne Smith; Nature's Path and Arran Stephens; Eden Foods and Celeste Kukla.

FOOD ALLERGY SURVIVAL GUIDE

WITHDRAWN

Surviving and Thriving with Food Allergies and Sensitivities

Vesanto Melina, MS, RD
Jo Stepaniak, MSEd
Dina Aronson, MS, RD

Healthy Living Publications
Summertown, Tennessee

Cover design: Warren Jefferson, Cynthia Holzapfel
Interior design: Gwynelle Dismukes
Cover photo: Warren Jefferson
Food styling: Barb Bloomfield

Published in the United States by
Healthy Living Publications
an imprint of
Book Publishing Company
P.O. Box 99
Summertown, TN 38483
1-888-260-8458

Printed in the United States

ISBN 1-57067-163-X

09 08 07 06 05 04   6 5 4 3 2 1

Pictured on the cover from left:

cherry pie with Perfection Pie Crust, pp. 196-97,

Gluten-Free Pizza Crust, pp. 190-91,
    with Pizza Party options, pp. 312-13,

Pumpkin Spice Bread, p. 194

Melina, Vesanto, 1942-
    Food allergy survival guide: surviving and thriving with food allergies and sensitivities / Vesanto Melina, Jo Stepaniak, Dina Aronson.
        p. cm.
    Includes bibliographical references and index.
    ISBN 1-57067-163-X
    1. Food allergy. 2. Food allergy–Diet therapy–Recipes. I. Stepaniak, Joanne, 1954- II. Aronson, Dina L. III. Title.

RC596.M45 2004
616.97'50654--dc22

                    2004014203

The information in this book is presented for educational purposes only. It is not intended to be a substitute for the medical advice of your healthcare professional.

Introduction

There was a time when people believed that a health-supportive diet had to be centered on animal products. Eggs were revered as the gold standard among proteins. Milk was described as nature's perfect food. Fish was included in menus at least once or twice a week. Balancing this mix with a little plant food was wheat, considered the staff of life.

In recent years, our attitudes towards every one of these foods have changed. Health professionals now are concerned about the cholesterol and saturated fats in eggs, dairy, and other animal products. Fish and other seafood are so contaminated by mercury, pesticides, and other unpleasant substances that pregnant women are cautioned about their use or advised to avoid them entirely. Foods of animal origin, including seafood, dairy products, and eggs, come with a hefty price tag in terms of environmental damage. Wheat sensitivities have become so common that many pasta houses serve optional rice noodles, and mainstream supermarkets stock rice cakes.

Nowadays, it is clear that centering one's diet on vegetables and fruits gives us the leading edge when it comes to protection against chronic disease. These colorful items give us more total vitamins, minerals, antioxidants, and other protective phytochemicals per calorie than any other categories of foods. It has become trendy to eat a significant amount of one's diet as raw foods and to balance the veggies and fruits with gluten-free grains and legumes. Simple fare and a plant-centered diet provide a firm foundation for overall health—and this same approach serves us well when it comes to food allergies.

This book combines the professional expertise of two leading dietitians with that of one of the best cookbook writers and recipe developers of our time. Here you will find a unique combination of the latest scientific information, culinary expertise, practical tips, and wisdom based on experience. You'll discover how to avoid the foods and ingredients that trigger reactions. You'll learn to create menus that meet your nutritional requirements; this is a tremendously important aspect of maintaining good health while dealing with food sensitivities. Using these recipes will help you stay well nourished with delicious meals. With each recipe you will find a nutritional analysis showing the protein, dietary fiber, minerals, vitamins, and essential fats provided in every serving.

The three authors are not only experts in their field, but they have personal experience with the topics in this book. Each brings a unique perspective, based on different geographical locations, talent, and experience. Vesanto is a wise woman of the west, with a wealth of experience, wisdom, and scientific expertise. Jo is sensitive, shy, and poetical by nature. She has an extraordinarily well-developed sense of taste and texture; for this and her culinary skills, you can thank the recipe treasures that you will find here. Dina is young, fiery, and a whiz with computers and research; she started out as a fast-paced New Yorker and hasn't slowed down since.

It is our sincere hope that this book will provide a wealth of practical information and support for you and your family. We wish you abundant health, joy, and peace.

Vesanto, Jo, and Dina

For author contact and biographical information,
please see pages 363 and 382–383.

Chapter 1

WHAT ARE FOOD SENSITIVITIES?

*D*uring the course of a lifetime each of us is likely to eat an estimated two to three tons of food. Yet when food sensitivities arise, it seems probable that we'll drop far below our quota. Longtime favorites may be banned from our menus. Familiar choices on restaurant menus now are impossible. The easy ways in which we put meals together in the past have become fraught with difficulties. If we knowingly or unsuspectingly consume a forbidden ingredient, we pay a terrible toll. We weep when we view the discomfort experienced by our children who have food allergies.

This book is designed to bring a large measure of relief to these difficult situations. It will provide you with a new world of delicious and nourishing foods and help you with challenges that may at first seem almost insurmountable. One of our goals is to help you achieve and maintain a nutritionally adequate diet, despite your restrictions.

Reactions to food can be experienced in many different parts of our body and range from mild irritation to life-threatening anaphylactic responses. In this book we distinguish between food allergies, intolerances, and sensitivities. The accepted scientific meanings of these words are shown in the box on the next page.

True food allergy, also known as food hypersensitivity, is actually a case of mistaken identity. Our symptoms are an inappropriate (and often very uncomfortable) response by the immune system to an otherwise harmless substance in food, typically a protein. If our immune system failed to respond as it does, that food would not pose a threat to us. Our response is like that of the knight-errant Don Quixote, who attacked windmills under the notion that these were dangerous giants, who righted "wrongs" (where none existed), and who attempted "rescues" with disastrous results.

Beyond these immune system responses is a broad group of food intolerances, which are reactions to small molecules that are digested or tolerated well by some of us, and not by others.

Whether appropriate or not, food sensitivities certainly can wreak havoc in our lives! Fortunately, much can be done to avoid or minimize symptoms and discomfort without using drugs that have unwanted side effects. Despite food sensitivities, we can enjoy an extensive and varied diet. In fact, with a little know-how, being well nourished becomes simple. Instead of viewing with despair a list of forbidden foods, we can plan flavorful and appealing meals for the day. Our food sensitivities may shepherd us to a path of excellent health, a diet of nourishing whole foods, and a lifestyle that steers clear of problematic situations or that manages them gracefully. In other words, our food sensitivities may turn out to be a blessing.

> - **Food allergy** is the reaction of the body's immune system to a food or food ingredient that it recognizes as "foreign."
>
> - **Food intolerance** is an adverse reaction to a food, food ingredient, or additive that does not involve the immune system. It typically involves the digestive system.
>
> - **Food sensitivity** includes both allergy and intolerance.

The Immune System: Our Protection Against Disease

The "Defense" Process: An Inside Look at Chemical Warfare

To understand food allergy, it is useful to observe the immune system's reaction to foreign organisms, such as bacteria and viruses that would harm us. The immune system effectively defends our cells against potential disease-causing organisms in this manner:

- recognize the invader;
- classify it as dangerous;
- prepare a tailor-made defense; and
- destroy the invader.

When a *phagocyte*, which is a large white cell found in the blood, encounters a bacterium or virus, it engulfs the foreign cell and creates a "pocket" around that cell, into which powerful destructive chemicals are released. As a result, the foreign cell is broken down into fragments. The large white cell then displays the fragments of the destroyed cell on its outside surface.

The cells that belong in our bodies also display fragments. These are the equivalent of identification cards, indicating the right of these cells to be present in the body.

Other white cells called *T cells* are circulating in the blood and are on the lookout for anything foreign. They examine these fragments. If foreign material is detected, the T cells determine whether to mount a counterattack specific to that type and species of foreign cell. T cells take on roles as controllers of operations, overseeing the defense process from beginning to end. When they receive a message from T cells, another class of white blood cells called *B cells* do their part. In response to foreign fragments called *antigens* (which are protein or protein-sugar molecules), the B cells create *antibodies* that will immobilize the type of virus or bacterium carrying that antigen. The antibody is a precision weapon, tailor-made to lock onto that antigen and allow the destruction of those particular foreign cells. On some future occasion, when foreign cells carrying that antigen enter the body, the result is chemical warfare.

Chemical weapons are supplied by cells that are armed with an arsenal of destructive chemicals known as *inflammatory mediators*. Some of these cells are continually circulating in the blood, ready to release their arsenal at any time. Others, called *mast cells*, are present in our skin and in the moist mucus membranes that line the lungs, nasal passages, and digestive tract.

When foreign cells that can cause disease invade the body, these immune system cells release inflammatory mediators in an attack on the invaders. While this is happening, our symptoms arise. We feel feverish, chilled, or ill; we experience aches and pains. These symptoms do not come from the foreign virus or bacteria; they result from our immune system fighting the foreign cell. When we develop a rash, as in measles or smallpox, the rash is caused by the immune system producing and releasing inflammatory mediators. When we cut our hand, inflammation develops at the wound site and we observe reddening, swelling, and pain. These symptoms are evidence of our immune system in action as it mounts an attack on potential disease-causing organisms that may enter the cut. At the time of the cut, these responses may seem bothersome; however, they play a part in our protection.

Food Allergy: Defense at Our Own Expense

The actions of the immune system against food allergens have many similarities to its actions against foreign bacteria or viruses. Again, they follow this sequence:
- recognize the invader, in this case, a food fragment or molecule called an *allergen*;
- classify it as dangerous;
- prepare a tailor-made defense; and
- destroy the invader by unleashing destructive chemicals.

The first time an allergen (which is typically a protein) enters the body, it does not trigger an allergic reaction; however, the body becomes *sensitized*. During sensitization, the immune system is alerted to the presence of the allergen, determines that this substance poses a threat, and prepares its defense. The next time the allergen enters the body, the immune system is ready to launch its counterattack. A complex series of events occurs, with each successive stage dependent upon the preceding stage.

At the beginning of this chapter, we said that the food allergy response is inappropriate. Here's why. Food components are not there to cause disease, as is the case with foreign bacteria and viruses, and do not warrant this massive defense.

Nonetheless it occurs in those of us who experience food allergies. The immune system reacts to food proteins (allergens) by producing antibodies. These in turn cause mast cells and similar immune system cells to release chemicals, causing inflammation. As in the protective response against potential disease, our tissues heat up. Access routes (blood vessels) widen to allow more chemicals to come to the defense. Our body quickly produces more cells to join our army. Body tissues may become red, swollen, and warm with increased flow of blood and body fluids. Symptoms differ depending on which part of the body is the site of the action: the skin, head, muscles around the lungs, mucous membranes in the nose or digestive tract, or other regions as shown in table 1.1. The weapons of defense hurt our body's own cells and result in mild to severe symptoms on the skin or in the respiratory, nervous, or digestive system. For theories on why these reactions occur in some of us and not in others, and why the incidence has dramatically increased in recent decades, see pages 14–18.

Our Arsenal of Chemical Weapons

The inflammatory mediators that we release include histamine, prostaglandins, leukotrienes, and bradykinins, each with specific effects. Enzymes that may cause tissue damage are also released. Histamine is a powerful mediator that can
- cause blood vessels to widen;
- allow fluids and proteins that are normally contained by blood vessels to leak through;
- increase the secretion of mucus by mucous membranes;
- cause muscles (such as those around the lungs) to contract; and
- stimulate nerves, creating an "itch."

Histamine can be created and released by mast cells in many parts of the body. Exactly what we experience depends on the area in which the histamine is acting.

Prostaglandins and leukotrienes (hormone-like chemicals made from fatty acids), and bradykinins (chains that are nine amino acids in length), can
- control the dilation of blood vessels;
- increase the secretion of mucus by mucous membranes;
- cause constriction of muscles around the lungs;
- control pain, swelling, and muscle contraction;
- move cells containing inflammatory mediators from one place to another; and
- act on the nervous system and gastrointestinal tract.

Allergy Symptoms with No Allergen

Symptoms might occasionally occur though no food allergen has recently been consumed. For example, when we are under stress we may release hormones that make our immune system more likely to react. Cold air can lead to a runny nose or asthma attack. Skin may react to physical irritation. Chemicals other than food allergens can result in intestinal inflammation and irritable bowel syndrome.

Symptoms of Food Sensitivity

Adverse reactions to foods can appear in various target areas of the body, as shown in table 1.1. A reaction will appear in one location for one individual, while another person has an entirely different experience. For one person, the skin may be particularly vulnerable to attack. Patches near the mouth or on another part of the face swell, redden, break out in hives, and itch; or eczema may develop on the hands. For another, the nose becomes stuffy and runny, or the lungs go into spasm. Some people develop mild or severe headaches. A common target area is the digestive tract, which can react to allergens from one end to the other. Many people show symptoms in more than one of these areas.

TABLE 1.1. FOOD SENSITIVITY SYMPTOMS AND CONDITIONS	
Skin and mucous membranes	Eczema; hives; redness; swelling of deeper tissues in the mouth and face; itching.
Respiratory tract	Runny nose; sneezing; itchy, watery, and reddened eyes; earache with fluid drainage; throat tightening (due to tissues swelling); asthma (recurring attacks of labored breathing, chest constriction, lung spasm, and coughing).
Nervous system	Migraines or other headaches; dizziness; spots before the eyes; listlessness; hyperactivity; fatigue; lack of concentration; irritability; depression.
Digestive tract	Nausea; vomiting; diarrhea; constipation; belching; indigestion; stomach or abdominal pains; bloating.
Other	Muscle aches; dark circles under the eyes; sweating.

Severity of Symptoms

Symptoms range from mild irritation to severe responses involving the whole body. For an individual, various conditions can affect the severity of reactions. If more than one type of allergen is encountered at once, more inflammatory chemicals may be released, heightening the response. Inflammation in the digestive system due to infection, for example, can make it easier for allergens to get into our bodies, increasing the impact. Alcohol, when consumed at the same time as an allergen, can result in greater absorption of an allergen. While exercise is generally a health benefit, vigorous exercise following exposure to an allergenic food may stimulate an allergic reaction for some people (for more information about this, see page 127). Under stressful conditions, allergy symptoms seem to appear or worsen.

In contrast, there is some scientific evidence that stress-management and relaxation techniques may reduce symptoms in a variety of conditions that may be linked with food sensitivities, such as dermatitis. It has been demonstrated that serum levels of histamine can be altered by relaxation. Studies of asthmatics have shown that improved control of breathing, by practicing yoga or breathing exercises, may contribute to the successful control of asthma. Research indicates that programs that include relaxation techniques can reduce pain in people with various forms of arthritis. Scientists have shown relaxation, biofeedback, and stress-management techniques to be effective in reducing headache activity by 35–50 percent. Chapter 7 provides additional tips for fostering a nurturing, supportive environment in spite of food sensitivities.

Anaphylactic Reactions

Anaphylactic (originally meaning "no protection") reactions are severe, rapid reactions involving most organ systems of the body. In the most extreme cases, the reaction turns into anaphylactic shock, cardiac collapse, and death. Fortunately, some protection is now available for people who face the possibility of these serious, potential reactions. They must take great care to avoid their specific allergens and always

> ## Important Reading for Those with Serious or Anaphylactic Reactions
>
> If you or someone you love has a potential for these reactions, we advise you to familiarize yourself with in-depth food allergy information that reaches beyond the scope of this book. We recommend the excellent book *Dealing with Food Allergies: A practical guide to detecting culprit foods and eating a healthy, enjoyable diet*, by Janice Vickerstaff Joneja. Bull Publishing, Colorado, 2003.

carry with them a kit containing injectable adrenaline (epinephrine) and an oral antihistamine in case of accidental exposure. (To read more about this, see chapter 7, page 125.) Foods most commonly implicated in anaphylactic reactions are peanuts, tree nuts, shellfish, and fish.

Apart from anaphylactic reactions, the symptoms of food allergy tend to be similar to those of food intolerance and occur in the same parts of the body. Some reactions, such as those to gluten (a protein complex in wheat and certain other grains) and histamine, may span the accepted definitions of both food allergy and food intolerance.

Food Intolerance

Most adverse reactions to food fall into the category of food intolerance. Though symptoms of food allergy or intolerance may be very similar, the latter do not involve the immune system and are typically triggered by molecules that are consid-

TABLE 1.2. SOME COMMON CAUSES OF FOOD INTOLERANCE REACTIONS

Substance	Description
Lactose	The sugar in cow's milk and human milk. To be digested and then absorbed, it requires the enzyme lactase to be broken down into simpler sugars that can be absorbed.
Sucrose; maltose	Sugars requiring enzymes for digestion into simpler sugars that can be absorbed.
Histamine; tyramine	Substances created during the fermentation process in aged cheese, processed meats, wines, beer, vinegar, and soy sauce; these also occur naturally in a few other foods.
Salicylate	A salt that is naturally present in some foods and is used in making aspirin.
Tartrazine	An artificial food color.
Benzoates; BHA; BHT; sulfites	Preservatives that are added to foods.
MSG (monosodium glutamate)	A naturally-occurring or added flavor enhancer.

erably smaller than proteins. The triggers are substances that are naturally present in foods, arise from processing methods, or are added during processing (table 1.2).

The substances in table 1.2 trigger adverse reactions in some of us, but not in everyone. (Food intolerance does not include food poisoning, which can affect everyone.) Food intolerance typically involves variations in some aspect of digestion from one person to another. For example, we differ in the quantities of enzymes we have available to break down tyramine or lactose, when these substances enter our digestive system. In the case of lactose intolerance, about 75 percent of the world's population loses, to some degree, the ability to digest milk sugar (lactose) after the "normal" time of weaning, about four years of age. Infants produce adequate amounts of the enzyme lactase, which breaks down lactose into simple sugars that are then absorbed. When most humans mature beyond the age of weaning, production of the enzyme lactase declines. If milk is consumed, undigested lactose remains in the intestine, resulting in digestive problems. Thus the inability of adults to digest milk that nature designed for a baby calf can be viewed as a normal human condition, and not as a disease or system failure. (For more on lactose intolerance, see pages 56–57.).

It's a bit of an academic distinction to divide our reactions into food allergies and intolerances, in that the treatments will often come down to a similar strategy. The most important thing is to avoid the allergen or offending food, no matter what the trigger, no matter what the reaction, and no matter what the mechanism that mediates the reaction. Whether it's histamine release or a local inflammatory response to gluten protein, the number one treatment is to avoid the offending substance that sets off the reaction.

—*Michael Klaper, MD*

Our ability to digest various substances is often dependent on the condition of our intestinal lining. Here are some examples:

- Someone whose intestinal membrane is damaged and functioning poorly because of a reaction to gluten, cow's milk, or soy protein may then have trouble breaking down (digesting) sugars and other food components.
- Overgrowth of bacteria, such as E. coli or salmonella, or infection with giardia or viruses can lead to digestive problems.
- An infant's immature digestive system may lack enzymes or substances required to transport the smaller molecules that are the products of digestion.

Individual Variation in Symptoms

Reactions to sugars occur within the digestive tract and include gas, bloating, abdominal pain, diarrhea, and sometimes nausea. For other substances, symptoms may appear in various parts of the body: the skin, mucous membranes, respiratory system, digestive tract, or nervous system, as shown in table 1.1, page 11.

For some people, the reaction is barely noticed; for others the symptoms are severe. Variations in level and type of response often depend on how much of the offending food or substance was consumed. For example, our body may have a limited amount of lactase enzyme, and a tablespoon of cow's milk causes no apparent symptoms, but a half-cup of milk brings abdominal bloating and distress.

Why Do Food Sensitivities Occur in One Person and Not Another?

An obvious question arises. Why me? Why do these adverse responses to food take place in some of us and not in others? This is the subject of considerable research, and the answers from science tend to be theoretical rather than exact. These answers are linked to our genetics, history since birth (or even conception), and current lifestyles.

Inherited Patterns and Family Patterns

We may inherit a tendency toward allergies in general. Furthermore, families pass along their eating patterns. For example, we may learn from mom when to introduce certain foods in infancy; what are the essentials for stocking the family fridge; and recipes for chowder, omelets, or biscuits. It's not surprising that sensitivities to milk, eggs, or wheat would show up among family members. Also, we may inherit a greater vulnerability in one system of the body, such as the digestive system, or perhaps in the skin or nervous system. Family members share a home environment that has pollutants (such as cigarette smoke) or other factors that can increase our susceptibility to food sensitivity. We also pass along habits of relaxation and reactions to stress that may moderate our symptoms. As you will see in chapter 2, the types of bacteria in our intestine (which family members are likely to share) can influence our response to foods.

Breast-feeding a child, without any supplementary foods or formula, for the first six months of life or longer is one course of action that is likely to reduce the risk of eczema, asthma, and gastrointestinal problems. This is a wise choice for infants whose parents, brothers, or sisters have allergies (and for other infants, too). For a breast-feeding mom with allergies herself, it's also important to avoid foods to which she is sensitive. Breast milk provides protective factors; plus it promotes the gradual maturation of the intestinal wall, increasing its ability to block allergens. For an allergy-prone infant who must receive formula, a hydrolyzed or partially hydrolyzed formula is likely to reduce risk.

Why Now?

We may wonder why these reactions have suddenly surfaced. For certain people, the food sensitivity, and even the symptoms, have been there all along, unnoticed. Sometimes a period of stress or overexposure to a certain food is enough to push our symptoms from a slight undercurrent to a raging torrent. Odd as it seems, food sensitivities may come to our attention at a time in our life when we become more health conscious and take the time to observe our responses.

How Many of Us Have Food Sensitivities?

First, it is necessary to differentiate between true food allergies and food intolerance. According to some surveys, one person in three has reported that she or he has a food "allergy." Yet such self-reporting is not always confirmed in clinical trials or laboratory tests. The National Institutes of Health estimate that between 5 and 8 percent of children have true food allergies involving the immune system. The incidence of food allergies gradually decreases over time, reaching the adult rate of 1–2 percent in late childhood.

What if we include nonallergic food sensitivities (food intolerance)? One could perhaps say that the number of people with some sort of food sensitivity is quite literally 100 percent. Who has not experienced some sort of adverse reaction to food, even a minor one, at one time or another? Yet with food intolerance, there are none of the objective laboratory indicators that occur with an immune response, where antibodies to a particular food protein can be seen in a blood sample. We may suspect that a reaction is linked with a certain food. However, when we have consumed a mixture of foods and beverages, it's hard to determine exactly what caused the reaction, and it may not happen every time or under all circumstances. The data are less clear and are subjective. Thus, estimating the prevalence of food intolerance is rather tricky.

Food intolerances seem to be more widespread than true food allergies. In one study that followed newborns to the age of three years, 28 percent of the infants were reported to have some sort of adverse reaction to a food. One-quarter of these were allergies that involved the immune system. Overall, one household in four adjusts its food habits due to food sensitivities.

Food Sensitivities Through Life

Most true food allergies are acquired during the first year of life. At one year of age, about 6–8 percent (or, by some reports, as many as 10 percent) of infants have developed food allergies. Since most gradually outgrow these reactions, about 1–2 percent of the adult population is affected by food allergy.

If we experience allergies to certain foods (fish, shellfish, peanuts, or tree nuts) or a sensitivity to wheat gluten, the situation is typically with us for life, though variations occur. (For example, recent research has shown that one person in five may outgrow an allergy to peanuts.) Yet when it comes to other foods, some children or adults outgrow their reactions. One person in three loses his or her clinical reactivity after completely avoiding an allergen for one to two years. It seems that the immune system can forget to launch its adverse reaction to an allergen after there has been no contact for years. (However, those who are anaphylactic should not test this out without medical supervision!)

Infants experience true allergies to various proteins in milk; these responses may be outgrown sometime during the next decade. A Danish study showed that 35 percent of infants with one food allergy went on to develop allergic reactions to other foods and that many developed allergies to inhaled substances. Males seem about twice as likely to develop food allergies as females. Considering all types of allergies, including those to inhaled substances and to food, if both parents are allergy free, there is a 5–15 percent chance of their child having allergies. If both parents have allergies, the risk jumps to 20 percent or as much as 60 percent.

Lactose intolerance appears after infancy. Thus we find difficulty in digesting the sugar in cow's milk among older children, teens, and adults. This is more common in some population groups than in others; about 20 percent of people of northern European descent and about 80 percent of most other ethnic groups show some degree of gastric distress in response to the sugar in milk and milk products.

Increased Frequency of Food Sensitivities

Food allergy and intolerance have increased at alarming rates in recent decades. For example, it is estimated that allergies have tripled during the last three decades in developed countries. Plausible theories for the cause of these changes span the spectrum from too much cleanliness in our lives, on the one hand, to the lack of it (in air quality, for example).

Hygiene Theory. Scientists suggest that our overprotected and hygienic lifestyles may play a role. According to this theory, children who are exposed to many foreign cells right from the start, as would be the case if they lived on a farm or closer to nature, develop an immune system that has turned its attention to effectively fighting off bacteria and viruses, and away from fighting off food proteins. According to the theory, when children begin life in a clean, sanitized world, their immune systems may focus their reactions on food particles, rather than on bacteria. It seems that having bacteria in our environment right from the start, even including a few germs, stimulates our immune system to protect us properly.

Pollution. Though the hygiene theory presents an interesting perspective on lifestyles with few bacteria, some types of pollution seem to promote more food sensitivities. Early exposure to dust, pets, cigarette smoke, pollen, and other allergens can increase our risk of developing allergies.

Modern Agricultural Methods. Innovations such as genetic modification can produce protein molecules that are resistant to digestion. According to the Food and Agriculture Organization and the World Health Organization, these may be more likely to stimulate allergic reactions. Their international panel of experts has emphasized that all foods derived from biotechnology should be assessed for allergenic potential. However, this group lacks the power to enforce such a recommendation on food corporations, which conduct considerable food research. Yet the topic of long-term damage to human health due to genetically modified organisms (GMOs) or pesticides seems to attract relatively few of their research dollars.

An example that alerted us to potential problems is that of StarLink corn. This genetically modified grain was intended to be used only for animal feed. Yet in the year 2000, this corn found its way into the human food supply, primarily in the form of taco shells. Some people with no history of corn allergy reported anaphylactic reactions to corn. The reactions were eventually traced to StarLink corn. The allergen turned out to be a protein that had been added in order for the corn to act as its own pesticide. Following these allergic reactions, the government placed a ban on the genetically modified corn (though other types of genetic modifications have not been banned). Unfortunately, some effects of this contamination are irreversible. At the end of 2003, the banned StarLink corn still contaminated over 1 percent of the United States corn crop.

Extensive use of pesticides and herbicides (which are, by definition, substances designed to destroy life) are being blamed for some of our reactions to foods. Some scientists and members of the public think that more research is needed about the novel foods, proteins, and chemicals that are constantly being added to our environment.

Skin Testing for Allergies. Certain experts believe that skin testing for allergies, as described in chapter 4, pages 66–67, may occasionally increase the range of foods to which a potentially allergic individual develops reactions. When a food allergen is allowed to reach the bloodstream through broken skin or particularly via injection, it bypasses mechanisms in the intestinal wall that nature has designed to protect us from the allergic response. Our natural protective mechanisms in the intestinal wall lead to oral tolerance for food proteins, described in the next chapter, and the handling of foods without an allergic response.

Influenza vaccines, used in flu shots, are grown on egg embryos and may contain a small amount of egg protein that could potentially lead to an allergic response to egg.

Intestinal Well-Being. Our intestinal lining is beautifully designed to be a semipermeable membrane, like a sieve, that allows small molecules, the products of digestion, to pass through, and blocks the larger molecules. These larger molecules may then travel through our intestine and be eliminated in feces. When functioning as intended, the intestinal lining (gut wall) is a barrier that prevents these large molecules from stimulating food sensitivity reactions. Unfortunately, certain factors in our lifestyles can create and sustain unwanted holes in this barrier. Maintaining the health of the gut wall, and avoiding a "leaky gut" (or restoring it to good health), may play a role in minimizing food sensitivities and preventing the development of further reactions to foods. A diet that includes fermented foods (or probiotics supplements) and the whole plant foods that sustain beneficial bacteria in our intestine may also be our ally, as you will discover in chapter 2.

Of the above explanations, none is conclusive. The good news is that more and more research is being dedicated to identifying prevention, management, and treatment strategies for food allergies.

Chapter 2

CREATING AND MAINTAINING A HEALTHY INTESTINAL BOUNDARY

By Vesanto Melina, M.S., R.D. with Michael Klaper, M.D.

I have finally come to the konklusion that a good reliable set ov bowels iz worth more to a man than enny quantity of brains.
—*Josh Billings (also known as Henry Wheeler Shaw, 1818-1885)*

*I*n recent years there has been an explosion of interest among medical researchers in the protective role played by the inner lining of our intestine. Lifestyle choices that support the well-being of this part of our body can strengthen our defense against food sensitivities.

Our digestive system may not be the most glamorous of organs. Yet this long tube that runs from one end of us to the other plays a pivotal role in our health and is certainly worth a closer look. Because of its immense surface area, it is the main interface between "us" and the outside world. Among its myriad functions, its surface operates as a series of doorways through which the nutrients from the foods we eat gain access to the cells throughout our body. This surface discriminates between particles that are actively welcomed, those that are tolerated, and those that are denied access. The complex assortment of immune system cells interspersed along this surface provides a beehive of surveillance and protection activities, twenty-four hours a day, seven days a week. To start, let us follow the fate of food from beginning to end as it travels on its two- to three-day journey along our digestive tract.

The inner workings of the digestive system can be compared to an assembly line, or more accurately, a disassembly line. In the mouth, the breakdown of food begins with the act of chewing and the release of salivary enzymes. This breakdown continues in the churning, acidic environment of our stomach and reaches its peak in the small intestine, where the final stages of chemical digestion occur and where most nutrients are absorbed. In the process, large molecules (proteins, fats, and starch) are broken down into small molecules (amino acids, fatty acids, and simple sugars, respectively), which can be absorbed through the wall of the intestine (the intestinal membrane or gut wall) and into the circulatory system for distribution throughout our body. From the liver and gallbladder the small intestine receives secretions that support fat digestion. From the pancreas it receives enzymes that break down proteins and carbohydrates, along with alkaline juices that aid digestion and control acidity. The products of digestion, as well as vitamins and minerals, are absorbed at various receiving sites along the small intestine. What remains passes into the large intestine, where water is absorbed, bacterial fermentation of fibrous material from plant foods takes place, and feces are formed for excretion.

The intestinal wall plays a complex role in determining which particles of food will gain access to cells throughout our body and which will be excluded. It acts as a sieve, permitting desirable substances to pass through for distribution to our cells. At the same time, this wall blocks unwanted large molecules, which eventually are eliminated at the other end of the long tube; it also blocks the entry of organisms such as bacteria, which remain in the intestine or are eliminated. The intestinal wall is home for much of our immune system, defending us from disease-causing bacteria and toxic substances. In recent years, scientists have recognized its role in determining whether to tolerate specific food particles or to react against them with an allergic response. The gut wall, the bacteria that live in proximity with it, and their relationship to food sensitivities are the focus of a great deal of research.

The wall of the intestine is composed of five main layers. Starting with the outer edge of the intestinal wall and moving toward its interior, or *lumen*, we find two layers of muscles: an outer layer that extends lengthwise, and a circular layer. These muscles provide the powerful action that mixes food and juices and propels the mixture along the intestinal tract. Inside the circular muscles is a *submucosa*, a layer of cells supporting the next layer, which is a *mucous membrane*. The fifth layer, the *epithelium*, covers the inner surface of the intestine and is closest to the food that is being digested in the lumen. Separating the food from the epithelium is a coating of mucus. The entire intestinal wall is a busy complex of activity. Blood vessels, lymph vessels (which carry fats, immune system cells, and other substances), and nerves are liberally dispersed throughout the layers that surround our intestinal tract, with immune system cells throughout the inner layers.

The mucous membrane is so named because of the presence of mucus-secreting cells known as *goblet cells*. Goblet cells extend to the lumen and secrete a highly beneficial, thick layer of mucus inside the intestinal epithelium. This mucus allows food and, farther down, fecal material, to move along smoothly. Mucus forms a protective layer that is home for many "friendly" bacteria, with whom we coexist. It acts as a gummy filter that blocks many other cells and particles from reaching the intestinal wall.

One role of the immune system cells lining the intestine is of immense interest to scientists: its function of distinguishing between friend and foe. These cells can either initiate an immune system (allergic) response to a particular food protein or not take this action. When they *do not* act, the response (actually, the lack of response) is called *oral tolerance*, a tolerance to substances that came in via the mouth. It seems that signals are sent back and forth between immune system cells and friendly bacteria. These signals may, for example, stimulate us to react with a vigorous defense against disease-causing bacteria yet tolerate molecules that pose no threat. Our abilities to keep out unwanted bacteria, destroy any that might get through the intestinal barrier, and decide which substances (such as food proteins) to tolerate develop gradually during infancy.

Surface Area of the Intestine

Our small intestine is about 20 feet (7 meters) long. Yet the layer of cells that lines it covers an enormous surface area. If it were to be spread flat, it would cover a sidewalk the length of two football fields. (Compare this with the surface area of our skin, which is about 2 square yards, or 1.75 square meters.) This vast interface with the contents of our intestine, allowing digestion and absorption, is created by:
- large folds of the intestinal mucosa, extending into the central lumen;
- fingerlike projections on the mucosa, called *villi*;
- tiny hair-like projections on the villi, called *microvilli*.

The intestinal wall is the largest interface between the cells of our body (including our blood circulation) and substances that are not part of the body. A healthy and unbroken intestinal barrier, with its protective layer of mucus, is essential to our well-being; it affords protection against numerous diseases and food sensitivities. During the last decade, the established medical literature has come to appreciate the variable and vulnerable state of our intestinal membrane. It is clear that many of the lifestyle choices we make can have an impact on this membrane and the many microorganisms that dwell there.

Bacterial Flora

The moist layer of mucus and the inner lumen of the intestine, especially at its lower end, are home to more than four hundred species of one-celled organisms. The intestine contains approximately ten times as many of these bacterial cells as the number of other cells in the human body. Some of these are "friendly" types of bacteria, whereas others have the capacity to produce toxic substances, invade the intestinal wall, encourage allergic responses, or promote diseases such as cancer. This complex and dynamic community is known as our *bacterial flora*.

Our relationship with the friendly bacteria is one of symbiosis, or mutual benefit. The bacteria benefit because they have access to food and water that pass down the intestine. We benefit because these bacteria perform a myriad of functions for us:

they destroy toxic substances; they aid us in digestion; they produce certain B vitamins (folic acid, biotin, vitamin B_{12}, and pantothenic acid) and vitamin K; and they help protect us from unfriendly organisms. Colonies at various locations along our intestine perform specific functions, each holding on to its own niche or location in the mucous membrane barrier. The helpful bacteria, with names such as lactobacillus and bifidobacterium, are of special interest.

The balance of types of organisms in our intestine varies at different stages of life, from newborn to old age. This balance depends on many factors, including diet, use of antibiotics and alcohol, the acidity (pH) of our intestinal contents (which can be affected by the use of antacids), the amount of stress in our life, and various aspects of our overall health.

Normally the numbers of "unfriendly" organisms are kept in check by the "friendly" bacteria, and relatively few are able to move into the mucus layer. However, if anything decreases the friendly flora, a relative "microbial vacuum" is created. Unfriendly organisms—such as *Clostridium*, *Hafnia*, *Citrobacter*, and *Candida*—seize the opportunity, move into the niche that was vacated, and multiply. The result is intestinal *dysbiosis*, signifying an overgrowth of harmful bacteria. "Dys" means bad and abnormal; "biosis" means life. As these aggressive organisms occupy the space right next to the intestinal membrane, they produce metabolic byproducts such as acids, peptides, and other potentially toxic, interfering substances that set off a chronic, low-grade, inflammatory reaction, injure the intestinal membrane, and make it more permeable or "leaky."

Our Intestinal Wall, "Leaky Gut," and Food Sensitivity

When healthy, our intestinal wall has many features that make it an effective barrier against unwanted substances. This protective wall can be compared with the most modern security system. Desirable molecules can be pumped in or escorted through certain channels within cells and get through the gut wall; other molecules are excluded. Between cells are "tight junctions" that block the passage of particles, and our bodies can adjust the degree of tightness. The covering layer of mucus adds another formidable barrier.

"Leaky gut" syndrome is a term that was used in the popular press and is now in use by medical researchers. It applies to an intestinal wall with increased permeability, allowing some of the contents (such as toxins and antigens) that would normally be excluded to pass through. Naturally, this can place a greater burden on our body's system of detoxification and on the immune system.

Certain conditions and substances can injure the intestinal wall or change its environment in such a way that allows large molecules to leak through. This may lead to food sensitivities. Conditions that can increase intestinal permeability are

- inflammation;
- injury to the intestinal wall from drugs, chemicals, or radiation;
- injury to the friendly bacteria living in the intestine;
- stress; and
- immaturity of the intestinal lining (in infants and young children).

Here are details showing how these conditions and substances may support the development of "leaky gut."

1. Inflammation

Conditions such as Crohn's disease and ulcerative colitis affect the permeability of the gut wall. It is a well-known phenomenon that 35–40 percent of people with Crohn's disease, ulcerative colitis, or other types of chronic inflammation of the intestinal lining also have aggressive, inflammatory arthritis. Their joints tend to be red, painful, and sore. Inflammation makes the intestinal lining more permeable, allowing protein fragments from undigested food and from the breakdown of intestinal bacteria to leak through into the bloodstream. It is believed that when these protein fragments in the blood reach a person's joints, they may trigger inflammatory reactions in the joint membranes.

2. Injury to the Intestinal Wall From Drugs, Chemicals, or Radiation

Certain medications can cause increased intestinal permeability. These include:

a. Chemotherapy Treatment Agents. Cytotoxic drugs ("cyto" means cell) are toxic to cancer cells and are used for that purpose in chemotherapy. However, they can damage cells in the intestinal lining too, creating a leaky gut. Radiation therapy to the abdomen also can increase intestinal permeability.

b. Non-steroidal Anti-inflammatory Drugs. Many non-steroidal anti-inflammatory drugs (NSAIDs) are notorious for injuring the gut lining, making it more permeable. Recent research indicates that these drugs may disrupt the functioning of cells along the intestinal wall. Increased permeability in the intestine allows food proteins to leak through into the bloodstream. These may stimulate inflammation, for example in joint membranes. This creates a strange and often frustrating situation in which the treatment may become a cause of further injury. Many people take NSAIDs because of arthritis and sore, inflamed joints. NSAIDs can injure their intestinal lining and make it more permeable, allowing food proteins to leak through. Their joints get sore so they take more NSAIDs, and around and around they go. Aspirin, ibuprofen, naproxin sodium, and many arthritis medications are examples of NSAIDs.

3. Injury to Friendly Bacteria That Live in the Intestine

Certain substances, such as antibiotics and colloidal silver, used with the intention of supporting our health, can actually injure it by destroying beneficial intestinal bacteria, disrupting the balance of bacteria, and increasing intestinal permeability. High intakes of sugar and/or alcohol also affect the colonies of bacteria that reside in the gut.

a. Antibiotics. "Anti" means opposed to or against; "bios" means life. We swallow antibiotics with the intention of killing off forms of life that are unwanted, specifically those organisms that cause infection. Unfortunately, antibiotics will kill off many of the "good" bacteria too. This can create a vacant niche into which unfriendly organisms—which can be somewhat resistant to common antibiotics, such as *Clostridium, Hafnia, Citrobacter,* and *Candida*—can move. A common example is when women develop a vaginal yeast infection following a round of antibiotics for an unrelated ailment.

b. Silver. Colloidal silver is widely advertised for its antibiotic (bacteria-killing) properties. This characteristic of heavy metals, such as silver and gold, has been known through history. In past millennia, Roman soldiers would throw a silver coin into the horse troughs in order to prevent algae and moss from growing in the water. People took silver salts for rheumatism and other complaints; these were used to such an extent that their skin would turn gray. If we consume colloidal silver, or heavy metals such as gold, we may destroy far more bacteria than we intend to, including some that we need.

c. Sugar. Our balance of "good" and "bad" intestinal organisms can be tipped in a harmful direction when we ingest a high-sugar diet. Friendly bacteria thrive on a diet that includes plenty of unrefined plant foods; they love the fiber present. Diets that are high in refined sugar foster the growth of less beneficial organisms such as yeast *(Candida albicans)* and encourage dysbiosis.

d. Alcohol. Alcohol consumption can affect the intestinal membrane and its balance of intestinal bacteria; the impact can be severe in alcoholics. Drinking one large shot (50 ml) of a 40 percent alcoholic beverage such as whisky has been shown to increase intestinal permeability in healthy people. If we consume alcohol and an allergenic food at the

> One may say, "Doctor, I have hives; I don't know why." When asked if he/she has taken any antibiotics lately, the reply may be, "Yes, several months ago I had a dental infection and was put on antibiotics. A few weeks later, I started having hives."
>
> This sequence may not be an accident. While antibiotics kill off the bacteria causing the infection, they also destroy the beneficial bacteria, setting off a chain reaction that permits more injurious bacteria (which tend to be more hardy) to enter the gut lining and allow foreign proteins to leak into the bloodstream. Adverse reactions may ensue, such as allergic reactions in the skin.
>
> —*Michael Klaper, M.D.*

same time, alcohol may increase our rate of absorption of food components. The combination of an alcohol-containing beverage and our allergen-containing food may result in an intensified allergic response.

4. Stress

In ways that are not fully understood, possibly involving higher levels of circulating stress hormones such as cortisol, various stresses may adversely affect the intestinal wall's permeability and its ability to heal itself.

5. Immaturity of the Intestinal Lining (in Infants and Young Children)

Our remarkable intestinal membrane, with all its complexities, is immature at birth and until at least two years of age. Many of the features that make this mucosal membrane an effective barrier are not fully functioning during infancy and early childhood. For example, the mature intestinal barrier plays complex roles in distinguishing between organisms and substances that truly pose a threat to our health and those that are neutral or protective and can be tolerated. The immature intestinal barrier of an infant is not so skilled at managing these processes and tends to opt for an allergic response. This is a primary reason for the higher rates of food allergy in infancy and early childhood. This is also the reason that dairy products and solid foods should not be introduced into the diet too early in life. According to Hugh Sampson of the Department of Pediatrics at Mount Sinai's Medical Center in New York, a direct relationship has been shown between the number of solid foods introduced into the diet by four months of age and the development of atopic dermatitis (skin reactions to foods). Delaying the introduction of solid foods until six months of age is widely recommended. Research also has shown that the early introduction of solid foods during infancy is linked with increased rates of eczema when children reach ten years of age.

Breast-feeding lowers the risk of developing allergies in several ways. First, the infant is not being fed a potentially allergenic cow's milk or soymilk formula. Second, breast milk reduces the absorption of allergenic molecules; it may accomplish this by providing protective factors and by promoting maturation of the intestinal wall. Third, breast milk passes to the infant numerous substances, including antibodies. These actively stimulate the child's development of a healthy, strong immune system and are specifically targeted to help protect the infant from potentially harmful organisms. At the same time they seem to aid oral tolerance, thus helping to avoid allergic reactivity to foods.

Formula-fed infants do not have these advantages. However, researchers in Finland and other parts of the world are studying ways in which their situation can be improved, particularly for bottle-fed infants at risk for eczema, asthma, and other allergic reactions. (For more on this, see page 156.)

As adults, our intestinal barrier still allows a small proportion of large food molecules to pass through. However, with maturity most of us have developed a tolerance to these and are able to handle them without too much difficulty. It is possible to assess the degree of permeability of our intestinal wall by methods explained in the section that follows.

Laboratory Testing

Testing for Intestinal Permeability (Leaky Gut)

The Intestinal Permeability Assessment Test is a laboratory test designed to determine the degree of intestinal permeability. The test begins with an overnight fast, followed by consumption of a drink containing two unusual sugars: lactulose (a large molecule) and mannitol (a small molecule). Where the intestinal wall is intact, very little lactulose is absorbed. If, during the next six hours, a significant amount passes through the intestinal wall and travels through the blood to reach the kidneys, it will be excreted by the kidneys. Therefore, lactulose in a urine sample indicates a "leaky gut." Mannitol appears in the urine as a standard of comparison.

> ## Check these sources for laboratory testing
>
> Great Smokies Lab
> Intestinal permeability assessment, digestive analysis, and more.
> Phone: 800-522-4762.
> Web: www.gsdl.com
>
> Metametrix Clinical Laboratory
> Nutritional, metabolic, and toxicant analyses, including analysis of markers of intestinal dysbiosis.
> Phone: 800-221-4640.
> Web: www.metametrix.com
>
> Now Leap
> Screening for migraine headaches and irritable bowel syndrome and services for other food sensitivity-related conditions.
> Phone: 888-669-5327.
> Web: www.nowleap.com

Testing for Intestinal Dysbiosis

Urine tests also may indicate intestinal dysbiosis by showing byproducts from the overgrowth of "bad" microorganisms. Tests used to show bacterial overgrowth are those for benzoate, hippurate, phenylacetate, phenylpropionate, p-cresol, p-hydroxybenzoate, p-hydroxyphenylacetate, indican, and tricarballyate. *Clostridia* overgrowth, for example, can be indicated by the presence of dihydroxyphenyl-propionate in the urine. Compounds that show yeast and fungal overgrowth are tartarate, and citramalate, and B-ketoglutarate D-arabinitol in the urine. The indican test also can show dysbiosis and indirectly indicate the degree of intestinal permeability.

Healing the Intestinal Wall

Are you ready for good news? Here's some. Our intestinal membrane has an immense capacity to regenerate and heal itself quickly.

If we wish to restore a "leaky gut" to health, it makes sense to avoid the medications, antibiotics, and colloidal silver that may destroy beneficial bacteria, and minimize or avoid sugar and alcohol. It also makes sense to provide a nutritious diet of cell-building materials. In the next few pages we will mention supplements that are sometimes used. *However, the foundation of our success is likely to be a balanced diet of cell-building plant foods that supply a wide range of nutrients and protective substances.*

Two over-the-counter supplements, available from natural food stores, are sometimes taken in an attempt to make the gut less permeable. These are the amino acid glutamine and the bioflavonoid quercetin. In both cases their use is based on theory, as little conclusive research has been done to establish their effectiveness in repairing a leaky gut wall. The value of zinc and other nutrients and supplements mentioned on the next few pages is also being investigated. Note that all of these substances also are available naturally in plant foods.

1. Glutamine

A supplement that is being promoted to help build, maintain, and transport substances across our intestinal wall is glutamine. (Note that this is different from glucosamine.) A typical dosage is 250–500 mg of glutamine taken three times a day. When our diets have been severely inadequate, our supply of this amino acid may be short. Yet glutamine is the most abundant amino acid in the bloodstream; we can make it ourselves from other amino acids, and it is present in plenty of plant foods. A good and economical way to increase your supply of glutamine is to build your diet around a variety of the following plant foods, choosing those to which you do not have sensitivities: greens (asparagus, broccoli, cabbage, green beans, kale, parsley, spinach), potatoes, other vegetables, legumes (peas, lentils, beans), grains, seeds, and nuts. You'll receive glutamine, plus plenty of other amino acids, minerals, and vitamins, too.

2. Quercetin

The wisdom behind "An apple a day keeps the doctor away" may lie, in part, with this protective bioflavonoid that is present in the skin of apples. In theory, we may be able to make our gut less leaky and tighten up the junctions between cells by using 250–500 mg of quercetin two or three times per day. Formulations that contain mixed bioflavonoids including quercetin may be used as well. Yet we also get quercetin from oranges, grapes, green beans, and from other fruits and vegetables. Amounts in supplement are much higher than those in plant foods; however, if our food sensitivities have led us to rely on plenty of fruits and vegetables, our quercetin intake may be greatly increased.

3. Zinc in Food or Supplements

The mineral zinc is known to be important for the immune system to function effectively and to maintain the epithelium that lines the intestine. One study showed it to improve "leaky gut" in those with Crohn's disease. The diets of many people are low in this mineral. Of course, illness, dietary restrictions due to gastrointestinal problems, or food sensitivities may have decreased our zinc intake even further. It makes sense to support our immune system by meeting recommended zinc intakes, which are shown on page 370. Single mineral supplements that provide only zinc can throw off the balance of copper and other minerals and excess zinc may even disturb immune system function. Here are some wise courses of action:

- Make sure that your diet includes any and all of the following zinc-containing foods that are not problematic for you: legumes, seeds, nuts, and whole grains. (See chapter 8, and read more about zinc in *Becoming Vegan* by B. Davis and V. Melina, the Book Publishing Company, 2000.)
- Take a multivitamin-mineral supplement that contains at least 15 mg zinc (for non-allergenic brands, see page 365). The supplement should also contain at least 1–2 mg of copper.

4. Other Nutrients

A great many nutrients—minerals, vitamins, protein, and essential fats, as well as protective phytochemicals—are needed to build, maintain, and repair the many cells that line our intestinal wall. Researchers are exploring the roles played by specific amino acids (the building blocks of protein, such as arginine, glutamate, glutamine, glutathione, and glycine) and by vitamin A, other antioxidants, and omega-3 fatty acids. Complex carbohydrates, which contain plenty of fiber, nourish the beneficial bacteria in our intestines, as you will see in the section on prebiotics, page 32. Whereas a certain supplement may hit the headlines, the truth is that we require a diverse team of food components. Our best insurance for getting a full spectrum of these is not to splurge on dozens of bottles of costly supplements. *A balanced diet of whole plant foods will provide the many nutrients that we require.* Of course, when food sensitivities arise, this may seem like an immense challenge, because some of the foods that have been part of our diet are now prohibited. However, the range of foods available to us is massive. Our job now is to explore some alternatives that are new to us, while avoiding foods to which we react. In this venture, you will find many of the recipes in this book to be your new allies in putting together a health-supporting diet as outlined in chapter 8. *Beyond this, a multivitamin-mineral supple-*

ment can help to "top up" your nutrient intake; this can be particularly important when your system has been depleted.

> Probiotics are live microorganisms in fermented foods or supplements that promote good health by improving the balance of intestinal bacteria.

Restoring Friendly Bacteria: Probiotics

The bacterial population in our intestinal lumen and in the intestinal mucosa can change depending on our food, other lifestyle choices, and "friendly" bacteria that we introduce through cultured or fermented foods and supplements. Mixtures of beneficial organisms called probiotics (as opposed to antibiotics) can be ingested in foods or in pill or powder form.

Fermented and cultured foods are generally recognized as safe because they have been used safely in human diets for many centuries. During the last decade, the health potential of cultured foods, and the bacteria they contain, has caught the attention of scientists worldwide. Those that may improve our intestinal health are known as probiotics. In order to do this, some of the microorganisms must withstand the rigors of passage through the acidity of the stomach, and the alkaline environment at the upper end of the small intestine, and get past the bile salts in the intestine. It has been established that this is possible. For centuries, the health benefits of cultured and fermented foods have been acknowledged in Asia. Fermented beverages and foods have a long history of use in Japan, Korea, Russia, India, and Indonesia, to name a few regions. Examples of foods that may be cultured or fermented include vegetables, grains, beans, fruits, and tea. Throughout the world, diets include foods that are preserved by fermentation or drying and contain beneficial microorganisms. Probiotics have been recognized in the West for the last hundred years, since Nobel Prize winner Metchnikoff hypothesized that the long, healthful lives of Bulgarian peasants were due in part to their use of fermented foods, including dairy products such as yogurt.

It is believed that probiotics may "calm down" allergic reactivity without diminishing our ability to fight off disease-causing organisms. The most frequently used bacteria in probiotics are those in the lactobacillus and bifidobacterium species (such as *L. acidophilus, L. bulgaricus, L. casei, L. salivarius*; and *B. bifidum* and *B. lactis*). Mixtures of these, in pill and powder form, are available at natural foods stores and at many pharmacies.

Though research is at an early stage, we are likely to see the development of standards for optimal doses and the content of live bacteria at the end of the shelf life of products. We can expect more research about bacterial survival from ingestion through to the intestine and the ability of microorganisms to remain there and form colonies. With the flurry of research on these topics, we are gaining more insight into specific actions of specific probiotics. Studies of seniors have shown a decline in bifidobacteria; therefore, the use of probiotics may be beneficial as we age. There may be cautions about use for people with compromised immune systems, such as HIV. In the future, we may expect the inclusion of probiotics with a wider range of foods, such as energy bars, cereals, juices, and infant formulas. We are also likely to see promotional claims that go far beyond actual effects.

Probiotics Pointers

1. Take probiotics before a meal. Probiotics consist of live bacteria. To do the job we want them to do, it is important that enough of them pass through the stomach and reach the intestine alive. At mealtime our digestive juices, including hydrochloric acid, start flowing; these can destroy many bacteria. Your probiotic bacteria may stand a better chance if they are taken fifteen to thirty minutes before a meal.

2. Make sure that your probiotics are alive. Though the probiotics supplement that we purchase may have contained live cells when it was first produced, storage en route or in a hot warehouse may have killed off many cells. The shelf life of probiotics supplements is generally twelve months; however, the number of active cells is likely to drop toward the end of the year. In a probiotics mixture that contains *L. acidophilus*, we can determine whether the bacteria are still alive through a simple experiment in our kitchen. This is based on the fact that *L. acidophilus* bacteria can curdle milk. For this experiment, you will need the following:

- two small bowls
- about ½ cup of soymilk or cow's milk (these may be discarded later)
- a heaping teaspoon of the probiotics (if it comes in capsules, open 4 or 5 capsules)

Pour about one-quarter cup of milk into each bowl. Into one bowl, place all of the probiotics. Stir it into the milk with a fork so that none remains on the top of the milk. The second bowl contains milk alone, with no probiotics. Leave both bowls on the counter overnight. The next day, lift and swirl the bowls. If the probiotics are live and active, we will see a difference. The bowl containing live bacteria will show signs of bacterial activity, such as coagulated milk with the consistency of yogurt, a film of curdled milk, or bubbles of carbon dioxide. If the contents of both bowls look the same, you may continue the experiment, leaving both bowls for a second night, in case growth increases by the second night. If both bowls continue to look the same, then your acidophilus is not live; it should be returned to the store for a live batch.

3. Take your live probiotics daily for three to six weeks. Daily use for this period is likely to restore your bacterial balance.

4. Follow up with occasional or regular probiotics use. It is possible that some probiotics may stay in the intestine and establish a colony. However, the research shows they tend to pass through and need to be replenished on a regular basis.

Intestinal Bacteria in Infants

Though an unborn baby's intestine is bacteria free, that situation changes quickly at birth due to bacteria gained from the mother and various other sources in the environment. (Infants born via the birth canal have a head start in terms of bacterial population compared with those born by Caesarian section.) Breast-fed infants soon have plenty of bifidobacteria in their intestines, whereas bottle-fed infants do not. This decreases the opportunity for "bad" bacteria to gain a foothold, a factor that may play a role in the increased immune protection of breast-fed infants.

For bottle-fed babies, there has been a burst of research, led by Finnish scientists, on the addition of probiotics to infant formula. Probiotics-fortified infant formulas may encourage a healthier balance of intestinal bacteria, more like the beneficial pattern in breast-fed infants and less like that of infants given formula without probiotics. It is possible that probiotics-fortified formulas may improve the balance of intestinal bacteria and reduce the risk of atopic eczema in allergy-prone infants. One example of current use is Nan 2 Probiotico formula, which is now in use in Portugal.

> People who are particularly sensitive to histamine and tyramine should avoid fermented and cultured foods that are high in these compounds, including cultured dairy and soy products and miso (see pages 102–103).

Use of Probiotics in Adults

If you are an adult considering using probiotics, for example in supplement form, here are a few practical comments. As we have said, the research is in its early stages, and the effectiveness of these supplements for young and old invites more investigation.

Most of the current research on probiotics is devoted to supplement forms or to cultured products such as yogurt and kefir. For centuries, Asian countries have used various fermented land and sea vegetables. Their value to the digestive system tends to be part of cultural tradition, with little investigation by Western research scientists.

Natural food stores carry an assortment of fermented or cultured foods; here are a few examples. Soy yogurt and kefir (such as Wholesoy, Lifeway, Soy Treat, O'Soy, and Silk brands) are sold with live bacteria. Soy miso is readily available, though the strains of bacteria used are entirely different from those in yogurt and kefir. Miso is also made from chickpeas (Miso Master and South River brands), lentils, or adzuki beans (South River). Refrigerated miso that has been properly stored contains live bacteria, whereas unrefrigerated miso in airtight packages does not.

Feeding Our Friendly Bacteria: Prebiotics

Not surprisingly, what we eat determines what our intestinal bacteria have on their menu. Some favorite items for our beneficial bacteria are the soluble fiber and related carbohydrate materials that are coming to be known as *prebiotics*. These

> Prebiotics are food substances that pass undigested into the lower intestine and support our health by feeding and thereby encouraging a favorable balance of beneficial bacteria.

substances are naturally present in many plant foods. Obvious examples of soluble fiber are the gummy liquid in a can of kidney beans, the sticky quality of oatmeal, and the pectin in fruit. (Pectin is the substance that allows fruit jelly to gel.) Prebiotics are naturally present in vegetables (asparagus, broccoli, garlic, Jerusalem artichokes, leeks, okra, onions, summer squash), fruits (bananas, apples, citrus fruits, and many others), legumes (beans, peas, lentils), and grains (corn, barley, oats, wheat). Changing our diet to include prebiotics may be even more important than using probiotics.

Prebiotics can be purchased as supplements. Yet we don't need a supplement to avail ourselves of prebiotics; they are present in our gardens, produce departments, and on grocery store shelves. Though carbohydrates have taken a beating in the popular press, that beating should rightly go toward overuse of sugar and refined carbohydrates. The complex mixture of carbohydrates that is present in whole plant foods provides a wide range of health benefits, including the nourishment of our friendly intestinal bacteria.

As a bonus, when we get our prebiotics from a varied diet of plant foods, as outlined in chapter 8, rather than from an expensive supplement, we get an assortment of amino acids, minerals, vitamins, and other nutrients that maintain our intestinal lining and the rest of our body.

For infants, prebiotics such as FOS (fructo-oligosaccharides) and inulin have been added to formulas that are available on the market. FOS are naturally occurring carbohydrate chains of molecules of the sugar fructose. These are present in many vegetables and grains, such as leeks, onions, garlic, oats, barley, and rye. Inulin is a longer-chain type of FOS. Though we absorb simple fructose molecules high up in the intestine, FOS passes undigested to the lower end, where it can support bifidobacteria.

Why Has the Role of Intestinal Permeability in Food Sensitivities Been Downplayed or Ignored by Some Health Professionals?

In the past, physicians and dietitians learned that proteins and larger molecules generally do not pass through the intestinal wall. The lectures and texts in medical schools, dietetics programs, and other health sciences gave several reasons:

1. Our intestinal membrane was described as a formidable barrier that would *entirely block* large molecules like proteins from passing through the intestinal membrane and into the bloodstream. At the same time, this membrane would act like a fine sieve, allowing small molecules like amino acids and sugars, which are the products of digestion, to pass through.

2. Textbooks stated that in the gastrointestinal tract, *all* food proteins are broken down by strong stomach acid (hydrochloric acid) and then by intestinal enzymes (proteases) to form the individual building blocks of protein, the amino acids. The process of digestion was understood to be complete.

Allergist and immunologist Dr. Theron Randolph was considered a renegade several decades ago when he broke with traditional thinking and presented theories on the subject of increased intestinal permeability and on environmental illness. Yet years of investigative research by other scientists have gradually led to validation, understanding, and acceptance in medical centers worldwide of many of the general concepts he introduced. During the last decade, scientists have recognized the variable and vulnerable state of our intestinal membrane. It is clear that lifestyle factors can have an impact on the permeability of this membrane. Though the research is in its early stages, there is recognition that our gut wall can indeed be "leaky" and that we also may be able to restore it to a state of well-being.

Can Our Vulnerability to Food Allergens Decrease?

Whether our allergic response is lost over time depends on several factors: the allergen, the individual, and in some cases, complete avoidance of the allergen for a period of time. Reactions to fish, shellfish, peanuts, or tree nuts typically persist through life, though some reports show that at least one person in five may outgrow peanut allergy. Celiac disease and gluten sensitivity requires exclusion of gluten from the diet for life. *Note that those with serious allergic reactions should not attempt reintroduction of their allergens without medical supervision.*

Some other foods that lead to allergic and sensitivity reactions often can be reintroduced later in life. It is estimated that one person in three will lose his or her reactivity to a particular allergen after avoiding that substance for one to two years. This is true for both children and adults. Some children get over a milk allergy after months on a diet free of milk and its products; others take eight or ten years. A careful and complete exclusion of foods that trigger reactions has been found to be a key factor in helping us to lose our reactivity. The recipes in this book are designed to make your meals delicious and pleasurable, while excluding common triggers for reactions.

Beyond this, if our intestinal membrane is in poor health, we may be able to nourish it back to health. With time, it may recover its ability to block the passage of proteins and other large molecules. A favorable balance of intestinal flora may be restored, and our tendency to develop new food sensitivities may diminish. Though these aspects of dealing with food allergy have been recognized only recently, they may be of primary importance. Those of us with food sensitivities can change lifestyle factors that increase our intestinal permeability. This is good news, because if the gut wall regains its power of selective permeability, the continual onslaught of molecules getting through to trigger reactions could be reduced. Otherwise, one may develop sensitivities to an ever-increasing range of foods. There can be a vicious cycle involving intestinal permeability, poor digestion, an increasingly limited diet, nutritional deficiencies, and poorly nourished intestinal cells. In this situation, intake becomes increasingly limited, with poor nutrition contributing to the severity of the problems. (For information on meeting nutrient needs despite allergies, see chapter 8.)

Yet if we avoid the culprit foods that trigger our reactions *and* maintain our cells in good health, a world war may be reduced to a few skirmishes. Overall health and vitality could be greatly improved.

Chapter 3

FOOD SENSITIVITIES AND VARIOUS CONDITIONS

*F*ood allergies and intolerances have long been suspects in a wide range of conditions. For some, such as asthma and dermatitis, the links are clear and well established, whereas for arthritis and migraine headaches, the burst of research backing up the association has occurred within the last few years. In this chapter, we give an overview of nine of these conditions. Food allergies and intolerances play a role in other conditions as well. For example, research has shown that food sensitivities and diet can trigger symptoms and affect the behavior of some people with a genetic predisposition to illnesses such as schizophrenia and autism.

Arthritis

There are over one hundred forms of arthritis, all of which have something to do with the joints in the body; the causes are complex and sometimes not well understood. Here we will focus on what little is known about the relationship between diet and several forms of arthritis. Diet revision may be viewed as an experiment, not a guaranteed cure. Yet there is evidence that for a significant number of people, food plays a role. Three broad subject areas are being explored:

- Some individuals find that avoiding foods to which they seem to have sensitivities reduces symptoms of rheumatoid arthritis, osteoarthritis, and fibromyalgia.
- Ensuring that our diet includes adequate amounts of essential nutrients— omega-3 fatty acids, vitamin D, vitamin B_{12}, and others—can improve overall health and may alleviate some symptoms.
- Weight management can be important. Losing excess pounds may reduce the burden on joints in those with osteoarthritis and minimize the symptoms of gouty arthritis.

The potential role played by food sensitivities is often neglected in the research on arthritis, probably for a number of reasons. First, the causes of the different forms of arthritis can vary from one person to another and may involve multiple origins.

Second, reactions triggered by food intolerances are likely to be delayed compared with true allergic responses that may be more immediate. Thus symptoms related to food intolerance are more difficult to track. Third, for those whose symptoms are triggered by food sensitivities, the degree of reaction can be affected by other lifestyle factors such as medications, intestinal infections, general health, exercise, and the amount of a food culprit that is eaten. Fourth, entirely different foods and food groups seem to trigger reactions in different individuals. Among a group of people with similar symptoms, some may be adversely affected by dairy products; for others the culprits are meat, wheat, citrus fruits, or plants in the nightshade group. Some find their condition improves with increased intakes of foods containing omega-3 fatty acids. Many are unaffected by dietary modifications. Thus no single dietary change helps everyone with arthritis.

Research on several types of arthritis indicates that pain and inflammatory reactions are diminished for some people when they avoid certain foods or when they undergo a supervised fast. Yet fasting is certainly not a long-term solution; most of us can barely manage to do it between meals, and depleting ourselves of nutrients would create more problems than we had in the first place! There is a need for careful and well-designed studies so that the role of diet in the treatment of arthritis may be better understood.

One of the first reports on diet and arthritis appeared in the *British Medical Journal* in 1981. The study involved a woman whose symptoms of rheumatoid arthritis were triggered by corn and disappeared when corn was removed from her diet. Since that time, increasing numbers of scientific studies suggest that dietary manipulation may help at least some people. Scandinavians and other Europeans are among the leading researchers in this field. Here are a few examples from the existing research:

✓ In Norway, fifty-three people who had rheumatoid arthritis were divided into two groups. During the next four months, half of the group followed an experimental though nutritious diet that was free of animal products (meat, fish, poultry, eggs, dairy products), gluten, citrus fruit, sugar, caffeine, and alcohol. The rest of the group remained on their regular diet and could include all of these items. About half of those who followed the experimental diet showed a significant improvement and reduction of symptoms compared with similar changes in only two of the people following their regular diet. In the following months, those on the experimental diet who detected food-related responses gradually reintroduced these foods to determine their individual triggers. (For more information on "food challenges," the process of carefully testing our responses to potential food triggers, see chapter 4.)

✓ Swedish scientists found that following a vegan diet (a diet that contains no animal products), along with avoiding gluten, improved the signs and symptoms of rheumatoid arthritis for 40 percent of the small group of people who followed this diet for nine months. The effects on arthritis were linked with a reduction in antibodies to food antigens (for dairy products and for gluten).

✓ Although data are limited and more follow-up is needed before conclusions can be drawn, studies suggest that a vegan diet containing plenty of raw foods may reduce the symptoms of fibromyalgia in certain people.

✓ Joint pain has been associated with the consumption of meat, dairy products, chocolate, and nightshade vegetables for various individuals.

✓ Adequate intakes of dietary fiber, folate, and vitamin C, all found in plant foods, and avoiding obesity and excess alcohol consumption may reduce the risk of gout. In the past, people with gout were advised to avoid legumes; however, recent studies show that these wholesome foods can be included as valuable and nutritious parts of the diet.

✓ The amount and type of polyunsaturated fatty acids we consume, such as omega-3 fatty acids, affect the functioning of our immune system. An optimal intake may have beneficial effects in inflammatory disorders such as arthritis. Taking borage oil or evening primrose oil also may have anti-inflammatory effects; however, they should not be used during pregnancy.

✓ Ginger, fresh and in extracts, has a long tradition of use in China, India, and Tibet in the treatment of osteoarthritis and rheumatoid arthritis. Recent research using ginger extracts supports its potential usefulness in reducing inflammation and joint pain. Furthermore, sliced, fresh ginger certainly can pep up a stir-fry!

✓ Finnish researchers are investigating use of probiotics in people with juvenile chronic arthritis and with mild rheumatoid arthritis. These may improve the balance of beneficial intestinal bacteria, reduce symptoms, and enhance quality of life. Findings are encouraging, though not yet conclusive.

Medications, Arthritis, and Nutrition

Medications used for arthritis affect various aspects of nutrition and intestinal health. For example:

• NSAIDs (nonsteroidal anti-inflammatory drugs), which are used for several forms of arthritis, may disturb the balance of beneficial intestinal bacteria (for more on this, see chapter 2, page 23). NSAIDs may also affect our absorption of, or requirement for, different nutrients.

• Bacterial infections with Salmonella, Campylobacter, or Yersinia can result in reactive arthritis and joint pain. These organisms are found in raw, undercooked, and improperly refrigerated chicken, beef, seafood, and eggs, and in dairy products and other items. They also can contaminate the foods they come in contact with at home and in restaurants. Though use of antibiotics has certain drawbacks, it can be an effective treatment in such cases.

- The drug hydroxychloroquine, used for patients with systemic lupus erythematosus and fibromyalgia, may affect vitamin D levels, and thus inhibit the absorption and utilization of calcium.

Diet

While we await further definitive research on the relationship between arthritis and food, here are some diet-related actions you may wish to try. The bottom line is that most people are likely to improve their overall health when they consume an adequate supply of essential nutrients. If you have sensitivities and can effectively track down and avoid trigger foods, and thereby reduce your symptoms, so much the better.

Avoid foods that are your personal triggers. For various types of arthritis, certain changes in diet may help to reduce inflammatory reactions. If you find that certain types of foods are linked with your symptoms, it makes sense to avoid these foods. The solution and its success at mitigating symptoms will vary from one individual to another.

Increased symptoms have been linked to dairy products, other animal products, nitrites (found in cured meats), wheat and gluten, soy, citrus fruits, yeast, refined sugar, corn, and nightshade vegetables. Examples of foods in the nightshade family are tomatoes, potatoes, eggplant, bell peppers, and hot peppers; tobacco is also in this family. For more information on these foods, see chapter 5. It is unlikely that one individual would have all of these as triggers. To try this approach, eliminate the suspected foods or food groups one at a time and see if your symptoms subside. It is possible that the culprit could be an item that is not listed here. Note that a trigger food may be one of our favorites that we crave. When we stop consuming the reactive food, we may undergo a period of "withdrawal," analogous to what occurs when caffeine consumption is abruptly stopped. Within seven to ten days of completely avoiding the food in question, positive changes should be apparent. In most cases, more time is not necessary, though some experts suggest eliminating a suspected culprit for as long as four weeks. To verify your findings, you may want to follow up with a food challenge, as described in chapter 4, pages 73–74, and see if your symptoms return.

Include sources of omega-3 fatty acids. Omega-3 fatty acids tend to be anti-inflammatory, whereas omega-6 fatty acids are mainly pro-inflammatory. We need both types of fatty acids in our diet; however, most people get an imbalance, with excess omega-6s and too few of the omega-3s. Sources of omega-3 fatty acids include flaxseeds and flaxseed oil, hempseeds and hempseed oil, walnuts, tofu, canola oil, and leafy green vegetables. (See chapter 8.) Long-chain omega-3s are also available in supplement form in veggie caps (see page 367).

Be sure your overall diet meets the recommended intakes for nutrients. A diet that nourishes cells throughout the body will keep us in better health overall. We need adequate but not excessive amounts of protein and iron. If you include rice milk or soymilk in your diet, it is important to use products that are fortified with vitamin D, calcium, and vitamin B_{12}. Meeting the recommended intakes of calcium and vitamin D (which helps us absorb and use calcium) is important to counteract osteoporosis that may accompany some forms of arthritis and the use of certain medications in treatment. Centering our intake on vegetables, grains, legumes, and other healthful plant foods provides the nutrients, protective phytochemicals, and antioxidants, such as vitamins E and C and selenium, that we need. These fiber-rich foods help to sustain a balance of "friendly" intestinal bacteria. A plant-based diet reduces the risk of cardiovascular disease, which can be a complication of arthritis. High intakes of sugar and alcohol are not beneficial and their inclusion may replace important nutrient-rich foods. If desired, you may use a nonallergenic multivitamin-mineral supplement to "top up" your intake.

Probiotics may help. Probiotics, in supplement or food form, may assist in restoring the balance of beneficial intestinal bacteria and may help to reduce inflammatory reactions. However, before using probiotics, be sure to check with your doctor, because they may not fit with the rest of your treatment plan.

Achieve a healthy weight. Overweight individuals can reduce the burden on their joints by losing weight. Also, being overweight is associated with an increased risk of diabetes, cancer, and heart disease, which complicates matters by worsening overall health.

Exercise

Suitable exercise, planned with the guidance of your doctor and/or other health professionals, will assist in weight management and improve overall well-being. Outdoor exercise that includes moderate skin exposure to sunlight can increase our production of vitamin D, resulting in better absorption and utilization of calcium.

Supplements

Glucosamine sulfate is found naturally in the body. It stimulates the formation and repair of the type of cartilage found in our joints and is sometimes recommended as a supplement for osteoarthritis. Glucosamine that is sold in natural food stores and pharmacies often comes from animal sources. Note that glucosamine of non-animal origin (made from rice) is available from Freeda Vitamins, 1-800-777-3737, or www.freedavitamins.com.

SAM-e (S-adenosyl-methionine) is a natural form of the amino acid methionine that is found in most body tissues and fluids. It is a nutritional supplement that can provide pain relief and may contribute to joint health for those with osteoarthritis and fibromyalgia. It is recommended that people taking SAM-e insure a good intake of folic acid (folate) by including plenty of dark leafy green vegetables or checking that their multivitamin supplement provides 200 mcg (0.2 mg) of folate per day, as this vitamin helps the SAM-e to do its job. If no improvement in symptoms is seen in six weeks, discontinue use of SAM-e.

MSM (methylsulfonylmethane) is another natural compound that contains sulfur. It is being investigated for its possible effectiveness in pain relief.

Asthma

Asthma, which affects over 4 percent of North Americans, is a chronic disease that causes the airways to become temporarily blocked or narrowed, making it difficult to breathe. Asthma attacks, which usually require prompt drug treatment to reverse inflammation and open the airways, often involve a variety of triggers. The role of food allergies and intolerances in asthma is controversial, but it is clear that certain foods cause reactions in some asthmatics. When these foods are avoided, the frequency and/or severity of asthma attacks may be reduced. When a food sensitivity triggers an allergy attack, the asthma usually is not the only symptom; frequently gastrointestinal or skin reactions occur as well. While it is difficult to determine the prevalence of true food-related asthma, it has been estimated that food-triggered asthma affects 6–8 percent of asthmatic children and about 2 percent of asthmatic adults. However, these figures may be underestimated, because according to a 1996 study, almost half of a group of 914 asthmatics reported adverse reactions to food. When people with asthma who also have food sensitivities identify and remove trigger foods from their diets, the results can be quite impressive.

While asthma is distinct from food allergy, the two conditions commonly coexist. The biological pathways—particularly those involved in the inflammatory response—that characterize asthma are quite similar to those seen in food allergy responses. People with asthma appear to be at a higher risk for food sensitivities than the general population. Likewise, the presence of food allergies early in life can help predict the risk of asthma in children. The connection between asthma and food allergies is still unclear, but clinical trials and population studies provide us with many clues. Interestingly, recent studies have shown a genetic similarity between food allergy sufferers and asthmatics, but the association still warrants more study. Despite data showing associations, it is certainly possible, in fact common, for food allergy sufferers to have no trace of asthma, and for asthmatics to have no accompanying food allergies.

What we do know is that when people with asthma work with food allergy specialists and dietitians to pinpoint food issues, the condition is improved for many. One 2003 study showed that asthmatics who seek regular treatment from an allergy specialist are about one-quarter less likely to need hospital care than those who do not see an allergy specialist. Another study of ninety adult asthma patients in which half were placed on elimination and rotation diets and the other half maintained their customary diets showed that those on the special diets needed considerably less medication and had much better lung function. This study also determined that 70 percent of the asthma was provoked by foods alone! The link between asthma and allergies is undeniable yet difficult to pinpoint; thus it is important for people with asthma to identify and avoid problem foods where a link is suspected.

The following are the most common trigger foods and food components for people with asthma:

- Sulfites, which are used as a food preservative and also occur naturally in some foods, are found in shrimp, wine, some dried fruits and vegetables, lemon or lime juice, some other fruit juices, pre-sliced potatoes, pectin, frozen dough, and some pickled foods. Other common sources are packaged potato and rice mixes.
- Tartrazine (FD & C Yellow No. 5) is an approved azo dye present in many drugs and food products. It is produced synthetically from petroleum and is a complex molecule that has been shown to cause reactions in susceptible individuals. On a product label, tartrazine may be listed as "color" or "artificial color." Processed foods are most likely to contain tartrazine.
- Other food dyes.
- Benzoate/benzoic acid is used as a food preservative and is also found naturally in small amounts in some foods, such as berries and some spices.
- Monosodium glutamate (MSG)
- Aspirin, though not a food, is a drug that is known to trigger attacks among some people with asthma. (Note that related compounds called salicylates, which occur naturally in foods, do not seem to have an important effect on the course of asthma.)

• Cow's milk	• Tree nuts
• Eggs	• Wheat
• Soy	• Fish
• Peanuts	• Shellfish

The following is a partial list of additional foods and food components that may also trigger asthma in some people:

- BHA/BHT
- Banana
- Potatoes

- Aspartame
- Avocado
- Tomatoes

- Nitrites
- Citrus fruits

Any food that triggers a skin response could also provoke an asthma attack.

Managing Asthma

If you suffer from asthma, you are probably well aware of many of the triggers that provoke an attack, especially those that lead to an immediate reaction. But what about those attacks that seem to come out of nowhere? Is there anything you can do to alleviate these attacks?

Performing a careful elimination diet (as outlined in chapter 4) that avoids foods known to trigger asthma attacks, as well as other suspected culprits, may provide valuable insight into the successful prevention of your symptoms. Though many foods are possible triggers for an allergic reaction leading to an allergy attack, you may be tempted to eliminate an extensive list of items. While investigating your food sensitivities, it is important also to focus on a healthy diet in order to stay as well-nourished as possible. Use fresh produce, an assortment of grains and legumes, and the recipes in this book as the basis of your diet while you track down those foods that aggravate your symptoms. Some studies indicate that low intakes of certain nutrients (in particular, vitamin C, magnesium, antioxidants, and healthy fats) may weaken lung function. To ensure optimal nutrient intake, we recommend a hypoallergenic, daily vitamin-mineral supplement (see brand suggestions in the resources section on page 365).

Because asthma is caused by inflammation of the tissues, it makes sense to follow a lifestyle that minimizes physiological inflammation. Practices that help include eating plenty of fresh foods; staying well (for example by avoiding infections); refraining from smoking and steering clear of smoky environments; and avoiding foods that promote inflammation (see pages 35–39).

Have you tried yoga? Many people with asthma have found that practicing yoga regularly leads to a significant improvement in their asthma symptoms and a reduction in their need for medication. This may be due to improved breathing methods, better lung function, stress reduction, or a combination of these benefits. Whatever the reason, if you're physically able and your doctor agrees to it, try a beginner's yoga class two or three times a week and see if you feel better.

As with any ailment, a balanced diet, fresh air, appropriate exercise (tailored to your individual needs), enough (but not too much!) sleep, and a balance of work and play are of utmost importance in asthma management.

Attention-Deficit Hyperactivity Disorder (ADHD)

ADHD is an increasingly common condition that responds to a multifaceted approach to treatment. Medications may be effective, yet in some cases they do not address the underlying problems. Though not always the solution, dietary changes can make a significant, positive difference for some children and adults. One reason that diet may be neglected as a part of most treatment plans is that it can be very challenging to determine exactly which aspect of diet is involved for each individual. Research points to nine areas of possible concern:

- Allergies to specific foods
- Sensitivities to food colorings and other additives
- High intakes of sugar and refined carbohydrates
- Toxicity from heavy metals and other environmental toxins
- Mineral imbalances
- Deficiencies of essential fatty acids
- Deficiencies of amino acids
- Deficiencies of B vitamins
- Thyroid disorders

In general, the solution to these concerns can be addressed by the following approaches: avoiding the foods and substances that trigger unwanted behavior, and building a diet that includes necessary nutrients.

Avoiding Food Culprits

There is growing evidence that many children with behavioral problems are sensitive to one or more food components. Tracking down the food culprits and eliminating them from the diet can make an enormous difference for those with ADHD. A brief period on a "few foods" trial elimination diet, or several weeks on a simple but nutritious diet devoid of suspected food culprits, is often beneficial. A dietitian can help you steer clear of possible food triggers while providing guidance for maintaining adequate nutrition. If the foods that are responsible for the hyperactivity are reintroduced, you may observe some symptoms of food sensitivity such as itching (with or without hives), wheezing, a runny nose, or red ears, in addition to behavioral changes.

In one small New York study, 73 percent of the children with ADHD reacted to various combinations of foods, artificial food colors, and preservatives; their behavior improved on the days when these were eliminated from their diets. British researchers found that the foods to which children with ADHD most commonly had allergic reactions were milk products (including cow's milk, cheese, yogurt, and ice cream), corn (an additive in many prepared foods), wheat, soy, and eggs. Altogether, forty-eight different foods were implicated as triggers for hyperactivity. For some, nuts or specific fruits (raisins, apples, or oranges) were linked with problem behavior. Australian scientists have demonstrated that in cases where ADHD is food-related, the consumption of a trigger food can noticeably alter the electrical activity of the brain.

Though sugar often is blamed for causing hyperactivity, its presence in the diet may not be the actual, or only, trigger for behavior changes. Sugar reduces the nutritional quality of the diet by displacing foods that provide vitamins, minerals, protein, and essential fats. It also may aggravate other food intolerances. Interestingly, a New Zealand study found that children with ADHD had twelve times the incidence of dental caries (tooth decay) compared with those who did not have ADHD.

Meals for those with ADHD should revolve around whole, minimally processed foods. Therefore, you may find yourself opening fewer boxes and chopping many more veggies. Fortunately, once food triggers are removed from their diet, children with ADHD may enjoy taking part in this aspect of food preparation with you. Using the recipes in this book, you can create entrées and snacks that will appeal to the whole family, while avoiding food colorings, additives, and many potential allergens.

Building a Nutritionally Adequate Diet

To function at optimal levels, our brain and the cells throughout our body require a wide assortment of nutrients. In addition to avoiding problematic foods, we must build a diet that includes the nutrients that keep our whole body running smoothly: minerals, omega-3 fatty acids, vitamins, protein, and other nutrients. A diet based on vegetables, legumes, whole grains, and fruits (while avoiding added sugars, food colorings, additives, and specific items that trigger reactions) can play a central role in the treatment of ADHD. A multivitamin-mineral supplement may be an important addition, as it can help prevent deficiencies. The supplement should include magnesium, calcium, zinc, and vitamin B_{12} (for sources of hypoallergenic supplements, see page 365). For a few individuals, specific B vitamins may increase hyperactive behavior; thus reactions to supplements should be observed. Limited research has shown probiotics to be helpful for children with ADHD; these may help nutrient absorption or decrease the likelihood of allergic reactions (see chapter 2).

Omega-3 fatty acids are specifically involved in the function of our central nervous system and have clear links to behavior. These essential fats tend to be low in the diets of many people, including those with ADHD. Foods from vending machines and fast-food restaurants and items that are refined, highly processed, or have plenty of additives are notably lacking in omega-3 fatty acids. Omega-3 fatty acids are present in relatively few foods; good sources are flaxseeds and flaxseed oil, walnuts, canola oil, soybean oil, and tofu. They are present in small amounts in fresh produce and tend to be found in items that require refrigeration. Some research indicates that those with ADHD may have low blood levels of highly unsaturated omega-3 fatty acids (for sources of omega-3 fatty acids, see page 367).

In general, diet modification can play a major role in the management of ADHD and should be considered as a potential part of the treatment. Similar approaches may also prove to be beneficial for some children with autism. Effective nutrition management for behavioral disorders tends to be unique for each person. All the same, creating a more nutritious way of eating for one child or adult can have ripple effects, improving dietary patterns for the whole family.

Candida

Candida albicans is a type of yeast that can become overgrown in the digestive tract and in other parts of the body, leading to a *C. albicans* infection. It is important to know that *Candida albicans* is found naturally in our bodies, and we can expect small amounts of this microorganism to be present in the mouth, intestines, vagina, urinary tract, and on the skin. The levels are kept in check in healthy people by other microorganisms in the digestive tract, such as bacteria. However, sometimes the healthy balance of these microorganisms, or "gut flora," becomes thrown off during periods of illness or as a result of medications, usually antibiotics. When this occurs, the yeast can multiply beyond normal levels and cause symptoms such as skin rashes, oral thrush, and inflammation. Unfortunately, this condition is often overlooked by health professionals because the symptoms mimic so many other conditions, so a diagnosis is not always straightforward.

As with many other illness-and-treatment relationships, treating *C. albicans* involves a catch-22 often seen in Western medical approaches. When we are sick, we might be prescribed antibiotics, which destroy not only the bacteria that are making us ill, but also many of the "friendly" bacteria residing innocuously in our bodies. When these bacteria are destroyed, *Candida albicans* seizes the opportunity and multiplies, because the yeast growth is no longer kept in check by the "friendly" bacteria. This can occur when we take antibiotics or other drugs, such as birth control pills.

Yeast overgrowth isn't the only problem that occurs. *Candida albicans* releases toxic by-products, which may build up in the body and weaken the immune system when *C. albicans'* growth is out of control. When this occurs, new symptoms arise, and we may end up taking more antibiotics for our problem. The cycle must be broken in order to restore health!

Long-term effects of *C. albicans* overgrowth may lead to increased intestinal permeability (see chapter 2) and may cause symptoms in other parts of the body. For some people who have only occasional medication-induced bouts of *C. albicans* infection, a temporary skin rash may be the only symptom. However, the condition can be quite debilitating, leading to a variety of symptoms in different parts of the body, such as fatigue, headaches, and increased sensitivities to certain foods.

Because different people have such diverse reactions to *C. albicans* infection, it is difficult to establish cause and effect. However, knowing that there is a problem with *C. albicans* gives sufferers the power to observe their symptoms and attempt to remove any food triggers that lead to these symptoms. You can get a simple blood test that will determine whether your body is over-infected with *Candida albicans*. Your local clinic may have the test available, or you can use Metametrix lab (www.metametrix.com), which tests the urine for possible by-products of *C. albicans* overgrowth, or Great Smokies lab (www.gsdl.com), which offers blood tests as well as urine and stool tests.

The link between *C. albicans* and food allergies is most commonly noted with wheat or gluten intolerance (see chapter 6), but other food sensitivities have been associated with *C. albicans*. This yeast grows in a carbohydrate-rich environment; its favorite foods are sugars and refined carbohydrates, such as white flour, that are easily broken down to sugar. Thus, avoidance of sugar and sweet foods is advised. Those suffering from *C. albicans* overgrowth may discover that certain foods trigger symptoms. Some that have been reported are dairy products, especially cheese and buttermilk, fermented foods (such as soy sauce, vinegar, and wine), yeast and yeasted items, malt, and mushrooms. However, research on this topic is limited.

Avoidance of the foods that trigger reactions is intended as a strategy to rid your body of *C. albicans* overgrowth and not necessarily as a permanent diet, though limiting sugar and refined carbohydrates may be wise. When your condition improves and a healthy balance of microorganisms has been restored in your intestine, you may reintroduce healthful foods that you are able to tolerate. However, pay close attention to your symptoms so that you are able to determine whether any of these foods indeed trigger *C. albicans* overgrowth.

If you have been diagnosed with *Candida albicans* overgrowth, elimination of foods that you suspect to be problematic, especially sugar and refined carbohydrates, can support other treatments, such as the use of antifungal medications. In addition to the dietary restrictions, garlic (as a food or supplement) and the herb goldenseal may help. Restore your gut to good health by following the guidelines in chapter 2; the use of probiotics is very promising as part of the overall treatment for

C. albicans infections. Keep your diet in tip-top shape by following the approach outlined in chapter 8. Remember to be patient; your illness did not materialize overnight, so healing will not be immediate. By eliminating problem foods and restoring the health of your intestinal tract, you should expect to see an alleviation of your symptoms within a few weeks.

Dermatitis

Dermatitis is the general term for inflammation of the skin ("derma" means skin; "itis" means inflammation). Skin reactions are one of the most common consequences of food allergy and sensitivity; in many cases, food allergy and dermatitis go hand in (itchy, uncomfortable) hand. For some highly allergic people, just touching an allergenic food can lead to contact dermatitis. Dermatitis can also result from a reaction occurring hours after a problem food is digested and absorbed by the body. The most common type of food allergy-related dermatitis is eczema (pronounced EG-zima).

Eczema

Eczema, also known as *atopic dermatitis,* is a chronic skin condition that usually appears in infancy. About 10–20 percent of all infants have eczema; however, in nearly half of these children, the disease will improve greatly by the time they reach five to fifteen years of age. Atopic dermatitis is often the first clue of a disposition toward allergies and asthma; in fact, over 50 percent of people with this condition later develop asthma, and 75 percent develop allergic rhinitis, or hay fever. Food allergies and intolerances are not primary causes of eczema, but certain foods can worsen preexisting eczema.

The symptoms of eczema are intense itching, inflammation, and sensitivity of the skin. The appearance and location of the rash may depend on age. In infants, eczema often appears as a bubbling or oozing rash on the face, hands, and feet. In older children and adults, it may appear as a red, scaly, and itchy rash on the neck, hands, feet, and creases of the elbows and knees. During severe outbreaks, the rash may appear all over the body.

People who have eczema are more prone to skin infections because the skin is often raw and open from scratching. These secondary infections, caused by bacteria, fungi, or viruses, can make controlling dermatitis difficult.

Psoriasis

Psoriasis is an immune-mediated, genetic disease manifesting in the skin and sometimes in the joints (called *psoriatic arthritis*). Symptoms, typically patches of raised, red skin covered by a flaky white buildup, can be mild to severe. Psoriasis appears most often in young adults, rather than infants, and the disease typically attacks the knees, elbows, scalp, hands, feet, or lower back. Itching and burning are common.

Though eczema and psoriasis are considered autoimmune disorders, and the appearance of the skin is often similar, they are distinctly different conditions. Eczema can be the result of external contact with allergens or an allergic reaction to food, while psoriasis is believed to have only internal origins. However, people with either disease may find that certain dietary changes improve the condition.

Food and Dermatitis

Allergic reactions to certain foods have been identified as triggers of dermatitis; the leading culprits are milk, eggs, and peanuts. Emotional stress, high temperatures, and exposure to irritants also can worsen existing skin problems due to food allergy or intolerance.

Dermatitis is one of the many conditions that may be triggered by a food allergy. Unfortunately, determining the offending foods is not always easy, even with sophisticated laboratory testing. Studies have shown that some types of tests are accurate for one food (eggs, for example), while other types of tests are accurate for another food (milk, for example). Though it takes time and attention, an elimination diet, as outlined in chapter 4, is considered to be the most reliable method for narrowing down the food or foods that trigger the skin reactions. In many cases, removing the problem food or foods eliminates the skin disorder completely.

Parents who have a history of allergy in the family can take steps to prevent the risk of dermatitis in their babies. A 2003 study, for example, observed over one thousand at-risk infants and determined that infants who were exclusively breast-fed for the first four months of life had a significantly lower risk of dermatitis than those who were given infant formula. Delaying the introduction of known allergens, along with maternal avoidance of foods like cow's milk and peanut products during lactation (where there is a family history of food allergy), have also been shown to be effective.

The following foods and food components are some of the ones most frequently associated with dermatitis, particularly eczema:

- Certain fruits (berries, citrus)
- Wheat and other glutenous grains
- Azo dyes (synthetic colorings used in food, clothing, and drugs that have nitrogen in their structure) and other food dyes

• Cow's milk	• Eggs	• Peanuts
• Soy	• Tree nuts	• Benzoates
• Sulfites	• Fish	• Shellfish

Managing Dermatitis

Rarely is dermatitis the sole symptom of a food intolerance (though it is one of the most obvious). Typically, your body has gone through a cascade of immune system reactions, starting in your mouth or gut and appearing at last on your face, arms, or chest. Even if red, itchy skin is your only noticeable symptom, the underlying immune response may be wreaking havoc on your body. Perhaps your food sensitivity is causing fatigue, increased susceptibility to infections, or even depression. The bottom line is that if your skin reacts to a particular food or a food component, your effective response is to remove that food from your diet. Sometimes the trigger food is obvious (for example, your neck may break out in a rash whenever you eat strawberries), but sometimes you have to play detective to get to the root of the problem. Fortunately, you have this book to guide you through your sleuthing, to help you identify the clues necessary to determine what you need to do to restore healthy skin, and to provide recipes that are free of common allergens.

First and foremost, nourish your body with whole foods: fruits, vegetables, whole grains, legumes, and tree nuts. See chapters 5 and 6 for more information if you are allergic to gluten-containing grains, peanuts, or tree nuts. Eliminate the foods you suspect to be at the root of your problem; use the guidelines in chapters 4 and 5 as your main tools. Take a daily multivitamin and mineral supplement; be sure to choose a hypoallergenic brand (see the list on page 365). Make sure you are getting enough essential fatty acids in your diet. Omega-3 oils in particular are effective in reducing inflammation and preventing dryness. The easiest way to get more omega-3s into your diet is by drizzling cold-pressed, organic flaxseed oil directly on salads, soups, vegetables, or cereals. (Never heat the oil, as this will destroy the delicate fatty acids.) Try one of our delicious flaxseed oil dressings (pages 291, 293, and 296). You can also take DHA supplements (see page 367). Make your health your priority: minimize stress; get enough fresh air and sunshine (some people find that a few minutes of direct sunlight every day improves their skin conditions); get adequate sleep, rest, and exercise; and take time out for activities you enjoy.

Of course, foods are not the only trigger for dermatitis. Environmental pollutants, airborne allergens, infections, microbial imbalances such as candida (see page 45), body care products, and even certain fabrics, such as wool, may cause an outbreak. Even dyes in clothing have been linked to dermatitis. Keep a detailed diary of your symptoms as well as everything you consume and everything that touches your skin, and soon you should discover patterns that lead to possible causes of your dermatitis.

Often, topical skin ointments can provide relief from the itching and pain associated with dermatitis, but it is important not to become dependent on these medications, especially steroid creams, which can be toxic when used for long periods of time. Use them sparingly and only when needed. Getting to the root of the problem will minimize your need for further intervention.

Depression

A solution to the puzzle of depression is unique for each and every person who struggles with this condition. Diet is just one piece of the puzzle, along with underlying physical conditions, medications, exercise, bodywork, psychotherapy, and other forms of treatment. However, dietary changes can be a significant part of preventing episodes of depression and may play an important role in its treatment for some individuals. In this brief section we review food-related aspects of recovery from depression.

Depression and Food Sensitivities

Studies have shown that some depressed people who have food sensitivities can significantly alleviate their depression by avoiding the items to which they react. Milk, wheat, eggs, sugars (even fructose, the sugar extracted from fruit), and pesticides are culprits that are often cited, though there are many other possibilities. Have you noticed any immediate or delayed reactions to foods? (Some symptoms may not appear until hours after a trigger food is consumed.) Are there foods you crave and eat compulsively? These may be items to which you have sensitivities. Keep a food diary, and if you suspect that a particular food or additive is affecting you, follow an elimination diet as described on pages 70–74. Though this process takes time, your detective work may pay off.

Keeping Well Nourished

Healthful eating—or eating anything at all—may hold little appeal when we're depressed, tired, and unmotivated. Yet adequate protein, vitamins, and minerals will nourish our stressed brain cells even when we don't care what is on our plate or find it a struggle to eat. Without these nutrients, there can be a downward cycle, with malnutrition worsening depression and depression worsening nutrient intake. Depression can result from deficiencies of any of the minerals, vitamins, and essential fatty acids listed in the next section. Shortages of these can be a key element in triggering depression, and restoring optimal levels can be an important part of recovery. The diets of many chronically depressed people fail to meet recommended intakes or are at borderline levels; further food restrictions due to food sensitivities or poor appetite can worsen the situation. Not only can good nutrition help to relieve depression directly, it provides a buffer so that when our mood begins to lift, our whole system is ready to perform. Eating well also helps us to avoid chronic diseases, such as diabetes and heart disease, which could hurl us deeper into pain and depression or provoke new episodes after we've recovered. A diet built around vegetables, fruits, whole grains, legumes, seeds, and nuts delivers a multitude of substances that are essential to our mental and physical well-being. This can be achieved even while avoiding foods to which we have sensitivities. (For more on nutrition, see chapter 8.) Here are a few suggestions to improve our overall nutrition.

Minerals. Magnesium is required for our nerves to function properly. *Zinc* is one of the building blocks of our immune system. It also plays a role in our ability to taste and smell; a symptom of deficiency is loss of appetite. Studies have shown zinc deficiency to be common among people with eating disorders and women with depression. *Chromium* supports the action of the hormone insulin and helps us to utilize carbohydrates. These and other minerals are lost when grains are refined. When much of our calories come from products made of white flour, sugar, and fats, intakes of these minerals can be very low. *Iron* is responsible for the delivery of oxygen to cells; iron deficiency anemia is associated with apathy, depression, and rapid fatigue. Adequate *calcium* intakes (along with vitamin D, which helps us absorb this mineral) improve hormonal balance and may alleviate the depressive symptoms of premenstrual syndrome (PMS) for some women. We require *iodine* in order to manufacture thyroid hormone. Low thyroid function (hypothyroidism) is a common cause of depression and has many underlying reasons. Thyroid function can be affected by too much or too little iodine, by certain depression-related medications, and by particularly high intakes of certain foods, such as soy products, vegetables in the cabbage family, and flaxseeds (though these foods pose little or no risk if iodine intake is adequate). Iodine deficiency has become rare in many parts of the world since the fortification of table salt, which is a common practice in the United States, Canada, Australia, and New Zealand.

> For a valuable overview of depression that is packed with practical information, see *Dealing With Depression Naturally*, by Syd Baumel, Second Edition, 2000, Keats/McGraw-Hill.

Vitamins. B vitamins (thiamine or B_1; riboflavin or B_2; niacin or B_3; folate or folic acid; pyridoxine or B_6; and cobalamin or vitamin B_{12}) are central to our energy metabolism and are required for normal brain function. Numerous studies with individuals who are depressed have pinpointed deficiencies of one or more of these, especially vitamin B_3, vitamin B_{12}, and folate. Correcting the deficiency can be both therapeutic and preventive. With the single exception of vitamin B_{12}, the full range of B vitamins is found in whole grains and legumes. Vegetables provide additional sources of riboflavin and folate. Excellent sources of folate are leafy greens (the name for this vitamin is related to the word "foliage," meaning leaves), legumes, and oranges. Vitamin B_{12} helps with neurotransmission and brain function; two common symptoms of B_{12} deficiency are fatigue and depression. Like most of the B vitamins and some of the minerals, vitamin B_{12} is a coenzyme that assists in the synthesis of mood-related neurotransmitters. Vitamin B_{12} should be included in the form of a supplement or in fortified foods. *Vitamin C*, widely distributed in fruits and vegetables, strengthens our immune function and enhances the absorption of iron from plant foods; a symptom of vitamin C deficiency is depression. People in northern climates may have low levels of *vitamin D*, especially during winter months. Increased blood levels of vitamin D have proven to be helpful for some people with depression and seasonal affective disorder. Be sure to choose varieties of rice milk or soymilk that are fortified with vitamin D (and calcium), or use a supplement that includes vitamin D. Heading for sunnier latitudes for a few weeks during winter can make a difference, too! You can create your own private Hawaii wherever you are by using phototherapy lamps (for details on how to do this, read *Dealing With Depression Naturally*, by Syd Baumel).

Omega-3 fatty acids are integral components of cell membranes in the brain. They aid in the transmission of nerve impulses and are needed for normal brain function. For many people with depression, a rich dietary source of omega-3s, such as flaxseed oil, is sufficient to meet their needs. However, some may do better by adding another member of the omega-3 family known as DHA. (For more about the sources of omega-3 fatty acids, see chapter 8, pages 138–139, and the resources section, page 367.)

Multivitamin-mineral supplements. A supplement offers us protection when our diets are insufficient, as it can raise our vitamin and mineral intakes to recommended levels. Certain antidepressants may increase our need for certain nutrients.

Replace sugary foods with more nutritious choices. Depression is often linked with carbohydrate cravings, and people who are depressed tend to consume foods that are high in sugars and refined starch. Sugar may provide a brief, immediate lift, or have a soothing effect (related to the mood-stabilizing neurotransmitter *serotonin*), or lead to drowsiness or exhaustion. After the initial rise, blood sugar (glucose) levels can plummet, causing a variety of symptoms, and low blood glucose triggers the release of stress hormones.

Some people with depression also have impaired insulin sensitivity; this means that the hormone insulin cannot do its job of delivering energy to cells. Though more and more insulin is produced, blood sugar levels remain high, and these factors can lead to a myriad of problems such as diabetes and heart disease. Larry Christensen, chair of the psychology department at the University of South Alabama, says, "My research has revealed that eliminating added sugar and caffeine from your diet will not only help you control your depression in the short term, but also that these beneficial effects will last over time."

While coffee can give a lift, for some people this may be followed by a drop in mood. Appealing though sugar may be, there are plenty of excellent reasons to avoid it. For example, limiting your intake of sugar and refined starches (which quickly break down to sugar) may also help to prevent the feast-or-famine fluctuations of serotonin. (Prozac and other popular antidepressants usually work by boosting serotonin.) Another benefit of sugar avoidance is to cut off the food supply to *Candida albicans* (page 46) and undesirable intestinal bacteria, thereby limiting overgrowth of these microorganisms. Foods with added sugar and fats but little nutritional value also displace more beneficial foods from the diet. Over time, we become depleted of nutrients that could help to alleviate depression.

Keep your blood sugar level. Legumes (beans, peas, lentils, and soyfoods) are particularly good at keeping our blood sugar level. These and whole grains and vegetables contain complex carbohydrates that are rich in fiber. Such foods are digested slowly and the energy from them is delivered to cells in a gradual and gentle manner that is easier for our system to handle, instead of being dumped into our bloodstream all at once, as is the case with sugar. (Also see the section on fatigue, page 58.)

Medications and Diet-Related Side Effects

Antidepressants such as SSRIs (selective serotonin reuptake inhibitors), TCAs (tricyclic antidepressants), and MAOIs (monoamine oxidase inhibitors) can cause major weight gain or require that certain foods and beverages be strictly avoided while taking them; be sure to discuss these with your physician. St. John's wort, 5-HTP (5-hydroxytryptophan), SAM-e (S-adenosyl-methionine) and other herbal and nutritional antidepressants tend to have much fewer and milder side effects. Because these can interact with certain drugs, including antidepressants, consult your doctor before using them.

Exercise and Lifestyle Choices

Though exercising may be the last thing you want to do when you are depressed, it is crucial to remember that regular physical activity can gradually shift your brain chemistry in a positive direction, much like antidepressant drugs and supplements. Do you remember the adage, "It's the last straw that breaks the camel's back"? When it comes to depression, becoming sedentary can be that straw. Or, perhaps one's habit of being sedentary is among the last straws, if inactivity leads to being overweight and if a poor self-image leads to low self-esteem.

Instead, picture each positive (even if small) lifestyle choice as helping you build a healthy buffer against depression. Take a walk in the sunlight. Get to the gym. Eat a meal that keeps your blood sugar from bouncing up and down, such as lentil soup and whole grain bread. Lunch on a colorful salad that provides your cells with antioxidants. Prepare food that you know to be nutritious. If you suspect that you have food sensitivities, plan a program to track down the culprits. Take the opportunity to share your feelings with supportive people. Watch your intake of alcohol and caffeine—both of these can be depressants. Breathe fresh air—and breathe it deeply to boost your vitality. Stick to your routine and get enough sleep, but not too much. Take a mental step back from dark thoughts; cognitive therapy as described in *Feeling Good, the New Mood Therapy*, by David Burns (Avon Books, 1999) may be helpful. Remember that as with the weather, change is inevitable and sunnier days lie ahead. Each of these actions, taken day after day, is a block in building a viable shelter from depression.

Digestive Disorders

Given the complexities of the digestive system, the immune system, and their relationship to each other, plus the fact that the intestinal tract is the first to confront an offending food, it is not surprising that we see multiple relationships between food sensitivities and digestive disorders. Because symptoms tend to be general in nature (nausea, vomiting, abdominal pain, cramping, and diarrhea), and because there are so many different potential causes for each of these symptoms, these types of disorders are notoriously difficult to diagnose and treat successfully. In addition, diet, lifestyle, and physiology, all of which play various roles in the development of digestive problems, vastly differ from one individual to the next. Successful treatment—not only of the symptoms but also of the underlying problem—depends on accurate diagnosis of the root cause and, when food sensitivities are involved, avoidance of the problematic foods. This can do a great deal to allow our troubled digestive tract to regain its health.

Like adverse food reactions, digestive disorders may be immunological in nature (caused by inappropriate immune response) or nonimmuniological (not involving the immune system). The relationship between food sensitivity and digestive disorders, unfortunately, is often overlooked by physicians. It is quite possible that food sensitivity is the root cause of a digestive problem, while the problem (actually, the symptom) is treated with unnecessary medications (the side effects of which may worsen the condition) or even surgery. When this is the case, the true cause and solution may escape notice for years.

The good news is that awareness of the relationship between food sensitivities and digestive disorders is growing. Medical professionals are seeing vast improvement in the digestive health of patients who discover certain foods to be the basis of their discomfort and eliminate these foods from their diets.

Inflammatory Bowel Disease

As discussed in chapter 2, an unhealthy intestine often goes hand in hand with food sensitivities. "Leaky gut" (increased intestinal permeability), bacterial imbalance, and inflammation are all possible indicators of a sensitivity to one or more foods. These same problems are also the main symptoms of both ulcerative colitis and Crohn's disease, inflammatory diseases of the gut referred to individually and collectively as inflammatory bowel disease (IBD). The main difference between these two diseases is the location of the inflammation: in Crohn's disease, both the small and large intestine are affected, while in ulcerative colitis, only the large intestine is affected. There are other telltale differences, such as the clinical appearance of the gut wall, which doctors use to make an accurate diagnosis. People with Crohn's disease seem to respond better to diet than people with ulcerative colitis.

The major symptoms of IBD are diarrhea (including bloody diarrhea, especially in ulcerative colitis), frequent bowel movements, severe cramping, fever, fatigue, loss of appetite, and weight loss. Susceptibility for IBD appears to be genetic, yet there is no known cause. However, research suggests that IBD patients have a weakened immune response in the intestine. The majority of the cells of our immune system are located along the intestinal wall. The immune system will react to foreign proteins, but with IBD the reaction fails to subside after it begins. The result is an inflammatory overreaction, causing pain, gastrointestinal discomfort, and tissue damage.

It is worth mentioning that Crohn's disease, specifically, may be linked to a bacterial infection. Scientific evidence suggests that the bacterium *Mycobacterium paratuberculosis* may play a significant role in Crohn's disease. Indeed, one study showed that 65 percent of Crohn's patients tested positive for this bacterium, whereas only 4 percent with other inflammatory intestinal disorders, such as ulcerative colitis, tested positive. Research has determined that one of the possible ways to contract this infection is through the consumption of cow's milk. Laboratory tests of pasteurized milk (taken from store shelves) have shown that some cartons contain live cultures of *Mycobacterium paratuberculosis*; the bacteria can be traced to infected dairy cows. While not all people exposed to this bacteria go on to develop Crohn's disease, and not everyone with Crohn's disease tests positive for the bacterium, the link is so strong that some experts recommend that people with a family history of Crohn's disease avoid using dairy products.

Because symptoms of food sensitivity can parallel those of IBD, it often is difficult to decipher which is the cause and which is the effect. Idiopathic (meaning "of unknown origin") IBD may lead to leaky gut, resulting in food allergies; or allergies to certain foods may lead to symptoms of IBD. Fortunately, the treatment of these problems, as discussed in chapter 2, show much promise. If you have been diagnosed with IBD, pay special attention to your diet and symptoms. Keep a food log along with detailed notes on bowel habits, flare-ups, and other symptoms (as outlined in chapter 4). If an offending food is discovered or eliminated, symptoms of IBD may improve in the long run.

Celiac Disease

Celiac disease is a digestive disease in which the small intestine becomes damaged, interfering with nutrient absorption. People who have celiac disease cannot tolerate a protein called *gluten*, which is found in wheat and several other grains. Because damage from celiac disease results from the body's own immune response, there are several possible causes and accompanying conditions, including food allergy. Celiac disease is covered in more detail in chapter 6, pages 108–118.

Irritable Bowel Syndrome

Irritable bowel syndrome (IBS) is a complex gastrointestinal condition affecting up to one-fifth of the population. Common symptoms are abdominal pain, gas, unpredictable bowel habits, constipation, diarrhea, and bloating. About two-thirds of people with IBS have diarrhea (IBS-D), whereas one-third of those with IBS suffer with constipation (IBS-C). IBS-D is often triggered by nonallergic but immunologic hypersensitivity to foods or food additives. While there is no confirmed relationship between actual food *allergy* and IBS, food *intolerance* may well be an underlying cause of or a contributor to IBS. Disruption of the normal flora in the intestine due to food sensitivity (particularly abnormal fermentation of food residues in the colon) is another proposed mechanism for IBS. Eliminating the offending food(s) and restoring the gut flora to normal, as described in chapter 2, may help alleviate IBS symptoms.

Lactose Intolerance

Another common digestive condition is lactose intolerance, in which the mature intestinal lining lacks an enzyme necessary to digest lactose, the sugar found in human milk, cow's milk, and other dairy products. Lactose intolerance affects about 70 percent of the world's adult population. In those who are lactose intolerant, lactose remains whole in the small intestine rather than being split, so its components are not absorbed through the intestinal wall. Instead, the lactose molecules stay intact during its journey to the large intestine, where bacteria eventually go to work breaking it down, causing gas, bloating, and diarrhea. Treatment of lactose intolerance is simple, but eternal vigilance is necessary. Lactose is also dose related for many people, so a small amount may be tolerated with no symptoms, but larger doses create symptoms. Limiting or avoiding dairy products is the first step; however, lactose and lactose-containing milk derivatives are added to many packaged foods, so it is important to read labels. (For more on this see page 79.) Fortunately, soy, rice, and nut-based "milks" are acceptable substitutes for cow's milk. Be sure to select milks that are fortified with calcium, vitamin D, and vitamin B_{12}, when possible. In addition, natural food stores and large supermarkets carry nondairy yogurts, cheeses, and sour cream, many of which are lactose free. Some people have transient lactose intolerance, where the condition is caused by a bacterial infection but then reversed upon the successful healing of the intestinal wall, usually via treatment with probiotics.

Fructose Intolerance

Fructose intolerance is similar to lactose intolerance, but in this case a person lacks the enzyme needed to absorb fructose, another form of simple sugar. Symptoms of fructose intolerance include bloating, abdominal pain, diarrhea, headache, weight loss, and fatigue. Fructose intolerance is diagnosed via breath tests.

Fructose is found naturally in fruits, honey and some vegetables and baked products. It is found in especially high amounts in fruit juices, soda, juice drinks, and sports drinks. High fructose corn syrup (HFCS) is a common ingredient in processed foods, which is another source of dietary fructose.

Managing Digestive Disorders

While many food culprits may trigger or worsen a digestive disorder, and culprit foods vary widely from person to person, the following items may be particularly problematic for those with diseases affecting the gastrointestinal tract:

- wheat
- red meat
- very fatty foods
- dairy products

- caffeine
- alcohol
- processed foods
- sugars and sweets

- soft drinks
- other sugary beverages
- yeast (brewer's and baker's)

By avoiding these foods and basing your diet on fresh and frozen vegetables (many people with chronic intestinal problems find that cooked vegetables are better tolerated than raw), whole fruits, beans and other legumes, and whole grains, you may find some relief from your symptoms. Give it a try; the power of healing foods is tremendous! Keep in mind, however, that during an acute flare-up, it is imperative that you follow the nutrition guidelines of your doctor and dietitian.

When it comes to disorders of the intestines, there is no single approach that is right for everyone. It takes time and patience, often with much pain and frustration, to determine the treatment that works best for you.

To support a healthy intestine, depending upon how severe your condition is, you may wish to try the probiotics regimen outlined in chapter 2. Also, because the absorption of nutrients may be impaired with digestive disorders, take a daily multivitamin and mineral supplement (be sure to choose a hypoallergenic brand; see the resources on page 365). If you cannot tolerate a supplement in tablet form, use a powdered form instead. Avoid smoking at all costs; studies show that smoking worsens the symptoms and increases the risk of surgery among people with Crohn's disease.

Stress, anxiety, and other negative emotions often exacerbate the symptoms of digestive problems. To combat the damaging effects of these emotions and find some relief, try engaging in daily activities that relax and comfort the body and mind. We all are better equipped to manage stress when we make it a priority to balance work, rest, sleep, and exercise.

Fatigue

Our body's wisdom naturally insists that we rest when our energies are required for healing and similar processes. Thus, numerous conditions and illnesses can be at the root of fatigue. Here are some food-related causes along with suggestions that may help you to regain your energy.

Food Sensitivities

Fatigue that arises from a few minutes to several hours after eating can be an indication of food sensitivities or digestive problems. Keep a record of your food and reactions; observe which foods trigger reactions, and note the length of time between symptoms. (For more on keeping your food diary, see chapter 4, page 69.)

Fibromyalgia and Rheumatoid Arthritis

In diseases such as fibromyalgia and rheumatoid arthritis, fatigue is a common symptom. These conditions involve food sensitivities for some individuals (see page 36). One study found that when people with fibromyalgia adopted a predominantly plant-based diet that included plenty of raw foods, there was a marked improvement in fatigue and sleep patterns. The high intakes of fruits and vegetables resulted in high intakes of fiber, folate, potassium, and magnesium, and antioxidants such as vitamins C and E. Such a diet must be balanced to include sufficient protein, iron, vitamin B_{12}, and other nutrients.

Insulin Resistance and Blood Sugar Imbalance

In order for food energy (such as glucose) to gain entry to our brain, muscles, and nerve cells, we require the action of insulin, the pancreatic hormone that allows glucose to pass through cell walls. Yet the ability to produce sufficient insulin begins to falter in certain people. Others produce enough insulin but their cells do not respond to insulin's presence.* When the fluids in our blood vessels and around our cells contain abnormally high levels of insulin and glucose, damage occurs. Cells become even more resistant to insulin's action, leading to a condition called *insulin resistance*. This can lead to the development of *prediabetes*, in which blood sugar levels are higher than normal. New fat cells are created to accommodate the extra glucose coursing through our blood vessels. (In cells, this glucose is changed into fat.) Insulin resistance and prediabetes are steps along a pathway toward high blood pressure, increased abdominal fat, cardiovascular problems, and diabetes. In diabetes, our body fails to produce or to use insulin properly.

Whereas blood sugar levels normally provide cues about our need to eat or not to eat, when we develop insulin resistance and prediabetes, our system becomes confused. We may feel an urge for sugar, hoping for a burst of energy, but the energy doesn't last long. At times, the high levels of insulin move glucose out of the bloodstream and into cells and we become *hypoglycemic* (low in blood sugar). We tire easily and tend to "run out of gas," both mentally and physically. As a person progresses toward diabetes, fatigue becomes overwhelming. With high sugar levels, our immune system loses its ability to defend us against invading germs, viruses, and yeast infections.

Preventing (and reversing) this cascade of events involves many aspects of our lifestyle. One of the keys is to center our diet around whole plant foods instead of refined sugars and starches, animal fats, and hydrogenated fats. It is crucial that we control our weight; thus exercise plays an important role. (Keeping fit also builds our oxygen delivery system. Even a short walk is a step in the right direction.)

Sugar, Refined Carbohydrates, and Fatigue

Nature did not design or bodies to run on a lot of refined sugar; in our blood vessels it becomes a sticky substance that causes problems. If sugar is frequently present in our arteries, the result can be damage to blood vessels in the heart, kidneys, eyes,

---

*Note that this failure of cells to respond to insulin commonly occurs in people who are overweight. With weight loss, the situation is often resolved and insulin's effectiveness returns.

and many other parts of the body. And when it comes to energy and fatigue, sugar really can take us on a roller-coaster ride.

Are all forms of this seductive substance (such as refined sugar, raw sugar, fructose, honey, maltose, and maple syrup) bad for us? Though there are minor differences among various types of sugars, the answer is yes on all counts, unless we limit the amounts. The carbohydrates in refined starchy foods also tend to enter our system with a rush, followed by a quick drop in blood sugar.

Why Whole Foods Are Better

In the past, carbohydrates were divided into two broad categories: simple carbohydrates (sugars) and complex carbohydrates (starches, which are long chains of simple sugars). We have since realized that another way of dividing carbohydrates is more helpful and that we should distinguish between those that come to us in highly refined foods versus those found naturally in whole foods. Refined starches and sugars are assimilated into our body very differently from the starch that is delivered to us in lentil soup or brown rice and the sugar in a piece of fruit. The starch in "whole" grains and lentils is accompanied by fiber, B vitamins that help us to process the food energy, other nutrients, and protective phytochemicals. When energy-producing starches are packaged together with this very complex blend of substances, the delivery of energy is gradual

> For an excellent book on controlling blood sugar, and related topics, read *Defeating Diabetes*, by B. Davis and T. Barnard (Healthy Living Publications, 2003).

and has a more gentle effect on our systems. Similar advantages are present when we absorb and use the sugar molecules that come to us in a piece of fruit.

In this book, you will find excellent recipes that are free of wheat, animal products, and common allergens. However, take care to limit your sugar intake even with the relatively healthful desserts you'll find here and in some natural food stores. Instead, rely on the wide range of whole plant foods to which you do not have sensitivities (see chapter 8).

Omega-3 Fatty Acids

Insufficient intake of essential fatty acids has been linked to chronic fatigue syndrome. See page 138 for recommendations on optimal intakes of omega-3 fatty acids.

Caffeine

Caffeine enhances the effect of two hormones (adrenaline and glucagon) that release stored sugar from the liver, resulting in high blood sugar. When there's a drop in blood sugar, hypoglycemia can follow. It's like withdrawing too many of our energy reserves from our energy bank.

Vitamin B_{12} and Insufficient or Excess Iron

Vitamin B_{12} and the mineral iron are crucial building blocks for our oxygen delivery system. Fatigue can indicate a lack of one or both of these nutrients. Iron deficiency is the most common nutrient deficiency among women who menstruate, pregnant and lactating women, teens, and children six months to four years of age. We need adequate but not excessive amounts of iron. Good sources of iron include leafy greens, beans and other legumes, and whole and fortified grains and cereals. At the other extreme, high levels of stored iron (high serum ferritin and hemochromatosis, related to high meat intakes and other medical factors) also induce fatigue. Good sources of vitamin B_{12} are fortified foods and supplements. For more about how to build these important nutrients into your diet, see chapter 8.

Migraines and Other Headaches

Not everyone can prevent headaches with a change in diet. However, for some of us, altering what we eat may lessen the frequency of headaches and possibly eliminate them.

Migraine Headaches

Many migraine sufferers discover that their symptoms can be triggered by a single food or specific combinations, for example, foods with a glass of wine. Certain circumstances, such as rainy weather or times of stress, can trigger a migraine as well. Studies point a finger at about a dozen possible offenders, and the food culprits vary from one individual to another. These may affect phases of the migraine process by influencing the release in our bodies of substances such as serotonin and norepinephrine. Blood vessels constrict and then expand and nerves in the head are stimulated, leading to throbbing, prolonged pain, nausea, and sensitivity to light and sounds.

Research from many parts of the world implicates fatty foods, animal products, several allergenic plant foods, and certain additives. Tyramine (found in cheese and red wine) is a common culprit. Alcoholic and caffeinated beverages (wine, beer, colas, coffee, and tea) are known triggers for reactions. A Brazilian researcher investigated why some people might react to the placebos used in studies as well as to the foods being investigated. In order to disguise the item being offered, both the placebo and food being tested were given in gelatin capsules. He found that migraines could be triggered by the gelatin protein (derived from animal bones and hooves) that is often used to make capsules.

In a classic English study of eighty-eight children who had migraine headaches at least once a week, 93 percent became symptom free when they followed a very restricted hypoallergenic diet. Gradually foods were reintroduced in an effort to identify the specific food or foods responsible. Interestingly, while the children avoided the foods that provoked their reactions, they became resistant to other triggers that had been thought to activate migraines, such as emotional distress, physical activity, and temperature changes.

When it comes to migraines, consider three aspects of your diet.

1. For those with food sensitivities, avoid the items that trigger headaches. The "dirty dozen" culprit foods for migraines are:

- chocolate
- wheat and gluten
- corn
- onions
- meat (including fish and poultry)
- eggs
- nuts
- tomatoes
- apples
- citrus fruits
- peanuts
- milk, cheese, ice cream and other dairy products

Some people find their headaches are triggered by other culprits. Food additives may set off these painful and prolonged reactions; these typically include MSG (monosodium glutamate), aspartame (Nutrasweet), or nitrites (found in hot dogs, salami, pepperoni, and cured meats). Tyramine is often a trigger; it is present in aged and fermented foods such as cheese and red wine (also see pages 13 and 102–103). Underage drinking of wine and beer is a significant cause of recurrent headaches among some of today's adolescent patients.

Medical researchers suggest that migraine treatment should begin with a detailed headache and diet diary, followed by a diet that eliminates potentially problematic foods. Take into account point three below. If you eliminate too many items at once, you might go hungry and trigger migraines with low blood sugar! Of course, it also is important to eliminate non-food triggers such as perfumes or cigarette smoke. If desired, individual challenge tests can be done to confirm whether or not a specific food stimulates attacks.

2. Overall nutrition makes a big difference. When you become headache free, don't celebrate with a bottle of wine, a cheese and salami pizza, or chocolate cake. In addition to being common triggers for headaches, alcoholic beverages and foods that are high in fat, sugar, and additives replace more nutritious items. Plant foods (apart from those to which we have sensitivities) are our best choices because of their high nutrient density. In other words, they deliver plenty of vitamins and minerals per calorie. Our brain cells and cells throughout our body depend on this supply of nutrients. Magnesium is present in all whole grains and is lost in the refining process. Where there is reliance on refined foods and sugar, intakes can be low. Magnesium is the central atom in the chlorophyll molecule, so, of course, greens are good sources. This mineral is also found in other vegetables, nuts, seeds, legumes, and fruits. Riboflavin and niacin affect brain chemicals and metabolism. These B vitamins are essential to keep our bodies running smoothly, and magnesium assists them in these processes. These and other nutrients have been shown to play a role in brain function, and low levels are sometimes suspects in research on headaches. For more on designing a well-balanced diet, see chapter 8. If your intake of these nutrients is sometimes marginal, it's a good idea to take a multivitamin-mineral supplement (for nonallergenic brands, see page 365).

Some women find that their migraines are linked with a certain stage of the menstrual cycle and with extreme fluctuation in levels of the hormone estrogen. The fiber in vegetables, whole grains, legumes, and fruits can help rid our bodies of excess estrogen and keep estrogen fluctuation within limits.

3. Keep your blood sugar level and avoid fasting and skipping meals. Prolonged hunger combined with hypoglycemia (low blood sugar) is a recognized trigger for migraines. Lentils, split peas, soyfoods, and all sorts of beans are not just great sources of protein, iron and zinc; they can play a role in keeping us headache free. These legumes are superstars when it comes to leveling out our blood sugar, as they deliver a steady stream of energy.

Consumption of Related Substances

Caffeine. An Israeli study found headaches to be linked to caffeine in thirty-three of thirty-six children with high intakes of cola beverages. Caffeinated beverages are peculiar in that they trigger headaches for some people, yet for others they seem to improve the situation. For example, caffeine is also known to provide a "cure" for the dull headache that can signal caffeine withdrawal in those who are accustomed to their daily dose.

Feverfew. This herb has anti-inflammatory effects and inhibits the release of chemicals in the brain that are linked with migraine headaches. In some sufferers, feverfew has been found to prevent migraines and associated nausea and vomiting. The dose that is useful varies considerably from one research study to another. Feverfew is not to be used during pregnancy, lactation, for infants, or for people allergic to chrysanthemums, marigolds, daisies, and ragweed, which are in the same botanical family. Amounts suggested are 50–114 mg per day, or two to three fresh leaves per day.

Cluster, Tension, and Sinus Headaches

For other types of headaches, common triggers are MSG (monosodium glutamate), aspartame (Nutrasweet), nitrites (found in hot dogs and cured meats), benzoic acids, tyramine, red wine, and other alcoholic beverages. When we keep leftover foods (especially fish) and eat them a few days later, the amount of histamine increases with time; histamine may trigger some types of headaches. An Italian study investigating tension headaches as well as migraines found that of the 309 people studied, one-third were aware of a link between specific foods or beverages and the onset of their symptoms. Three common culprits were alcohol, chocolate, and cheese. Sinus headaches can be related to milk, wheat, and other food allergens.

Relaxation and Fitness

Relaxation, stress reduction, and related techniques have proven their worth in reducing the frequency and severity of headaches, and even in preventing them. It is important to consult with your doctor regarding changes in diet and exercise, and to ask about diet-related side effects of any medications used.

Chapter 4

DISCOVERING WHAT AILS US:
TESTING FOR FOOD SENSITIVITIES

O ne of the most challenging and often frustrating aspects of having food sensitivities is the process of determining exactly which foods are causing our problems. Since we typically eat more than one food at a time, and often include a beverage, it can be very difficult to pinpoint which item or items in a meal or snack are the culprits. A reaction can occur immediately or as long as several hours after we eat an offending food. In addition, our body may not necessarily react the same way to a problem food every time we are exposed to it. This may be due to variable qualities regarding the food itself, for example, the food's freshness or origin. Further complicating matters, accompanying foods and beverages may influence the way our body reacts to certain foods. Reactions also may be due to the state of our body. Other illnesses, medications, stress, and even hormonal imbalances may change the degree to which a food triggers a reaction.

Laboratory Testing for Food Sensitivities

Allergy testing

Historically, when people have suspected a food allergy, their doctors have referred them to an allergy specialist for testing. While testing has some value as part of our overall detective work, alone its value is limited because of a high level of false positives (we may test positive for a food allergy but have no problem eating that food) and false negatives (we may test negative for a food allergy and experience no symptoms when that food is eaten, but we indeed have antibodies to that food). Experts concur that for the most accurate results, a detailed medical history, family history, and physical exam should always accompany testing. In diagnosing a food allergy, the allergist should ask:

- Which food or foods are suspected to have caused a reaction?
- What quantity of that food or foods is necessary to cause a reaction?
- What is the length of time between ingestion and the development of symptoms?
- How often does the food produce the symptoms?

- What other factors, such as exercise or alcohol, affect the reaction?
- When was the last time a reaction occurred?

One of the most significant limitations of traditional allergy testing is that it does not reveal food sensitivities or intolerances, only IgE-mediated allergies (that is, sensitivities that cause the immune system to react). In tracking down the culprit foods, it is important to remember that we and our doctors or other health professionals must work as a team. Our awareness about the reactions we experience and the conditions surrounding them is a tremendously important part of the detective work.

Skin tests. Skin tests are usually the first approach used by allergists. There are three types of skin tests:

- *Prick test.* This is the most common skin test. It involves placing a drop of liquid containing the test allergen on the skin. This is followed by a skin prick underneath the drop.
- *Scratch test.* During this test the skin is lightly scraped and the liquid is dropped on the site.
- *Intradermal test.* For this test the liquid containing the allergen is injected just under the skin with a syringe.

The allergist looks for redness and swelling at the site, which is considered the basis for a positive result in each case. A control substance such as saline is often used to rule out a general skin reaction to the irritation. A positive test does not confirm the diagnosis of a food allergy; rather, it indicates the presence of antibodies to the test food, a mere clue in the quest for the root of the problem. It is important to remember that a negative test is more reliable than a positive test. In other words, a negative test is good news: you probably don't have an allergy to the test food. But a positive test result is only "suggestive" of the presence of an allergy (unless the response is acute, as with an anaphylactic reaction); it may or may not mean that you're allergic to the food. Thus, to clarify the diagnosis, a positive test is usually followed by a food challenge (see page 68).

Most experts agree that skin testing is only one piece of the puzzle, since it has many limitations including false positive and false negative results. We must remember that the skin and the intestine are two separate organs, and the cells of each may react differently to the same protein. The food extracts used for the test may lack the proteins that cause a reaction when the food is eaten. Patients with skin conditions, such as eczema, are not good candidates for skin tests. Also, skin tests, particularly the intradermal test, may cause a systemic and/or anaphylactic reaction. There is concern among some experts that intradermal testing could potentially be the initial trigger for a food allergy.

It is important to know that skin tests are not useful for detecting allergies to foods that cause a delayed reaction. This is a significant limitation. Skin testing for a large number of foods is rarely necessary or helpful. If you decide to go for testing, be wary of clinics that suggest testing for twenty to thirty foods. Testing should be tailored to you, based on your symptoms, history, and state of health.

Blood tests. Blood tests are simpler and safer than skin tests, but their value is limited by false results. The most common blood tests are the RAST (an abbreviation for radioallergosorbent test) and ELISA (short for enzyme-linked immunosorbent assay). These are less invasive than skin tests, because although a blood sample is drawn, the test itself takes place outside the body and thus does not pose the risk of a reaction. These tests measure the presence of food-specific IgE in the blood, the globulin protein that our immune system generates for that specific food protein. However, blood tests have limitations similar to skin tests. Even when the test is negative, most allergists will tell you that this does not necessarily rule out the diagnosis of an allergy.

For both skin and blood tests, it is common for a patient to test positive to several members of the same botanical family of plant foods or animal species, yet they may have a true sensitivity to only one food in the family.* This is one reason why positive tests should be viewed with a degree of skepticism; the unnecessary elimination of foods can result in nutrient deficiencies, increased social challenges, and decreased quality of life.

Novel tests. A few controversial tests may or may not show promise in detecting food allergy. The first is patch testing. For this test, the allergen is placed in contact with the skin and then covered with a patch, which remains in place for forty-eight hours. This test is best for delayed-onset reactions. The second is the In Vitro Assay for Lymphocyte and Eosinophil Activation. This is a blood test that measures the activity of certain immune cells. It appears to be best suited for people who suffer from intestinal inflammation. The third is Total Serum IgE Screening, another blood test that measures the levels of IgE antibodies in the blood. It is known that IgE levels are elevated in people with certain allergic syndromes, such as allergic asthma, but due to the wide range of what is considered to be a "normal" lab value, the test is not effective in predicting food allergy.

---

*For this reason, the formerly common approach of automatically avoiding all other members of a botanical family when we are diagnosed with an allergy to one member of that family has been revised. It now is considered preferable to determine actual and existing food sensitivities rather than ruling out entire groups.

Food Intolerance Testing

There are few laboratory tests for nonallergic food sensitivities, but they are becoming increasingly popular. Research on these tests is sparse, but as technology advances, we are sure to see more and more information about these innovative techniques.

One test that has shown promise in detecting sensitivity reactions, but not in detecting classic allergic reactions, is called the Mediator Release Test, or MRT for short. Because mast cells, the primary allergy cells, are found in the tissue and not circulating in the blood, MRT is not able to identify allergic reactions. Instead, MRT measures the cumulative reaction of the circulating immune cells after specific individual foods or chemicals are exposed to a patient's blood sample. Because testing is done on a blood sample, there is no worry of being exposed to allergens or chemicals. Reactions are measured and then categorized as being "reactive," "moderately reactive," or "nonreactive." In one study published in Europe, MRT showed a high level of accuracy when protein fractions of cow's milk were tested on milk-sensitive children and a control group of children who were not sensitive to cow's milk. In this study, MRT was found to have a sensitivity of about 95 percent and a specificity of about 92 percent, meaning that the results are quite accurate. Thus MRT provides a potential method of easily identifying sensitivity-type reactions for at least some proteins. Following a test such as this, a food challenge is the best way to confirm the results.

Dietary Approaches for the Diagnosis of Food Allergy

Practitioner-Guided Food Challenges

The oral food challenge is the most reliable test known for food allergies. Simply stated, this test involves the elimination of specific foods from the diet for a certain period of time (during which symptoms may subside), followed by a "test dose" of this food to see if symptoms develop. Some practitioners take this procedure one step further by prescribing the double-blind, placebo-controlled food challenge (DBPCFC), considered the "gold standard" test.

In the DBPCFC, the food being tested is taken in a swallowed capsule, with neither the practitioner nor the patient knowing what food is in the capsule. (Thus both patient and tester are "blind" to what is being tested, which helps keep our opinions at bay and makes the test objective.) A placebo, or food that is known to be nonallergenic, is also taken. The placebo is given at a different time. If the patient exhibits symptoms following the pill with the food capsule yet no symptoms following the pill with the placebo, then the test is positive.

The DBPCFC, which some believe is the only valid test, has its drawbacks. First, the amount of food in one or several capsules may be insufficient to cause a reaction. Second, the actual sight, odor, and taste of a food might be necessary for a reaction to occur. A third disadvantage, discovered during testing for migraine headaches, is that the material of a capsule itself may cause reactions. For example, gelatin, an animal product used in some capsules, is known to trigger migraine headaches in some individuals; thus the gelatin-cased placebo also can cause reactions. For these reasons, following a negative DBPCFC, some allergy specialists will ask the patient to eat the food while being observed.

Done properly, an oral food challenge takes quite a bit of time and effort, but the rewards of good health certainly are worth the energy expended in the quest to identify problem food(s). The oral food challenge involves three steps: the use of a food diary, an elimination diet, and an oral challenge

Food diary. Detailed food diaries often have proved successful in providing the clues necessary to pinpoint problem foods. A food diary should involve a detailed list of all the foods eaten, the quantity of each food, the ingredient lists of foods when possible, and a notation of the time the food was consumed. Foods placed in the mouth but not swallowed, such as chewing gum, must be included as well. Also important is a record of any symptoms and when they occur. A food diary should be kept for as long as possible before, during, and after the elimination diet phase. It may be helpful to list any activities or recent circumstances that could be involved, for example, your current state of health including any illnesses; your exercise regimen; any medications and/or supplements you are taking; and any particularly stressful events in your life.

Elimination diet. During the elimination diet we should eat as we normally do, except that we completely avoid the food or foods that we suspect are causing problems. It is imperative that we eliminate all possible sources of these food(s). For example, if we suspect a soy allergy, we must avoid all foods containing soy, including those that may have "hidden" sources of soy, such as flavor enhancers (for a complete list of hidden sources of commonly suspected problem foods, see chapter 5). Typically, four to six weeks of complete avoidance of the suspected foods is recommended. For details on how to perform your own elimination diet, see pages 70–74.

Oral challenge. The oral challenge involves consuming the suspect food, whether in a capsule, extracted and placed in a beverage, hidden in other foods, or simply eaten in the regular manner. If this is done in a clinic, a clinician will observe whether or not symptoms develop. If we are investigating our response to more than one food, it is important that the eliminated foods be gradually reintroduced one at a time. Several days should elapse between each food challenge to allow sufficient time for symptoms to develop and subside and for the test foods to exit the system.

Becoming a Master Sleuth: Tracking Down Your Food Sensitivities

Since sensitivities to food involve a release of chemicals in the body, the reactions may be tested via the methods described above; sometimes a successful diagnosis is made. However, because laboratory testing is generally not precise or definitive, figuring out the culprit food or foods can be tricky, especially when it involves a sensitivity that is not a classic allergic reaction. Some people eat the same food every day for years without realizing that it is causing a problem. They go from doctor to doctor, trying to figure out why they feel sick or fatigued day after day. It is only after strict avoidance of a food, followed by a reintroduction of that food, that the mystery is solved.

Do-It-Yourself Elimination Diet and Food Challenge

Whether or not you decide to visit a clinic to undergo formal laboratory testing, if you suspect that food is at the root of your poor health, one powerful strategy you can undertake yourself is the elimination diet and food challenge. This can be done on your own or with the assistance of a registered dietitian, who can help you meet your nutrient requirements while you are eliminating a number of potentially problematic foods. She or he also may help you identify hidden sources of the foods you are avoiding. If you have had a severe reaction to a food in the past, never try a food challenge involving this food without professional supervision.

Step 1: Your food diary. You may need to modify the traditional elimination diet used by allergists, because nonallergic food intolerances tend to have more subtle effects on the body than true allergies, and these effects tend to be related to the quantity of the food that is consumed. Therefore, we recommend that you keep a very detailed food diary that includes a list of the symptoms, feelings, and physical reactions that you experience immediately after, several hours after, and several days after eating. Make several photocopies of the Food

---

FOOD DIARY CHECKLIST

In your diary, be sure to include:

✓ Everything you eat, drink, and place in your mouth, listing each item by the date and time of day it is consumed.

✓ All the ingredients in the recipes you prepare.

✓ All the ingredients on the labels of any packaged foods you eat.

✓ All the ingredients in foods eaten away from home (limit these foods during your test, if possible).

✓ Any medications, prescribed or over-the-counter.

✓ Any supplements (herbs, vitamins, minerals).

✓ Your state of health and any illnesses you are experiencing.

✓ Any symptoms, including the time and length of the reaction.

Diary Form on page 368 for your convenience. Keep this diary for at least two weeks before you make any changes in your diet, and continue to keep it throughout the next two phases of the challenge.

Step 2: Elimination phase. Next you must choose which food or foods to eliminate from your diet during the elimination phase. The foods you select will depend on your symptoms, your diet, and your past experiences. Your diary and past history may provide clues to help you pinpoint the foods that are causing your discomfort. Keep in mind that you may need to eliminate the suspicious food or foods for several weeks before you notice a change in your symptoms. It is possible that you will initially feel worse after eliminating a problem food; this may mean that your body is readjusting to a new state where it is no longer dealing with that food. If this is the case, after a couple of days, the symptoms should subside. Be sure to continue keeping your detailed diary during the elimination phase.

For your elimination diet, you can take one of the following two approaches:

1. Eliminate a food or group of foods based on your suspicions that they are the root of your problem. This diet is typically followed for about four weeks.

2. Practice the "few foods" approach. This involves the elimination of practically every food that may cause a reaction, leaving your diet stripped down to only a few hypoallergenic foods. This diet is followed for only a short period of time because such restricted food intake cannot provide complete nutrition and may actually suppress the immune system. Due to the difficulty of sustaining the "few foods" diet for more than a few days, and because of the risk of nutrient deficiency, we recommend the first approach in most cases. The "few foods" approach is best suited for those with particularly severe symptoms who are unable to identify problem foods using traditional allergy testing or a regular elimination diet. If you would like to take this approach, be sure to discuss it with your healthcare provider. The "few foods diet" is not nutritionally adequate for extended periods of time and should be followed for no more than ten days (usually seven days is sufficient).

If you follow the "few foods" elimination diet for a short period, you will discover that even one type of grain, plus a few fruits and vegetables, still allows variety in textures and flavors. Crunchy rice cakes (plain or salted) can be spread with pear sauce; cream of rice cereal and puffed rice are tasty with cranberries and juice; rice flakes make a topping for a cranberry-pear crumble; and rice salad can be dotted with chopped vegetables. Rice noodles or vermicelli can be served with cooked vegetables or used in a vegetable soup. Rice wrappers, available from Asian food markets, can be dipped in cold water to rehydrate them and wrapped around a cooked rice and chopped vegetable filling to form a sandwich. Winter squash (hard

"Few Foods" Elimination Diet

Permitted foods:

Grains: rice, tapioca, millet

Vegetables: squash, parsnips, sweet potatoes, yams, lettuce

Legumes: dried lentils, rinsed well and boiled

Fruits: pears, cranberries

Oils: canola, sunflower (select the cold-pressed variety)

Condiments: non-iodized sea salt

Beverages: Distilled water and juice from allowed fruits and vegetables

Desserts: pudding made from tapioca or rice, sweetened with the juice of allowed fruits (no milk or eggs). Agar-agar, a bland sea vegetable, often called "vegetable gelatin" due to its jelling abilities, may be used as a thickener. (Agar-agar is available in natural food stores and Asian markets. It must be simmered in a liquid, preferably water, on the stovetop for about 5–10 minutes or in the microwave until it is dissolved. It will thicken more as it cools. To jell about 2 cups of liquid use 2 tablespoons agar flakes or 1½ to 2 teaspoons agar powder, which equals about 1 tablespoon of animal gelatin. Some fruit juices interfere with the jelling abilities of agar, so you may need to add a little more agar.)

✓ Wash and cook foods with distilled water only.

✓ Use glass, iron, or aluminum cookware and utensils; avoid stainless steel, plastic, and nonstick-coated materials.

✓ Consult your doctor about medications that must be continued versus those that can be avoided during the diet.

Adapted from *Dealing With Food Allergies*, by J. V. Joneja (Bull Publishing, 2003).

---

shell squash), with the seeds removed, can be stuffed with cooked grains and baked. Cooked brown rice can be combined with four times as much water and blended to make a milk. (After blending, let the mixture rest for one hour, then strain and refrigerate.) Several types of rice are available: long-, medium- and short-grain brown rice, basmati, Arborio, jasmine, and glutinous (sweet) rice. For grain cooking charts, see page 168. Brown rice contains B vitamins, iron, zinc, and other trace minerals, as well as fiber. About 9 percent of the calories in rice come from protein; white rice is less nutritious.

Lentils can be made into a variety of soups, cooked and served alone as a main dish, or cooked along with the allowed vegetables and grains. Mashed lentils mixed with cooked mashed vegetables, a little fruit juice, and salt make a tasty spread for rice crackers. Lentils are a good source of protein and will help keep your blood sugar level, providing energy between meals.

If you plan on trying the "few foods" approach, we recommend that you take a nutritional supplement during the elimination and reintroduction phases. See the resources section for a list of hypoallergenic vitamin-mineral supplements.

Most people will be successful in pinpointing problem foods using the first approach (that is, by eliminating a specific food or foods that seem to be problematic). Depending on your symptoms, it might be wise not to eliminate too many foods all at once. Avoiding too many healthful foods may rob you of essential nutrients, leaving you feeling sluggish and fatigued and making it increasingly difficult to pinpoint the original source of your symptoms. However, if you have multiple food sensitivities, the symptoms may not go away if you eliminate only one food at a time. (This is typical of migraine headache sufferers; symptoms are often triggered by several foods, not just one food.) Because of these competing issues, there is no single approach that is suitable for everyone. One solution may be to try eliminating one food at a time in an attempt to pinpoint the culprit; but if this does not work, eliminate several foods you may suspect are causing your symptoms. If neither of these approaches is successful, the "few foods" elimination diet is the next step.

Based on your personal experiences, reactions, and food diary, you may already suspect which food or foods are the offenders. To help formulate an appropriate elimination diet, refer to chapter 5 for specific guidelines and tips on avoiding the following potentially problematic foods:

• Dairy	• Eggs
• Soy	• Peanuts
• Tree nuts	• Corn
• Yeast	• Fresh and dried fruit, sulfites, and citrus
• Nightshades	• Wheat (see chapter 6)

See pages 100–104 for a discussion of other food culprits: fish and shellfish; sesame seeds and other seeds; chocolate; histamine and tyramine; salicylate; MSG (monosodium glutamate); BHA and BHT (butylated hydroxyanisole and butylated hydroxytoluene); banana, kiwi fruit; avocado; and chestnuts.

Step 3: Your food challenge. The most important thing to remember when attempting your food challenge is that you must reintroduce only one eliminated food at a time. Except for the one food being challenged, your diet should be exactly the same as it was during the elimination phase. If you reintroduce several eliminated foods at once, it will be nearly impossible to determine which of the foods is the culprit.

Here's the recommended approach for initiating the challenge. At breakfast, reintroduce a small amount of only one of the foods you eliminated and wait until lunchtime to see if your symptoms return. If you don't have any reaction, try a larger portion of the same food at lunch. Again, wait it out until dinnertime and try once more with a still larger portion. If you still have no adverse symptoms, wait two days and repeat the process with your next test food. For each food tested, the day after the first test do not consume any more of the test food until the entire testing is completed. Keep in mind that you may experience a delayed reaction. If you do experience a reaction at any point during the test, discontinue the food. Continue to record in your food diary all the foods you have eaten and any symptoms experienced.

If you are eliminating a group of foods, such as tree nuts, this test may reveal that you can tolerate only some foods but not others in the group (for example, almonds may cause symptoms but pecans do not). You also may discover that you have a tolerance for a certain amount of a food before you begin to experience symptoms—for example, one-half ounce of cashews can be tolerated but symptoms begin to appear if you eat an ounce or more. Using this careful approach should lead to success in identifying problem foods.

You may find that you feel so much better on your elimination diet that you don't wish to reintroduce problem foods; after all, why make yourself sick again after achieving remission? It is perfectly okay if you have eliminated only one food. If you have eliminated many foods, it is important to figure out which one or ones are triggering your symptoms. We can't emphasize enough the importance of maximizing variety in your diet and removing only the foods that you truly suspect are causing your problems. For more information on building a healthful diet (without your allergens), see chapter 8.

Chapter 5

FOODS, LABEL READING,
AND ALTERNATIVES

Hidden Culprits

When we have food sensitivities, or care or cook for those who do, we soon discover that problematic ingredients can sneak into our diet in all sorts of unexpected and mysterious ways. Taking precautions to avoid these hidden culprits is important; for some of us this detective work can be life saving.

Cross-Contamination

A common scenario occurs when people accidentally consume a "hidden" substance that has contaminated an otherwise safe food. This is known as cross-contamination. This can happen, for example, if the same serving utensil is used for different foods. At a salad bar, restaurant buffet, or potluck meal, we may have little idea where the scoop was sitting a few minutes before we picked it up. Cross-contamination occurs at deli counters and sandwich shops when the same knife or slicer is used for meat, cheese, hard-boiled eggs, and vegetables. It also occurs when a restaurant or fast-food shop uses the same oil to fry various items.

Cross-contamination can take place when a manufacturing plant uses the same equipment to make or package various products (such as ice cream and milk-free sorbet; milk chocolate and dairy-free dark chocolate; or soymilk and cow's milk) without adequately cleaning the equipment between runs. It can happen when gluten-free grains and gluten-containing grains are processed in the same mill or cereal plant. Fortunately, some companies take a great deal of care to avoid this sort of cross-contamination; however, many do not. Those with serious allergies are wise to become familiar with companies whose practices they can trust.

Ingredient Substitution

Another source of concern with manufactured food products is ingredient substitution. This can occur when there is a shortage of an ingredient and a manufacturer makes a temporary replacement (such as using peanut oil instead of 100 percent corn oil) or when a company permanently changes ingredients without making this clear on the label.

Consumer Error

Mistakes take place when consumers assume that a brand of food has similar formulations for a range of products (such as a line of soups, cereals, veggie burgers, or nondairy milks). To avoid unwanted milk or dairy proteins, soy, nuts, wheat gluten, or other allergens, it is crucial that we read all product labels. Companies change their formulations from time to time, so it's wise to check even those products we purchase regularly.

Food Packaging

It is possible that a nonallergenic food is packed in material that contains a food allergen. For example, some manufacturers use starch dust to prevent packaging from sticking to itself. Others may use foil coated with a wheat ingredient. While it is rare that packaging material causes an allergic reaction, highly sensitive individuals should be aware of the possibility.

Regulatory Loopholes

Loopholes in current labeling regulations allow for allergens to be hidden in a food product when a manufacturer is excused from listing an ingredient that is present at less than a specific percentage of the total product.

Misleading Labels

Product labels that are deceptive or ambiguous may hide the presence of allergens. For example, coffee creamer or margarine labeled "nondairy" may actually contain milk protein. Soy or egg products may be used in processed foods to "texturize" or emulsify but may be listed on the ingredient panel simply as "binder," "emulsifier," or "coagulant." Natural flavors, such as casein (a milk protein) or hydrolyzed soy protein, may be listed as "flavoring" or "natural flavoring."

Because food manufacturing practices vary throughout the world, imported foods can be a concern. Also, unknown ingredients may be present in raw materials. Fortunately, food producers are becoming increasingly aware of the potential seriousness of errors.

Labeling Regulations

Currently the U. S. federal Food, Drug, and Cosmetic Act requires that products bear a full listing of all ingredients. However, the act allows for exemptions—exemptions that may wreak havoc on an unsuspecting person with food sensitivities. For example, spices, flavors, and certain colors used in a food may be declared collectively without naming each one. In some instances, these ingredients contain subcomponents that may trigger reactions. Additionally, many "incidental additives," such as processing aids, which may be present in a food at minute levels and do not have a technical or functional effect in the finished food, are exempt from ingredient declaration.

Because of these exemptions, food manufacturers have not been absolutely required to list known food allergens on product labels. A long history of proposed bills, laws, and regulations in the United States culminated with the proposed Food Allergen Labeling and Consumer Protection Act of 2003, which became law in August 2004. The law is designed to provide improved food labeling to better inform consumers who suffer from food allergies. The law, effective January 1, 2006, requires the top eight allergens (milk, eggs, shellfish, fish, soybeans, peanuts, tree nuts, and wheat) to be listed on food labels by their common or usual name, or by the source of the ingredient. In addition, it requires that the Food and Drug Administration (FDA) conduct inspections and issue a report within eighteen months to ensure that food manufacturers comply with practices to reduce or eliminate cross-contact of a food with any major food allergens that are not intentional ingredients of the food. The law also requires the FDA to issue final regulations for the use of the term "gluten free" on food labels. For updates about allergy alerts, see the Web site www.foodallergy.org.

The Canadian Food Inspection Agency works with the food industry in Canada to ensure that the same eight allergens plus sesame seeds and sulfites are declared in the list of ingredients on the food label and that manufacturers develop allergen prevention strategies. They run allergy alerts on their Web site at www.inspection.gc.ca. Also see the Calgary Allergy Network website at www.calgaryallergy.ca.

In Australia and New Zealand, new allergen labeling requirements came into effect in 2002 as part of the joint Australia-New Zealand Food Standards Code, with the aim of reducing the incidence of this same list of undeclared allergens as in Canada. For more information, check with www.allergyfacts.org.au and www.allergy.org.nz.

In the U. K., the new European Directive that improves allergen labeling has been approved. Allergens covered by the directive are the top eight allergens plus celery, mustard, sesame, and sulfites above a certain concentration. By November 2005, all major allergens must be labeled when they appear in packaged foods. See www.anaphylaxis.org.uk.

If you feel strongly about food companies requiring clear and accurate information on their food labels, make your voice heard by writing your legislator.

Unfamiliar Terms

Another major problem for people with food sensitivities is that an ingredient may be listed on the product label by an uncommon term. In each section of this chapter, we list many of the foods where you may find hidden food culprits and some of the various terms used for them. For wheat and gluten-containing foods, see chapter 6. Those with severe adverse reactions to certain ingredients must be vigilant, read labels carefully, and always avoid any questionable foods.

Dairy Products

Our friends and acquaintances may tell us of milk "allergies" in their families. Yet their symptoms and the milk components that trigger their reactions may differ considerably. Some, particularly infants and children, experience true allergic reactions to any of more than twenty-five proteins in milk, while adults tend to be intolerant to the sugar in milk. To distinguish between milk allergy and lactose intolerance, see page 56.

Allergic reactions to milk most frequently affect the skin and the digestive system. Cheese and ice cream have been reported as triggers for migraine headaches. Milk may trigger or worsen asthma attacks. For some children, milk consumption is linked with restlessness and difficulty sleeping. Milk-related inflammation along the intestine may induce fecal blood loss, resulting in iron deficiency. Furthermore, damage to cells along the intestinal wall can lead to the insufficient absorption of nutrients.

Lactose intolerance occurs when the amount of dairy products, specifically the milk sugar lactose, exceeds the ability of the intestinal enzyme lactase to digest or break down the sugar. Undigested lactose remains in the intestinal tract and causes water to be drawn into the intestine, resulting in abdominal distension and bloating. When lactose reaches the lower intestine, the bacteria that inhabit this area feast on the undigested sugar, producing gas and acid. This produces cramps, flatulence, and often diarrhea. Lactose intolerance does not affect the skin or respiratory system, as milk allergy does. Some degree of lactose intolerance is present in three out of four adults worldwide. After weaning, or about four years of age, our ability to digest lactose, which also is present in human milk, typically declines. Adults may have a limited ability to digest milk sugar, so symptoms often don't show up until the amount of milk consumed exceeds the small amount they can handle. Infants occasionally develop temporary lactose intolerance if a bacterial or viral infection in the intestine affects the ability of the intestinal cells to produce lactose; however, things return to normal as soon as the infection clears up. This temporary condition may occur in children and adults as well.

We can expect that 80 percent or more of those with cow's milk allergy will show a similar response to goat's milk because the proteins are quite similar. Lactose is present in the milk of all species. Thus, goat's milk cannot be substituted for cow's milk in cases of lactose intolerance, and it's seldom suitable for those with allergies to milk protein.

Tips for the Label Detective

Whereas we know to look for the word "milk" on ingredient panels, it comes in various disguises. Extracted milk proteins that are added to foods may be listed as casein, caseinate, whey, lactalbumin, or lactoglobulin; hydrolysates of these may also be allergenic. Though some proteins in milk are altered by heating, others are not and may trigger reactions. Caramel coloring and caramel flavorings are made out of burnt lactose and "natural flavorings," and brown sugar flavoring can be milk based. Also look for phrases that contain the words listed in table 5.1, except where a plant source, such as cocoa butter, rice milk, or soymilk, is specified. Lactic acid, lactate, and lactylate do not contain milk and do not need to be eliminated from the diet. However, a label listing of "lactic acid starter culture" may indicate that the product contains some milk.

TABLE 5.1. TERMS THAT INDICATE THE PRESENCE OF MILK OR MILK DERIVATIVES		
Artificial butter flavor	Dairy	Lactose
Butter	Feta	Milk
Butterfat	Ghee	Natural flavoring
Buttermilk	Half-and-half	Nougat
Caramel	High-protein flavor	Quark
Casein	High-protein flour	Rennet casein
Caseinate	Kefir	Ricotta
Cheese	Kosher symbol "D" or "DE"	Sherbet
Cream	Lactalbumin	Whey
Curd	Lactoglobulin	Yogurt

Milk and its derivatives are found in a large variety of processed foods, such as those shown in table 5.2. Some are fairly obvious, such as cream, skim milk, milk chocolate, cheese, ice cream, yogurt, and many baked goods. Less obvious and occasionally surprising are "nondairy" creamer and some dark chocolate. Margarine often contains milk protein, such as whey. Many soy cheeses contain casein, as this milk protein allows the product to melt well and have a characteristic cheese "stretch." Check the ingredient list on all soy products, even if they are marked as dairy free or milk free. Baked goods, deli items, candies, and confections, especially

TABLE 5.2. FOODS THAT SOMETIMES OR ALWAYS CONTAIN MILK INGREDIENTS

Batter-fried foods	Energy bars	Pasta sauce
Biscuits	Flavored teas	Pies
Bread	Gravies and gravy mixes	Pizza sauce
Breaded foods	Ice cream	Puddings
Breakfast cereals	Imitation sour cream	Rusks
Cakes	Instant potato flakes	Salad dressings
Cheese	Margarine	Sherbet
Chocolate	Mashed potatoes	Soup
Coated nuts or seeds	Muesli	Soup mixes
Cookies	Muffins	Soy cheese
Crackers	Nondairy "cheese"	Sports supplements
Cream sauces	Other baked goods	Sweets
Cream soups	Packaged soups	Whipped toppings
Custard	Pancakes	Yogurt

those sold in bulk or at counters, may not be labeled. If in doubt, ask the vendor for an ingredient list or check with the server at a restaurant.

Milk contamination of a product is possible if the same manufacturing or packaging equipment is used for various products. We should be careful when ordering sliced products from food outlets that use the same cutters or slicers for a variety of foods, such as cheese and tomatoes. Lactose, which may contain residual milk protein, often is used as a filler in the manufacture of medicinal capsules and pill tablets.

In hard cheeses and yogurt, the amount of lactose is reduced compared with the amount in the original cow's milk; little lactose is present in butter and in margarine that contains whey. Lactaid® and Lacteeze® milks still contain milk protein and may contain a small amount of lactose. Some people consume lactase tablets along with milk to help them break down milk sugar. However, people who are allergic to molds and fungus should use caution with these pills, as they may react to the fungus used to manufacture the lactase enzyme or to one of the additives in the tablets.

Going Dairy Free in the World

Restaurants and Traveling. Sensitivities to milk protein or lactose need not prevent us from enjoying a wonderful meal when we're out on the town or traveling. Chinese, Thai, and Japanese restaurants can accommodate us very well. Middle Eastern and African restaurants are likely to have many dairy-free entrées. Though not mentioned on the menu, some Indian restaurants use ghee (clarified butter) as a base for recipes, even for apparently dairy-free vegetable dishes, so check with your server. Vegan restaurants serve no animal products and are among the safest places for people with sensitivities to milk. Many vegetarian restaurants offer a number of nondairy items.

Most restaurants take care to deal with special requests for those with allergies. Let your server know of your food sensitivities. Often dairy is used in preparing a dish, though it may not be mentioned on the menu. It is important that your server check with the chef to determine which items are safe for you. In some cases, the butter, cheese, or dairy-based sauce can simply be omitted from a recipe.

Breakfast can be our most challenging meal. While traveling or visiting others, it helps to bring along powdered or fluid nondairy milk to add to cereal or to a hot beverage such as tea or coffee. Juice, such as apple juice, tastes good on cereal, too. When traveling with an allergic child, be sure to bring a few favorite beverages and foods.

Shopping and Food Preparation. In recent years, natural food stores and mainstream supermarkets have expanded their offerings of nondairy milks, cheeses, sour creams, puddings, and frozen desserts. Dairy-free margarines, such as Earth Balance, Soy Garden, and Spectrum are available. As long as you avoid the "reduced calorie" varieties, you can expect these products to taste delicious; they melt beautifully and can be used for cooking and baking, substituted measure per measure for stick margarine or butter. The quality and flavor of many of these products makes it a pleasure to go dairy free.

While most of us easily can do without milk, cheese may be another matter. The average North American goes through about thirty pounds of cheese every year, five times as much as in 1944. Many people find it difficult to break this habit—despite the connection with our escalating rates of obesity. Fortunately, substitutes that are vegan contain no milk products, including casein, and are readily available. The taste and texture of commercial products has been steadily improving (such as Road's End Organics Chreese, Soymage, Tofutti, and VeganRella). Vegan Gourmet melts well, and many people find that it tastes more like dairy cheese than the others. We find that the best tasting uncheeses are

For more on creating wonderful meals and menus without dairy products, see:

The Ultimate Uncheese Cookbook,
by J. Stepaniak

Dairy-free and Delicious,
by B. Davis, J. Stepaniak, and B. C. Grogan

For more on dairy-free nutrition, see:

The New Becoming Vegetarian,*
by V. Melina and B. Davis

Becoming Vegan,
by B. Davis and V. Melina

Raising Vegetarian Children,
by J. Stepaniak and V. Melina

*In Canada this is *Becoming Vegetarian,* published by Wiley Canada, 2003.

homemade (see the recipes in the first two books listed in the box on page 81). In this book, you'll discover wonderful recipes without a speck of dairy, including baked goods, breakfast items, spreads, sandwich fillings, creamy dressings and soups, and alternative pizza toppings. You'll even find a smooth, sensuous Berry Delicious Ice Cream (page 358); like the other recipes, it contains ingredients that are good for you!

Being Well Nourished Without Dairy

Cow's milk and milk products constitute an entire food group on some national food guides, but this is due largely to the powerful dairy lobbies in these countries. These items are not essential to human nutrition. In many parts of the world, dairy products are not on the food guides and are not part of everyday meals. We require calcium, vitamin D, and other nutrients, all of which are present in a variety of other foods. For more on this topic, see chapter 8.

Infants. Because it is their mainstay of life, the primary beverages for infants and children with milk allergies must be considered carefully; your healthcare provider should be consulted on this (also see pages 149–151). Breast milk is best, with an allergic mother avoiding her own allergens. For bottle-fed infants, hydrolyzed or partially hydrolyzed formula may be necessary. Hypoallergenic milk formulas have been used as a milk replacement for children with milk allergy. However, hypoallergenic milk formulas are not necessarily nonallergenic, and sensitive children may have a reaction to these, depending on the particular formula.

Today's vegetarian and vegan restaurants include everything from simple, family-style restaurants and fast-food outlets to romantic bistros and elegant gourmet establishments and can accommodate those sensitive to milk, eggs, and other allergens. To find out what's near your home or along a route you plan to travel, check www.vegdining.com, www.vegeats.com, or www.happycow.com. For long flights, many airlines provide special meals for those with milk, egg, and other allergies, or with lactose intolerance. Ask for a vegan or strict vegetarian meal when you make your reservation and reconfirm your order the day before you fly.

Children. For children aged two and older who can tolerate soy, fortified soymilks can be used; the amounts of calcium, vitamin D, and protein are similar to those in cow's milk. Some soymilks contain added vitamin B_{12} and riboflavin; in Canada, zinc is added as well. Note that one cup (250 ml) of soymilk contains 7–9 grams of protein, whereas rice milk (fortified or not) provides only about 0.5 grams of protein per cup. If your best option for a child or teen is fortified rice milk, it is important that the diet contains plenty of other protein sources.

Egg

Egg contains a number of proteins to which we may be allergic; most are in the white. Some of these proteins are heat stable and are allergenic in both the raw and cooked form. Egg can result in severe or anaphylactic reactions, especially in children under seven, and should be carefully avoided by those with this risk. Someone with a proven egg allergy should avoid both the white and yolk unless it is established that one or the other can be tolerated safely. Furthermore, even when white and yolk are separated, there is likely to be some cross-contamination. Eggs from various species contain similar proteins, so those who are allergic to chicken eggs should also avoid eggs from ducks, turkeys, and other birds, unless safety is established. Because the blood of the chicken is sometimes found in eggs, some people may be allergic to both hens' eggs and chicken flesh.

Tips for the Label Detective

A variety of terms in a food label may indicate the presence of egg protein. Check for egg as part of a phrase, such as "dried egg," and for the words listed in table 5.3. The term ovo comes from the Latin word for egg and is a clue to its presence, as it is often used as part of a word. In some cases, the ingredient itself is not mentioned; instead we are told the function that the egg performs, such as "binder," "emulsifier," or "coagulant." Many wines are clarified with egg whites, though the label will not indicate this. Since legislation may permit a manufacturer not to list an ingredient that constitutes less than a specific percentage of the total product, it may not show up on the label. For example, noodles containing egg may not have egg listed on the ingredient panel. Similarly, egg whites may not be listed when they are used to give bagels, pretzels, piecrusts, and other baked goods their shiny appearance. In most manufactured food products, the lecithin used is derived from soy, but

---

TABLE 5.3. TERMS THAT SOMETIMES OR ALWAYS INDICATE THE PRESENCE OF EGG PROTEIN

Albumin	Emulsifier	Ovotransferrin
Avidin	Globulin	Ovovitellin
Binder	Lecithin	Phosvitin
Coagulant	Lipovitelin	Powdered egg
Conalbumin	Livetin	Silici albuminate
Egg	Lysozyme	Vitellin
Egg white	Ovalbumin	Whole egg
Egg yellow	Ovamucin, Ovomucin	Yolk
Egg yolk	Ovomucoid	

---

occasionally the source may be egg. Provitamin A, which is extracted from eggs, may be used and described simply as a colorant, but it is not yet known whether this can cause an allergic reaction. In addition to food products, egg proteins also are found in some cosmetics, shampoos, nutritional supplements, and pharmaceuticals such as laxatives. Influenza vaccines, used in flu shots, are grown on egg embryos and may contain a small amount of egg protein.

Facing the World Without Egg on Your Face

Restaurants and traveling. Avoiding obvious egg dishes, such as omelets, quiche, or eggnog, is a simple matter. However, a small amount of egg is an ingredient in many manufactured foods; thus allergic individuals must ask. Eggs are a staple in most baking, so you'll find them in cakes, doughnuts, fancy pastries, glazed rolls, glazed nuts, and some biscuits, cookies, and breads. Eggs are often an ingredient in pastas (especially "homemade" or "fresh" pastas), commercial sauce mixes, soups, sausages, meat loaves and meat jellies, marshmallows, marzipan, icings, fancy ice creams, and other foods listed in table 5.4. Wines, soft drinks, and consommés often are clarified with egg whites. Avoid batter-coated items, such as vegetable tempura in Japanese restaurants. In Chinese restaurants, noodles typically contain eggs. Avoid buying fried foods from restaurants and vendors that use the same frying surface for preparing multiple types of food.

Food preparation. Read package labels carefully, looking for the words listed in table 5.3. In recipes, eggs act as a source of liquid; egg protein acts as a binder to hold together cakes, cookies, and burgers; and beaten eggs provide lightness by helping to incorporate air in little bubbles. It's a simple matter to replace eggs with a similar amount of liquid or wet foods, such as juice, nondairy milk, water, applesauce, or mashed bananas. In this book, we use nonallergenic alternatives, such as xanthan gum, as a binder for baked goods; other gums, such as guar gum, also work well. Ground flaxseeds, mixed with water, make an excellent replacement for eggs in baked items, pancakes, and waffles; plus this will boost your intake of omega-3 fatty acids. Use one tablespoon (15 ml) of ground flaxseeds to three tablespoons (45 ml) of water for each egg. To learn more about useful gums and similar substances, see Ingredients That May Be New To You on pages 171–178. For leavening, baking powder or soda are very effective. (Soda requires the presence of something sour, like vinegar or lemon juice, for its leavening action to work.) It's helpful to know that when we just omit the one or two eggs called for in some of our favorite baked goods recipes, such as muffins, the end result turns out just as well. You'll find tasty sandwich spreads, hearty entrées, creamy puddings, and some truly Divine Macaroons (page 207) in the recipe section of this book, all without eggs.

TABLE 5.4. FOODS THAT SOMETIMES OR ALWAYS CONTAIN EGG PROTEIN

Baked goods	Ice cream	Pavlova mix
Baking mixes	Instant Cream of Wheat	Puddings
Batters	Instant oatmeal	Quiche
Béarnaise sauce	Lemon curd	Salad dressing
Breakfast cereals	Malted cocoa drinks	Sandwich spreads
Cookies	Mayonnaise	Sherbet
Creamy fillings	Meringue	Soufflés
Custard	Mousse	Soups
Egg noodles	Muffins	Tartar sauce
Eggnog	Nougat	Tempura
French toast	Omelettes	Waffles
Hollandaise sauce	Pancakes	Wines

Being Well Nourished Without Eggs

Eggs provide protein, several vitamins (such as riboflavin, folate, pantothenic acid, and vitamin B_{12}), and iron. However, these nutrients can easily be supplied by other foods, so avoiding eggs should not create any risk of deficiency (see chapter 8).

Soy

Soybeans are a legume and are botanically related to other legumes, including peanuts and beans. Nonetheless, people who cannot tolerate soy frequently can eat other legumes without adverse reactions. In skin testing for allergies, a legume mix (such as peanut, soy, and green peas) often is used. In such cases, if a reaction occurs, the test results will indicate that a patient is sensitive to legumes as a group. The fact is that the proteins in various legumes differ, and the sensitivity to all legumes based on a reaction to an individual legume has not been established. Some clinics and labs test for individual beans, peas, and lentils, and it is worthwhile to ask about this so that some of these highly nutritious foods can be included in your diet.

Soy allergy most frequently is seen in infants. It is less common than allergies to eggs, milk, peanuts, tree nuts, fish, and wheat, and is frequently outgrown by the age of three. Fortunately, soy rarely causes anaphylaxis; but unfortunately, people with soy allergy or intolerance may suffer from varying degrees of asthma, stuffy nose, intestinal inflammation and discomfort, and skin reactions. Because symptoms may be mild (but aggravating nonetheless), it is possible to go for years without realizing that soy is the root of poor health.

TABLE 5.5. TERMS THAT SOMETIMES OR ALWAYS INDICATE THE PRESENCE OF SOY

Bulking agent	Shoyu	Starch
Carob	Soy flour	Tamari
Emulsifier	Soy nuts	Tempeh
Guar gum	Soy panthenol	Textured soy protein
Gum Arabic	Soy protein	Textured vegetable protein (TVP)
Hydrolyzed vegetable protein (HVP)	Soy protein isolate or concentrate	Thickener
Lecithin*	Soy sauce	Tofu
Miso	Soya	Vegetable broth
Monosodium glutamate (MSG)**	Soybean	Vegetable gum
Protein	Soybean oil	Vegetable starch
Protein extender	Stabilizer	Vitamin E

* Mostly produced from soy but may be manufactured from egg.

** Sometimes produced from soy or wheat but is commonly synthetic.

Tips for the Label Detective

In the processed-food industry there has been almost unlimited use of soy and soy derivatives, making it a particularly ubiquitous and menacing hidden allergen. As with many other food allergens, a reaction may occur with exposure to very small quantities of soy protein. Some sources of soy are fairly obvious: soy-based veggie burgers, soymilk, tofu, tempeh, soy flour, soy oil, and the beans themselves are easy to avoid. What is challenging is the fact that soy is used in the manufacture of various foods in a wide variety of ways, including as a "texturizer," emulsifier, and protein filler. Consequently, soy may be listed on the ingredient panel according to its use (for example, "hydrolyzed protein" or "lecithin").

Soy protein isolate and concentrate are commonly used to emulsify fat in food products. Therefore they may be present in ice cream, mayonnaise, and a variety of other liquid fat- or oil-containing foods. They also may be used in soymilk and as a protein concentrate added to "health foods" and high-protein bars, powders, and beverages. Other foods that may contain soy include puréed baby foods, cereals, margarine, and white and brown bread (for example, whole wheat, rye, or pumpernickel). Additional uses of soy in the processed food industry include tofu, soy-based "ice cream," nondairy "cheese," textured vegetable protein, meat extenders, and vegetarian meat alternatives.

Soybean flour often is added to cereal grain flours and is used extensively in the baking industry. The majority of commercial breads contain some amount of soy flour. Pastries, cakes, biscuits, and baby foods also may contain soy flour. Fermented soybeans are commonly used in the preparation of soy sauce or Worcestershire sauce, and fermented soy products in various forms are widely used in Asian cuisines.

Soybean oil has many uses and can be found in salad dressings, margarine, baby foods, and many nonfood items (such as linoleum, paint, plastics, soap, and glue). Labels are not always clear about its presence; often "vegetable oil" is an oil blend containing soy. Although it was initially thought that soybean oil was safe for soy-sensitive individuals, soy proteins may be present in the oil depending on the extraction process and the oil's purity. Cold-pressed or expeller-processed soy oil is more likely to contain soy protein than soy oil that has undergone the hot-solvent extraction process. The vitamin E in many multivitamin supplements is derived from soy.

Soy may find its way into food products where it is added as a "compound" ingredient. For example, if margarine is added to a food product, it will be listed as such, but soy that may be present in the margarine itself will not be listed on the ingredient panel. Because of this, complete avoidance of soy is a tricky task.

TABLE 5.6. FOODS THAT SOMETIMES OR ALWAYS CONTAIN SOY PROTEIN

Baby foods	Edamame (fresh green soybeans)	Salad dressings
Bakery goods*	Energy and "health" drinks	Sauces (such as Worcestershire, sweet and sour, hoison, teriyaki)
Bread (esp. high-protein bread)*	Gravy (sauce) powders*	Seasoned salt
Breakfast cereals (some)	Hydrolyzed vegetable protein**	Shortenings
Butter substitutes	Ice cream	Shoyu
Cakes	Infant formula (including cow's milk formula)	Snack and "energy" bars
Candy	Liquid meal replacers	Soups (canned and mixes)
Canned or packaged soups	Margarine	Soy pasta products
Cheese (nondairy) made from soybeans	Meat alternatives (such as vegetarian burger patties, tofu dogs, deli slices)	Soy sauce
Chinese food	Muesli	Soy sprouts (Asian restaurants)
Chocolates (cream centers)	Nondairy frozen desserts	Soybeans
Cookies	Pies*	Sports bars
Cooking oils	Powdered meal replacers	Stock cubes (bouillon cubes)
Crackers		Tamari
Desserts		Tofu

* May be present because of soy in the flour used.

** May be wheat.

TABLE 5.7. OTHER POSSIBLE SOURCES OF CONTACT WITH SOY		
Adhesives	Enamel paints	Nitroglycerine
Blankets	Fabrics, fabric finishes	Paper
Body lotions and creams	Fertilizers	Printing inks
Cosmetics	Flooring materials	Shampoos
Dog food	Lubricants	Soaps

Going Soy-Free in the World

Soy is a relatively recent addition to the cuisine of Western countries and thus is less commonly used as a basic ingredient in recipes and home-prepared foods compared with eggs and dairy products. When you shop, read ingredient labels carefully. You're more likely to encounter hidden sources of soy in foods prepared outside the home and in processed foods.

Restaurants and traveling. Check out Web sites of chain restaurants; many have allergy information and will indicate which restaurant items are free of soy. However, be aware that busy restaurants are a common source of cross contamination. If you are very sensitive to soy, it is best to avoid chain or fast-food restaurants. Your best bets are restaurants that make everything from scratch. Italian, Middle Eastern, and Indian eateries may be able to accommodate you, but Chinese, Thai, Korean, and Japanese restaurants rely heavily on soy ingredients and thus are best avoided. Diners and American eateries often use soy oil for frying; ask the manager if you can get foods that do not depend on soy oil or other soy derivatives.

Being Well Nourished Without Soy

Soy is a major source of protein in many vegetarian diets and a considerable source of fat (via soybean oil) in most diets. Some excellent soy-free, high-protein ingredients for main dishes include beans, peas, lentils, and wheat gluten. Grains, nuts, and seeds provide protein as well. Refer to pages 307–333 for some delicious soy-free main dishes. Fortunately, giving up soy oil may be a blessing, because much of the soy oil found in processed foods is hydrogenated, a form best avoided by all. The healthiest sources of fats are nuts and seeds and their oils, including canola and flaxseed oils, avocados, olives, and olive oil.

If you are able to eat neither dairy nor soy products, good cereal toppers are rice milk, almond milk, or other nut milks. Look for varieties with added calcium, vitamin D, and vitamin B_{12}.

Formula-fed infants who cannot tolerate formulas made with cow's milk or soy may be given Alimentum or Nutramigen formulas, which are hypoallergenic.

Peanuts

Peanuts are one of the most allergenic foods and the leading cause of severe allergic reactions in the United States and Canada. The prevalence of peanut allergy has climbed dramatically over the past few years: An estimated 1.5 million Americans are peanut sensitive. Peanut allergy is outgrown about 20 percent of the time and occurs more commonly among people with asthma, skin conditions, or other food allergies. About one-third of peanut-sensitive individuals have severe, life-threatening reactions to peanuts. People with peanut allergies often are concerned about possible reactions from tree nuts; however, tree nuts are botanically unrelated to the peanut, which is a legume. It is estimated that 25–35 percent of people with peanut allergy also have a sensitivity to tree nuts. If tree nuts are tolerated and desired, sources that are not contaminated with peanuts should be sought, as nuts can make important contributions to a healthful diet including protein, energy, vitamin E, trace minerals, and protective phytochemicals.

The most notable symptom of peanut allergy is anaphylaxis (see page 150). However, those with a less severe sensitivity to peanuts may experience hives, stuffy nose, watery eyes, wheezing, asthma, or nausea.

Recent research has indicated that mothers should wait until a child is at least three years old before introducing peanut products and do so in tiny amounts at first, especially if there is a history of peanut allergy in the family or if the child has a history of asthma, intestinal disorders, or skin problems. An infant may react to peanut proteins through the mother's milk; in this case the mother should avoid peanut-containing foods until after weaning.

A minute amount of peanuts—for example "peanut dust" in the air resulting from a nearby peanut muncher)—may cause a severe reaction in sensitive individuals. As a result, many airlines have become peanut free, and many schools do not allow peanuts or peanut butter sandwiches in the classroom or cafeteria.

Tips for the Label Detective

Peanuts are added to a large variety of processed foods (see table 5.9). These include cookies and cakes, marinades, sauces (especially Asian sauces), dressings, dairy and nondairy frozen desserts (as a flavoring), vegetarian burger patties, and a wide range of snack foods. Some individuals with peanut allergy also have shown reactions to sweet lupine seed flour, which may be added to some pastas, gluten-free baked goods, and other specialty food products.

Many manufacturing plants that process tree nut and seed butters also process peanut butters and other peanut products. Cross-contamination often is unavoidable. Thus, individuals who are not allergic to tree nuts but are very sensitive to peanuts may not be able to eat prepared foods or other nut and seed butters that contain tree nuts.

Because food companies do not want to be responsible for an unforeseen peanut allergy reaction, many voluntarily place information about peanuts on food labels, such as: "Produced on shared equipment that processes products that contain peanuts," or "Produced at a facility that produces peanuts," or "May contain trace amounts of peanuts." This is a source of great comfort as well as great frustration to many peanut allergy sufferers. It is important to note that because including allergy information on labels is voluntary, the lack of such a statement on a food product does not mean that it is free of peanut products. As the demand for peanut-free foods increases, we will be seeing more statements like, "Produced in a peanut-free facility."

Although peanut oil has been considered to be "safe," like soy oil, its allergenicity appears to be related to the way the oil is processed. Cold-pressed peanut oils may contain peanut allergen, and the residual peanut proteins in it may become more allergenic with heating. Peanut oil often is used to fry foods and is common in the preparation of many food and nonfood products, which can affect extremely sensitive individuals just through contact. Peanut oil may also be called "arachis oil."

Some skin lotions and hair products may contain peanut proteins. Those sensitive to peanuts should select hypoallergenic cleansers and lotions whenever possible.

TABLE 5.8. TERMS THAT SOMETIMES OR ALWAYS INDICATE THE PRESENCE OF PEANUTS

Asian dressing	Groundnut	Peanut
Asian sauce	Loratamine	Peanut butter
Flavoring	Mandalona	

Going Peanut Free in the World

When dining out of your peanut-free home, make it clear to the host or server and the restaurant management that you have a peanut allergy that is severe. Ask if peanuts, peanut butter, and peanut oil are used and to what extent. Ask for recommendations that are peanut free. If you are at risk for anaphylaxis, always take your EpiPen with you in the case of unforeseen cross-contamination. Eateries that are most likely to use peanuts in many dishes include Thai, African, Chinese, Indonesian, Mexican, and Vietnamese restaurants.

Even though it is recommended that people who are hypersensitive to peanuts avoid *all* tree nuts (because of potential cross-contamination with peanuts), it is possible to find nuts that are "pure"—in other words, that have never come into contact with peanuts via shared equipment or packaging facilities that also process peanuts. We contacted almond, pistachio, and other tree nut processors and discovered that some brands are peanut safe but don't necessarily say so on the label. We encourage you to call nut growers and manufacturers to find out which nuts are safe to buy in your area. You may find ways to purchase nuts directly from the growers.

Being Well Nourished Without Peanuts

Fortunately, the absence of peanuts from the diet poses no special risk of nutrient deficiencies. Peanuts are a good source of unsaturated fats, protein, vitamin E, and trace minerals. These nutrients also are abundant in tree nuts. If you can tolerate other nuts (and know of a reputable brand produced in a peanut-free facility), include them in your diet. If you wish to enjoy a peanut butter–like spread and you can tolerate other tree nuts, try almond butter, cashew butter, sunflower seed butter, and others. Be sure to purchase products processed in a peanut-free facility (one peanut-free brand of almonds, walnuts, and almond butter is Four K Farms, www.4kfarms-almonds-walnuts-driedfruit.com). You may be able to find other fresh nuts that are from a peanut-free facility; with these you can make your own nut butters at home using a grinder, sturdy food processor, or juicer (several brands are suitable for making nut butters). Seeds can also be ground to make tasty, nutritious butters. See page 354 for instructions on making your own seed and nut butters at home. If you are sensitive to other nuts as well as peanuts and wish for a nutty spread, you have at least three options. One is I.M. Healthy brand soy nut butter (www.soynutbutter.com), which is made in a 100 percent peanut- and tree nut–free facility. The other is No Nuts brand Golden Pea Butter (www.peabutter.ca), made from special peas in a nut-free environment. SunButter (www.sunbutter.com) makes a sunflower seed butter made in a peanut- and tree nut–free factory.

TABLE 5.9. FOODS THAT SOMETIMES OR ALWAYS CONTAIN PEANUTS

Baked goods	Cookies	Pastry
Baking mixes	Egg rolls	Peanut butter
Battered foods	Ice cream (dairy and nondairy)	Satay sauce and dishes
Breakfast cereals		Soups
Candy	Mandalona nuts	Sweets
Cereal-based products	Margarine	Thai dishes
Chili	Marzipan	Vegetable fat
Chinese dishes	Milk-based formula	Vegetable oil

Tree Nuts

Tree nut allergies are common and are potentially life threatening for some individuals; they often tend to persist for life. Tree nuts include almonds, Brazil nuts, cashews, hazelnuts (filberts), macadamia nuts, pecans, pine nuts (pignolias), pistachios, and walnuts. Almonds appear to be the least problematic of all common tree nuts. Some people suffer reactions from all of these nuts, and others from one or several. For those who experience anaphylaxis from exposure to one type of nut, all nuts should be avoided, because all too often nuts are cross-contaminated with each other. Coconuts, peanuts, nutmeg, and water chestnuts are not examples of tree nuts. People allergic to peanuts often can eat tree nuts, and people allergic to tree nuts often can eat peanuts; some individuals are allergic to both.

Those sensitive to tree nuts may or may not be sensitive to seeds. Sesame seed allergy is more common than in years past, and other seeds have been identified as culprits as well. Allergy to one seed does not necessitate the avoidance of all seeds, unless the reaction is severe. See page 101 for more information on seed allergy.

Symptoms of tree nut sensitivity range from tingling of the lips to anaphylactic shock. People sensitive to tree nuts may experience contact dermatitis (especially in the mouth); itching of the mouth, eyes, and ears; throat tightening; skin reactions; asthma; and intestinal discomfort.

TABLE 5.10. TERMS THAT SOMETIMES OR ALWAYS INDICATE THE PRESENCE OF TREE NUTS

Almond paste	Macadamia nuts	Nut pieces
Almonds	Marzipan	Pecans
Artificial nuts*	Natural nut extract	Pesto
Brazil nuts	Nougat	Piñolia nuts
Chestnuts	Nut butters (such as	Pine nuts
Filberts	almond or cashew butter)	Piñon nuts
Gianduja	Nut meal	Pistachios
Hazelnuts	Nut oil	Pralines
Hickory nuts	Nut paste	Walnuts

* Artificial nuts can be peanuts that have been deflavored and reflavored with a nut, such as pecans or walnuts.

Tips for the Label Detective

Allergic reactions to nuts most often are caused by eating unlabelled foods, by not checking food labels carefully, or by consuming foods that contain hidden sources of nuts. The most common types of foods that cause allergic reactions due to nuts are chocolates, cookies, candies, granola bars, and ice cream.

Nuts may be found as a hidden, unlabelled part of a food because of accidental cross-contamination during manufacturing. Companies often label their products with the statement "may contain nuts" if they cannot guarantee that a food they are producing is free of nuts. This usually is because nuts are being used in the same machines for other foods. A company that makes similar foods—some that contain nuts and some that do not contain nuts—may have difficulty removing all traces of nut allergens when cleaning the machines between processing different items. This type of cross-contamination is most likely to occur with cookies, candies, cereals, chocolate, ice cream, dried soups, and nut butters. Chocolate and mint ice cream are most likely to contain undeclared nuts since leftover ice cream can be added to these without changing the flavor. European chocolates are permitted to be made with leftover chocolate, which may contain nuts and may not be declared on the label.

Unpackaged foods, such as those in a cookie jar or tin, may contain traces of nuts from nut-containing cookies that were previously stored in the container. Bulk foods, buffet meals, and potluck dishes may also be dangerous because of cross-contamination. Cross-contamination can occur during food preparation when a cutting board or knife is used to chop nuts as well as other foods. It also can happen when the same oil is used to fry different foods, the same batter is used for different foods, or the same frying utensils are used for different foods without washing them carefully in between uses. Other possible sources of cross-contamination are grinding nut-flavored coffees in a coffee grinder; baking muffins with and without nuts if the leftover batter is used for the other muffins or if the baking pans are not properly cleaned; using the same scoop to take scoops of different ice creams, some of which may contain nuts; and using the same knife to cut a nut-containing dessert and then to cut another dessert.

TABLE 5.11. FOODS THAT SOMETIMES OR ALWAYS CONTAIN TREE NUTS

Nut	Food
Tree nut	almond paste, candies, cereal, chocolate, cookies, desserts, donuts, European chocolates, granola bars, gianduja, hamster and gerbil food, liqueurs, marzipan, milkshakes, muesli, pesto sauce, popcorn, specialty cheese spreads, specialty coffees, sundaes, sweets, trail mixes
Walnut/pecan	chocolate "turtles," nut muffins, pecan pie, pesto sauce, pralines, walnut oil, Worcestershire sauce
Hazelnut/filbert	nougat, chocolate bars, Frangelico liqueur, hazelnut coffee, hazelnut liqueur
Pistachio/cashew	candies, cashew butter, pistachio ice cream
Almonds	almond mocha, almond paste, amaretto, marzipan, pure almond extract

Allergic reactions also can happen when candy vending machines contain different foods at various times. Some candies may become contaminated with traces of nuts if there were nuts or other nut-containing foods previously in the vending machine.

Oils (such as safflower and canola) do not need to be avoided unless someone is specifically allergic to these as well. It is believed that most tree nut oils probably contain enough allergenic protein to cause allergic reactions. These are "cold pressed" (unprocessed, extruded, or expressed) oils and generally are not safe for nut allergic people.

Going Without Nuts Without Going Nuts

Unless you are sensitive to all nuts, seeds, and soy, you can get creative in the kitchen with your cooking and baking. Try swapping a nut butter for a seed butter (such as tahini or sunflower butter) or soy nut butter for baking and some sauces. Snack on chickpea "nuts" (page 352) or roasted soybeans for a nutty crunch.

Once you are aware of the myriad ways nuts can sneak their way into your diet, you should be able to dine outside your home without a high risk of exposure. Always ask your host or your restaurant server as well as the restaurant manager what options are available, and voice your concerns regarding your food sensitivities. Depending upon the severity of your reaction, you may need to avoid restaurants that use nuts as an ingredient in their dishes.

Being Well Nourished Without Tree Nuts

Tree nuts provide protein, unsaturated fats, vitamin E, and the minerals zinc (especially in cashews), calcium (in almonds), and selenium (in Brazil nuts). If you cannot tolerate any nuts at all, be sure to include a regular source of unsaturated fat, such as olives, avocados, and vegetable oils that you can have. Legumes such as peanuts, soy, and beans provide similar nutrients as nuts and are suitable substitutes in many main dishes. Pages 307–333 provide several nut-free main dishes for you to try, many with variations to suit your taste and tolerances.

Corn

Corn, which is often thought of as a vegetable, actually is a versatile grain. In addition to its widespread use in soups and chowders, side dishes, breakfast cereals, corn bread, grits, corn chips, tacos, nachos, and corn tortillas, not to mention corn on the cob, corn is used as an inexpensive source of sweetener (corn syrup), thickener (cornstarch), and fat (corn oil) in the processed food industry. People who are corn sensitive may suffer from intestinal distress, stuffy nose and sneezing, or skin hives after eating a food with corn in it. Corn allergy is relatively rare, but reactions may be severe among hypersensitive individuals. Nonallergic intolerance appears to be more prevalent than a true corn allergy.

Tips for the Label Detective

Diets without corn are difficult to plan because corn and corn derivatives are used in many prepared foods and packaged products, mostly in the form of sweeteners or cornstarch. While it is easy to avoid obvious uses of corn where corn is the featured ingredient (as with corn chips, corn tortillas, popcorn, and cornflakes), many processed foods contain corn derivatives that are more difficult to spot. Many packaged cereals and beverages are sweetened with corn syrup, and many other pantry staples, such as spaghetti sauce, baked beans, and canned soups, contain corn sweetener, corn oil, or cornstarch.

Commercial food producers often make caramel flavoring with corn syrup instead of cane or beet sugar. Corn is used in maple, nut, and root beer flavorings for ice cream, ices, confections, and baked goods. Many soft drinks and fruit drinks contain corn syrup in the flavoring. Grits, polenta, hominy, and maize also are sources of corn. Marshmallows are dusted with cornstarch to keep them from sticking together, and cornstarch is added to most brands of confectioner's sugar and baking powder to keep them from caking or clumping.

Corn may or may not be in food starch, modified food starch, vegetable gum, or vegetable starch. Contact the product manufacturer if these terms appear on an ingredient label to determine if they are corn derived. Distilled white vinegar, bleached white flour, and iodized table salt also may contain corn allergens.

TABLE 5.12. TERMS THAT SOMETIMES OR ALWAYS INDICATE THE PRESENCE OF CORN

Baking powder	Dextrin	Malt extract
Caramel	Dextrose	Malt syrup
Caramel coloring	Food starch	Maltodextrin
Corn	Fructose	Modified food starch
Corn alcohol	Golden syrup	Monosodium glutamate (MSG)
Corn flour	Grits	Starch
Corn oil	High-fructose corn syrup	Syrup
Corn sweetener	Hominy	Treacle
Corn syrup	Hydrolyzed corn protein	Vanilla extract
Corn syrup solids	Invert sugar or invert syrup	Vegetable gum
Cornmeal	Lactic acid	Vegetable oil
Cornstarch	Maize	Vegetable starch
Dextrates	Malt	Xanthan gum

Dextrin and maltodextrin, often made from cornstarch, are used in sauces, dressings, and ice cream as a thickening agent. Dextrose may be used in cookies, sports drinks, and crispy foods such as French fries, batter-fried foods, and potato puffs. Dextrose (also known as glucose or corn sugar) may be listed on labels as dextrin, dextrates, maltodextrin, caramel, or malt syrup.

Corn derivatives are used in a wide range of everyday products. These include general household goods, cosmetics, personal care products, and pharmaceuticals. Sometimes corn oil is used in emollient creams and toothpastes. Corn syrup often is used as a "texturizer" and carrying agent in cosmetics. Corn derivatives also may be

TABLE 5.13. FOODS THAT SOMETIMES OR ALWAYS CONTAIN CORN

Alcoholic beverages (ale, beer, gin, whiskey)	Corn chips	Pancake syrup
	Corn flakes	Pancakes
Artificial sweeteners (such as Equal)	Corn flour	Peanut butter (commercial sweetened)
	Corn oil	
Baked beans	Corn syrup	Pickle relish
Bakery products	Cornmeal	Pickles, sweet
Baking powder	Cornstarch	Pie fillings
Barbeque sauce	Custard	Polenta
Biscuit, cake, and pancake mixes	Doughnuts	Puddings
	Frozen desserts	Salad dressing
Biscuits	Graham crackers	Sauces (thickened, clear, Asian-style)
Bleached flour	Gravy	
Blended sugar	Grits	Sherbet
Bread	Hominy	Soda
Cakes and cake mixes	Iced tea (canned or bottled)	Soup
Candied fruit	Instant coffee	Spaghetti sauce
Candy	Iodized salt	Succotash
Caramels	Jam	Syrup
Carbonated beverages	Jelly	Tortillas
Carob	Juice drinks (canned or bottled)	Vanilla extract
Cereals (presweetened)	Ketchup	Vanilla flavoring
Cheese (imitation and nondairy)	Maize	Vegetable shortening
Coffee creamers/whiteners	Malt	Vegetables (mixed, frozen)
Condiments	Malt syrup	Vinegar (distilled white)
Confectioner's sugar or powdered sugar	Margarine	Waffles
	Nachos	Yogurt (dairy or soy)
Cookies	Nondairy "creamers"	
Corn		

found in adhesives, plastic wrap, paper cups, recycled plastic eating utensils, and paper plates. Other possible hidden sources of corn are aspirin, lozenges, ointments, suppositories, vitamins, laxatives, bath powders, and medicinal capsules. Medications in liquid or tablet form may contain cornstarch or corn syrup.

Going Corn-free in the World

Restaurants and traveling. Corn-sensitive individuals can still eat out, but it would be best to avoid Mexican restaurants, where corn ingredients are very common and cross-contamination may be inevitable. Asian restaurants may or may not be acceptable; ask the chefs what they use for sauce thickeners and sweeteners. Pizzas often are placed on a bed of cornmeal to prevent sticking, although you may be able to find a pizzeria that does not use cornmeal. You may have the most success at restaurants that take pride in using fresh ingredients and preparing everything to order; they may avoid processed ingredients that contain corn derivatives. Make your allergy or sensitivity clear to the restaurant management or host.

Shopping and food preparation. Although ingredients like cornstarch and corn syrup are quite common in cooking and baking, acceptable substitutes are available. You will find a wonderful recipe for corn-free baking powder on page 183. For recipes that call for cornstarch as a thickener, you may substitute potato starch, tapioca starch, arrowroot, or kuzu. Instead of corn syrup, you may use golden syrup made from sugar cane, maple syrup, brown rice syrup, concentrated fruit juice, or molasses (these may affect the flavor and color of your finished product). Check out the sweeteners at your natural food store or gourmet market for other corn-free options. You may make your own corn syrup alternative with the following recipe:

IMITATION CORN SYRUP

MAKES ABOUT 2 CUPS (500 ML)

2 cups	cane sugar	500 ml
¾ cup	water	185 ml
¼ teaspoon	cream of tartar	1 ml
	Dash of salt	

Combine all the ingredients in a heavy saucepan. Stir well and bring to a boil. Reduce the heat, cover, and simmer for 3 minutes. Uncover and cook, stirring often, until the syrup has thickened to the consistency of corn syrup.

You don't need to give up snack foods that are typically corn based. Next time you watch a movie at home, try popped rice (available online and at many gourmet food stores), rice crisps, baked potato chips, or even soy chips. Roll up your favorite fillings into a flour tortilla instead of a corn tortilla. Make some bean chili with our no-corn Ricebread Squares, page 191.

Being Well Nourished Without Corn

Avoiding corn is not typically a cause for concern, nutritionally speaking. Multiple grain allergies, however, may be problematic. In this case, it is important to focus on whole foods that you are able to tolerate. Starchy vegetables such as potatoes, sweet potatoes, beets (don't throw away the greens!), parsnips, radishes, and turnips are particularly well tolerated. These veggies provide a nutritious source of complex carbohydrates for grain-sensitive folks. You also may wish to try lesser known but equally tasty starchy vegetables such as taro, cassava, rutabaga, and Jerusalem artichokes.

Yeast

Yeast is a type of fungus. Its most popular functions in foods are as a rising agent in baked goods and as a key player in the fermentation process of beer, vinegar, and other fermented foods. People who are sensitive to yeast are often sensitive to mold as well.

It is unlikely but possible to be allergic to the specific proteins found in yeast. However, sensitivity to yeast is typically not allergy related.

Candida albicans is a yeast that is naturally present in our bodies. However, this yeast can become overgrown, upsetting the balance of healthful microorganisms in the intestine. The result can be unpleasant symptoms such as itching, intestinal discomfort, and headaches. One way to bring our bodies back into balance is to avoid sugar, which is a favorite menu item for yeast. See chapter 3, pages 45–47 for a more complete discussion on candida and how it relates to food allergies.

Some people are sensitive to foods with yeast or mold because of their histamine or tyramine content. See pages 102–103 for more about histamine and tyramine.

TABLE 5.13. TERMS THAT SOMETIMES OR ALWAYS INDICATE THE PRESENCE OF YEAST OR MOLD		
Au gratin	Flavoring	Vinegar
Breaded	Malt	Yeast (including nutritional,
Enriched flour	Mushroom	brewer's, active dry, and
Enzymes	Sour	torula yeasts)

TABLE 5.14. FOODS THAT SOMETIMES OR ALWAYS CONTAIN YEAST OR MOLD

Alcoholic beverages	Enriched flour	Pickles
Baking mix	Ginger ale	Pretzels
Barbecue sauce	Grapes	Relish
Biscuits	Horseradish	Rolls
Bread crumbs	Kefir	Root beer
Breads	Ketchup	Salad dressing
Buns	Luncheon meats	Sauerkraut
Buttermilk	Malted milk	Sour cream
Cake	Marmite or Vegemite	Soy sauce
Cheese	Mayonnaise	Spice mixes
Chili sauce	Miso	Stuffing
Chutney	Morels	Tea
Cookies	Mushrooms	Tomato sauce
Crackers	Mustard	Truffles
Croutons	Olives	Vinegars
Dried fruits	Pastry	Worcestershire sauce

Fruit, Dried Fruit, Sulfites, and Citrus

People experience several types of reactions to fruits. One is Oral Allergy Syndrome, an instant response experienced in the mouth and throat when one or more types of raw fruit are consumed. Cooked fruit is usually less allergenic. Thus oranges, grapefruit, or apples may cause a reaction, whereas marmalade may not. Grapes and raisins (which are dried grapes) may cause a reaction; yet if raisins are present in a baked item, they may have no effect.

Commercially produced raisins and other dried fruits often contain sulfites, which are added to preserve or bleach the color. Sulfites also are added to many other foods, beverages, salad bar ingredients, and medications for a variety of reasons. Sulfite agents commonly used are sulfur dioxide, sodium sulfite, sodium bisulfite, potassium bisulfite, sodium metabisulfite, and potassium metabisulfite. People with asthma, particularly steroid-dependant asthmatics, tend to be sensitive to sulfites, as do some migraine sufferers. Dried fruit that is sulfite free is available at natural food stores. A commercial test kit (Sulfitest) is available to help detect the presence of sulfites in foods. It consists of chemically treated paper strips that turn red in the presence of sulfites or green in the absence of sulfites. Some problems with the test have been reported (for example, it may give false-negative and false-positive results), thus its use is not recommended.

Though these types of sensitivities are classified as food intolerance rather than an allergic response (because they cannot be confirmed by immunoglobulins in the blood), some people report that citrus fruit exacerbates their arthritis or triggers headaches. Ironically, citrus contains a phytochemical (nobiletin) that may be anti-inflammatory. At this time there is little scientific research to shed light on the situation. Dietary triggers that are reported for various forms of arthritis, and for migraines, seem to differ from one person to the next.

Nightshades

The nightshade family has long been blamed by some health practitioners and in the popular press for triggering arthritic reactions (osteoarthritis, rheumatoid arthritis, and gout) in some individuals—though not in everyone who has these conditions. Foods from this plant family include tomatoes, potatoes, eggplant (aubergines), huckleberries, bell peppers, and hot peppers. It also includes products made with these foods, such as ketchup, cayenne, chili powder, paprika, pimento, and Tabasco. (Black pepper is not a nightshade.) Tobacco, morning glory, and medicinal plants, such as mandrake and belladonna (deadly nightshade), are also related. The components in these plants that cause reactions are present in relatively small amounts in the foods listed, compared with medicinal plants and tobacco.

Though there is little firm scientific research to explain these reported experiences, sensitivity to certain alkaloids that are naturally present in these plants may cause pain and swelling in a significant minority of individuals with degenerative arthritis. To determine whether nightshades truly are a trigger, it is recommended that they be eliminated from the diet for three to six months, along with the avoidance of tobacco exposure in any form. During this elimination phase, it is important to observe whether symptoms recede. Following this period, nightshade foods may be reintroduced to see whether symptoms return.

Cooking may reduce the alkaloid content of nightshade foods by about 40–50 percent. The green spots and sprouts on potatoes usually reflect a high alkaloid content (the green color is due to chlorophyll, not to alkaloids). It is wise for sensitive individuals who wish to occasionally eat potatoes to thoroughly remove sprouted areas before cooking, or to discard green or sprouted potatoes. Exposure to light increases alkaloid formation in potatoes. Like tobacco, eggplant and tomatoes (green and red) contain the alkaloid nicotine, though in smaller amounts.

Other Food Culprits

There are many other foods to which we may develop sensitivities. In this section we briefly refer to some other triggers for food allergies and intolerances.

Fish and Shellfish

Fish, crustaceans (such as crab, crayfish, lobster, and shrimp), and mollusks (such as clams, mussels, oysters, and scallops) are among the most potent allergens. Those who have a potentially life-threatening anaphylactic reaction are advised to avoid all fish, due to the proteins they contain known as *parvalbumins*. Those who are sensitive to one crustacean are likely to be sensitive to all types of crustaceans; the same is true for mollusks. Though once highly regarded as health food, much seafood now is contaminated with various waste chemicals that are dumped into our oceans and rivers. Fortunately, plenty of other protein-rich plant foods are available to us. The omega-3 fatty acids that contributed to the "health food" status of fish can be obtained from flaxseeds, hempseeds, walnuts, and soyfoods. Long-chain omega-3s are available in O-Mega-Zen3 vegetable-based capsules (rather than gelatin capsules) through Pangea at www.veganstore.com or 1-800-340-1200, and Vegan Essentials at www.veganessentials.com or 1-866-88-VEGAN.

If you are allergic to fish, note that Worcestershire sauce contains anchovies and may be found in pasta sauce, cocktails, caponata relish, and Caesar salad dressing, and on pizzas. Asian food may contain oyster sauce or Worcestershire sauce. Avoid French fries from restaurants that use the same oil for fries and fish. Shampoos, conditioners, and other skin care products may contain fish oils. In fish and seafood restaurants there is a risk of cross-contamination from utensils and cooking surfaces in the food preparation areas. Fish protein can become airborne; some individuals have had reactions just from walking through a fish market.

> For additional information on food culprits, see *Dealing with Food Allergies: A practical guide to detecting culprit foods and eating a healthy, enjoyable diet*, by Janice Vickerstaff Joneja, Bull Publishing, Colorado, 2003.

Sesame Seeds and Other Seeds

Sesame seeds may be a cause of allergic reactions, typically around the mouth or in the digestive or respiratory systems. They may be anaphylactic for some individuals. Someone who has experienced an anaphylactic reaction to seeds should avoid all types of seeds that are eaten as foods or as seasonings. Those with milder reactions may find that one type of seed is problematic, whereas others cause no reaction. Seeds that are consumed as foods, for example, as part of breads, other baked items, and energy bars, are flax, melon, pomegranate, psyllium, pumpkin, sesame, sunflower, and cottonseed. Those consumed as seasonings include mustard (white, yellow, and black), celery, and poppy seeds. Flaxseed oil and sesame oil may contain traces of protein allergens.

Sesame seeds are present in tahini, hummus, and halva. Sesame seed oils are present in the herbal beverage Aqua Libra and sometimes in Chinese stir-fries. The antioxidant vitamin E, also known as a *tocopherol*, is sometimes extracted from seeds such as sesame seeds.

Chocolate

The list of foods that may trigger migraine headaches includes chocolate. Like red wines and certain cheeses, chocolate contains *phenylethylamine,* a substance that can dilate blood vessels in the brain. To test for chocolate sensitivity, do not use milk chocolate or filled chocolates, as doing so will make it difficult to determine if you are reacting to the dairy ingredients or fillings rather than the chocolate; instead use dark, unsweetened baker's chocolate. (If desired, you may melt it and mix in a little sweetener to which you are not sensitive.)

Sugars

Some people have difficulty digesting sugars other than the lactose sugar in milk. As a result, undigested sugar can draw water into the intestine, where intestinal organisms will ferment the sugar, leading to gas, bloating, and diarrhea. Foods that may cause this type of problem include white table sugar (sucrose), refined grains (which contain maltose), and products that contain either of these. Sometimes, a small amount of sugar is tolerated, yet with larger quantities, symptoms arise. The inability to digest sugars may be a temporary condition related to an intestinal infection, food allergies, or the use of antibiotics.

Histamine and Tyramine

Two substances, *histamine* and *tyramine*, derived from amino acids in proteins, can cause problems when amounts get so high that our body has difficulty ridding itself of these compounds. Both of these substances are naturally present in our bodies and in a wide range of foods.

Histamine. You may recall from chapter 1 that histamines are the substances made in our body that are responsible for the symptoms of allergy, such as nasal congestion, hives, swelling, itching, headaches, and digestive upsets. Yet histamines are also normal components of body fluids that regulate important functions in our bodies and play protective roles in the immune system. Our bodies remove excess histamine; however, the maximum amount we can tolerate varies from person to person. Reactions may occur when we consume too many dietary sources of histamine. Our tolerance for it can be reduced through the use of certain medications for depression, asthma, or hypertension.

Histamine is present in spoiled foods, particularly fish. As a result of bacterial action, histamine is present in fermented foods, such as cheese, yogurt, kefir, fermented processed meats (salami, pepperoni, bologna, wieners), and smoked or pickled meats. People who are sensitive to histamine may need to avoid eating leftovers, which could contain increased levels. Histamine can be released by shellfish, alcohol, egg whites, and strawberries. It is naturally present in tomatoes, eggplants, and spinach. Dyes such as tartrazine (in foods or medications) may trigger the release of histamine from mast cells in our bodies. So can benzoates, which are added to foods as preservatives, emulsifiers, or as bleaching agents for flour.

Tyramine. As with histamine, we have natural mechanisms in our bodies to rid us of tyramine, and our tolerance for this substance is uniquely individual. Symptoms such as hives or migraine headaches may arise when the amount of tyramine present exceeds our ability to break it down. Certain drugs used for depression or for Parkinson's disease can limit our ability to break down tyramine. Tyramine is present in aged cheeses, yeast extract, wines (especially red), beer, and vinegars. Some tyramine is present in chicken liver, tomatoes, eggplant, avocados, raspberries, and red plums.

Salicylate (Aspirin, Acetylsalicylic Acid)

Salicylates naturally are present in an immense variety of plant foods. They may cause no problems at these levels, even in sensitive individuals. However, when salicylate is concentrated to form a pain-killing medication such as aspirin, amounts exceed tolerable levels for some people. The result can be hives and swelling. Reactions are particularly common among asthmatics.

MSG (Monosodium Glutamate)

When we think of MSG we may have an instant association with Chinese foods. Yet MSG is used as a flavor enhancer at many other types of restaurants, in many packaged and prepared foods, and in dozens of seasonings such as Accent and Zest. The listing of MSG on labels is voluntary. MSG may appear on labels as "hydrolyzed protein," "hydrolyzed vegetable protein," "hydrolyzed plant protein," "glutamic acid," "flavoring," "Kombu extract," and other names. Sensitive individuals must ask about its use at restaurants and in packaged and prepared foods. MSG can affect the respiratory and digestive systems and increase heart rate. It also can cause flushing, mood changes, headaches, and other symptoms. Drinking alcohol at the same time increases the speed of absorption of MSG.

BHA and BHT (Butylated Hydroxyanisole and Butylated Hydroxytoluene)

Though most people tolerate these common additives, the antioxidants BHA and BHT trigger rashes and hives in sensitive individuals, particularly those with aspirin sensitivity. BHA or BHT are added to processed foods to keep fats from going rancid and developing objectionable odors. They are found in oils, margarines, lard, shortening, and items containing these fats (such as potato chips, doughnuts, pastries, roasted peanuts, and other foods). The presence of BHA or BHT is shown on the ingredient list on labels. Some packaging materials for cereals, crackers, and convenience foods contain these antioxidants.

Latex, Banana, Kiwi Fruit, Avocado, or Chestnut

Though this may seem an odd grouping, remember that rubber comes from a tree. Those who are allergic to latex rubber (in baby bottle nipples, balloons, dental dams, gloves, or condoms) are sometimes allergic to certain foods, most notably bananas, avocados, or chestnuts, and sometimes kiwi fruit, mango, peaches, and certain other foods. Not everyone with latex allergy will react to the whole list; at least twelve potentially allergenic proteins can be involved. Latex reaction can be anaphylactic.

Cross Reactivity Among Plant Families

Prior to the 1980s, the popular assumption was that a person allergic to the edible part of one plant was allergic to other plants within the same botanical family, or would become so if foods from the other plants were ingested. It has since been learned that we react to specific allergenic proteins in a particular food. A particular food often contains several proteins that may be antigens, and we may react to one, or several, but not all of those antigens. Plant A may contain one protein that is also present in plant B; whereas a second allergenic protein may be found in plants A and C but not in B. We need not assume that we are allergic to plant foods in related botanical families and need not excessively restrict foods. To find out which foods are our triggers, see chapter 4, Testing for Food Sensitivities, page 65. Our response pattern is unique and is not necessarily identical to that of someone we know who reacts to one of the same foods that we do.

Chapter 6

WHEAT AND GLUTEN SENSITIVITIES AND CELIAC DISEASE

$\mathcal{W}$heat is the primary grain eaten by humans. Around the world, consumption of wheat has doubled in the last thirty years to reach nearly 600 million tons per year. In 2002, the average American consumed about 137 pounds of wheat flour. More foods are made with wheat than with any other cereal grain.

Europeans and North Americans love their wheat in countless foods: breads, cereals, pancakes, waffles, pastries, bagels, sandwiches, pastas, crackers, biscuits, pretzels, cookies, cakes, and myriad other ways that are not always so obvious. Unfortunately for many people, wheat is food enemy number one. Some wheat-sensitive people seem to be able to tolerate a small quantity of wheat, while others get sick if they consume even a minuscule amount.

Wheat sensitivity manifests in a variety of ways, depending on the person. These include:

- Mild symptoms (such as fatigue and gastrointestinal discomfort).
- Aggravation of a pre-existing condition (such as asthma or eczema).
- Acute allergic reaction (such as abdominal pain, diarrhea, hives).
- Celiac disease.

Some people react to one or more proteins that are specific to wheat, while others are sensitive exclusively to gluten, a protein that makes up about 86 percent of the overall protein in wheat and is found in many other grains as well.

Wheat Allergy

Prevalence

True wheat allergy is relatively uncommon. It is thought to affect fewer than 1 percent of infants, most of whom outgrow the allergy by the age of three, and it affects far fewer adults. However, self-reported sensitivity to wheat is becoming more common. Though the reason for the latter condition is not well understood, it appears that some people who are not actually allergic to wheat find that they feel better when they eliminate or cut down on wheat.

Symptoms

Like any food allergy, a wheat allergy may manifest as a respiratory reaction (such as wheezing), a skin response, or gastrointestinal distress. People who are severely sensitive to wheat may have reactions when their skin comes into contact with a wheat-containing food, when they breathe in wheat flour dust at a bakery ("baker's asthma," for example, is a respiratory allergy to inhaled flour), or inhale the allergen while harvesting wheat. Anaphylaxis to wheat is rare but does exist among some people. For those who have a tendency to this severe reaction, the anaphylaxis may be induced by exercise.

Diagnosis

Although we can be tested for wheat allergy at our allergist's office (using the methods described in chapter 4), the test results might not paint an accurate picture. Studies show that many people who test positive for a wheat allergy can eat wheat with no evidence of allergic symptoms. Conversely, people who exhibit obvious symptoms of allergy after consuming wheat may test negative for a wheat allergy. The best way to determine whether you are sensitive to wheat is to perform a careful elimination diet, followed by a food challenge (see chapter 4, page 70). During the elimination phase of the diet, it is important to avoid all possible sources of wheat. See tables 6.1 and 6.2 for foods and ingredients that sometimes or always contain wheat.

Living Well with a Wheat Allergy or Sensitivity

After testing foods and observing your symptoms, you and your healthcare providers may determine that eliminating wheat is a solution to your food-related troubles. Living wheat-free is challenging but certainly not impossible.

TABLE 6.1. TERMS THAT SOMETIMES OR ALWAYS INDICATE THE PRESENCE OF WHEAT

Bran	Flour	Seasoning
Bread or bread crumbs	Gluten	Seitan
Bulgur	Graham	Semolina
Cereal extract	Hydrolyzed plant protein	Spelt
Couscous	Hydrolyzed vegetable protein	Stabilizers
Crackers and cracker meal	Kamut	Surimi
Dextrin	Maltodextrin	Triticale
Durum	Matzoh	"Wheat" as part of a phrase
Farina	Modified food starch (unless otherwise specified)	

Tips for the Label Detective

Never assume that a product is wheat free simply because it appears to be so at first glance. For example, wheat proteins are common in seasoning mixtures and some food additives, the sources of which may not be identified on a food label. See tables 6.1 and 6.2 for terms to look out for when seeking wheat-free foods. Unless the product label specifically states "wheat free" and there are no ambiguous ingredients, it is possible that there are traces of wheat in the product. As discussed in chapter 5, there may be traces of wheat in a food that was produced in the same facility as a wheat-containing food. You might find that you can tolerate such tiny amounts of wheat; vigilance of your intake along with observing any symptoms you experience will help you determine how much wheat, if any, your body can handle without consequence.

Fortunately, there is an enormous market for wheat-free products, so your prospects for enjoying a wheat-free life are excellent and improving all the time. See page 117 for a list of Web sites and resources for wheat- and gluten-free products. Also, be sure to explore the many recipes in this book, particularly the section on baking, pages 179–212, as all the recipes we've included are free of wheat.

TABLE 6.2. FOODS THAT SOMETIMES OR ALWAYS CONTAIN WHEAT INGREDIENTS

Baked goods	Granola	Processed meats
Baking powder	Gravies	Salad dressings
Battered foods	Icings	Sauces
Breaded foods	Instant cocoa	Sausages
Burgers	Luncheon meats	Seasonings
Candy	Meatloaf or meatballs	Soy sauce
Cereal	Ovaltine	Stuffing
Corn bread	Pâté	Tamari (unless designated wheat free)
Croquettes	Pie crust	
Grain coffee substitute	Postum	Tempura

Going Wheat Free in the World

Probably the most challenging aspect of following a wheat-free diet is dining outside your home. Our kitchens are safe havens where we know exactly how our food is prepared. When eating at the home of a friend or relative, or at a restaurant, we must be especially careful. If you are very sensitive to wheat, it's best to avoid places that make their own bread or pasta because wheat flour can contaminate foods that are otherwise wheat free. Talk to the manager of the restaurant you're visiting; be specific about what you can and cannot eat. Your best option may be to order basic foods such as salads, grilled or steamed vegetables, rice, and fresh fruit. Because dressings, sauces, and condiments are common sources of hidden wheat or gluten, it's wise to bring along your own dressing, sauce, or wheat-free seasonings. Many natural food restaurants now offer wheat-free delicacies like quinoa salad, rice pilafs, and millet-bean burgers. As awareness of wheat sensitivity grows, so will our food selections, both in and out of our homes.

Thanks to the myriad wheat-free products available, and the recipes in this book and other books, you can eat almost "normally"—that is, much like a person who eats wheat does! For breakfast, you might enjoy a wheat-free cereal topped with fortified rice milk or soymilk and fresh fruit. For lunch, how about one of the hearty bean soups from this book (see pages 299–301) with some wheat-free bread (either store bought or from one of our recipes, pages 187–195)? For supper, enjoy one of our entrées (pages 307–333) or perhaps some wheat-free noodles with sautéed vegetables in a succulent sauce, accompanied by a crisp garden salad.

Being Well Nourished Without Wheat

Wheat provides protein, carbohydrates (including fiber, if the whole grain is left intact), B vitamins including folic acid and riboflavin, vitamin E, calcium, iron, magnesium, and zinc. Fortunately, alternative grains provide similar, and often superior, nutritional quality—quinoa and amaranth are two excellent examples. Include plenty of wheat-free grains: millet, quinoa, buckwheat, and amaranth. See table 6.7 for a full list of the grains allowed on a wheat- and gluten-free diet. For descriptions of these grains, see Ingredients That May Be New To You, pages 171–178, and to learn about grain cookery, see and pages 165–168. Consume plenty of fresh fruits, vegetables, legumes (lentils, peas, and beans), and include a good source of omega-3 fatty acids (see page 138). Be sure to incorporate reliable sources of vitamin B_{12} and vitamin D; you will find more details about planning your diet in chapter 8. See the list of wheat- and gluten-free supplements, pages 363–364.

Gluten Intolerance and Celiac Disease

About one in 133 Americans suffers from celiac disease (CD), also known as *celiac sprue, gluten-sensitive enteropathy,* and *gluten intolerance.* Just what is gluten? Gluten is one of the primary proteins found in wheat (as well as various strains of wheat, such as spelt and kamut), rye, and barley. Gluten gives bread its elasticity and helps baked goods retain their shape. For people with CD, eating a food containing gluten leads to a wide array of adverse symptoms ranging from general discomfort to malnutrition and growth failure in children. Wheat is the primary but not only grain that people with celiac disease must avoid. They must also avoid all foods that contain gluten naturally or to which gluten has been added (see tables 6.6 and 6.8).

What Is Celiac Disease?

Celiac disease is characterized by chronic inflammation of the small intestine, resulting in structural damage to the intestinal mucosa, which is the inner lining of the small intestine. The result of this injury is that the small intestine has a hard time absorbing nutrients, which leads to malnutrition and other complications. Also, it is thought that CD leads to increased intestinal permeability (see chapter 2), which may lead to other food intolerances and possibly allergies. Dietary gluten is thought to be the main culprit in the progression of CD.

TABLE 6.3. SYMPTOMS ASSOCIATED WITH CELIAC DISEASE

Abdominal pain, bloating, and flatulence	Fatigue	Muscle wasting
Anxiety	Hair loss	Nausea and vomiting
Bone and joint pain	Infertility	Nerve problems
Depression	Lactose intolerance	Nutrient deficiencies, including iron, vitamins A, D, E, K, and B_{12}
Developmental delays (children)	Loss of coordination	
Diarrhea	Mental problems	Skin rashes
Failure to thrive (children)	Migraine headaches	Steatorrhea (fat in the stools)
	Mouth ulcers	Weight loss

Symptoms

The widely variable symptoms of untreated celiac disease are listed in table 6.3. Various people experience different combinations and levels of severity. Because the disease originates in the small intestine, which is where we absorb much-needed nutrients from food, CD can wreak havoc on our health. The symptoms of CD tend to mirror the symptoms of other diseases (see table 6.4). Unfortunately, this often causes people to live with their disease for a long time before a correct diagnosis is made.

TABLE 6.4. CONDITIONS WITH SYMPTOMS SIMILAR TO CELIAC DISEASE

Bacterial overgrowth syndromes	Effects of some drugs
Cow's milk allergy/intolerance	IBD
Crohn's disease	IBS
Diverticulosis	Lactose intolerance

Even though CD has its origins in the small intestine, it tends to manifest in systems and organs throughout the body. This is because our intestines are central to the absorption of nutrients as well as being the main center of immune activity. At first glance it might not be obvious why symptoms such as anxiety or migraine headaches would be caused by gluten intolerance. Once we understand the role our small intestine plays in both our nutritional status and the function of our immune system, we can see how damage to that part of our body can lead to a host of other problems.

Diagnosis

Blood tests are commonly used to test for CD, even though they are not 100 percent accurate. The most accurate way to diagnose CD is by a biopsy of the jejunum, a part of the small intestine that is especially prone to injury from CD. The doctor examines the tissue for abnormalities, also taking into account symptoms, diet history, family history, and other health issues. A diagnosis of CD should not be made without a biopsy, because the actual cause of symptoms may be a different disorder. Furthermore, the unnecessary avoidance of foods can compromise our health. A misdiagnosis of CD is not something to take lightly. When you get tested (whether via blood tests, biopsy, or both), it is important that you are following a gluten-*containing* diet prior to testing; otherwise, a false-negative result may occur.

Gluten Sensitivity Without Celiac Disease

Some people appear to be sensitive to gluten but test negative for celiac disease. Sensitivity to gluten is a continuum, not a black-and-white issue. You don't need a confirmed diagnosis of CD to benefit from a gluten-free diet. Even if the biopsy of the intestine is normal and blood tests are negative, it is possible that the body has become sensitized to gluten in different ways that are not detected by these indicators. There is a debate in the scientific community regarding whether there are forms of gluten intolerance that are distinct from celiac disease. The only way to know for sure that you are sensitive to gluten is to perform an elimination diet followed by a food challenge (see chapter 4). Bear in mind that there's a difference between gluten sensitivity and wheat sensitivity, and while the diet therapy for each overlaps, it is an important distinction. If you test negative for CD but find that you are ultra-sensitive to gluten, follow the dietary advice given for celiac disease. However, some gluten-sensitive people appear to be able to tolerate small amounts of gluten or only certain types of gluten-containing foods. For example, you may be able to tolerate sprouted grain bread but not regular bread. The only way to know with certainty is to follow a controlled test diet and carefully track your symptoms. Some researchers postulate that gluten-sensitive people who test negative for CD will eventually contract the disease; in this case the disorder is referred to as "latent celiac disease." Others believe that certain cases of gluten sensitivity (without celiac disease) can be overcome if the intestinal lining can be healed. (See chapter 2.)

Dermatitis Herpetiformis

Dermatitis herpetiformis (DH) is a chronic skin condition characterized by lesions and intense itching and burning sensations. DH is a form of celiac disease, as it is usually associated with the same abnormal mucosal lining of the small intestine as seen in those who have CD. In DH, the skin on the outside of our body is also affected. Most people with DH have few bowel complaints, while a small percentage may have diarrhea, bloating, bulky stools, or abdominal cramps. DH, which can be diagnosed with a skin biopsy, is often discussed together with celiac disease because both conditions respond well to a gluten-free diet. If you have been diagnosed with dermatitis herpetiformis, follow the same treatment plan given for those diagnosed with celiac disease.

Is There a Cure for Celiac Disease?

There is no known cure for celiac disease. Complete and permanent avoidance of gluten is the only treatment that will avert symptoms and heal the intestine (additional measures may support this treatment; see chapter 2). It is important to note that for a significant number of people with CD, sensitivity to cow's milk may complicate remission. If you have celiac disease and cannot get relief from strict gluten avoidance, you may find success by avoiding dairy products as well. You may be sensitive to the protein in cow's milk, or you may be suffering from lactose intolerance. Almost half of those diagnosed with celiac disease are also lactose intolerant, so it makes sense to try to eliminate lactose and dairy products from your diet to see if you get relief from your symptoms. See chapter 5 for details on how to eliminate dairy products. The recipes in this book are free of both gluten and dairy products.

Who's at Risk for Celiac Disease?

Celiac disease runs in families; over half the people with CD have a close relative with the disease. Some experts believe that CD can result from an injury to the small intestine, such as *Candida albicans* overgrowth (see chapter 3) or parasitic, viral, or bacterial infections. CD is thought to be caused by an inappropriate immune response (scientifically speaking, the immune reaction is mediated by T cells rather than Immunoglobulin E, which is the main player in classic allergic reactions). Therefore, those with other immune disorders, particularly autoimmune disorders

TABLE 6.5. CONDITIONS THAT ARE OR MAY BE ASSOCIATED WITH CELIAC DISEASE		
Autoimmune disorders	Liver disease	Addison's disease
Diabetes (type 1; insulin-dependent)	Iron-deficiency anemia and other anemias	Congenital heart disease
Down syndrome	Osteomalacia and osteoporosis	Epilepsy
Rheumatoid arthritis		*Candida albicans* infection
Kidney disease	Thyroid disease (autoimmune)	Gall bladder disease
		Lymphoma

such as rheumatoid arthritis and type 1 (insulin-dependent) diabetes, are more prone to the disease than the general population (see table 6.5). Symptoms among those predisposed to CD may be triggered by emotional stress, pregnancy, or surgery.

"Silent" Celiac Disease

Because of the increased prevalence of screening for celiac disease among those at risk (for example, children with insulin-dependent diabetes), more and more diagnoses of CD are being made. However, some people with confirmed celiac disease present mild symptoms or none at all; this is known as "silent" celiac disease. Some researchers postulate that these people will inevitably fall victim to related symptoms and associated conditions as outlined in tables 6.3 and 6.5, respectively. Having an accurate diagnosis of celiac disease is essential, regardless of the symptoms that occur. Knowing that you have this disease provides knowledge that your family members are at risk, since CD has a genetic basis. Even "silent" celiac disease may progress into associated conditions such as osteoporosis and lymphoma. On the other hand, it is important to rule out a diagnosis of CD when other conditions are the cause of symptoms, because a gluten-free diet can be a challenge to follow and may not be appropriate if gluten sensitivity is not the problem.

The Gluten-Free Diet

For a complete resource guide on the gluten-free diet, we recommend dietitian Shelley Case's tremendously helpful book, *Gluten-Free Diet: A Comprehensive Resource Guide* (Case Nutrition Consulting, 2004; www.glutenfreediet.ca). This book

TABLE 6.6. GLUTEN-CONTAINING GRAINS		
Barley	Kamut	Spelt
Einkorn	Oats (see box on page 114)	Triticale
Emmer		Wheat (including wheat bran, wheat germ, and wheat starch)
Farro	Rye	

TABLE 6.7. GLUTEN-FREE GRAINS

Note: These grains are gluten free by nature but may contain gluten if they have become cross-contaminated by gluten-containing grains; for example, via processing in a facility that also processes wheat.

Amaranth	Flax (also considered to be a seed)	Rice (brown and white varieties)
Buckwheat (kasha)*	Job's tears	Sorghum (milo)
Cassava (arrowroot)	Millet	Tapioca
Chickpea (technically a legume but its flour may be used for batters and other recipes)	Montina™ (Indian rice grass)	Taro
		Teff
Corn	Quinoa	Wild rice

* Pure buckwheat flour is gluten free, but many products labeled "buckwheat flour" might contain buckwheat and wheat flours. Read labels carefully.

lists over 1,600 gluten-free products, plus recipes, nutrition information, shopping guidelines, and resources. Here we will cover the basics.

Since gluten is found in grains, it is important to distinguish acceptable grains from unacceptable grains. Table 6.6 lists grains that contain gluten; these are to be strictly avoided. Table 6.7 lists grains that are gluten free and are thus acceptable on a gluten-free diet.

Other Foods to Avoid

All of the foods and ingredients listed in tables 6.1 and 6.2, which are sometimes or always made with or derived from wheat, are off-limits with a gluten-free diet, unless their source is specified as gluten free. If you're gluten sensitive, take care to avoid all wheat-containing items and all of the gluten-containing grains and products made from them that are listed in table 6.6. With a straightforward wheat allergy, many of the items in tables 6.1 and 6.2 may be appropriate if they are explicitly from a non-wheat source. However, people with CD need to be extra vigilant because the source of a questionable ingredient may be wheat or another gluten-

TABLE 6.8. FOODS THAT SOMETIMES OR ALWAYS CONTAIN GLUTEN BUT NOT NECESSARILY WHEAT

Barley malt	Candy	Baked beans and other ready-to-eat entrées with added thickeners or flavorings
Beer	Soymilk and other nondairy milks sweetened with malt	
Ale		
Lager	Dried dates dusted with flour	Grain additives in some teas and coffee alternatives
Malted liquor	Soups and broths with vegetable protein added	Chips and other crispy snack foods with added seasonings
Malt vinegar		

The Oat Controversy

It is generally recommended that gluten-sensitive individuals avoid oats due to the potential for cross-contamination with gluten-containing grains. Historically, oats have been forbidden on a gluten-free diet because of the protein they contain. Recently, however, doubt has been cast on this theory, as the protein in oats does not appear to elicit the same reaction as the gluten protein in wheat, rye, and barley. Current studies have supported this: Researchers have discovered that a significant percentage of gluten-sensitive people seem to be able to tolerate oats just fine. A recent study in Finland followed two groups of people with celiac disease for five years. One group consumed oats and the other group did not. The conclusion of the study was that people with CD could eat oats without suffering any aggravation of their disease.

A new study from Holland sheds light on why oats do not lead to the same symptoms caused by other gluten-containing grains. The researchers found that the protein in oats has a different molecular structure than the gluten found in wheat, rye, and barley. Furthermore, the researchers determined that among people with CD, the immune response to gluten is significantly different from the immune response to the similar protein in oats.

If you know you cannot tolerate gluten, should you eat oats? If you can tolerate them, yes, because including oats in an otherwise limited-grain diet would be wonderfully convenient and a valuable nutritional boon. However, if you find that you cannot tolerate oats, the symptoms you experience may be extremely unpleasant. If you are not sure whether you can tolerate oats, you may want to introduce "pure oats" into your diet in small amounts and keep a detailed food diary to track your responses. "Pure oats" refers to sources that have not been contaminated with traces of wheat or other troublesome grains. If you find that you can tolerate oats, be sure to use oat products that are milled and processed in a dedicated facility (one that does not mill or process any gluten-containing foods). Although research indicates that oats are safe, celiac organizations in the United States and Canada do not recommend oats because it cannot be guaranteed that oats are pure and uncontaminated.

containing grain. For example, a wheat-sensitive person may be able to tolerate malt made from barley, but a gluten-sensitive person cannot, because barley is a prohibited grain. Unfortunately, the statement "wheat free" on a food label does not necessarily mean "gluten free." However, legislation appears to be favoring those with gluten intolerance; new bills are calling for more specific information about gluten-containing ingredients on food labels. See table 6.8 for food items that may contain gluten but are not necessarily derived from wheat.

Baking and Cooking

If you have been disappointed by the gluten-free baking mixes on the market (or maybe you haven't tried them because of their price), we have a treat for you! Jo's

Gluten-Free All-Purpose Flour (page 182) is for you! This flour has been tested time and time again, and is the basis of most of the baked goods in this book. You can use this alternative to all-purpose wheat flour for most of your baking needs. See page xx for tips on how to use this flour.

Table 6.9 provides useful substitutes for common foods that contain gluten. Using these and similar alternatives will streamline your cooking and enable you to follow many conventional recipes while keeping them gluten free. Remember to always check labels for possible gluten-containing ingredients and additives.

Dining Out

For tips on dining away from home, refer to the wheat allergy section on page 107.

TABLE 6.9. COMMON GLUTEN-CONTAINING FOODS AND SUITABLE ALTERNATIVES

GLUTEN-CONTAINING ITEMS	ALTERNATIVES
Semolina or durum wheat pasta	Rice, corn, or quinoa pasta
Udon noodles	Rice linguine or 100 percent buckwheat soba noodles
Soy sauce	Wheat-free tamari, Bragg's Liquid Aminos, or wheat-free miso thinned with a little water
Worcestershire sauce	Bragg's Liquid Aminos or miso thinned with a little water
Seitan ("wheat meat")	Tempeh*, baked tofu, or legumes (peas, beans, or lentils)
Bulgur (in tabouleh salads and some chilis)	Quinoa
Couscous	Quinoa or millet
Barley	Brown rice
Oatmeal	Rice flakes (see resources section, pages 363–64) or corn grits
Flour tortillas (also the base for most "wraps")	Gluten-Free Chapatis, page 192, or corn tortillas
Regular corn bread	Ricebread or Cornbread Squares, page 191
Flour for frying	Jo's Gluten-Free All-Purpose Flour, page 182, rice flour, fine cornmeal, or chickpea flour
Thickening for soups	Jo's Gluten-Free All-Purpose Flour, page 182, arrowroot, cornstarch, kuzu, potato starch, rice flour, or toasted chickpea flour
Wheat Flour	Jo's Gluten-Free All-Purpose Flour, page 182
Baking Powder	Gluten-Free Baking Powder, page 183

* Tempeh may be made with gluten-containing ingredients such as soy sauce or wheat grain. Choose an unflavored, 100 percent soy tempeh, and carefully check the label.

Healing the Gut in Celiac Disease

The following three-pronged approach is the best way for those with celiac disease to reclaim excellent health:

1. Avoid gluten.
2. Replenish nutrients, particularly those that are absorbed by the jejunum, which is the part of the intestine most damaged by the disease.
3. Heal the intestinal wall.

Avoid gluten. This is described in detail on pages 106–108 or 112–115 in this chapter.

Replenish nutrients. The nutrients that are absorbed by the jejunum are amino acids, fatty acids, zinc, potassium, calcium, magnesium, phosphorus, iodine, iron, copper, vitamins D, E, and K, most of the B vitamins, and vitamin C. Thus there are many nutrients to consider. This second aspect of healing is best accomplished by combining a wide variety of nutritious whole foods (see chapter 8 and our wonderful collection of recipes) and a gluten-free dietary supplement. Since so many nutrients are involved, the regular use of a multivitamin and mineral supplement is strongly recommended (see page 365 for a list of acceptable products). Because CD involves inflammatory reactions, and because fatty-acid absorption may be reduced in CD flare-ups, it is important to pay special attention to your intake of omega-3 fatty acids. Ground flaxseeds and flaxseed oil are excellent, concentrated sources of omega-3 fatty acids. If you use ground flaxseeds you'll obtain not only the beneficial oil but also fiber, amino acids, and lignans, which help soothe the damaged intestinal lining. For details on amounts and for other sources of omega-3 fatty acids, see pages 138–139 and 367.

Heal the intestinal wall. The methods for healing the intestinal wall are described in detail in chapter 2. Because CD is thought to increase intestinal permeability, it is of prime importance to restore the intestine to good health.

Recent Research Findings

Probiotics. These "friendly" bacteria, which are discussed in detail in chapter 2, have been making the celiac news! It turns out that their ability to transform intestinal flora may be powerful enough to eventually allow a person with CD to actually eat bread made with wheat flour. According to a 2003 study that was published in the *Journal of Applied and Environmental Microbiology*, a sourdough bread containing wheat and nontoxic oat, millet, and buckwheat flours mixed with *lactobacilli* ("friendly" bacteria) and fermented for twenty-four hours was well-tolerated by CD patients. Though you may not necessarily wish to try this (and if you did, it should only be done under the supervision of your physician or healthcare provider), it is

encouraging to know that introducing "friendly" bacteria to ou
improve the health of this part of our body.

Immunotherapy. This exciting new approach just might be th
defense against celiac disease. Promising research indicates that admi
tain proteins into the body may control the immune response to gluten
that clinical trials will begin within a few years.

"Glutazyme" Therapy. This treatment was recently developed in Australia and
is being looked at as a potential shield against damage to the small intestine caused
by gluten. This product is a pig-derived enzyme extract that breaks down gluten.
Fragmented gluten does not appear to damage the small intestine the way that
whole gluten proteins do. More research is needed to determine whether this will be
a useful therapy.

Oral Medication for Celiacs. This highly anticipated treatment may soon
become a reality. Researchers recently discovered that celiac patients fail to break
down a specific protein in gluten. A newly developed bacterial enzyme, taken as an
oral medication, may in fact break down the protein that is toxic to those with celiac
disease, making gluten digestible and safe for those with the disease. For any medication intended to break down gluten, the biggest challenge is that all of the toxic
proteins are broken down (as opposed to most of the proteins).

Resources for Gluten Intolerance and Celiac Disease

Books

Case, Shelley. *Gluten-Free Diet: A Comprehensive Resource Guide.* Saskatchewan, Canada: Case
   Nutrition Consulting, 2004. www.glutenfreediet.ca
Crangle, Claudine. *Living Well With Celiac Disease: Abundance Beyond Wheat or Gluten.* New
   Bern, North Carolina: Trafford. 2002.
Korn, Danna. *Kids With Celiac Disease.* Bethesda, MD: Woodbine House. 2001.
   www.glutenfreedom.net
Korn, Danna. *Wheat-Free, Worry Free.* Carlsbad, CA: Hay House Inc., 2003.
   www.glutenfreedom.net
Lowell, Jax Peters. *Against the Grain: The Slightly Eccentric Guide to Living Well Without Gluten
   or Wheat.* New York: Henry Holt & Co. 1996.
*The Official Patient's Sourcebook on Celiac Disease: A Revised and Updated Directory for the Internet
   Age.* Edited by James Parker and Philip Parker. San Diego, CA: Icon Group, Inc., 2002.
Tessmer, Kimberly A. *Gluten-Free for a Healthy Life.* Franklin Lakes, NJ: New Page Books. 2003.

Online Stores

www.enjoylifefoods.com
www.glutenfree.com
www.glutenfreedelights.com
www.glutenfreemall.com
www.glutenfreemarket.com

www.glutenfreepantry.com
www.glutenfree-supermarket.com
www.glutensolutions.com
www.glutino.com
www.missroben.com

Canadian Celiac Association/L'association Canadienne de la Maladie Coeliaque, Toronto, Canada, 800-363-7296. www.celiac.ca

Celiac Disease and Gluten-Free Diet Support Page. www.celiac.com

Celiac Disease Foundation, Studio City, CA, 818-990-2354. www.celiac.org

Celiac Sprue Association of the USA, Omaha, NE, 402-558-0600. www.csaceliacs.org

The Coeliac Society of Ireland. www.coeliac.ie

Friends of Celiac Disease Research, Inc. www.friendsofceliac.org

Gluten Intolerance Group (GIG), Seattle, WA, 206-246-6652. a nonprofit organization working toward increased awareness of gluten-intolerance diseases. Complete with information, event listings, advocacy, and education materials. www.gluten.net

Glutenfreeda's Online Cooking Magazine. www.glutenfreeda.com

R.O.C.K. Raising Our Celiac Kids, Encinitas, CA, 858-395-5421. www.celiackids.com

The Savory Palate, Inc. Cookbooks for people with food allergies, celiac disease, and autism. www.savorypalate.com

Special Diets Resource Guide. Local celiac support groups in your area. www.specialdiets.org/usorgs.htm

University of Maryland School of Medicine Center for Celiac Research, 410-706-8021. www.celiaccenter.org

Online Message Boards and Discussion Groups

Assortment of celiac-related discussion groups: www.lsoft.com/lists/listref.html (click "search" and use the keyword "celiac.")

Celiac.com message board: www.glutenfreeforum.com

Food Allergy Living Forum (specifically for gluten intolerance): http://foodallergyliving.com/community/start/login.php?msg=:

Glutino message board: www.glutino.com/english/interieur/index.cfm?myMenu=msg_board

Newsletters

Gluten-Free Living: National Newsletter for People with Gluten Sensitivity. www.glutenfreeliving.com

Scott-Free Life Without Gluten Newsletter. www.celiac.com (click on "Newsletter")

Grassroots Action

Food Allergy Initiative (FAI). A nonprofit organization that raises funds for food allergy treatment and cure. Complete with information, resources, advice, downloads, and news. www.foodallergyinitiative.org

Food Allergy Research and Resource Program (FARRP). Helps the food industry reduce allergy risk. Complete with an allergen database, library, newsletter, workshops, more. www.farrp.org

Gluten Intolerance Group (GIG). A nonprofit organization working toward increased awareness of gluten-intolerance diseases. Complete with information, event listings, advocacy, and education materials. www.gluten.net

Chapter 7

LIVING WITH FOOD SENSITIVITIES: FEELINGS, SAFETY, AND EXERCISE

*H*ave you ever been told, "It's all in your head," or, "Just wait it out; you'll feel better"? For many of us, an unfortunate consequence of our food sensitivities is the lack of understanding from friends and family who don't know what it is like to have such unpleasant symptoms and discomfort caused by food. Though well intentioned, their responses may be far from helpful. In some cases, those closest to us may feel discouraged or powerless to help, and they respond by making light of the situation. Others may offer advice that is unproven or speculative. Unfortunately, rather than making things better, our frustration and distress may be increased.

Most people take for granted their ability to eat virtually everything. When they're hungry; they simply chow down on whatever they want. Yet for those of us who must scrutinize every food label, interrogate every server, and question every host, the simple act of getting and eating a "safe" meal can be downright exasperating. We may feel judged and regarded as needlessly fussy. Perhaps we find one or two foods we know we can tolerate and stick only to those for months on end. However, we might suspect that such severe restrictions could be risky for our health. Having such limitations imposed on us can be demoralizing and make us feel isolated and sad about our situation and our restricted food choices.

Allergies and Our Children

When adults are afflicted with food allergies, we can explain what we are experiencing and draw upon a host of clues to help us identify the culprit, remove it from our diet, and ease our symptoms. Yet as parents and caregivers of little ones with food allergies, we face special challenges. When our babies react to foods, we must rely on our eyes and ears to figure out the cause and determine what to do to relieve their discomfort. When our youngsters grab a trigger food before we can stop them, we have to witness their pain and discomfort or, with severe allergies, be prepared for emergency intervention. When our toddler is given a cookie by well-meaning teachers or friends before we can intervene, we must watch as a rash develops on his face and hands because of troublesome ingredients. When our child acts out at a family picnic because the potato salad contained a food additive to which she is sensitive, we have to deal with the behavior as well as our embarrassment, knowing that others may not understand that the food was the cause of the outburst. Our occasional feelings of helplessness and frustration are accompanied by a strong sense of responsibility to prevent further attacks. However, as hard as we try, it is not always possible to monitor every morsel of food that goes into our child's mouth. And of course, we do not always know which foods will cause a reaction.

Fostering a Supportive Environment

Having food allergies can make us feel cut off from other people and left out of social situations. It can be difficult to go to parties, family gatherings, or even out to lunch with colleagues or friends. Celebrations and meals at restaurants may no longer seem like fun, and every event that involves food can seem like an ordeal.

How can we improve the situation? A crucial component of thriving with food allergies is to have supportive allies. Finding even one person who understands what we are going through can bolster us during low times. Local support groups, online message boards, national associations for people with foods allergies, and organizations for parents of children with food allergies can provide a tremendous amount of encouragement, friendship, and practical tips (see table 7.1 and the resources at the end of this chapter). For some of us, fear and depression may be a "side effect" of having to cope with food sensitivities. When our emotions pull us down, a counselor or therapist can be useful in helping us come to terms with our situation and assisting us with developing an effective plan of action.

Take command of your (or your child's) diet and health. By using the guidance provided in this book, you can learn how to identify food culprits, remove them from your diet, and replace them with healthful, delicious foods and recipes.

If you suspect that emotional problems are playing a role in your symptoms, talk it over with a trusted friend or seek out a therapist to help you sort out the root of your symptoms. Research shows that stress, anxiety, and other difficult emotions can bring about skin rashes, upset stomach, headache, and other symptoms that mimic those of food intolerance.

Direct Psychological Effects of Food Allergies

Can food allergies cause changes in our behavior, mood, and emotional state? Yes! This was discussed in chapter 3 in the sections on ADHD and depression. However, we can expect food allergies to affect our perception, attitude, and feelings in more subtle ways as well. Apart from the more obvious reactions to certain foods, our sensitivities may also result in emotional and/or behavioral changes. After all, when the immune system is stimulated by a trigger food, various biologic messengers are released that impact us both mentally and physically.

Indirect Psychological Effects of Food Allergies

Even if an offending food doesn't directly cause psychological imbalances, it is common for those who have food sensitivities to experience grief, sadness, and depression as a result of dealing with so many restrictions.

Stress

Those of us with food sensitivities typically experience more anxiety, particularly around mealtimes. But when we know our personal food triggers we can have more control over our stress, because we can take effective action to avoid these foods. In contrast, if we suspect that we have food sensitivities but are unsure which foods are the offenders, stress management is much more difficult. This is why it is so important to learn more about our body and how it responds to different foods. Knowledge is power. To detect which foods are at the root of your discomfort, use the tools in chapter 4 to determine which ones are culprits for you. Then, with the information in chapter 8, design a health-supportive, allergy-free eating plan.

Guilt

If our child has food allergies, we may experience guilt about the child's problem and may wonder if we could have prevented it if we had done something differently. Mothers may worry about their dietary choices during pregnancy or lactation. These reactions are understandable (in fact, with or without allergies, isn't motherhood almost a synonym for guilt?) but are based on unrealistic expectations. Food allergies are common and unpredictable. The most loving and caring parents and caregivers have children with allergies. By the same token, those of us with food allergies may feel that our special dietary needs place a heavy burden on our loved ones. Like diabetes, a broken bone, or any medical problem, food sensitivities are a fact of life that must be accepted, understood, and dealt with head on. As family members or friends, we can help most by being supportive of our loved ones with food allergies and learning about the dietary guidelines they need to follow to prevent reactions and stay well. If we feel guilty about our food sensitivities or misunderstood by our loved ones, gently explaining our feelings to them may make a great deal of difference. If necessary, we may want to seek the help of a counselor. We owe it to ourselves and our loved ones to share our needs with them so that we can devote our energies to being happy and healthy.

Fear

When something as innocent but essential as food causes pain and discomfort, it is a scary situation. When foods that others can eat without ill effect give us a splitting headache, nausea, or other distressing symptoms, it is easy to feel apprehensive about eating. Understandably, some people with food sensitivities become afraid to eat almost anything. As a result of avoiding foods for fear of the reaction they may produce, some allergic people become malnourished or develop eating disorders. To a certain extent, fear is necessary and our ally, as it drives us to be careful about what we eat. It can motivate us to find and consume only foods that we can tolerate. However, fear may be overwhelming and lead to feelings of loss of control, dread at the thought of going out, and terror at the thought of having to eat food prepared by someone else. If our children are the ones with food allergies, we feel a special fear and responsibility for their health, happiness, and well-being. While these fears are not unfounded, they also are not productive. It is possible to regain control and shed our feelings of helplessness. This book is your tool. Use it to pinpoint the cause of your ills, empower you to take control of your condition, and rebuild your diet so it is not only free of trigger foods but is health-supportive and delicious.

Coping Day-to-Day with Food Allergies

For those with severe food allergies, such as anaphylaxis to peanuts, the psychological burden can be overwhelming. Avoidance strategies must be in place at all times, and it is never acceptable to "slip." Such eternal vigilance is extremely demanding and exhausting. But even when our food sensitivities are not life-threatening, we may experience hardships with food management and difficulty living life to the fullest. Indeed, studies have shown that the quality of life among allergy sufferers can be poorer than those without allergies, greatly impacting how we perceive our own health. Food sensitivities have emotional effects on other family members (particularly parents of children with food allergies), as they limit activities outside the home.

When our food sensitivities are not life-threatening (even though they may be exasperating), we should approach them in a similar manner to other problems we face. Here are some tips:

Educate yourself. Learn everything you can about your particular condition. Read this and other books on food sensitivities. Research Web sites and join online message boards and local support groups to discover others with similar problems. (See the resources at the end of this chapter.) Talk to your healthcare providers. If you need to figure out more about the cause of your symptoms, try an elimination diet, as outlined in chapter 4. Find out as much as you can about the problems that you (or your child) are experiencing.

Minimize the impact of the problem. Perhaps healing the intestinal wall, as described in chapter 2, will help curtail reactions. If you have a permanent allergy or intolerance, learn how to eliminate trigger foods using the guidelines in chapter 5.

Maintain your health. Start with a nutrient-rich, balanced diet as described in chapter 8. Join an exercise class, take a daily walk, or engage in whatever activity you enjoy that will get you moving. Take a daily multivitamin-mineral supplement (see resources, page 365, for hypoallergenic brands). Nurture your relationships and find joy in what you do each day.

Seek support. There are many people who are able and willing to support you. Surround yourself with understanding people: loved ones, therapists or other health professionals, and others suffering with similar issues. Join a support group. Check with your local health clinic, spiritual group, library, community center, natural food store, local bulletin boards, telephone directory, and newspaper. If you find a lack of organized support, start your own support group. Even if you have a hard time finding somebody in your area, there is a wide range of support groups on the Internet. See the box below for just a few suggestions and where to go online to join them. They all are free. You may later bless your food sensitivities for the wonderful folks you have met because of them!

TABLE 7.1 ONLINE SUPPORT GROUPS AND MESSAGE BOARDS

Parents of Food Allergic Kids	health.groups.yahoo.com/group/POFAK
Allergies Message Board	www.healthboards.com/allergies
Allergy Discussion Group	www.immune.com/allergy/index.html
Parents Of Allergic Children	www.parentsofallergicchildren.org
SAFE-Support (SAFE=Society for Anaphylaxis from Food and the Environment)	au.groups.yahoo.com/group/SAFE-Support
Baby Centre Food Allergy Message Boards	www.babycentre.co.uk/bbs/545216
Food You Can Eat Forum	www.foodyoucaneat.com/food/forum/default.asp
Food Allergy Living Forum	foodallergyliving.com/community/start/login.php?msg=

For more information and support, please see the resources at the end of this chapter.

Life-Threatening Aspects of Food Allergies: Prevention Is Key

Rarely does the consumption of food threaten one's life. The leading cause of death from food is actually contamination of food with dangerous foodborne bacteria, usually due to improper handling or undercooked foods such as meat. However, food allergies do take the lives of 150–200 people per year in the United States and are believed to cause 30,000 emergency room visits annually.

Once it is known that a food causes a life-threatening reaction, prevention is of utmost importance. The best way to prevent a dangerous reaction to food is effective communication with everyone you come in contact with so they thoroughly understand the situation and the food can be avoided.

Tell Everyone

If your child has a severe food allergy, explain the allergy and its consequences to all the adults and children in her life. In school and at camp, teachers, school nurses, foodservice workers, and counselors need to be made aware. In your child's social circles, all of the neighborhood parents, other children, and anyone who would possibly give food to your child must be informed. Teach your child to tell others about her allergies and to politely decline food that has not been approved by you or another informed caregiver. If you have a food allergy, be sure to let people know if they are planning on serving you food. Always tell the people you are with, so that in the case of an accidental exposure, they will know what is going on and how to act accordingly.

Get the Word Out

Prepare a letter on your computer so you can easily print it out and send it to people. Give a talk at your child's school. Write a letter to the editor of your local paper. Give a seminar on food allergies at your local library. Give a cooking demonstration at your natural food store and ask them to carry more allergy-safe foods as part of their regular stock.

Be Extra Cautious when Served Food Outside the Home

At restaurants and at friends' homes, call in advance to discuss your concerns with those who will be preparing the food. For restaurants and hotels, be sure to speak with management. If you feel that you are burdening others, remember that you are doing what is necessary to protect your life; for this, any slight inconvenience is worth the peace of mind. Furthermore, others will feel much more burdened if an unfortunate reaction occurs. At restaurants, it is generally safer to order simple items such as a baked potato (instead of a potato casserole) or steamed vegetables (instead of a vegetable stew). One study of allergic reactions at restaurants found that half of the reactions were caused by foods "hidden" in dressings, egg rolls, and sauces. How strictly you adhere to this rule depends on your particular allergy and your risk of a severe reaction. If you prefer your food seasoned, bring your own safe seasonings, sauces, and salad dressings. Remember that restaurants, pizzerias, bakeries, candy shops, fast-food outlets, and delis pose a considerable risk of cross-contamination. In some cases, it's best to avoid places that serve a food (such as fish) that you are allergic to, even if you do not order it. See chapter 5 for more details.

Use Common Sense when Eating Outside the Home

Bring a meal or contribution to the meal with you whenever possible, even when a celebration or gathering is centered around a particular menu. On daily outings, while en route to a destination, or at an event that might serve food (such as a ballpark), bring your own food along rather than grabbing something at a restaurant. If you plan to fly on a plane, avoid eating the food served, as medical help won't be immediate should you need it.

Wear a Medical Alert Bracelet

Should you have an emergency, rescue workers will look for a bracelet containing allergy information. Wear it at all times; it can save your life!

Create an Action Plan and Stick to It

An action plan outlines what actions a caregiver should take in the event of an emergency. An example of an action plan for a child with anaphylactic allergy can be viewed at the Food Allergy and Anaphylactic Network's Web site, www.foodallergy.org/actionplan.pdf. If your child has food allergies, use this and other action plans to design one of your own, and share it with other caregivers and parents of your child's friends. If you are the one with an allergy, use it for yourself to share with others in your life. Having a plan of action on paper not only reduces stress and educates others, it also may save your life or your child's.

If You Have an EpiPen, Carry It with You at All Times

If you are at risk of anaphylactic shock from food, you must take your EpiPen (a medical device that serves as an auto-injector for epinephrine) with you wherever you go. Unexpected cross-contamination or accidental ingestion is always a possibility. If children are at risk for anaphylaxis, they must carry their EpiPen with them at all times. Teach your child (four years and older) how to inject the EpiPen; it can be administered through clothing. Make sure your child's teacher and other caregivers have an EpiPen of their own. Make sure to keep the EpiPens current (within the expiration date); the drug loses its effectiveness over time, so regularly check that the product is fresh.

Keep up with Product Recalls

Sometimes, due to manufacturer error, an allergen is introduced into a product that is labeled as being free of that allergen. Occasionally a product is placed into the wrong packaging or is labeled with incomplete information. When these oversights are discovered, the manufacturer must pull these products from store shelves. To read about the latest recalls and alerts, visit the very timely and useful Special Allergy Alert page of the Food Allergy and Anaphylaxis Network, www.foodallergy.org/alerts.html.

Responsibility of the Hospitality Industry

Anyone who serves food needs to be well educated about the risk of allergy. Airline, restaurant, and hotel employees are trained to heed the requests and special needs of their customers. However, this training isn't always sufficient, and sometimes mistakes happen. Horror stories abound. For example, a few years ago a woman ordered a dish at an Italian restaurant, but not before asking the server if the dish contained nuts. The server said it did not, though the kitchen staff were not asked. Unfortunately, the sauce was nut-based and the woman suffered anaphylactic shock and ultimately died. In cases where anaphylactic shock is a possibility, we are literally putting our lives in the hands of complete strangers. This is why it is imperative that wherever food is served, we must make our needs and risks clear not only to the servers but also to the cooks and managers. Keep in mind that no matter how clear we may be, errors and cross-contamination are always possible. Go out, socialize, and enjoy your meals. But communicate clearly and carry your EpiPen at all times.

Barriers to Others' Acceptance

Those around us may find it difficult to comprehend how a food that most people can eat without problem may actually lead to severe illness or death. A common example is when others (such as extended family or babysitters) are asked to care for children with food allergies. They may not believe that the threat of food allergy is that dangerous and thus may not be as careful as necessary. Whether due to denial, lack of understanding, or other reasons, such scenarios illustrate the importance of clear, effective communication about the serious nature of food allergies.

Because food intolerances are uniquely individual and vary widely, most people don't have a clear idea what a food allergy is or know the facts. Many claim they are "allergic" to foods they don't like or that they are opposed to eating; unfortunately this "overreporting" tends to undermine the threat that true food allergies pose to those afflicted.

Exercise-Induced Anaphylaxis: A Unique Form of Allergy

Regular exercise is one of the basic tenets of good health and longevity. This holds true for those with or without food sensitivities. However, for a small percentage of the population, exercising after eating certain foods (that otherwise are well tolerated) can induce allergic reactions. Exercise-induced anaphylaxis is a rare, distinct form of allergy. During an attack, which typically occurs one to four hours after ingesting a trigger food, the person affected may experience a range of possible symptoms from skin rash to severe anaphylaxis. The reaction may occur during any activity or level of physical exertion. For some people, certain foods or medications taken before an activity can trigger this response. Common food culprits include celery, seafood (especially shellfish), wheat, cheese, and others. About two-thirds of those who have exercise-induced anaphylaxis have a family history of atopy (hypersensitivity reactions, such as hay fever, asthma, or chronic hives). The immediate treatment for exercise-induced anaphylaxis is termination of the activity and rest; sometimes antihistamines or epinephrine is given if the symptoms are severe. Long-term treatment for exercise-induced anaphylaxis involves, first and foremost, an understanding of the condition on the part of the sufferer as well as the sports medicine team (if the person is an athlete). If you have exercise-induced anaphylaxis, wearing a medical alert bracelet is essential, and you should always carry an EpiPen. It may help to exercise during cooler times of the day, and always exercise with at least one other person present. If you find that food is related to your condition, the trigger foods should be avoided if possible. Should you eat an offending food, avoid exercise within four hours of the meal.

If you have trouble figuring out which food or foods cause symptoms when you exercise, keep a detailed food diary as described in chapter 4. Be sure to also keep close track of your activities, how soon you are active after eating, and the onset of any symptoms.

Restaurants and Travel

Today's vegetarian and vegan restaurants include everything from simple family style restaurants and fast food outlets to romantic bistros and elegant gourmet establishments. Most are happy to accommodate patrons who are sensitive to milk, eggs, and other allergens. To find out what's near your home or along a route you plan to travel, check www.vegdining.com or www.happycow.com, or do a search at www.ivu.org.

For long flights, many airlines provide special meals for those with milk, egg, and other allergies, or with lactose intolerance. Ask for a vegan or strict vegetarian meal. Be sure to explain your allergy when you make your reservation, and reconfirm your food order the day before you fly.

More Online Information and Support

Academy of Allergy, Asthma, and Immunology: www.aaaai.org
Action Against Allergy to help people with allergies (UK based): www.actionagainstallergy.co.uk
All Allergy: http://allallergy.net (Start here if you need to search for something in particular. Features thousands of resources, including Web sites in different languages, support groups, clinical trial information, databases, products, and events.)
Allergic Child: www.allergicchild.com.
Allergies (on About.com): www.allergies.about.com
Allergy Net Australia: www.allergynet.com.au
Allergy New Zealand: www.allergy.org.nz
Allergy Support: www.allergysupport.org
Anaphylaxis Australia Incorporated: www.allergyfacts.org.au
The Anaphylaxis Campaign (U.K.): www.anaphylaxis.org.uk
Anaphylaxis Canada: www.anaphylaxis.org
Asthma and Allergy Foundation of America: www.aafa.org
Food Additives Guide: www.foodag.com
The Food Allergy and Anaphylaxis Network: www.foodallergy.org
Food Can Make You Ill: www.tigmor.com/food
Food You Can Eat: www.foodyoucaneat.com
Special Diets Resource Guide: www.specialdiets.org

Additional Online Message Boards and Discussion Groups

Allergen-free Recipe Exchange: http://groups.yahoo.com/group/foodallergykitchen
Allergy Support: www.allergysupport.org (click on "Discussion Groups" to get started)
Food Can Make You Ill discussion board: http://groups.yahoo.com/group/fcmyi

Grassroots Action

Food Allergy Initiative (FAI), a nonprofit organization that raises funds for food allergy treatment and cure. Complete with information, resources, advice, downloads, and news. www.foodallergyinitiative.org
Food Allergy Research and Resource Program (FARRP), helps the food industry reduce allergy risk. Complete with an allergen database, library, newsletter, workshops, more. www.farrp.org

Chapter 8

NUTRITION PLANNING FOR ADULTS AND CHILDREN

One cannot think well, love well, sleep well, if one has not dined well.
—Virginia Woolf, 1882–1941

*O*ur discovery of food sensitivities may be the dawn of a new way of eating that over time will reveal benefits far beyond what we anticipate. Thus, while some items are off the menu, our food horizons may just be opening up. Our allergic reactions can inspire (or force) us to adopt simple habits that will eventually prove highly beneficial. Though our diet may be somewhat different from the eating patterns of those around us, ours can be wonderfully healthful and provide every nutrient we require. It is important that we focus not just on foods to avoid, but also take care to build our diet around highly nutritious items. If it is our children who have allergies, we will help them immensely by setting a good example with our own food choices.

In this chapter, we take a journey through the various food groups while avoiding the common culprits that provoke reactions. We discuss variations and menus for different ages and activity levels and offer practical tips. In the process, you can map out a nourishing way of eating that will help you and your family members survive—and thrive.

Vegetables: Vital and Protective

When we discover food sensitivities, we may start to view vegetables with fresh eyes and a new enthusiasm. This immensely varied group of foods is least likely to trigger our allergic reactions, so now is an excellent time to explore its benefits. Research from all over the globe has driven home this message: *centering our diet on vegetables is our best insurance policy against chronic disease.* These colorful foods provide more total vitamins, minerals, antioxidants, and protective phytochemicals per calorie than other category of foods. Thus, if food sensitivities force you to pile your plate with a variety of vegetables, you're assured of abundant intakes of a great many protective nutrients. Recommended ranges for protein, fat, and carbohydrates are given in table 8.1 and can be used as a standard of comparison. Compare these figures with the values for vegetables and other foods given in table 8.2 on page 132. It may come as a surprise to learn that vegetables contain significant amounts of protein, if we eat enough of them. Why isn't this fact better known? Perhaps because vegetables aren't big protein providers for all the people whose main—and perhaps only—choices from this food group are French fries with tomato ketchup.

> The word "vegetable" has no precise botanical meaning in reference to food plants, and we find that almost all parts of plants have been employed as vegetables—roots (carrot and beet), stems (Irish potato and asparagus), leaves (spinach and lettuce), leaf stalk (celery and Swiss chard), bracts (globe artichoke), flower stalks and buds (broccoli and cauliflower), fruits (tomato and squash), seeds (beans), and even the petals (Yucca and pumpkin).
>
> —Charles Bixler Heiser, *Seed to Civilization: The Story of Food*, Harvard University Press, 1990.

Vitamins

Orange, red, yellow, and green vegetables are excellent sources of *vitamin A* (as beta-carotene), which we need for good eyesight, reproduction, growth (as in the lengthening of bones), fighting infection, and the production of red blood cells. Vegetables also provide the powerful antioxidant *vitamin C*, which protects molecules throughout our body from damage by free radicals and greatly increases our absorption of iron. Rich sources are peppers, leafy greens, cruciferous vegetables (such as broccoli, cabbage, and cauliflower), and potatoes.

The next three vitamins are various shades of yellow; their rich pigments contribute to the deep color of green vegetables. *Vitamin K* was named for the German word for coagulation (in reference to blood). It helps mend our wounds when we have a scratch or cut and is found in deep green leafy vegetables, broccoli, cabbage, asparagus, and sea vegetables (seaweeds). *Riboflavin* (vitamin B_2) is found in asparagus, avocados, lotus root, mushrooms, sea vegetables, sweet potatoes, and spinach and other greens. *Folate*, with a name related to the word "foliage," is found in leafy greens as well as asparagus, avocados, beets, broccoli, Brussels sprouts, cauliflower, corn, parsnips, squash, sweet potatoes, and tomatoes.

Minerals

As mineral contributors, green veggies again take center stage. *Calcium*-rich greens are kale, collards, broccoli, okra, Napa cabbage, turnip greens, mustard greens, and Asian greens such as bok choy. In fact, we absorb calcium from these twice as readily as from cow's milk. *Iron* is tremendously important during growth for our oxygen delivery system and to fight fatigue. *Zinc* plays important roles in our immune system; it may come as little surprise that leafy greens are good sources of both of these minerals, as are bean sprouts, broccoli, green and yellow (wax) beans, and mushrooms. *Magnesium* is the central atom in the chlorophyll molecule; thus greens, again, are good sources. Magnesium is present in many other vegetables, too. *Iodine,* needed for thyroid function, is found in varying amounts in many vegetables but is most concentrated in sea vegetables and in the iodized salt we may sprinkle on our food. We need *potassium* for the transmission of nerve impulses and for muscle contraction, and although bananas have become famous as "the" potassium-rich food, in fact mushrooms, tomatoes, potatoes, and green beans all have more potassium per calorie than bananas. Other minerals provided by vegetables are *chromium* (in asparagus and mushrooms) and *copper* (in sweet potatoes).

Phytochemicals and Fiber

In both cooked and raw forms, vegetables are rich storehouses of numerous phytochemicals that protect us against chronic diseases. As if all this isn't enough, vegetables come packaged with fiber, a complex mixture that provides food for friendly intestinal bacteria and helps to carry waste materials and toxins out of our body.

Protein, Fat and Carbohydrate

One way to view our overall diet is to look at the percentage of our total caloric intake that comes from each of three nutrients that provide calories: protein, fat, and carbohydrate. Protein and carbohydrate provide approximately four calories per gram, whereas fat, a highly concentrated form of energy, provides nine calories per gram. Table 8.1 shows the general recommendations for adults based on guidelines from The World Health Organization and The Dietary Guidelines for Americans.

TABLE 8.1. RECOMMENDED DISTRIBUTION OF CALORIES FROM PROTEIN, FAT, AND CARBOHYDRATE		
Protein	Fat	Carbohydrate
10–20%	15–35%	50–70%

Keep in mind that babies and children require diets that are relatively high in fat. In fact, 55 percent of the calories in breast milk comes from fat, and this proportion should gradually decrease as they get older and include other foods in their diets.

Vegetables are well-known allies when it comes to weight control; one of the most effective ways to lose weight yet remain well-nourished is to pile our plate with vegetables.

However, this isn't the whole story. Those who need concentrated sources of calories can rely on higher fat choices such as avocados and olives, along with salad dressings and higher fat foods in other food groups. Dense foods such as potatoes also help those who need to increase their caloric intake.

TABLE 8.2. PERCENTAGE OF CALORIES FROM PROTEIN, FAT, AND CARBOHYDRATE IN FOODS

	Protein	Fat	Carb.
Vegetables			
Artichokes	24%	2%	74%
Asparagus	33%	67%	0%
Avocados	5%	78-81%	14-17%
Beans, green/yellow (wax)	20%	3%	77%
Beets	14%	3%	83%
Bok choy	36%	11%	33%
Broccoli	34%	9%	57%
Brussels sprouts	26%	5%	69%
Cabbage	19%	8%	73%
Carrots, yams, baked potatoes	8%	1–3%	89–91%
Cauliflower	26%	15%	59%
Celery	16%	7%	77%
Corn	13%	10%	77%
Eggplant	14%	5%	81%
Kale	22%	11%	67%
Leeks	9%	4%	87%
Mushrooms	32–50%	0–6%	50–62%
Okra	21%	2%	77%
Olives	3–4%	89–91%	4–7%
Parsnips	6%	3%	91%
Pepper, red, green, yellow	11%	6%	83%
Potato	10%	1%	89%
Rutabaga	12%	5%	83%
Salad greens	31%	11%	38%
Squash	7–17%	2–10%	74–91%
Spinach	40%	11%	49%
Sweet potatoes	6%	3%	91%
Turnips	12%	3%	85%
Zucchini	27%	7%	66%
Legumes: Beans, Peas, Lentils and Soyfoods			
Beans*	23–27%	2–4%	70–73%
Lentils	30%	3%	67%
Garbanzo beans (chickpeas)	21%	14%	65%
Kidney beans	28%	1%	71%
Peanuts	15%	71%	14%
Soybeans	33%	39%	28%
Soy protein isolate	91%	9%	0%
Tofu, firm	40%	49%	11%
Veggie "meats," low fat	69–85%	1–4%	14–30%
Veggie "meats," higher fat	56–75%	7–17%	18–28%

	Protein	Fat	Carb.
Seeds, Nuts, and Their Butters			
Flaxseeds	15%	59%	26%
Pumpkin or sunflower seeds	17%	71%	12%
Sesame butter (tahini)	11%	75%	14%
Almonds	14%	74%	13%
Cashews	10%	68%	21%
Hazelnuts (filberts)	9%	81%	10%
Pine nuts	10%	82%	8%
Walnuts	9%	83%	8%
Grains			
Amaranth	16%	15%	69%
Barley	10%	7%	83%
Brown rice	7–9%	4–8%	83–87%
Buckwheat	15%	8%	77%
Corn	9–11%	4–9%	80–86%
Cornmeal	9%	7–9%	82–84%
Millet	11%	7%	82%
Oatmeal	17%	16%	67%
Quinoa	13%	15%	72%
Rye	18%	8%	73%
Wheat	15%	5%	80%
White rice	8–9%	2%	89–90%
Wild rice	16%	3%	81%
Fruits			
Apples	1%	5%	94%
Bananas	4%	4%	92%
Dates, figs, raisins	3–4%	1–2%	94–96%
Melons	5–9%	2–11%	82–93%
Oranges	7%	2%	91%
Raspberries, strawberries	7%	9–10%	83–84%
Animal Products			
Beef, regular ground	33%	67%	0%
Cheddar cheese, medium	25%	73–74%	1–2%
Cod fish	92%	8%	0%
Cow's milk, 2%	27%	35%	38%
Eggs	34%	63%	3%
Salmon, sockeye	52%	48%	0%
Other Foods			
Sugar	0%	0%	100%
Oil	0%	100%	0%

*anasazi, black, cranberry, Great Northern, lima, mung, navy, pinto, red, or white; black-eyed or split peas

Protein Powerhouses:
Legumes (Lentils, Beans, and Peas), Seeds and Nuts

Legumes

> *I used to visit and revisit it a dozen times a day, and stand in deep contemplation over my vegetable progeny with a love that nobody could share or conceive of who had never taken part in the process of creation. It was one of the most bewitching sights in the world to observe a hill of beans thrusting aside the soil, or a rose of early peas just peeping forth sufficiently to trace a line of delicate green.*
>
> —*Nathaniel Hawthorne, 1804–1864,* Mosses from an Old Manse

Since proteins are the food components that commonly trigger allergic reactions, getting enough high-protein foods can present a challenge for those with allergies. Legumes (foods that grow in pods) tend to be our allies. These concentrated protein sources provide an excellent assortment of amino acids, along with folate, iron, zinc, and other minerals, and dietary fiber. Many legumes, especially black turtle beans, white beans, and soybeans, are good sources of calcium. These hearty (and heart-healthy) foods are tremendously important because along with their nutritional contribution they give us staying power between meals by delivering food energy in a gradual manner. The soluble fiber in legumes (which can make them a little gummy when cooked, as shown in the thickened liquid in a can of kidney beans) is an indication of their value as a prebiotic; in other words, they provide food for our friendly intestinal bacteria. The protective phytochemicals in legumes have anticancer activity.

Allergy testing clinics often use a legume mix when assessing reactions. When the results are positive, they inform their patients that they are allergic to legumes and soyfoods as a group, when in fact testing for individual legumes has not been done. In such cases, this entire group may be eliminated even though the patient is allergic to only one of these valuable foods. Those who rely on legumes as important protein sources are well advised to request that the clinic or lab test for legumes individually.

If you are not accustomed to eating legumes, begin with the smaller ones (lentils, peas, and adzuki beans). Rinse beans after soaking, cook legumes well, rinse them well, chew them thoroughly, and start with small portions. Lentils tend to be among the least likely members of this food group to trigger reactions. People commonly eat about twenty different legumes, most of which are mentioned in table 8.2.

Seeds and Nuts

Seeds and nuts trigger allergies for some people. However, for those who can include seeds and/or nuts, these life-generating little bundles make a valuable contribution in terms of both nutrition and texture.

The value of seeds in human nutrition is often underestimated. Pumpkin, sesame, sunflower, poppy, flax, and hemp seeds are high in copper, iron, magnesium, and selenium, and are outstanding sources of zinc. The fat present is a concentrated source of energy and is rich in the antioxidant vitamin E as well as many protective phytochemicals. Seeds also contain protein, though less than legumes (see table 8.2). Seed butters make delicious spreads and form a creamy base for sauces. (For details on making seed butters, see page 354.) Seeds and their butters add richness to a diet that is free of or low in animal products. Unlike the fat in animal products, seeds contain no cholesterol or trans fats and are low in saturated fats.

Nuts have similar qualities. Almonds are particularly high in calcium; Brazil nuts in selenium; cashews in zinc; and pecans in chromium. Walnuts are uniquely high in omega-3 fatty acids.

In nature, nuts are a way of storing energy so that as the nut develops into a small seedling it will have the stored energy to grow. There are storage proteins in nuts (a group of proteins called *albumins*) that tend to be highly allergenic. The albumin in each nut is unique; thus someone who reacts to one nut will not necessarily

> To learn more about cooking various vegetables, legumes, and grains, see pages 159–168.

react to others. However, people with anaphylactic reactions to one nut should avoid all nuts in the interest of safety. Similarly, those with anaphylactic reactions to seeds should avoid all seeds.

Grains: Our Energy-Givers

> *Grains Around the Globe. Europeans have cultivated spelt for the last 9,000 years and this relative of wheat is referred to in the Old Testament. Corn was grown in Mexico 7,000 years ago. Millet was among the first grains to be cultivated by man (or woman), with records dating back to 5500 B.C. in China and even earlier in Africa. Amaranth was harvested for thousands of years by Mayan and Incan civilizations. Quinoa, grown for 5,000 years in the South American Andes Mountains, was called "the Mother Grain" by the Incas because it was believed to impart long life. Farmers grew kamut in Egypt (grains were found in the pyramids) and in Asia Minor. Wheat and barley originated in the Middle East, and buckwheat came to us from central Asia.*

Grains constitute the base of the American Food Guide Pyramid and form the largest group on each of the food guides of Canada, the U.K, Australia, and New Zealand. This gives the impression that we require large quantities of this food group. However, our diet can be well constructed with considerably less emphasis on these foods. This de-emphasis is often appropriate for those with sensitivities to wheat and gluten. And whether or not we can tolerate wheat, it is worth our while to explore the gluten-free grains: millet, corn, amaranth, quinoa, and buckwheat. (For more on these, see Ingredients That May be New to You, pages 171–178, as well as recipes in the recipe section.)

Though they are seldom regarded as protein providers, grains supply half of the world's protein. A comparison of the grains in table 8.2 with the recommended ranges in table 8.1 shows grains to have an ideal balance of protein, fat, and carbohydrate. (Note that we're talking about whole grains, not croissants and Danish pastries.) Whole grains have their full complement of trace minerals, such as magnesium, selenium, chromium, iron, and zinc, and B vitamins. B vitamins work in concert to release the food energy that is stored in whole grains. In contrast, refined grains have been depleted of the majority of their nutrients. While it is true that refined grains often are fortified with some of the nutrients that were lost in processing (notably several B vitamins and iron), the vast majority of the nutrients (such as fiber, vitamin E, calcium, selenium, calcium, zinc, magnesium, and other minerals) are gone forever.

From a nutritional perspective, whole grains are particularly beneficial for those with food sensitivities because their dietary fiber (including resistant starch and oligosaccharides) directly affects the gut environment and supports our friendly intestinal bacteria. Whole grains modulate the glycemic response, meaning that they deliver energy to us in a gentle and gradual manner. Whole grains are rich in antioxidants, and extensive research shows them to be protective against cardiovascular disease and cancers of the gastrointestinal tract. Some people react to components in the bran layer that surrounds the whole grain and is removed during processing; in these cases refined grains (including those that are enriched with vitamins and iron) are preferable.

Fruits: Sweet Protectors

The sun, with all those planets revolving around it and dependent on it, can still ripen a bunch of grapes as if it had nothing else in the universe to do.
—Galileo, 1564–1642

Fruits are nature's candy and are by far the best sweet treat we can give ourselves between and after meals. They are among the least likely foods to trigger sensitivity reactions, although some people must avoid citrus fruits or eat only cooked fruits.

While the multitude of fruits that nature offers is too extensive to list in table 8.2, you can quickly get the idea that fruits are generally low in protein and fat and high in carbohydrate. The carbohydrate includes fruit sugar (fructose) and pectin, the substance that helps fruit jelly to gel. Pectin is considered to be a prebiotic and is a favorite food for our "friendly" and health supportive intestinal bacteria.

Fruits are not quite as nutrition packed as vegetables; however, they make outstanding contributions of several vitamins, a few minerals, and numerous phytochemicals. Our richest sources of vitamin C are citrus fruits, other tropical fruits, berries, and melons. Orange fruits, such as papaya and peaches, also provide beta-carotene, a form of vitamin A. Oranges and citrus juices are high in folate. Figs are sources of calcium, and calcium-fortified juices can boost your intake of this mineral. Dried fruits (such as currants, raisins, figs, and apricots) are high in iron. Fruits also contain phytochemicals with fancy names and impressive credentials as cancer fighters (flavonoids and terpenes in citrus fruit; flavonols, lignans, and phenolic acids in berries) and protectors from heart disease (anthocyanins in berries and plums; coumarins in citrus fruit; resveratrol in grapes). Quercetin, found in berries, apples, and many other fruits, is mentioned in chapter 2 for its role in supporting the health of our intestinal wall. On the basis of its antioxidant activity, the "champion protector" among fruits and vegetables has been found to be the blueberry.

Research has established high dietary intakes of antioxidants, including vitamin C, beta-carotene, and many phytochemicals, to reduce the severity of asthma attacks. For example, one Italian study found fruits and vegetables are protective against shortness of breath and wheezing in asthmatic children, whereas diets high in bread and margarine increased the severity of these symptoms. Antioxidants are needed to protect and repair our skin, and low intakes of vitamin C have been linked with atopic dermatitis (eczema).

Native Americans across the United States and Canada use a term they call "the Three Sisters" to describe the Native American way of life through the gardening technique of planting corn, beans, and squash together on the same mound. These Three Sisters—corn, beans, and squash—supplement and complement each other. The vines of the bean plant grow up the corn stalk. The huge leaves of the squash vines keep the ground moist for all of the roots. The nutritious vitamins from each of the plants escape into the soil so that they each benefit from one another.
—Deborah Champlain, Native American Gardening,
http://newigwam.com/garden.html

Calcium-Rich Foods and Vitamin D: Bone Builders

What are good sources of dietary calcium? If you said "a combination of calcium-rich foods from various food groups," you'd be right. Advertising tries to convince us that cow's milk is essential to human health. But the truth is that people world-wide get this bone-building mineral by including choices from the food groups listed earlier in this chapter, which include:

- Certain green vegetables: kale, collards, broccoli, okra, Napa cabbage, turnip greens, mustard greens, and Asian greens such as bok choy. (Note that this list does not contain beet greens, spinach, and Swiss chard because the calcium they contain is bound by oxalates, making it less available for absorption.)
- Legumes, especially black beans and white beans. If you are not sensitive to soybeans, these are an excellent source of calcium, including the young green soybeans known as edamame. So is tofu that is set with calcium (look for calcium on the ingredient panel).
- Almonds and almond butter provide calcium.
- The grains quinoa and amaranth are particularly high in calcium.
- Figs and calcium-fortified juices are good ways to add calcium to your meals and snacks.
- Calcium-fortified rice milk and soymilk are excellent sources of calcium. (Check for vitamins D and B_{12}, too.)
- We also get calcium from blackstrap molasses (choose organic brands).

Vitamin D is necessary for us to absorb and utilize calcium. We can make adequate amounts of vitamin D in our bodies when our skin is exposed to sunlight. This synthesis cannot occur through sunscreen, glass, or clothes. In regions that are far from the equator, vitamin D synthesis is diminished or ceases during the winter months, even on sunny days. The childhood vitamin D deficiency disease known as rickets is on the rise in the United States, Canada, and other developed countries. People with light skin can create their day's supply of vitamin D with ten to fifteen minutes of exposure to sunlight (mid-morning to mid-afternoon) per day on the face and forearms. Those with darker skin need more, about half an hour per day. This sun exposure can be accomplished with a short walk on a lunch break, for example. At latitudes far from the equator and during winter months you can get your vitamin D from a fortified beverage or as part of a multivitamin-mineral supplement. For infants, whose delicate skin can burn with even ten minutes of sun exposure, dietary vitamin D is essential. Breast-fed babies should be given an additional supplement, just before or just after a feed. Formula-fed babies receive vitamin D as part of their formula.

We absorb this bone-building mineral most efficiently when small amounts of calcium-rich foods are eaten throughout the day, rather than when larger amounts are taken in one or two sittings. For example, we absorb more calcium from four half-cup servings of fortified rice milk consumed at different times of the day than if we had the whole two cups of rice milk at once. Over the course of the day, we might have two to four half-cup servings of fortified beverages (juice, rice milk, or soymilk). We might choose calcium rich greens, such as broccoli, with dinner and snack on figs. Beans at one or two meals provide additional calcium. Thus, over the course of the day, we can include six to eight calcium-rich foods.

Omega-3 Fatty Acids: Anti-Inflammatory Fats

We require two types of fatty acids in our diet: omega-6 fatty acids and omega-3 fatty acids. Fatty acids in the omega-6 family tend to be pro-inflammatory, performing necessary functions when there is injury or infection. Those in the omega-3 family provide a vital counterbalance and reduce inflammation; they may also have special health benefits for people with several types of arthritis and those with depression. Omega-3 fats also provide relief for people with eczema or other skin conditions. The diets of most people provide an imbalance between the two, supplying more than enough of the omega-6 fatty acids and insufficient amounts of the omega-3 fatty acids. This is because omega-6 fatty acids tend to be widely distributed in plant foods and commonly used oils, whereas omega-3 fatty acids are present in far fewer foods. We require at least 1.2 grams of omega-3 fatty acids per 1,000 calories in our diet. A simple way to get our day's supply of omega-3 fatty acids on a 2,000 calorie diet is to choose one of the following plant sources each day from table 8.3 at right.

Non-hydrogenated margarines made with canola or soybean oils are also sources of

TABLE 8.3. FOODS PROVIDING AT LEAST 2.4 GRAMS OF OMEGA-3 FATTY ACIDS	
Flaxseed oil	1 teaspoon (5 ml)
Ground flaxseeds	1 tablespoon (15 ml)
Hempseed oil	1 tablespoon (15 ml)
Canola oil	1½ tablespoons (22 ml)
Soybean oil	2½ tablespoons (37 ml)
Walnuts or butternuts	¼ cup (60 ml) or 1 ounce (30 g)

omega-3 fatty acids. Foods and oils rich in omega-3 fatty acids should be stored in the refrigerator or freezer. Flaxseed oil should never be heated or used in cooking; if added to foods, it should be stirred in just before serving. This is because heat will destroy the delicate omega-3s in the oil. If you use flaxseeds, be sure to grind them or purchase the ground form; whole flaxseeds have such a strong protective outer coating that they slide through our gastrointestinal tract whole, without our benefiting from the nutrients they contain. For those who are not sensitive to soy, one-half cup of soybeans or tofu will supply 25 percent of our requirement for omega-3 fatty acids. Dark green leafy vegetables and broccoli can make a contribution; two cups of either of these will provide 10 percent of our omega-3s for the day.

Highly Unsaturated Omega-3 Fatty Acids

The omega-3 "family" also contains the highly unsaturated fatty acids EPA (eicosapentaenoic acid) and DHA (docosahexaenoic acid). These are long molecules that we can make in our own bodies from the foods listed in table 8.3 and that come to us from certain foods, including seafood. However, in addition to the tendencies of fish and seafood to be allergenic, there are plenty of reasons to avoid these, including contamination with heavy metals such as lead, mercury, and cadmium; industrial pollutants such as PCBs, DDT, and dioxin; possible foodborne illness; and compelling ecological and ethical arguments.

DHA is needed by infants for eye and brain development and low levels are associated with depression and ADHD (attention-deficit hyperactivity disorder). While our bodies can make DHA, there is evidence that some people's ability to do this is limited. Direct sources of DHA (present in breast milk, for example) are required by premature infants. DHA may be valuable for some people with depression, several types of arthritis, and perhaps for pregnant and lactating women.

In fact, highly unsaturated fatty acids originate with plants (seaweed) and microalgae (not blue-green algae, but algae from deep in the ocean) that fish consume. DHA from these specific types of microalgae is available in the form of supplements providing 100–300 mg of DHA per capsule. These supplemental sources of highly unsaturated omega-3 fatty acids are available in O-Mega-Zen3 vegetable-based capsules (rather than gelatin capsules) through Vegan Essentials at www.veganessentials.com or 1-866-88-VEGAN, and Pangea at www.veganstore.com or 1-800-340-1200. This supplement is distributed across North America and in the UK, Australia, New Zealand, and other countries. Another source is Seroyal brand, which originates in the UK.

Vitamin B$_{12}$: Essential in Fortified Foods or Supplements

Vitamin B$_{12}$ originates from one-celled organisms. It is not present in clean plant foods and the B$_{12}$ that is present in animal products originates from bacterial contamination or from supplements given to the animals. To ensure your intake of this essential nutrient, rely on a supplement or on fortified foods, such as fortified rice milk. (Vitamin B$_{12}$ also is added to some brands of soymilk, veggie "meats," breakfast cereals, and nutritional yeast; check labels.) While essential for everyone, vitamin B$_{12}$ has special importance for those with a tendency toward depression, as depression is a deficiency symptom for this vitamin. It is essential that care be taken to achieve adequate intakes of vitamin B_{12} during pregnancy and lactation, and for infants and children. This vitamin plays a role in the division of cells that divide rapidly, such as red blood cells, and in maintaining the protective sheaths around nerves; it has special importance during the growing years.

Multivitamin-Mineral and Other Supplements

Even well-planned menus, such as those on page 143, can fall short of meeting our recommended intakes for one or two nutrients. A multivitamin-mineral supplement can save the day and is a reliable way to get trace minerals and vitamins B_{12} and D. Many diets fail to meet recommended intakes for vitamin E. This is especially true when seeds or nuts are not included, so check that your brand of supplement includes vitamin E. If our diet has been restricted due to food sensitivities, a multivitamin-mineral supplement can "top up" our intake. A supplement will help if our intestinal lining is damaged and absorption is decreased, or if medications increase our requirement for one or more nutrients. For examples of hypoallergenic brands, see resources, page 365.

You may need an additional calcium supplement in order for your combination of diet and supplements to meet recommended intakes (see pages 369 and 370 [appendixes A and B]). A multivitamin-mineral supplement is likely to provide less than 200 mg of calcium; if it contained more, the pill would be too big to swallow.

Rotation Diets

Rotation diets have been used in attempts to control food sensitivities. Menus are arranged so that biologically related foods are eaten on the same day and so that at least four days pass before foods from this family are reintroduced. Most experts, however, consider rotation diets to be controversial at best; their main benefit seems to be that they extend the range of foods we eat. Research has established that having a reaction to one food does not necessarily mean that we will react to others in that botanical family. Because rotation diets introduce unnecessary complications and restrictions, they may lead to malnutrition; thus we do not emphasize rotation diets in this book. Your best course of action is to follow a varied diet. For example, if you are sensitive to gluten, include the full range of gluten-free grains. However, it is not necessary to eat amaranth on day one (while excluding other gluten-free grains), rice on day two, buckwheat on day three, and so on.

Certain biologically related foods—specifically fish as a group, shellfish as another group, or nuts as a third group—are likely to have similar antigens. Thus a person who is allergic to fish may need to avoid more than one species of fish or avoid all fish completely. Of course, in this situation, fish must be excluded, not rotated. A similar situation applies for those who are allergic to shellfish or to tree nuts.

Meal Planning

When we have one or more food sensitivities, planning meals can be a challenge—but it can also be very easy. Natural, whole foods, such as vegetables, are good for us and are the least likely to trigger reactions. Our food sensitivities are apt to inspire us to try out vegetables, grains, legumes, and fruits that are entirely new to us. We can choose to do the bare minimum of preparation or we can decide to explore new recipes. This simple food guide will help you to meet your nutritional requirements.

> ### Guide to Meal Planning
>
> For each meal, choose at least one serving from each of the following food groups:
> - ✓ Vegetables or fruits
> - ✓ Legumes (lentils, beans, and peas), seeds or nuts
> - ✓ Grains
>
> When you make your choices, include plenty of calcium-rich foods.
> During the day include one good source of omega-3 fatty acids.

Your Allergen-Free Day from Morning to Night

To illustrate how this works in practice, see the menus on pages 143–144.

Breakfast. A good way to start your day is with calcium-fortified juice. This can be used on your cereal (which can be gluten free), or you might add a fortified rice milk or soymilk. You could sprinkle seeds, dried fruit, or nuts on cereal, or add a sliced banana (depending on foods included and omitted from your diet.) Your breakfast might include a seed or nut butter on rice cakes, or one of the bean-based spreads on pages 242–247. You may not always have a breakfast item from the Legumes, Nuts, or Seeds food group; however, when you do, it will increase your "staying power" until lunch.

Not everyone begins the day with cereal; be adventurous. People all over the world get off to an excellent start with lentil soup or with leftovers from last night's supper. When you need a grab-and go breakfast to take to work or school, a shake or smoothie (pages 236–238) and a muffin or other baked item are good choices. On mornings that allow time for a more leisurely brunch, try the Mini-Pancakes and topping (pages 231 and 235) or Banana Bread (page 195).

Lunch. Lunch could include a lentil, bean, or vegetable soup; this may be purchased at a cafeteria or restaurant or brought from home in a thermos. Bean-based dips served with raw veggies or spread on rice cakes are an easy choice. See the innovative sandwich ideas on pages 239–241. A Rice Vegetable Roll (page 325) is an appealing lunch item. The salad section in this book is a wonderful resource and will introduce you to gluten-free grain- and bean-based salads with outstanding flavor and appeal. To get your day's supply of omega-3 fatty acids, try out the flaxseed oil version of salad dressings on pages 291, 293, and 296. For bag lunches, invest in spill-proof containers; these make life a great deal simpler (page 364).

Supper. In the Main Dishes section (pages 307–333) you'll discover delicious and hearty entrées for your evening meal. These recipes are designed to keep you in excellent health while you steer clear of ingredients that are problematic. There are nonallergenic versions of old favorites: chili, sloppy Joes, tacos, burger-type patties, bean stews, curries, stuffed peppers, eggless quiches, stir fries, pad thai, and nori rolls. Complement these with one of the Simple Sides on pages 341–350, and a baked item or salad. You'll find plenty of ways to Build a Meal Around a Baked Potato on pages 326–327. The lunch ideas listed above also are good supper choices.

Snacks. Nutritious snacks can round out your choices during the rest of the day and add significantly to your overall nutrient intake. If your appetite at mealtimes is small, this is even more reason to ensure that your snacks are based on whole foods. Include dips (pages 239–254) served with raw vegetables or gluten-free crackers. Make a big batch of muffins, keep them in the freezer, and take one or two with you when you head out the door; these are particularly helpful in the diets of children and teens. You'll find a multitude of muffin variations, so you can make them every week or two without tiring of them (see the recipe on pages 184–186). Keep a tin containing scones (page 188) or a gluten-free bread handy; even if you bake only occasionally, you can always have a baked item ready. Keep dried fruit, gluten-free crackers, or some other standby that doesn't require refrigeration in your backpack, purse, briefcase, or glove compartment.

Entertaining. While testing recipes for this book, we tried our recipes out on friends and relations for miles around, including those with and without food allergies. Here are a few of our "Recipe Superstars" that proved to be big favorites with people who had no food sensitivities at all: Stuffed Squash (page 332), two types of gravy (pages 337 and 338), Chili Express (page 308), Lentil "Chopped Liver" (page 246), and Pumpkin Spice Bread (page 194). At birthday parties, children love to take part in preparing their own tacos (page 313) or pizza (page 312).

For dessert, serve Incredible Hot Fudge Sauce (page 362) on dairy-free frozen dessert. You'll find appealing cake recipes on pages 198–203. People who are experts in simplicity have had wonderful celebrations by just sticking a birthday candle in a watermelon and then carving up the melon.

MENU #1 (1,900 calories)

BREAKFAST

1 cup (250 ml) calcium-fortified beverage
(juice, rice milk, or ½ cup/125 ml of each)
1 cup (250 ml) Creamy Golden Porridge,
page 230, or rice flakes
2 tablespoons (30 ml) sunflower seeds
or dried fruit

LUNCH

1½ cups (375 ml) Lentil and Rice Soup,
page 299, or other lentil soup
2 rice or corn cakes or ½ cup (125 ml)
corn chips
1 cup (250 ml) tossed salad
2 tablespoons (30 ml) French Dijon
Dressing, page 296, or other dressing

DINNER

1 cup (250 ml) rice pasta
1 cup (250 ml) tomato sauce
1 serving Herbed Green and White Bean
Salad with Tomatoes, page 284

SNACK OR DESSERT

2 figs or 1 other fruit
1 cup (250 ml) fortified rice milk

MENU #2 (2,100 calories)

BREAKFAST

1 cup (250 ml) calcium-fortified beverage
(juice, rice milk, or ½ cup/125 ml of each)
1 cup (250 ml) Whole Grain Cereal, page 226
3 tablespoons (30 ml) toasted pumpkin seeds,
other seeds, or dried fruit
1 banana

LUNCH

1 cup (250 ml) Red Bean Hummus, page 244
4 brown rice cakes
1 cup (250 ml) carrot sticks or other
raw veggies
1 apple

DINNER

1 serving Chili Express, page 308
1 cup (250 ml) quinoa
1 cup (250 ml) steamed kale
1 serving mixed green salad
2 tablespoons (30 ml) Caesar's Best Dressing,
page 292

SNACK OR DESSERT

2 Ultra-Fudge Brownies, page 204, fruit,
or other dessert

MENU #3 (3,000 calories)

BREAKFAST

1 cup (250 ml) calcium-fortified beverage
(juice, rice milk, or ½ cup/125 ml cup of
each)
1 cup (250 ml) Muesli, page 225, or rice flakes
2 tablespoons (45 ml) sesame seed butter
3 rice cakes or 2 slices Sunny Seed Bread,
page 187

LUNCH

1 serving Chick-a-Dee Pea Salad, page 285
1 avocado, sliced
2 Scones, page 188, or Muffins (page 184)

DINNER

1½ servings Moroccan Millet, page 316
1½ tablespoons (22 ml) ground flaxseeds
1 cup (250 ml) broccoli
2 Gluten-Free Chapatis, page 192

SNACK

¾ cup (185 ml) Chickpea "Nuts," page 352

TABLE 8.4. NUTRIENTS PROVIDED IN MENUS #1, #2, AND #3

Nutrient	Recommended Adult Intakes*	Menu #1	Menu #2	Menu #3
Calories	Varies, depending mainly on weight and activity level	1,900	2,100	3,000
Protein	Typical: 45 g (women) 60 g (men) (0.8–1 g protein per kg body weight)	60 g	60 g	63 g
Fiber	Approximately 25–60 g	51 g	55 g	57 g
Omega-3 fatty acids	(1.2 g per 1,000 calories)	0.5–5.5 g**	2.3–6.1 g**	4 g
Percent of calories from:				
Protein	10–15%	12%	11%	10%
Fat	15–35%	29%	21%	34%
Carbohydrate	55–75%	59%	68%	56%
MINERALS				
Calcium	1,000 mg to age 50 1,200 mg after age 50	1,020 mg	1,000 mg	1,150 mg
Iron (on vegetarian diet***)	32 mg (women to age 50) *18 mg (men; women over 50)	22 mg	25 mg	25 mg
Magnesium	320 mg (women); 420 mg (men)	540 mg	600 mg	650 mg
Zinc	8 mg (women); 11 mg (men)	11 mg	12 mg	14.5 mg
VITAMINS*				
A (beta-carotene)	700 mcg (women); 900 mcg (men)	2,950 mcg	5,730 mcg	4,100 mcg
Thiamin (B$_1$)	1.1 mg (women); 1.2 mg (men)	2.2 mg	1.6 mg	2.4 mg
Riboflavin (B$_2$)	1.1 mg (women); 1.3 mg (men)	0.9 mg	1.2 mg	1.3 mg
Niacin equivalents	14 mg (women); 16 mg (men)	23 mg	25 mg	31 mg
Folate/folic acid	400 mcg	635 mcg	770 mcg	950 mcg
Pyridoxine/B$_6$	1.3 mg to age 50; 1.5 mg (women 50+); 1.7 mg (men 50+)	1.8 mg	2.8 mg	2.8 mg
B$_{12}$/cobalamin	2.4 mcg	0 mcg	0.1 mcg	0.8 mcg
C/ascorbic acid	75 mg (women); 90 mg (men)	180 mg	580 mg	360 mg
D**** (or sunlight)	5 mcg (to age 50); 10 mcg (to age 70); 15 mcg 70+	2.5 mcg	0 mcg	1.25 mcg
E	15 mg	18 mg	15 mg	18 mg

*For specific recommendations for different age groups including children, see Appendix A and B.

** Highest value applies when flaxseed oil is used in dressing.

***High values reflect recommendations that vegetarian intakes be 1.8 times regular levels, though not all experts agree that vegetarian iron intakes need to be this high.

****Note that for vitamin D, 1 mcg=40 I.U.

Menus

Menus #1, #2, and #3 on page 143 provide from 1,900 calories to 3,000 calories. (The latter will feed an active young man with a hearty appetite.) These sample menus have been planned in keeping with recommended intakes for various nutrients. While your menu may not necessarily meet your recommended intake for every nutrient each day, by following the Guide to Meal Planning (page 141) including plenty of variety over the course of a week, along with vitamin B_{12} in a fortified food or supplement, your needs will be met. Where variety is limited, enhance your diet with a multivitamin-mineral supplement.

Of course, you may adjust these menus according to your preferences. For example, a bean soup could be used instead of lentil soup, or try a different supper entrée or salad. Some people will eat the same amount of food but eat less at meal-times and use some items as snacks. For those who are very active or have bigger appetites, larger portions can be used and desserts or other items may be added to the basic menu. Including more of the calcium-fortified beverages will easily raise the intake of calcium, vitamin D, and other nutrients. For children and people with small appetites, serving sizes can be decreased. Following the menus, table 8.4 shows the nutrients provided by each menu. Where menu options are given, the analysis was done using the first item listed. For comparison, the recommended vitamin and mineral intakes for different age groups, including children, are given on pages 369 and 370.

Mealtimes

In this plate of food, I see the entire universe supporting my existence.
—a Zen blessing at mealtime

If your attention has been on avoiding foods, take care to shift your focus to gathering, preparing, and eating the most nutritious foods you can find, and eating them with enjoyment. In doing so, you will nourish the cells throughout your body. Relaxed mealtimes will increase your absorption of nutrients. Chew foods well; this begins the breakdown of food into small particles and ensures that saliva is mixed throughout. Enzymes in your saliva begin the digestion process and help to prepare the mix for absorption of nutrients when it reaches your intestine. Even when eating alone, arrange a pretty place setting, perhaps with flowers, a candle, or music.

Restaurant Eating

Fortunately, restaurants are becoming increasingly sensitive to meeting the needs of their patrons with food allergies. It's not unusual to see a line on a menu that reads, "Tell us about any special food needs." Some restaurants provide a "Pamphlet with the Pasta"—in other words, an ingredient list for menu items.

When eating is a matter of life and death for us or a family member, it takes courage to trust a restaurant. It also takes clear communication, preferably in advance of our visit. We need to feel secure that the person preparing our food thoroughly understands our situation and requirements, is fully knowledgeable about all the ingredients used in the food they prepare and serve, and is able to take the appropriate measures to avoid cross-contamination. If we're fortunate, we may find several local restaurants that will welcome our repeat business, where we can feel comfortable and safe, become known to the staff, and trust them to provide foods that fit our guidelines.

> # For more on nutrition, see:
>
> *The New Becoming Vegetarian*, by V. Melina and B. Davis, Book Publishing Company, 2003.
> (In Canada, *Becoming Vegetarian*, Wiley Canada)
> *Becoming Vegan*, by B. Davis and V. Melina, Book Publishing Company, 2000.
>
> For a detailed and comprehensive guide on nutrition, practical tips for infancy through adolescence, supportive information for families with various eating patterns, and family-friendly meal plans and recipes, see:
> *Raising Vegetarian Children*, by J. Stepaniak and V. Melina. McGraw-Hill, 2002.

Tips for Eating at Restaurants

- Begin by doing some research on the Internet. See if the restaurant you're considering has a menu posted on the Web.
- Check with allergy Web sites for recommended restaurants in your geographical area and at travel destinations that accommodate people with food sensitivities. Vegetarian and vegan restaurants also can be helpful in offering meals that are free of fish, dairy, eggs, other animal products. These typically feature menu items based on gluten-free grains as well. (For Web sites, see the resources at the end of chapter 6.)
- Call the restaurant during the least busy times, rather than during the lunch rush or dinner hours, and ask to talk to the head chef, owner, or manager. Explain your limitations and ask whether they are equipped to accommodate you and how the restaurant would handle your needs.
- Ask about food preparation practices. Are fresh cutting boards and utensils used to avoid cross-contamination? Is the same oil used to fry various foods?
- Explain clearly and politely why you cannot consume certain foods. No restaurant wants to be held responsible for making a customer ill.
- A new chef at a restaurant may change the recipe and add a "secret ingredient." If your allergies are life threatening, you should always take care to speak directly with the chef or person who actually will be preparing your

food, even regarding a dish that you order regularly. Do not rely solely on the person who takes your order.

- Dine out during off-peak hours, when you can have the full attention of the personnel.
- When you have a good experience, be sure to tip well and to express your appreciation.

Getting Off to a Good Start: Decreasing the Risk of Allergies for Infants

Diet and nutrition in early life can be crucial in helping to prevent food allergies that might otherwise last through childhood and into adulthood (though, of course, there's no iron-clad guarantee).

During pregnancy, the risk of causing a food allergy in our baby is small. If we have food allergies, we certainly should avoid the foods we are allergic to. At the same time, it is of primary importance to avoid unnecessary restrictions and to ensure that our diet meets our nutritional requirements. During times of growth, such as pregnancy, infancy, childhood, and adolescence, our nutritional needs are particularly high (see pages 369 and 370). These recommended intakes can be met while avoiding allergens, though planning a balanced and well-designed diet takes extra time and attention in the beginning stages. A multivitamin-mineral supplement is likely to help you meet your nutritional needs.

When confronting possible food allergies in a parent or child, the first step is to accurately identify the allergenic food (or foods). This involves keeping a record of your or your child's food intake and symptoms, as outlined in chapter 4. The next step is the complete removal of the suspected allergens to determine if this relieves the symptoms. Chapter 5 presents details about the many hidden sources of allergens. Third, when it is clear which foods are the culprits, eliminate them from your or your child's diet and ensure that a nutritionally adequate diet is provided. Enlist the expert assistance of your nurse, doctor, or a knowledgeable dietitian in these steps. Regular checkups can also give you reassurance about weight gain during pregnancy and normal rates of growth for infants and children.

Breast-feeding

Begin breast-feeding as soon as possible after your baby is born. Most healthy babies are born well hydrated and require nothing except the small amounts of colostrum and the transitional milk provided by the mother in the early days after giving birth. Exclusive breast-feeding, without any added foods or beverages (apart from water) for the first six months of life reduces the likelihood of allergies, including respiratory allergies and asthma, in several important ways. Numerous components in human milk support the normal maturation of the immune system. This maturation seems to include the development of oral tolerance to foods; in other words, it helps to avoid or reduce allergic reactions to foods. In chapter 2 we mentioned that an infant's intestinal lining takes time to mature (when mature it can selectively allow desirable products of digestion to pass through and be absorbed, while blocking large and unwanted molecules). This delayed maturation of the intestinal lining may have the positive function of allowing the immune system proteins that are present in the mother's breast milk to pass through the baby's intestinal wall and help the infant fight infection. An infant's digestive system is not designed to handle foods that are suitable for older children and adults, and offering these foods too early may result in allergies.

Breast-feeding represents an ingenious and natural team effort on the part of mother and child. For added protection with

Reducing the Risk of Food Allergies in Your Baby

1. Breast-feed your baby.

2. If you have food allergies and are breast-feeding, avoid foods to which you have allergies.

3. If your breast-fed child shows signs of a possible allergic reaction when you consume common allergens, such as cow's milk, eggs, fish, peanuts, and tree nuts, eliminate the offending food(s) from your diet and see if the baby's symptoms improve (for more on this, see table 8.5, page 150). If the symptoms do not improve after a few weeks of completely avoiding the allergen, you can assume that the food is not the cause of your baby's problems.

4. Maintain an overall balanced diet, including sources of omega-3 fatty acids.

5. If there is a family history of atopy* and you must use formula as the main food for your infant or to supplement breast-feeding, use a complete hydrolysate formula such as Nutramigen or Alimentum, particularly during the first six months of life.

6. Wait until six months of age to introduce solid foods.

7. When introducing solid foods, start with those that have a low allergenicity (see table 8.6).

8. Avoid tobacco smoke. Exposure to tobacco smoke during pregnancy and after the baby is born increases the risk of allergies.

*Atopy refers to a family history of allergic conditions, such as eczema, asthma, food allergies, or hay fever.

allergy-prone infants, continue breast-feeding for at least the first two years of life. Though prolonged breast-feeding may be uncommon in our culture, nature's plan certainly supports this practice for the first two years. The American Academy of Pediatrics encourages mothers to nurse for at least one year and as long after as both mother and baby desire. The World Health Authority, Health Canada, and the Canadian Paediatric Society all recommend that breast-feeding continue to age two and beyond. Infants weaned before twelve months of age should not receive cow's milk; instead they should receive iron-fortified infant formula.

The majority of the well-designed studies show that breast-feeding reduces the incidence and severity of food allergies in infants. (However, if a breast-feeding mom consumes foods to which she is allergic, it is possible that she could pass allergens to the baby through her milk and perhaps increase the risk of allergy to the breast-fed infant, as discussed on page 147.)

Vitamin D for infants. Breast-fed infants should be given a vitamin D supplement, beginning within the first two weeks of life and continuing until the child is consuming at least two cups (500 ml) per day of a vitamin D–fortified beverage. It seems that Mother Nature did not intend breast milk to be the primary source of vitamin D, but rather sunlight; breast milk contains little of this vitamin. Changes such as the thinning ozone layer, sun safety precautions, and living farther from the equator than our ancestors did have led health authorities to recommend that infants be given vitamin D through diet or supplements instead of relying on sunlight. Formula-fed babies receive vitamin D through infant formula.

Maternal Avoidance of Allergenic Foods During Breast-feeding

All experts are not of one mind regarding the extent to which potential allergens should be avoided during lactation. Factors to consider are the obvious need to be well nourished, the potential risk of allergy, and the immense value of continuing to nurse the baby. Breast-feeding mothers should eliminate from their own diets the foods they are allergic to. If a certain food seems to trigger reactions in the infant, with symptoms (table 8.5) occurring three to eight hours after that food is eaten by the mother, it can be eliminated from the mother's diet on a trial basis. **Note: Some of the symptoms in table 8.5 may be caused by other conditions, so check with your doctor before assuming that food allergy is the cause.**

If an infant is going to react to food in the mother's diet, this reaction often begins three to eight hours after eating the culprit food, though reactions have been delayed as much as two to three days, or up to two months in the case of allergic colitis (in which there is bloody, mucousy stool). Symptoms of reaction are more reliable indicators of food allergy than are skin or blood tests. There can be a single symptom, such as vomiting or hives, or several reactions may occur together. In cases of colic, consider feeding technique first, as your timing and alternation of breasts may play a role. (For assistance, check with your local public health unit or well-baby clinic.) Then consider food allergy. A lactating mother can start with a trial elimination diet by avoiding all dairy products, soy (60 percent of babies with milk allergy may also react to soy), and eggs. See if this helps. It may take up to four weeks for symptoms to resolve, though you should notice an improvement within one to two weeks if colic is related to these foods. For a list of foods and ingredients

Table 8.5. Possible Signs of Food Allergy

Gastrointestinal Symptoms (often occur right after eating or can be delayed)

• vomiting	• frequent excessive spitting up (reflux)
• abdominal pain (crying, drawing up legs, hard tummy)	• chronic inconsolable crying (colic)
• frequent diarrhea	• bloody, mucousy stool
• chronic constipation (hard, dry, painful stools) (Note that soft, infrequent stools are not signs of constipation.)	

Skin Symptoms (often occur right after eating or can be delayed)

• itchy skin rash	• eczema
• frequent scratching and rubbing	• diaper rash, redness around anus
• redness or rash on or around mouth, ears, or cheeks	
• hives, swelling, redness, swelling of lips, eyes, face, tongue, or throat	

Respiratory Symptoms (may occur right away or be delayed for six to eight hours or more)

• stuffy, itchy, or runny nose (clear mucus), nose rubbing	• chronic sneezing
• dark circles under eyes (due to nasal congestion)	• chronic coughing
• itchy, watery, reddened eyes	• noisy breathing, wheezing, asthma
• chronic earaches or ear infections	

Other Possible Symptoms

• ongoing poor weight gain, usually in combination with other allergy symptoms such as frequent spitting up, diarrhea, chronic constipation, or colic

• anaphylaxis (includes difficulty breathing, loss of consciousness, can be fatal)

containing these possible allergens, along with nutritious alternatives, see chapter 5. If baby's symptoms improve during a trial in which several foods have been eliminated, the foods can be reintroduced one at a time, one week apart, to determine which was the culprit.

It is appropriate for lactating mothers to avoid the most problematic foods (such as peanuts and tree nuts) when the risk of allergy is strong, for example, when food allergies, asthma, or eczema are present in two parents or in a parent and a sibling. (With more cases of allergy in the family, the likelihood of infant allergy increases.) The American Academy of Pediatrics has given this general advice for infants and children who have a strong risk of allergy: Mothers should eliminate peanuts and tree nuts (almonds, walnuts, etc), and consider eliminating eggs, cow's milk, fish, and perhaps other foods from their diets while nursing. This cannot be considered a guarantee for prevention of infant allergies, as the research results are unclear; however, it may help. Other experts advise that breast-feeding mothers should avoid or reduce allergenic foods ony if baby shows signs of allergy. **Meeting the nutrient requirements of the mother and infant is also a top priority and must also be**

taken into account. For example, if eliminating foods such as dairy products and eggs, it is important that the diet includes appropriate and nutritious alternatives for the nutrients found in these foods. (For more on this, see chapter 5.)

In some women, proteins that they eat pass unaltered into their breast milk. This does not happen in all women and is not a problem unless the baby has signs of allergy. As examples of the transmission of allergens, one study showed peanut protein to be present in the breast milk of about half of the women studied, two hours after the lactating mother ate peanuts. Similarly, egg or milk proteins appeared in breast milk two to six hours after lactating women ate egg or dairy products, respectively. Women with food allergies should avoid the foods to which they are allergic while breast-feeding; this is especially important during the baby's first six months of life.

If soy in the mother's diet seems to cause symptoms in her baby, a fortified grain beverage can be used by the mother for calcium and vitamin D. (Grain beverages are considerably lower in protein, providing only 0.5 grams of protein per cup/250 ml, compared with 69 grams per cup/250 ml in soymilk or cow's milk, so be sure to include other high-protein foods, such as legumes.) Breast-feeding mothers sometimes find it a challenge to get enough to eat (as they require about 500 extra calories per day), while avoiding potential allergens. Nutrition counseling is likely to help a lactating woman to meet her recommended nutrient intakes and will provide practical tips. If moms are finding it too much of a challenge to get enough to eat, it is better to continue breast-feeding and extend the range of foods in their diet than to switch the baby to formula. Unless the food allergy symptoms are severe, mothers who find the elimination diet too much should add foods back to their diet. Most babies will outgrow food allergies, but the risks of not breast-feeding are significant and lifelong.

Eating a Balanced Diet That Includes Omega-3 Fatty Acids

It is important that the mother's diet is adequate in calories and other nutrients during lactation. Be sure that your diet includes omega-3 fatty acids (for sources see page 138; this may or may not include DHA supplements [page 139]). These support the immune system and may encourage a nonallergenic response to foods during lactation (and pregnancy). A prenatal multivitamin-mineral supplement can provide vitamins B_{12} and D and help to meet recommended intakes for other vitamins and minerals. A supplement may be especially helpful for mothers when their diet is very limited because of food sensitivities.

Formula Feeding

If your baby is formula fed and reacts to cow's milk–based formula, consider a trial of complete hydrolysate formula, such as Nutramigen or Alimentum, for four weeks. If your baby improves on the complete hydrolysate formula, it is a good idea to keep him on this formula until he is at least six months old or even as long as nine to twelve months of age. If the cost of the formula is an issue, you may consider a trial of soy formula after at least four weeks on the hypoallergenic formula or after six months of age. Though soy formula is not hypoallergenic, it often can be used by infants who are allergic to cow's milk formula. Anaphylactic reactions are much less common with soy formula than with cow's milk formula. Alternatively, if your child's reaction to milk formula was not severe, you may consider a trial of partially hydrolyzed formula (Good Start) after six to nine months of age. For more details, see the publication *Hypoallergenic Infant Formulas*, by the American Academy of Pediatrics' Committee on Nutrition, available on the Internet at this address: http://aappolicy.aappublications.org/cgi/reprint/pediatrics;106/2/346.pdf.

Introduction of Solid Foods: Age Six to Nine Months

When introducing any foods or beverages to a baby it is important to be aware of any family history of allergy. To reduce the risk of allergy for any infant, avoid solid foods until six months of age, when your baby's digestive tract and immune system are more mature. Take care to add items gradually to the diet and identify allergens before symptoms become severe. The best way to develop tolerance for a food is to offer just a little. Then, when things go well, increase the amount, bit by bit. When first offering a food, try it early in the day so you have time to watch for symptoms. Dab a little on your baby's cheek and watch for redness, swelling, or itching. If after twenty minutes there is no sign of a reaction, dab a small amount on your baby's bottom lip and watch for redness, swelling, or itching. If after twenty minutes there is no reaction, offer some by spoon. Offer one-third teaspoon the first time and increase the amount to one teaspoon the second time. Gradually increase the amount over a few days so that by the fourth day your baby is taking as much of the new food as she wants. If your baby shows signs of allergy at any time, stop giving the new food. Talk with your doctor about severe reactions or about trying the food again at a later date. For babies with a family history of allergy, and those who have had reactions to foods before, wait six or seven days before trying a new food (this is longer than the two to three days that is suggested for those with no allergies in the family). Introduce new foods one at a time. If there has been a reaction, do not try a new food until two days after any allergic symptoms have gone away. Avoid mixtures until you have tried each item separately.

Starter foods for babies are single grains, iron-fortified grain cereals, and vegetables. Because baby's iron stores may be running low by six months, experts recommend starting with a food containing iron, such as an iron-fortified rice cereal. Table 8.6 contains a select list of starter foods that are less likely to trigger allergic reactions. Each baby is an individual, and there is no universal list of nonallergenic foods. Therefore, an infant may react adversely to something that is generally considered to be a "low allergenicity food" and tolerate others that are considered to be more allergenic. Soft-cooked, mashed vegetables, or in the case of "tough" or stringy foods like kale, blended to form a smooth purée, also provide an excellent introduction to the world of solid food. (Plus you'll get some colorful spots on your floor and walls, as the big adventure of feeding begins!) Kale and broccoli are high in iron and many other nutrients; all vegetables are high in protective vitamins and phytochemicals. To make sure your baby gets enough iron, you may use iron-enriched infant cereals, such as rice cereal, increasing the amounts to at least one-half cup (125 ml) per day by nine months of age. Check the label to see that the cereal does not include milk ingredients (listed in table 5.1, page 79). Check with your doctor, dietitian, or baby clinic about your baby's iron intake and growth.

TABLE 8.6 STARTER FOODS: FOODS OF LOW ALLERGENICITY

Food Group	Low Allergenicity Foods (all cooked)
Grains	Rice, quinoa, amaranth, tapioca, millet
Vegetables	Yams, sweet potatoes, squash (all types), parsnips, carrots, green beans, beets, broccoli, kale, potato, green beans, cabbage
Fruits	Pears, blueberries, peaches, banana, apricots

Even if a child's diet is restricted to a few basic foods during infancy, variety can be introduced in successive weeks. Sweet potatoes can be mashed, then diced, and later given as well-cooked chunks, and finally as French-fried sweet potatoes. This allows the child to experiment, develop feeding skills, and experience different textures.

As a general rule, try vegetables and fruits in the cooked form first, before introducing the raw form. Read labels carefully. For example, commercial baby food that is called "broccoli and cauliflower" may contain added butter, and thus traces of dairy; DHA that is added to a product may be derived from egg. Watch for symptoms that might suggest an allergic reaction (table 8.5), keeping in mind that these symptoms also may be due to other conditions.

Table 8.7. Sequence of Adding Solid Foods for Babies at Moderate to High Risk for Allergies

- For the first six months of life, feed baby breast milk only, plus a vitamin D supplement of 400 IU per day.
- Hydrolyzed formula may be used (such as Nutramigen or Alimentum).
- Offer vegetables and fruit in the cooked form first (or from a jar). Once the cooked food is tolerated, try the same food raw.
- At six months you may offer milk-free, iron-fortified rice baby cereal that is high in iron.
- Begin with foods that are the least likely to cause allergic reactions; these are found at the top of the chart.
- Breast milk helps to reduce the risk of allergies and infections. Continue to offer breast milk while adding solids; it can be mixed with cereal and other foods.
- Product ingredients may change so always check labels.

6 to 9 Months
At first, offer solids 1 or 2 times per day; then increase to 3 or 4 times per day.

Grains and Cereals	Iron-fortified infant rice cereal (aim for 8 tbsp. per day by age 9 months). Avoid cereals that contain milk ingredients (such as milk powder, whey, casein). Many infant cereals contain soy lecithin; however, this is often not a problem for allergic babies. Low-allergen grains include millet and amaranth, but these are lower in iron than fortified cereals.
Vegetables	Yams, sweet potato, squash (all types), parsnips, carrots, beets, broccoli, kale, potatoes, green beans, cabbage
Fruits	Pears, peaches, bananas, apricots, nectarines, blueberries. Use fruits cooked first, then try raw. Juices must be pasteurized or cooked.

9 to 12 Months
Offer solids 5 or 6 times per day.

Grains and Cereals	Oats, barley (e.g., iron-fortified cereal). Some cereals contain milk ingredients; avoid these. Bread, noodles, crackers and baked goods made from tolerated grains and flours.
Vegetables	Asparagus, avocados, cauliflower, brussels sprouts
Fruits	Plums, prunes, pineapple, grapes, apples, cranberries, raisins
Other	Canola oil, olive oil, milk-free nonhydrogenated margarine (Earth Balance, Soy Garden, Spectrum, and Fleischmann's Lactose-Free) See chapter 5.

Offer solids 5 or 6 times per day.

Grains and Cereals	Corn, wheat, spelt, kamut, rye, other grains
	Other commercial cereals
	Bread, noodles, crackers and baked goods made from tolerated grains and flours.
Vegetables	Green peas, spinach, tomatoes, celery, cucumbers, lettuce, onions, garlic, lima beans, broad beans
	Any raw vegetables
Fruits	Citrus fruits (orange, grapefruit, lemon, lime)
	Strawberries, raspberries, melons, mangoes, figs, dates, cherries (pitted)
	Any raw fruits
Other	Legumes (such as soybeans, tofu, lentils, navy beans, garbanzo beans, kidney beans, and others)
	Flaxseed oil, soy oil, safflower oil, sunflower oil
	Flaxseeds, sunflower seeds
	Continue to offer breast milk to age 2 years and beyond.

Solid Foods at Nine to Twelve Months of Age and Beyond

When your little one is nine to twelve months of age, you may add avocado, cauliflower, plums, prunes, cooked apple, and barley to the list, one at a time. If your baby has no signs of allergy by nine months, you can speed up the process and try a new food every four to five days instead of every six or seven days. Once a food is tolerated, keep it in the diet while trying more new foods. If your baby has reacted to many foods or has significant eczema, be more cautious.

Foods that sometimes trigger allergies—such as wheat, corn, citrus fruit, berries, melon, tomato, green peas, lentils, tofu, soybeans, and other cooked legumes (beans)—deserve special consideration. If no signs of allergy have appeared by ten months, you can gradually try adding these foods. If your baby has reacted to many foods or has significant eczema, wait until your baby is one year old to try these foods. For the sequence of adding solid foods for babies at moderate to high risk for allergies, see table 8.7.

At this age, your baby's need for omega-3 fatty acids is met by the combination of breast milk plus one tablespoon (15 ml) per day of canola oil, soybean oil, or non-hydrogenated margarines made from these oils.

Breast milk can be expressed and mixed with cereals and other foods; this will provide an excellent source of nutrition for toddlers. Infant formula, if used, provides a wide range of nutrients and can be used in food preparation and mixed into cereal long past infancy.

Dairy products are common triggers for allergies and should not be introduced during the first year. In a study of children ages eleven months to six years who had chronic constipation (and who had used cow's milk products), 68 percent improved on a dairy-free diet that included soymilk. Because soy is somewhat lower in fat than cow's milk, an additional tablespoon per day of fat, oil, or a high-fat food such as avocado is recommended. For infants at a high risk for allergies, the American Academy of Pediatrics recommends that eggs not be introduced during the first two years and peanuts (peanut butter), tree nuts, fish, and shellfish not be given before three years. If other allergies have been observed, it may be wise to also delay the introduction of sesame seeds and chocolate until after age two for these children.

Probiotics

Probiotics (described in chapter 2) appear to have antiallergic properties that may make their use beneficial during pregnancy and lactation as well as during infancy and childhood. Research on probiotics is in its the early stages, though the use of these bacterial supplements is promising. For formula-fed infants, they may support a population of "friendly" intestinal bacteria that more closely resembles that of a breast-fed infant. Since formula-fed infants have significantly fewer bifidobacteria than those who are breast-fed, probiotics can improve the situation for those who are formula-fed. Probiotics may promote maturation of an infant's intestinal wall, making it less permeable while decreasing intestinal inflammation. They may promote maturation of an infant's immune system and the development of oral tolerance, decreasing the likelihood of allergic reactions to foods. They also may help with the digestion of dietary proteins.

Finnish researchers discovered that women with allergies who were given probiotics during pregnancy and lactation reduced by half the risk of their babies developing atopic eczema. A plant-centered diet, including breast milk, helps to sustain the "friendly" bacteria that are naturally in the intestine or are introduced through supplements.

As Your Child Grows: Allergies During Childhood

Though 6–8 percent of children develop food allergies during their first three years of life, most have outgrown early allergies before they reach the age of five years. Eighty percent of children who are prone to food allergies are allergic to only one or two foods. Some have multiple allergies, however, and concern about what to feed them can give parents sleepless nights.

It may be a relief to know that despite all the dairy industry's advertising, our little ones can grow strong and tall without consuming a drop of cow's milk. Vegetarian youngsters can be robust and healthy without soy or wheat. In fact, there are nutritious alternatives to just about any food we can think of and countless ways to get the nutrients we need. Be reassured that a well-balanced diet can provide adequate protein, calories, and all the other essential nutrients even without dairy products, eggs, soyfoods, other animal products, or other allergens. This can be accomplished with an assortment of grains, legumes (lentils, peas and beans), vegetables, and fruits. For children who can tolerate them, soyfoods are valuable sources of protein, iron, zinc and other nutrients, though they are not essential. In some cases, an infant formula that has proven to be well tolerated can be used past infancy (for example, in the preparation of cereals, muffins, puddings, and casseroles). Fats, such as those in avocados, canola oil, flaxseed oil, and other plant oils, are vital as concentrated energy sources during these years of peak growth. The types of fat are important and must include sources of essential fatty acids (see chapter 8).

Supplementary vitamin B_{12} is required, and added vitamin D is necessary for youngsters if sun exposure is insufficient, especially during winter months, and year-round at colder latitudes. Those with dark skin require more sunlight to produce vitamin D and are more likely to need a vitamin D–fortified beverage or supplement year-round (also see page 149). A nonallergenic multivitamin-mineral supplement will prove helpful in meeting recommended intakes (see the resources section, page 365). Because all this takes planning, it is wise to enlist the help of a dietitian who is skilled in this area, as research has shown that such counseling can improve the growth of children with allergies.

Certain children may have increased requirements for particular nutrients due to the use of medications. Those with moderate to severe atopic dermatitis (eczema) may also have increased requirements for calories and protein.

The recipe for the Powerhouse Smoothie on page 238 was developed by a father whose youngster was a particularly picky eater. It has proven to be great fun for parents and other caregivers to make this tasty concoction together with their child. A toddler can climb onto a stool and help to toss ingredients into the blender, push the button, and then share the smoothie with the adult. Using this basic concept, you can be inventive and develop your own version based on foods that are well tolerated.

Whether or not your child has allergies, your own food choices will have a powerful influence, so inspire your little one to good health by example. Invite your child to prepare nourishing foods with you. Even when very young, toddlers have a great time cutting up an avocado with a plastic utensil. (Watching them is entertaining, too.) To get closer to the origins of healthful foods, take your child to a farmers' market. Together, seek out produce that you've never tried before. Learn the background and history of some of the grains, herbs, or spices that you use. Plant some seeds and create a garden on the balcony or kitchen window sill or in the backyard.

Whereas some children are fussy eaters, we often find that those with food sensitivities are thrilled to get their version of pizza, breads, and cookies that taste good and don't cause any symptoms. For wonderful examples, see the recipe section of this book. Many of these recipes have a special appeal for children and teenagers. You'll find creative examples for quick breakfasts, bag lunches, after school snacks, family dinners, and parties.

Though generally you may pack your child's lunch, you may also develop a contingency plan for the days it is forgotten or lost. Some parents collaborate with school cafeteria personnel or other staff to develop a suitable lunch or snack for such occasions. When our youngsters who have allergies visit friends or attend a social event, it helps tremendously if we can plan ahead and provide a few special food items that will fit in with what is served to make their visit go smoothly.

Chapter 9

KITCHEN BASICS AND COOKING FUNDAMENTALS

*W*hether you are a novice in the kitchen or a gourmet chef, this chapter will equip you to prepare the essentials of a wholesome diet. Tips about kitchen equipment and on making your own gluten-free flours will save you time and money. You'll learn how to cook gluten-free whole grains as well as legumes (peas, beans, and lentils). In addition to stovetop preparation we include the basics of pressure-cooking, because this is such a fast and simple way to prepare longer-cooking foods.

Grinding Your Own Gluten-Free Flours

It's easy to make a variety of gluten-free flours right in your own kitchen. You can use an electric grain grinder, which has blades designed specifically for this purpose, or you can use a sturdy and powerful blender. Although most high-quality blenders can do a reasonable job of grinding grains in small quantities, using them regularly for this purpose can take a toll on their blades. Therefore, you might want to look into blenders that have blades and blender jars designed specifically for this purpose, such as the K-Tec Kitchen Mill or K-Tec Champ HP3 Blender (www.ktec.com) or the Vita Mix (www.vitamix.com). These powerful appliances can also grind spices and seasoning mixes and transform nuts and seeds into butters as well as create purées, dips, and creamy desserts.

The appropriate machine can grind flours from gluten-free grains as well as from legumes (such as dried chickpeas). Thus, you can make flours fresh when you need them without loss of nutrients due to extended exposure to light or oxygen, both of which can deplete certain vitamins. It is much more cost-effective to grind your own flours, and you will have access to a greater variety of gluten-free alternatives than you will find commercially. You also avoid the possibility of contamination that can arise in a commercial mill where the same equipment may be used to grind wheat flours and gluten-free flours.

Fundamentals of Pressure Cooking

Pressure cookers cook food with astonishing speed—up to 70 percent faster than conventional methods and 40 percent faster than microwave ovens, saving both time and energy. And they can do things a microwave oven can't—cook the staples of a gluten-free vegan diet, grains and beans—and do so in a fraction of standard cooking times. They also can be used for pressure steaming vegetables, even longer-cooking ones, such as beets and winter squash, and complete the task in record time.

Pressure cookers work by superheating steam and trapping it inside. This builds up pressure and raises the internal temperature of the cooker from the standard boiling point of 212°F (100°C)–250°F (120°C). Once high pressure is reached (15 pounds or 7 kilograms of pressure is standard for most cookers), only a small amount of heat is needed to keep the pressure stabilized. This produces less heat in the kitchen, making the pressure cooker ideal for hot weather cooking. It also is the perfect "green" appliance because it uses less fuel than other cooking methods. Moreover, it requires less human energy, since the food does not need to be stirred, turned, or otherwise tended. Just set the timer and relax until it goes off.

Pressure cookers help to lock in and preserve the nutrients naturally found in vegetables and other foods. They also cook with less liquid than many conventional methods (between ¼ to 1 cup/60–250 ml depending on the manufacturer's specifications), so there is less loss of water-soluble vitamins. Most pressure cooker recipes can be made fat-free and, since flavors are sealed inside, less salt and seasonings are required as well.

Pressure Cooking Tips

- Most pressure cookers come with a steaming rack or trivet to keep certain foods, such as vegetables, from coming in contact with the cooking water. Alternatively, you can use any good quality stainless steel steamer basket that fits comfortably inside the pot of the cooker and permits the lid to close easily without touching the steamer.

- Start with boiling (rather than cold or room temperature) water or liquid whenever feasible. This will dramatically speed up the time it takes for the cooker to come up to high pressure. Set the cooker over maximum heat. The instruction manual that comes with your cooker will explain how to determine when high pressure has been reached.

- As soon as your cooker has come up to high pressure, lower the heat, set the timer, and begin cooking for the amount of time specified. Once high pressure is reached, the heat must be lowered; otherwise the pressure will continue to rise, causing the release of steam and loud hissing sounds. The heat should be lowered just enough to maintain high pressure.

- At higher elevations, dense foods such as brown rice and beans take somewhat longer to cook. This is because the temperature at which these foods come to a boil (and therefore cook) is lower than it would be at sea level. In order to compensate for the lower external pressure at elevations above 2,000 feet, pressure cooking times must be adjusted. For every 1,000 feet (0.3 km) above 2,000 feet (0.6 km) elevation, increase the cooking time by 5 percent.

- Because electric ranges are notoriously slow to respond to heat adjustments, it is a good idea to remove the cooker from the hot burner for about one minute once high pressure has been reached (you can place it on a cold burner or on a trivet) in order to allow the burner to cool down and prevent the cooker from overheating. The cooker should remain at high pressure for this brief time. If the pressure starts to fall below the high pressure indicator, return the cooker to the hot burner. Alternatively, heat a separate burner to low. Once the cooker has reached high pressure, transfer it to the burner with the lower setting and turn off the first burner. Adjust the heat, if necessary, to maintain high pressure.

- The times given in the pressure cooking charts on pages 164 and 168 are only approximate. It is best to err on the side of undercooking because it's easy to bring the pressure back up and continue cooking for a few more minutes if the food is significantly undercooked. You also can simmer the food briefly on the stovetop if minimal additional cooking is needed.

- Always open the lid of the cooker by tilting it away from you. Even when the pressure is completely released, there is still residual steam in the pot that could burn you.

Pressure Release Methods

Remove the cooker from the heat source as soon as the timer goes off. Then use one of the following methods to release the pressure from your cooker. Never attempt to open your cooker until all of the pressure has been released.

1. *Natural pressure release or allowing the pressure to come down naturally* means to remove the cooker from the heat source and allow it to rest with the lid locked in place until the pressure drops of its own accord. Depending on the type and quantity of food inside the cooker, this can take from about 1 minute to 20 minutes. The food inside the pot will continue to cook. (Approximately 5 minutes of natural pressure release equals 2 minutes of cooking under pressure.)

2. Sometimes a partial natural pressure release is indicated. For instance, when a recipe stipulates "10 minutes natural pressure release," remove the cooker from the heat source and allow it to rest for 10 minutes. Keep the lid in place the entire time whether or not the pressure has dropped completely. Once the specified time has elapsed, release any remaining pressure using one of the following methods before attempting to remove the lid.

3. *Quick-releasing the pressure* means to rapidly bring down the pressure by placing the cooker under cold water in the sink. This is done by running cold tap water around the rim of the cooker while holding the pot at a forty-five degree angle so the water runs down the side of the cooker and is directed away from the pressure regulator.

4. *Stovetop quick-release options* vary among manufacturers. This involves removing the cooker from the heat source and manipulating a button or lever to release the pressure. This method has drawbacks, however, because it releases a steady current of steam into the kitchen, which many cooks find objectionable. It also can cause sputtering at the vent, especially when cooking grains, beans, and other foam-producing foods. If sputtering occurs, use the cold water quick-release method described above.

Bean Cookery

Getting Started

The first step in successful bean cookery is finding the freshest beans possible. Seek stores with a high grocery turnover rate, so you aren't stuck with beans that have grown stale on the shelf. Whether sold in bulk or packaged, beware of beans that appear wrinkled; this may indicate that the beans are old. (The older a bean is, the longer it will take to cook.) Of course, dust on or around bulk bins and grocery shelves is a hint that the beans are not at their freshest.

Before you use dried beans in your recipe, it is important to sort them carefully. Pick them over and remove small stones, fragments of dirt, beans with holes, misshapen or wrinkled beans, and discolored beans. If you plan to cook the beans without soaking them, be sure to rinse them thoroughly in plenty of fresh water. Small beans that do not require soaking, such as lentils, split peas, or black-eyed peas, should always be rinsed.

Soaking Beans

Most experienced cooks consider soaking an essential step in bean preparation, though it is not essential for peas and lentils and is optional for very small beans such as adzuki beans. There are several excellent reasons for soaking beans. Once you get the knack of it, you'll find it easy to set a pot on the kitchen counter to soak several times a week. Scientists have discovered that pre-soaking beans increases the ease with which we can absorb minerals from these nutritious foods. Beans contain indigestible carbohydrates that are not eliminated simply by cooking. When beans are soaked first, however, most of these carbohydrates are released into the soaking water and are washed away when the beans are drained and rinsed. Effective soaking involves immersing the beans in water until the water permeates the center of each bean. There are three effective methods for soaking beans:

- *Long Soak:* Cover the beans with about triple the amount of fresh cold water and let them rest for 6–12 hours. If the soak time exceeds 8 hours, place the soaking beans in the refrigerator to keep them from souring.

- *Short Soak:* Place the beans in a large pot and cover them with about triple the amount of water. Bring to a hard boil. Remove the pot from the heat, cover, and let the beans rest for about 1 hour.

- *Pressure Soak:* Place the beans and water in a pressure cooker and bring to a boil. Lock the lid in place and bring up to high pressure. Reduce the heat just enough to maintain high pressure, and cook under pressure for 2–5 minutes (2–3 minutes for small beans, 3–4 minutes for medium beans, 4–5 minutes for large beans). Remove the cooker from the heat and allow the pressure to come down naturally. Although this will take only about 10 minutes, let the beans soak with the lid locked in place for a total of 20–30 minutes for small beans, 30–45 minutes for medium beans, or 60 minutes for large beans (this includes the natural pressure release time).

To check if beans have soaked long enough, remove one or two of them with a slotted spoon and slice them in half with a sharp knife. If the beans look evenly saturated and uniform in color, they are ready to be cooked. If the center is still opaque, more soaking is necessary.

> After soaking the beans, always discard the bean soaking liquid, rinse the beans well, and use fresh water to cook them. This removes some of the gas-forming compounds.

Cooking Beans

Beans need time or pressure to cook. If you have the time and inclination, simmering beans on the stovetop can be relaxing and enjoyable. However, if you serve beans often or your schedule is tight, pressure cooking is the speediest and most energy efficient way to go.

Tips for Cooking Beans on the Stovetop

- Beans must be completely covered with a liquid (water or unsalted vegetable stock) at all times during cooking. Usually 3 cups liquid to 1 cup soaked beans is sufficient.

- Salt and acidic ingredients—such as vinegar, tomatoes or tomato juice, lemon juice, and molasses—toughen the skins of beans and inhibit water absorption, preventing the beans from softening properly. Add salt and acidic ingredients to beans only after thorough cooking.

- Beans often create a lot of foam during cooking. This foam contains some of the carbohydrates that are gas producing; it may be skimmed off with a large spoon and discarded. An optional 2–3 teaspoons of oil (such as olive oil or organic canola oil) per cup of beans may be added to the cooking liquid to help keep foam under control.

Tips for Pressure Cooking Beans

- Fill the pressure cooker no more than halfway full, using at least 2½–3 cups liquid for each cup of soaked beans. Make sure there is plenty of liquid so the beans remain completely covered during the entire cooking time. Remove any floating bean skins so they won't clog the vent of the cooker.

- Add oil (2–3 teaspoons per 1 cup dried beans) and any flavoring options, but do not add salt or acidic ingredients. Oil is optional, although it helps to con-

Approximate Bean, Lentil, and Pea Cooking Times*
*Older beans will take longer to cook.

Beans, Lentils, and Peas (1 cup dry)	PRESSURE COOKING† Soaked	Unsoaked	STOVETOP COOKING Soaked	Unsoaked	Approx. Yield (cups)
Adzuki	1–2 min.	12–14 min.	1–1½ hours	2–3 hours	2¼
Anasazi	4–6 min.	16–18 min.	1½–2 hours	2–3 hours	2¼
Black	4–7 min.	15–22 min.	1½–2 hours	2–3 hours	2
Black–eyed peas	—	**10–12 min.	30 min.	45–60 min.	2¼
Cannellini	5–7 min.	18–20 min.	1–1½ hours	1½–2 hours	2
Chickpeas (garbanzo)	12–14 min.	25–35 min.	1½–2 hours	3–4 hours	2½
Cranberry	5–7 min.	25–30 min.	1½–2 hours	2–3 hours	2¼
Great Northern	4–6 min.	20–25 min.	1–1½ hours	2–3 hours	2¼
Kidney (red)	4–6 min.	15–20 min.	1½–2 hours	2–3 hours	2
Lentils (green, brown, or French)	—	**8–12 min.	—	30–45 min.	2
Lentils (red)	—	**4–6 min.	—	20–35 min.	2
Limas (baby)	2–3 min.	8–10 min.	45–60 min.	1½–1¾ hours	2½
Limas (large)‡	1–3 min.	8–10 min.	45–60 min.	1½–1¾ hours	2
Navy (pea)	1–3 min.	10–20 min.	1½–2 hours	2½–3 hours	2
Pinto (pink or white)	2–3 min.	18–20 min.	1½–2 hours	2–3 hours	2¼
Split peas (green or yellow)	—	**6–10 min.	—	45 min.	2

† Using Natural Pressure Release. Natural pressure release takes from 10–15 minutes. If you choose to use a quick–release method instead of natural pressure release, you will need to add 3–4 minutes to the pressure cooking time.

‡ Add ½ teaspoon salt to the soaking and cooking water of large limas to keep their delicate skins intact.

** Use only a quick release method; natural pressure release will overcook these delicate legumes.

trol foam that can clog the vent. Add salt and acidic ingredients to beans only after thorough cooking. There are a few exceptions to this rule, however. Large lima beans require a bit of salt to keep their fragile skins from breaking apart. A few other varieties of beans, such as black beans, calypso beans, and red kidney beans, may also hold together better when a pinch of salt is added to the cooking water because they tend to rupture under pressure.

- Bring to a boil. Lock the lid in place and bring up to high pressure. Reduce the heat just enough to maintain high pressure. Begin timing as soon as high pressure is reached. Approximate cooking times under high pressure are listed in the chart on page 164.

- Unless otherwise noted, always use natural pressure release (about 10–15 minutes) instead of a quick-release method, which can produce foaming or sputtering at the vent and cause beans to rupture.

- If the beans are not quite tender, cover the pot (but do not lock the lid) and simmer the beans without pressure over low heat until done. If the beans are still hard or require significantly longer cooking, return them to high pressure for a few more minutes and again allow the pressure to fall naturally.

- Clean the lid, vent, and rubber gasket thoroughly after each use to keep the pressure cooker functioning safely and efficiently.

Cooling Beans

For both the standard stovetop and pressure cooking methods, allow the beans to cool in their cooking liquid. To do this, transfer the beans and cooking liquid to a shallow metal, glass, or ceramic pan, and place uncovered in the refrigerator. Stir every 20–30 minutes to disperse the heat. Once the beans are completely cool, store them in their cooking liquid or drain them and save the liquid to use for making soup or cooking grains. Refrigerate or freeze cooked beans in a tightly sealed container. Beans may be frozen in ziplock bags.

Grain Cookery

Rinsing

If you've stood on a golden Nepalese hillside during the October millet harvest, or been present while other grains are gathered and threshed, you'll realize how easy it is for grains to include bits of husk, pebbles, and other debris. Most whole grains should be thoroughly rinsed before cooking to remove dust or natural coatings that may impart a bitter taste. Clean the grain just before you are ready to use it, rinsing only the quantity you are planning cook.

How to Rinse Grains

Method A

1. Measure the amount of grain you need.
2. Fill a large bowl with cold water. Transfer the grain to a fine-wire mesh strainer and plunge the strainer up and down into the water several times, stirring the grain with your fingers or a spoon while it is immersed.
3. Discard the dirty water and refill the bowl with clean water. Repeat the process as many times as necessary, replacing the water with fresh water until the water remains almost clear. (With some grains, it may not be possible to get the water completely clear.)
4. Rinse the grain under cold running water, stirring them with your fingers or a spoon. Allow the grain to drain before proceeding with the recipe.

Method B

1. Measure the amount of grain you need, and place it in your cooking pot.
2. Run cold water into the pot while swirling the grain gently, allowing bits of debris to rise to the surface and be tipped over the edge of the pot. Repeat, stirring the grain with your fingers, until there is no more debris to discard. Using the pot lid, drain the remaining water and proceed.

Toasting

Toasting grains refers to browning them in the cooking pot before they are cooked. This makes grains taste nuttier and promotes a fluffier, more pilaf-like texture. It is an optional step.

How to Toast Grains

1. Place the rinsed grain in a pressure cooker or in a large heavy pot over medium heat. Stir with a wooden spoon until the rinse water has evaporated and the grain looks dry.
2. At this time you can add one to three teaspoons of oil for each cup of grain used. Although it is optional, oil enhances the toasting process. It also coats each individual grain, which helps keep the grains separate and fluffy.
3. Reduce the heat slightly and continue stirring. Once the grain emits a roasted, nutty aroma and turns a shade or two darker, the toasting process is complete. This will take about 5–10 minutes.
4. Pour the cooking liquid into the pot and proceed with pressure cooking or stovetop simmering the grain. Stand back a bit when you add the liquid, as it will sputter.

Grain Cooking Tips

An advantage of the gluten-free grains is that most of them, apart from brown rice and wild rice, are very quick to cook, as you'll see from the charts that list pressure and stovetop cooking times, on page 168.

- Always cook grain in a pressure cooker or in a heavy pot with a tight-fitting lid. A loose-fitting lid is inefficient and may extend the cooking time or cause uneven results.
- The best liquids to use for cooking grains are water, bean broth (the water from cooked beans), or vegetable stock. Do not add salt to the grain if the liquid you are using contains salt.
- Cooking times for grains can vary greatly depending on factors such as age and storage conditions. If the grain is not completely cooked after the recommended cooking time has elapsed and the water has been absorbed, stir in a few tablespoons of boiling water. Cover the pot tightly and continue to cook the grain over very low heat (not under pressure) until it is sufficiently done.
- If liquid remains after the grain is tender, drain through a strainer. Then return the grain to the cooking pot and reheat it over very low heat to dry it out.

Tips for Pressure Cooking Grains

- To pressure cook untoasted grain, pour the liquid, oil (if using), and optional salt into the cooker and bring to a boil. Add the grain, lock the lid in place, and bring up to high pressure. Immediately reduce the heat just enough to maintain full pressure (15 lbs). Begin timing as soon as the cooker has reached full pressure.
- Never fill the cooker more than three-quarters full or beyond the manufacturer's recommended maximum.
- The texture of grains benefits from the final steaming, which occurs during natural pressure release. This also prevents the outer "skin" of grains from bursting.

Tips for Cooking Grains on the Stovetop

- To simmer grain on the stovetop, bring the water to a rolling boil before stirring in the grain or adding it to toasted grain.
- Make sure the lid of the pot fits tightly so that little to no steam escapes.
- For fluffier grain, put a clean towel under the lid of the pot during the standing time. The towel will absorb excess moisture instead of the grain and will help keep the grains separate and fluffy.
- When removing the lid of the pot, always tilt it away from you to avoid being burned by steam.

Grain Pressure Cooking Times

Grain (1 cup)	Liquid (Cups)	Optional Salt (teaspoons)	Minutes Under High Pressure	Yield (Cups)
Amaranth	1½–1¾	½ ‡	4 + 10 min. npr*	2
Buckwheat***	1¾**	½–¾	3 + 7 min. npr*	2
Millet***	2	½–¾	12 + 10 min. npr*	3½
Quinoa	1½	½–¾	0 + 10 min. npr*†	3
Rice, basmati white	1½–1¾	½	3 + 7 min. npr*	3
Rice, brown	1¾–2	½	20–40 + 10–20 min. npr*	2½
Rice, white	1½–1¾	½	3 + 7 min. npr*	3
Wild rice	2½	¼	20–28 min.	2½

*natural pressure release
**add 1 tablespoon oil to control foaming
***toast before boiling for improved flavor and more even cooking
‡add salt after cooking to ensure proper absorption of liquid
†a "0 minutes" cooking time means to cook just until high pressure is reached

Notes About Pressure–Cooked Brown Rice:

Wide variations in cooking times are given so you can custom cook the rice to your liking. For a firmer, chewier rice, use the shorter cooking times with a smaller amount of liquid; for a softer, creamier rice, use the longer cooking times with slightly more liquid. The smaller amount of liquid will produce a dry rice; the larger amount, a moister rice. Cook short-grain brown rice 25–40 minutes with 10–20 minutes natural pressure release. Cook long- or medium-grain brown rice 20–30 minutes with 10 minutes natural pressure release.

Grain Standard Stovetop Cooking Times

Grain (1 cup)	Liquid (Cups)	Optional Salt (teaspoons)	Minutes Standard Cooking	Yield (Cups)
Amaranth	2	½ ‡	20–25	2
Buckwheat**	2	½–¾	10–12 + 5 min. st*	2
Millet**	2½	½–¾	20–25 + 5 min. st*	3½
Quinoa	2	½–¾	15 + 5 min. st*	3
Rice, basmati white	2	½	15–20 + 5 min. st*	3
Rice, brown	2¼	½	45–60 + 10 min. st*	3
Rice, white	2	½	15–20 + 5 min. st*	3
Wild rice	2¼	¼ ‡	50–55 + 10 min. st*	2½

*standing time (covered)
**toast before boiling for improved flavor and more even cooking
‡add salt after cooking to ensure proper absorption of liquid

Chapter 10

RECItitle

Chapter 10

RECIPES

*A*re your former favorite foods now on a "banned" list? When you try to think of tasty meals that can be prepared quickly from available ingredients, do the prospects look bleak?

> ## Free of the Major Allergens!
>
> Every recipe in this book completely excludes these common allergens: dairy products, eggs, fish, shellfish, wheat and gluten, soy, peanuts, kiwi fruit, plus baker's, brewers' and nutritional yeasts. Strawberries and tree nuts are optional in a few recipes; however, in every case, one or more alternatives are suggested that can be used instead.

Take heart. In this section we open a doorway to a bountiful buffet of foods that will nourish and sustain you. These include delicious baked goods, hearty entrées, easy items for bag lunches, sauces that can make simple meals come to life, meals to make in moments, and even celebration foods that will appeal to a crowd.

Though the foods listed in this box are responsible for most of our responses, other foods can trigger reactions in one individual or another. Naturally, we couldn't exclude everything from our recipes. Here is our approach. Some recipes include one or more of the following ingredients: chocolate, citrus, corn, fermented foods (such as vinegar, miso, and ketchup), potatoes, tomatoes, and sesame. Readers who are sensitive to any of these items will find many recipes that exclude the problematic ingredient(s). Where an item is included, we have done our best to suggest alternatives. Where a food listed in this paragraph is an essential ingredient, a "Contains" list accompanies the recipe (below the nutritional analysis) showing its presence at a glance.

For example, below the Choco-Currant Cranberry Squares, page 359 (which are delicious, by the way), you will see:

***

CONTAINS: * Chocolate

The "Contains" list does not include sesame because sesame butter (tahini) is not essential; another seed butter or a nut butter may be used instead.

If you are sensitive to various sugars, seeds, mustard, or to culprits that we have not listed, just read through the ingredient list. In the extensive collection here, you'll find plenty of delicious recipes that are free of items that are problematic for you.

This book is based on whole, unprocessed foods. Thus many of the sensitivity reactions to artificial food colors, preservatives such as benzoates, or other additives will be minimized or avoided. Yet it's important to read labels, even in a "natural food" store. People sensitive to sulfites need to take care in selecting dried fruit and other foods. For more information on additives, see pages 99 and 103–104.

The recipes that follow are carefully designed to combine great taste and sensory appeal, simple preparation, and excellent nutrition. Serving sizes are suitable for adults. However, as we all know, suitable serving sizes can range from the mouse-like nibbles of a toddler to the gargantuan appetite of a teenager who can devour a whole pizza and then wonder when the main course is coming. Therefore, we have given the recipe yield in volume measure wherever possible.

Nutritional Analysis of Recipes

Each recipe also has a nutritional analysis. For example, below the recipe for Chickpea Flour Pizza (page 320) you will see:

Per pizza: calories: 218, protein: 10.5 g, fat: 8 g, carbohydrate: 28 g, dietary fiber: 5 g, calcium: 38 mg, iron: 2.7 mg, magnesium: 81 mg, sodium: 615 mg, zinc: 1.4 mg, folate: 203 mcg, riboflavin: 0.1 mg, vitamin C: 1 mg, vitamin E: 0.6 mg, omega-3 fatty acids: 0.1 g.
% Calories from: protein 19%,   fat 31%,   carbohydrate 50%

Protein, fat, and carbohydrates are shown in grams and also as a percentage of the total calories. Since protein and carbohydrate each provide 4 calories per gram, and fat provides 9 calories per gram, even a small amount of fat can result in a relatively high percentage of total calories. Minerals (calcium, iron, magnesium, sodium, and zinc), vitamins (folate, riboflavin, C, and E), and fatty acids (omega-3), are shown below each recipe. Humans require thirteen vitamins, twenty-one minerals, and two types of essential fatty acids. Not every one of these nutrients is listed in the analysis. We selected key nutrients that provide an overview of the nutritional value. We took care to include those for which it can be a challenge to meet recommended intakes, such as calcium, zinc, folate, riboflavin, and vitamin E.

You can learn more about the recommended intakes of minerals and vitamins for people of various ages on pages 369 and 370. For more detailed nutrition information, see *Raising Vegetarian Children*, by Jo Stepaniak and Vesanto Melina, McGraw-Hill, 2002, and *The New Becoming Vegetarian*, by Vesanto Melina and Brenda Davis, The Book Publishing Company, 2003 (in Canada, *Becoming Vegetarian*, Wiley Canada).

The nutritional analysis does not include optional ingredients. Where there is a range in amounts for an ingredient, the smaller amount is used for the analysis. Where two or more choices are given for an ingredient, the analysis is based on the first choice. In certain cases a footnote is given, for example, to explain the source of the calcium when a fortified food is used.

Ingredients That May Be New to You

Most of the ingredients listed in this section can be found in any well-stocked natural food store or via mail order from the specialty sources listed on page 363. If there is an Indian grocery store in your area, you may find some excellent bargains on arrowroot starch, chickpea flour, coconut oil, basmati rice, and rice flour. You'll also be pleasantly surprised by the array of exotic beans and spice mixtures, papadums (see page 356), and grated fresh gingerroot (in jars in the cooler). Other ethnic stores offer similar sensory adventures. You may discover that food sensitivities have fostered your introduction to a world tour of new ingredients and delicious foods.

Amaranth: Cooked like a grain, this is the seed of a gorgeous, red-plumed plant that is native to Central and South America. To the ancient Aztecs, amaranth was a superfood. It has regained this status in recent years as a result of scientific recognition of its nutritional attributes. These include its content of excellent quality protein (including the amino acids lysine and methionine, which are low in many grains), plus fiber, polyunsaturated fats, calcium, iron, magnesium, and zinc, and the absence of gluten. Its soluble fiber helps to lower cholesterol levels by carrying excess cholesterol through the digestive tract and out of the body in the same manner soluble fiber can rid us of toxins. This fiber imparts a sticky quality, so you may find amaranth most appealing when combined with non-sticky grains, as in our whole grain cereals, pages 226–229. Creamy Golden Porridge, page 230, is a great way to make the acquaintance of amaranth in the form of flour.

Arrowroot starch (also called arrowroot flour, arrowroot powder, or arrowroot): To make this starch, the rootstalks of the arrowroot plant are dried and ground into a very fine powder. This powder is used as a thickening agent for puddings, sauces, and other cooked foods. Arrowroot has about twice the thickening power of wheat flour, has no taste, and becomes clear when cooked. It can be used as a substitute for cornstarch, measure for measure. As with cornstarch, arrowroot should be mixed with a cold liquid before being heated or added to hot mixtures. Arrowroot can be found in some supermarkets, natural food stores, and Asian markets. Stored at room temperature in an airtight container, it will keep indefinitely. Its name is derived from its use by Native Americans to draw out poisons from arrow wounds.

Balsamic vinegar: Dark brown with an exquisite flavor and subtle sweetness, balsamic vinegar is made from sweet Trebbiano grapes. It acquires its dark color and pungency from being aged in wooden barrels for a minimum of ten years. Balsamic vinegar is available in supermarkets, Italian grocery stores, and gourmet and specialty food shops. Store at room temperature or in the refrigerator.

Buckwheat: Though cooked like a grain (in just 15–20 minutes), this triangle-shaped seed of a broad-leafed plant is in the same family as rhubarb and sorrel. Its slowly absorbed carbohydrates and excellent glycemic index make it valuable in diabetic diets and for the leveling of blood glucose. It contains phytochemicals that may protect us against heart disease and cancer. Buckwheat is unusually high in protein and provides riboflavin, niacin, copper, and magnesium. It has a natural sweetness, making it suitable for grain salads. Unhulled buckwheat kernels are known as buckwheat groats; when roasted they are called kasha, which has a nutty flavor. Groats can be ground into flour, which is popular as a pancake ingredient. In Japan, buckwheat has long been used in the form of soba noodles, though these typically are combined with wheat. Try 100 percent, wheat-free buckwheat noodles with the sauces on pages 337 and 338. Contrary to its name, buckwheat is not related to wheat at all, nor does it contain any gluten. If you are wheat or gluten sensitive, make sure that your buckwheat flour is pure and not mixed with wheat flour. Also, check that the buckwheat is processed at a facility that does not process gluten-containing grains. While it is possible to be allergic to buckwheat, most people who are sensitive to wheat or gluten can enjoy buckwheat grain without any problems.

Cashew butter: Similar to natural peanut butter, cashew butter is a paste made from ground raw or roasted cashew nuts. If the natural oil separates out, just stir it back in. Store briefly at room temperature or, for longer storage, in the refrigerator.

Chickpea flour (garbanzo flour): This versatile, delicious, gluten-free flour also is known as besan, gram flour, cici flour, chana flour, and garbanzo bean flour. Made from ground chickpeas, it is tan in color. Chickpea flour is commonly used in Indian, Italian, and some Middle Eastern cuisines. Look for it in Indian markets and natural food stores. For the longest shelf life, store it in an airtight container in the freezer.

Coconut oil: Coconut oil (also known as coconut butter) has received a lot of negative press because of its saturated fat content. However, modern research has shown that not all saturated fats are created equal. The fatty acids in coconut oil (the medium chain triglycerides) may not raise serum cholesterol or contribute to heart disease risk; instead, they may be protective and healthful. Coconut oil is an excellent hypoallergenic alternative to butter, animal fats, and artificially hardened margarines and shortenings for baking, frying, and sautéing. While its flavor is mild and unobtrusive, coconut oil adds richness to baked goods and prolongs their shelf life. In addition, it remains stable, even when heated at higher temperatures. Store your coconut oil in an airtight container at room temperature. Refrigerating coconut oil will make it too solid to use. To soften coconut oil, place the tightly sealed jar in a bowl of warm water.

Organic or virgin coconut oil may be found in natural food stores or you can purchase it online. Some recommended brands are Omega Nutrition (www.omeganutrition.com), Tropical Traditions (www.tropicaltraditions.com), and Spectrum Naturals (www.spectrumnaturals.com).

Corn: We first think of corn as a vegetable, served as niblets or on the cob or popped, as a movie or video snack. Its other forms are of value to those on gluten-free diets. When dried, corn can be ground into a coarse or fine meal or flour or made into pasta. Though relatively low in protein, corn contributes fiber, vitamin B_6 (pyridoxine), and selenium to our diets. Hominy grits are a refined product, with the hull, corn germ, and much of the nutritional content removed.

Guar gum: This stabilizer and thickening agent is obtained from the seeds of a plant in the bean family that is indigenous to India. It is valuable in unyeasted, gluten-free baked goods to improve structure and rise, qualities typically imparted by gluten-containing flours. Guar gum can have a mild laxative effect, so it is best used in small quantities. It makes a good replacement for xanthan gum for those who are sensitive to corn and may be substituted measure for measure. Look for guar gum through retailers that specialize in gluten-free products or in your natural food store. Stored at room temperature in an airtight container, it will keep indefinitely.

Kuzu: This thickener is made from the tuber of the kudzu plant. Also known as kudzu starch, it is a thickening agent similar to cornstarch, arrowroot, or potato starch. There are a number of characteristics of kuzu that distinguish it from other starches: kuzu starch creates a smooth, creamy consistency and a clear shine in jelled foods; its mild flavor does not conflict with delicate or subtle flavors; it produces a crispy texture when the powder is dusted over foods prior to deep frying; and its alkalinity allows the starch to harmonize well with sugars, which are acidic. Kuzu comes in small chunks. To measure, crush the chunks into a powder. To thicken a liquid, mix the powder with an equal amount of cold water, then stir the mixture into the hot liquid and simmer for a few minutes until the sauce is thickened. Look for kuzu in your natural food store. Stored at room temperature in an airtight container, it will keep indefinitely.

Millet: The October harvesting and threshing of millet grain in the Himalayan foothills makes a glorious picture. Cooked millet has a long history of use for the Nepalese and in China, India, Africa, and around the Mediterranean. Millet is gluten free, quick cooking, and rich in B vitamins: thiamine, riboflavin, and folate. Its importance in macrobiotic diets is also related to its alkalinity.

Miso (chickpea, lentil, or adzuki bean): Miso is a salty, flavorful, fermented paste that typically is made from soybeans along with rice, barley, or another grain or bean. Some specialty misos are made from chickpeas, lentils, adzuki beans, or other legumes instead of soybeans. Used primarily as a seasoning, miso's characteristics range from dark and strongly flavored to light, smooth, and delicately flavored varieties such as chickpea miso. The best varieties will be found in the refrigerated section of your natural food store, as they retain active enzymes. Store miso in a tightly covered container in the refrigerator, where it will keep for several months to a year (check the "use by" date on the container). If you are unable to have soy products, choose chickpea, adzuki bean, or lentil miso; these also are gluten free. Miso contains live bacteria that are beneficial to our intestinal health. To keep these bacteria alive, avoid overheating miso. For example, instead of adding miso to your soup pot while it's on the stove, stir a spoonful of miso into your soup at the table.

Potato starch: Potato starch is used as a thickener for sauces, soups, and stews. Potato starch tolerates higher temperatures better than cornstarch when used as a thickener. It attracts water, is a natural way to add moistness to many baked goods, and is an important ingredient in many gluten-free baking mixes. Be sure to purchase only pure potato starch, not potato flour, as the two are not interchangeable. Stored at room temperature in an airtight container, it will keep indefinitely.

Pumpkin seed butter: Pumpkin seed butter is a great source of omega-6 and omega-9 essential fatty acids; vitamins A, E, and C; zinc; and phytosterols. Pure pumpkin seed butter is made only from pumpkin seeds and sometimes salt. The color may at first surprise you: Green is the natural color of the pumpkin seeds. This rich, vibrant color is your guarantee of the butter's freshness. The first time you open your jar of pumpkin seed butter you may notice a layer of oil on top of a thick layer of seed butter. Just mix these two layers together and then refrigerate the butter; you will not have to mix it again. Like natural peanut butter, pumpkin seed butter divides into two layers because there are no additives or hydrogenated oils (trans-fatty acids) to prevent the natural oils from separating out.

Because it is a specialty item, some companies that make pumpkin seed butter do so in small batches in plants that do not process other nuts or seeds. This makes it ideal for people with nut and sesame allergies. Pumpkin seed butter is an excellent alternative to peanut butter, other nut butters, or sesame tahini in recipes, though it might turn some of your dishes an interesting shade of green. Omega Nutrition makes an excellent, smooth, high-quality pumpkin seed butter. Order it from them directly via their Web site (www.omeganutrition.com) or look for it at your natural food store. You also can make your own pumpkin seed butter. See page 354 for directions.

Quinoa: (pronounced KEEN-wah) This was a staple of the ancient Incas, who called it "the mother grain." Technically, it is not a grain but the seed of a plant in the same family as lamb's quarters. Gluten free and high in protein with an excellent balance of all eight essential amino acids, quinoa flour increases the protein quality of many baked goods in the recipe section of this book, providing a rich source of vitamin E, riboflavin, iron, magnesium, potassium, and zinc. Quinoa's tiny, bead-shaped grains are quick cooking and expand to four times their original volume. Its delicate, light flavor makes it suitable as a main dish, in soups, in salads, and even in puddings. Look for quinoa in most natural food stores and some supermarkets. It usually needs to be rinsed to remove the naturally occurring resin that coats its grains, though some quinoa is pre-rinsed.

Quinoa flour, flakes, and pasta: This gluten-free flour is made from ground quinoa (see above). It also is made into several forms of pasta. Look for quinoa flour, flakes, and pasta in your natural food store. For the longest shelf life, store quinoa flour in an airtight container in the freezer.

Rice: This grain has fed more people over a longer period of time than has any other crop known to mankind. It tends to be a mainstay of gluten-free, non-allergenic diets and is available in many varieties. Long-grain rice cooks up to be dry and fluffy, with distinct grains; short-grain rice is soft and sticky; and medium-grain rice has attributes of both. Long- and medium-grain rices generally are used for main courses, while short-grain rice is used for risottos, desserts, and Japanese foods, such as nori rolls, that require sticky rice. (See our recipe for Simple Nori Rolls on page 322.) Basmati rice is a unique, aromatic strain that is grown in the foothills of the Himalayas.

Rice flour: This finely ground flour can be made from either refined white rice or whole grain brown rice. It is popular for gluten-free baking and cooking. It also is made into several forms of pasta. Look for rice flour in natural food stores. For the longest shelf life, store it in an airtight container in the freezer.

Rice vinegar: This delicately flavored, amber-colored vinegar is made from either fermented brown or white rice or unrefined rice wine. It is available in natural food stores, Asian markets, and some supermarkets. Beware of most grocery store "seasoned" rice vinegars, as these typically contain added sugar. Stored at room temperature or in the refrigerator, brown or white rice vinegar will keep indefinitely.

Sesame oil, toasted: This oil is extracted from toasted sesame seeds and has a luscious, highly concentrated flavor. A few drops sprinkled over cooked grains, beans, pasta, or vegetables add outstanding flavor. It also comes in a spicy hot pepper variety. Do not use toasted sesame oil for cooking or sautéing, as it burns easily. You'll find it in natural food stores. Be sure to refrigerate it after opening to preserve its delicious flavor. If you cannot have sesame products, feel free to substitute another flavorful oil of your choice in the recipes in this book.

Sesame tahini: Sesame tahini is a smooth, creamy, tan-colored paste made from finely ground raw or roasted sesame seeds. It is an essential ingredient in many Middle Eastern recipes and adds a wonderful texture and nutty flavor to spreads, sauces, and dressings. Tahini may be very thick, like peanut butter, or thin and slightly runny, depending on the brand, and flavors vary considerably depending on the seeds used and whether they were roasted. As with all unrefined nut and seed butters, you'll want to store tahini in the refrigerator to prevent it from becoming rancid and to avoid separation. However, if the oil does separate, simply stir it back in. Sesame tahini is available in many supermarkets, Middle Eastern grocery stores, and natural food stores.

Please beware that sesame tahini usually is made on equipment that also processes nut butters. However, you can make your own sesame tahini at home. See the directions on page 354. If you cannot have sesame products, feel free to substitute any suitable seed or nut butter of your choice in these recipes.

Sorghum: This gluten-free cereal grain, similar to corn, grows in hot climates. The whole grain can be used in soups or puddings. Its bland flour tends to be dry. To improve its texture and moisture retention, it is recommended that ½–1 teaspoon (5–10 ml) of cornstarch or xanthum gum be added to a recipe for every cup of sorghum flour used, and that a little extra baking powder be added.

Sunflower seed butter: This nut-free spread makes a wonderful alternative to peanut butter, nut butters, and sesame tahini. Sunflower seeds contain appreciable amounts of vitamins E, B$_6$, niacin, folate, thiamin, and pantothenic acid. They are packed with minerals (magnesium, potassium, iron, zinc, and calcium) and protein. It currently is difficult to find commercial sunflower seed butter that is free of hydrogenated fats, but it is easy to make your own sunflower seed butter at home. See the directions on page 354.

Tapioca starch: A starchy flour that is extracted from the root of the cassava plant, it may be used as a thickening agent for soups, fruit fillings, gravies, and sauces, much the same as cornstarch and arrowroot. Tapioca starch is available from retailers that specialize in gluten-free products, some Asian markets, and natural food stores. Stored in an airtight container at room temperature, tapioca starch will keep indefinitely.

Teff (or tef or t'ef): This tiny grain, from a plant family called lovegrass and related to millet, is high in protein, fiber, calcium, and iron. It is completely free of gluten; however, if you are gluten sensitive, check with the manufacturer to make sure that the teff was milled and processed at a plant that does not process any gluten-containing grains. Next time you have the opportunity to visit an Ethiopian restaurant, welcome it! Or look for one in your phone book. You'll be able to try injera, the thin, porous, teff flatbread that also serves as plate and utensil at Ethiopian meals. Pieces of the crepe-like bread are held in your fingers and used as "grabbers" for deliciously seasoned lentil, spinach, and other vegetable dishes that are served in mounds on one large injera. The ingredients in injera traditionally are teff, water, oil, and salt. A small amount of "wild" yeast is present on the grain naturally. The batter is fermented for several days and then cooked on a hot stovetop or skillet.

Injera and teff can be purchased from Ethiopian stores and restaurants. Be sure to read the package label or inquire about ingredients to be certain your injera is made only with teff flour. It is not uncommon for restaurants to add wheat flour to their injera batter, so if you are allergic to wheat or are gluten intolerant, don't assume that all injera is safe. You can buy teff flour at many natural food stores and online from Bob's Red Mill (www.bobsredmill.com) and Gluten Free Mall (www.glutenfreemall.com). Or, you can skip the cooking and purchase prepared injera from Injera (www.injera.com).

Umeboshi vinegar: This unique vinegar is created during the processing of umeboshi plums with an herb called red shiso leaf. The vinegar and plums are condiments in Japanese and macrobiotic cuisine, valued for their alkaline qualities. The vinegar's salty, tart flavor makes a delightful seasoning. When using umeboshi, avoid adding salt to your recipe. Look for umeboshi vinegar in the macrobiotic section or condiment aisle of your natural food store. It may be stored indefinitely at room temperature. If you are avoiding vinegar but would like to use umeboshi flavoring, use an equal amount of umeboshi plum paste.

Wild rice: These dark brown kernels are not actually rice but are the seeds of a grain that is grown in the Canada prairies and in Minnesota and Wisconsin. It has almost twice the protein content of rice, is unusually rich in the mineral zinc, and is high in the B vitamins niacin and folate. It has a delicious, nutty flavor when cooked alone or mixed with brown rice.

Xanthan gum: Produced from the fermentation of corn sugar, xanthan gum is used as a thickener, emulsifier, and stabilizer in foods. It is used in unyeasted, gluten-free baked goods to improve structure and rise, qualities typically imparted by gluten-containing flours. Xanthan gum makes a good replacement for guar gum and may be substituted measure for measure. Look for xanthan gum through retailers that specialize in gluten-free products or in natural food stores. Stored in an airtight container at room temperature, it will keep indefinitely.

Resources for Unusual Ingredients

(For an extensive list of contact information for food manufacturers, see page 363–364.)

Online Stores

www.goodnessdirect.co.uk
www.nuworldfamily.com
www.shopbydiet.com

(especially for gluten intolerance and celiac disease)

www.enjoylifefoods.com
www.glutenfree.com
www.glutenfreedelights.com
www.glutenfreemall.com
www.glutenfreemarket.com
www.glutenfreepantry.com
www.glutenfree-supermarket.com
www.glutensolutions.com
www.glutino.com
www.missroben.com

Baking Basics

$\mathcal{B}$ aking is as much a science as it is an art. When it comes to baking without eggs or dairy products, it can be a little tricky. When it comes to gluten-free, soy-free, egg-free, and dairy-free baking, it becomes trickier yet. This is because gluten, eggs, and soy add structure to baked goods. Without this structure, cakes and cookies can become dry and crumbly, unable to hold together; and cakes, quick breads, and muffins will not rise properly or may fall or sink. These recipes have been carefully designed to give excellent results. Thus it is important to follow the directions carefully, always using the exact ingredients called for, using the proper type and size of pan required, setting the oven temperature precisely (and getting an oven thermometer to check your oven's temperature if you think it might need to be calibrated), and watching baking times closely. Small changes, such as substituting ingredients or not measuring accurately, can ruin an otherwise wonderful recipe.

To ensure a positive gluten-free baking experience, here are some tips:

- Do not sample the raw batter. Gluten-free batters contain uncooked bean flours that can cause severe gastrointestinal upset. Though the baked products are delicious, they do not taste very good before cooking.

- Always preheat the oven to the temperature specified. Quick breads (those that contain baking powder rather than yeast) will not hold well waiting until the oven is ready.

- Work quickly with recipes that contain baking powder. These recipes must be baked immediately or the baking powder will lose much of its punch.

- Double-acting baking powder will work best. "Double-acting" means that it reacts on contact with liquid and with heat. Be sure your baking powder is fresh (check the expiration date), as it will lose its leavening power over time. To test if your baking powder is still active, stir 1 teaspoon (5 ml) of it into ⅓ cup (85 ml) of hot water. If it bubbles vigorously, it is fine. (Note: If you cannot have corn derivatives, try our Corn-Free Baking Powder, page 183.)

- Use a metal baking pan or cookie sheet. Other materials (such as glass or ceramic) heat faster than metal and can cause gluten-free baked goods to become overcooked on the exterior and undercooked in the interior. All of the baked goods recipes in this section were tested using metal baking pans.

- When a recipe directs you to oil a pan, you'll get the best results with non-hydrogenated vegetable shortening or coconut oil. One brand of non-hydrogenated vegetable shortening is Spectrum Shortening, which is free of gluten and soy and is available in natural food stores. Organic or virgin coconut oil, which is soy free, may be found in natural food stores or you can purchase it online. Some recommended brands are Omega Nutrition (www.omeganutrition.com), Tropical Traditions (www.tropicaltraditions.com), and Spectrum Naturals (www.spectrum-naturals.com).

- Parchment paper is suggested as a liner for baking sheets and pans. Using parchment paper eliminates the need to oil bakeware, and it makes cleanup a breeze. If you prefer not to use parchment paper or have difficulty finding it, just use well-oiled and/or nonstick bakeware instead.

- When adapting any recipe (conventional or other) that specifies margarine, try to find a non-hydrogenated brand that suits your particular dietary restrictions. Alternatively, coconut oil may be used. When replacing margarine with coconut oil in a recipe, use one-quarter less the amount of coconut oil as margarine specified in the recipe. (For example, replace 1 cup/250 ml of margarine with ¾ cup/185 ml of coconut oil.)

- Most gluten-free baked goods fare better if a small amount of xanthan gum or guar gum is added to the dry ingredients. This replicates some of the properties of gluten-containing grains by helping gluten-free baked goods hold together better. Use approximately ¼–½ teaspoon (1–2 ml) xanthan gum or guar gum for each cup of Jo's Gluten-Free All-Purpose Flour Mix (page 182) when this mix is used to replace wheat flour in conventional recipes.

- Gluten-free flours will vary in their moisture content from batch to batch because of uncontrollable variables with cultivation, harvesting, and storage. As a result, at times you may need to add slightly more or less liquid than is called for in a recipe.

- When mixing dry ingredients for cakes, cookies, loaves, and other baked goods, you will achieve a lighter product if you sift the flours first. As old-fashioned as this might sound, adding a bit of air to gluten-free flours makes baked items lighter and more porous.

- Cool quick breads completely before slicing them to avoid a gummy texture.

- Gluten-free muffins, cakes, and quick breads will keep for one or two days at room temperature. After that, store them, loosely wrapped, in the refrigerator. Most can also be frozen for up to three months (cakes should be frozen without frosting). Cookies and biscuits can be stored at room temperature.

- If any of the recipe ingredients typically contain substances to which you are sensitive, be sure to use a suitable brand or alternative.

What to Use to Frost a Cake?

Confectioners' sugar, which is a staple in traditional frostings, usually contains corn-starch, making it off limits for those with corn allergies. It is possible to find corn-free confectioners' sugar, but you may have to contact several sources or special order it (please see page 363 for possible suppliers). If you can have confectioners' sugar (or are able to find a corn-free brand) and have access to suitable, non-hydrogenated margarine, then most conventional frosting recipes will work fine for you by just substituting margarine or three-quarters the amount of coconut oil for the butter called for in the recipe. Many conventional, packaged frostings are free of eggs and dairy, so that may be another alternative (just read the labels carefully beforehand). Here are some options you can use to top your cakes as an alternative to frosting:

- Incredible Hot Fudge Sauce, page 362
- In-A-Jiffy Breakfast Pudding or Fruit Sauce, page 235
- Hot Cinnamon Apple Topping, page 227
- apple butter
- applesauce (unsweetened or blended with a little pure maple syrup)
- fruit-sweetened jam
- finely shredded plain or toasted coconut
- dairy-free sorbet
- puréed ripe bananas
- puréed ripe berries (or blended bananas and berries)
- sliced fresh fruit
- well-drained crushed pineapple packed in juice
- dairy-free chocolate sauce or syrup
- brown rice syrup

Jo's Gluten-Free All-Purpose Flour Mix

Yields 8 cups (2 l)

Use this amazing mix for both cooking and baking. It's incredibly adaptable, very easy to prepare, and contains no soy or corn derivatives. Each starch and flour in the mix contributes unique qualities. Potato and arrowroot starches provide stickiness and adhesion. Chickpea flour is a source of protein and iron; rice flour is also, but to a lesser extent. Together they provide a mix that is neutral in flavor (when cooked) and ideal to replace wheat flour in your favorite recipes.

3 cups	potato starch or tapioca starch	750 ml
2 cups	chickpea flour	500 ml
2 cups	brown or white rice flour	500 ml
1 cup	arrowroot starch	250 ml

Place all the ingredients in a large bowl and stir with a dry wire whisk until evenly combined. Store in a sealed, airtight container at room temperature or in the refrigerator. Shake the container well before using in case any of the ingredients have settled.

VARIATION: When using potato starch as the major ingredient, 1 cup (250 ml) of tapioca starch may be substituted for the arrowroot starch, if desired.

TIPS: When using this mix to replace wheat flour in conventional recipes, reduce the oven temperature by 25°F (14°C) and bake a little bit longer.

- When adapting conventional recipes for baked goods, add ¼–½ teaspoon (1–2 ml) xanthan gum (or ½ teaspoon/2 ml guar gum, for a corn-free version) for each cup of flour called for in the recipe.

- This recipe may be doubled, if you want to keep a large amount on hand. The mix itself should not be frozen; however, chickpea flour and rice flour should be kept in the refrigerator or freezer for the longest storage. Potato starch and arrowroot should be stored in airtight containers at room temperature.

PER CUP (250 ML): calories: 525, protein: 8 g, fat: 3 g, carbohydrate: 108 g, dietary fiber: 4.5 g, calcium: 29 mg, iron: 2.7 mg, magnesium: 82 mg, sodium: 18 mg, zinc: 1.7 mg, folate: 107 mcg, riboflavin: 0.1 mg, vitamin C: 0 mg, vitamin E: 0.8 mg, omega-3 fatty acids: 0 g.

% CALORIES FROM: protein 7%, fat 5%, carbohydrate 88%

Corn-Free Baking Powder

If you are allergic to corn, use this simple baking powder to replace standard baking powder, which typically contains cornstarch.

Yields scant 1 cup (250 ml):

½ cup	arrowroot or tapioca starch	125 ml
⅓ cup	cream of tartar	85 ml
2½ tablespoons	baking soda	37 ml

Yields 2 cups (500 ml):

1 cup	arrowroot or tapioca starch	250 ml
⅔ cup	cream of tartar	170 ml
⅓ cup	baking soda	85 ml

Combine all the ingredients in a bowl and stir with a dry wire whisk until evenly blended. Store at room temperature in an airtight container.

PER TEASPOON (5 ML): calories: 7, protein: 0 g, fat: 0 g, carbohydrate: 2 g, dietary fiber: 0 g, calcium: 0 mg, iron: 0.1 mg, magnesium: 0 mg, sodium: 199 mg, zinc: 0 mg, folate: 0 mcg, riboflavin: 0 mg, vitamin C: 0 mg, vitamin E: 0 mg, omega-3 fatty acids: 0 g.

% CALORIES FROM: protein 0%,   fat 0%,   carbohydrate 100%

MAGICAL ONE-BOWL MUFFINS

Yields 6 or 12 muffins

Although these muffins are "plain," they are mighty tasty, especially when served with your favorite jam or fruit butter. Their magic comes into play with all the variations that are possible with them. You can make them sweet or savory with just a few additions, which makes them perfect for breakfast, snacks, or an alternative to bread with lunch or dinner. Of course, they always are a welcome standby with soups and salads, and with a little extra sweetener, they can be transformed into cupcakes for dessert!

These muffins are best served warm, fresh out of the oven. If you have leftovers, you might like to reheat them briefly in the microwave, standard oven (at around 300°F or 150°C), or toaster oven. For the oven or toaster oven, be sure to wrap them in foil so they don't dry out. These muffins freeze well.

FOR 6 MUFFINS:

1 cup	Jo's Gluten-Free All-Purpose Flour Mix, p. 182	250 ml
¼ cup	sugar	60 ml
1½ teaspoons	baking powder	7 ml
¼ teaspoon	xanthan gum or guar gum	1 ml
¼ teaspoon	salt	1 ml
1 cup	fortified nondairy milk or water	250 ml
¼ cup	organic canola, safflower, or coconut oil	60 ml

FOR 12 MUFFINS:

2 cups	Jo's Gluten-Free All-Purpose Flour Mix, p. 182	500 ml
½ cup	sugar	125 ml
1 tablespoon	baking powder	15 ml
½ teaspoon	xanthan gum or guar gum	2 ml
½ teaspoon	salt	2 ml
2 cups	fortified nondairy milk or water	500 ml
½ cup	organic canola, safflower, or coconut oil	125 ml

PER MUFFIN: calories: 222, protein: 1.5 g, fat: 10 g, carbohydrate: 31 g, dietary fiber: 1 g, calcium: 115 mg, iron: 0.5 mg, magnesium: 14 mg, sodium: 215 mg, zinc: 0.3 mg, folate: 18 mcg, riboflavin: 0 mg, vitamin C: 0 mg, vitamin E: 2.8 mg, omega-3 fatty acids: 0.9 g.

% CALORIES FROM: protein 3%, fat 41%, carbohydrate 56%

Preheat the oven to 375°F (190°C). Line a 6-cup or 12-cup muffin tin with baking cups. Combine the flour mix, sugar, baking powder, xanthan gum, and salt in a large bowl. Whisk in the milk or water and oil until smooth and well combined. Spoon equally into the baking cups (do not overfill). Bake on the center rack until lightly browned and a cake tester (or toothpick) inserted in the center of a muffin tests clean, about 25 minutes. Turn out onto a rack to cool. Best when served warm.

VARIATIONS: The following variations provide amounts for twelve muffins. If you are only making six muffins, cut the amounts in half.

- For Maple Corn Muffins, replace 1½ cups (375 ml) of the flour mix with yellow or blue cornmeal. Omit the sugar and combine ½ cup (125 ml) pure maple syrup with the milk or water and oil.

- For Maple Rice Muffins, replace 1½ cups (375 ml) of the flour mix with coarse rice flour or grits. If a "corn" yellow color is desired, add ¼ teaspoon (1 ml) turmeric to the dry ingredients. Omit the sugar and combine ½ cup (125 ml) pure maple syrup with the milk or water and oil.

- For Quinoa-Corn Muffins, replace 1½ cups (375 ml) of the flour mix with 1¼ cups (310 ml) plus 2 tablespoons (30 ml) yellow cornmeal and 2 tablespoons (30 ml) quinoa flour.

- For Quinoa-Rice Muffins, replace 1½ cups (375 ml) of the flour mix with 1¼ cups (310 ml) plus 2 tablespoons (30 ml) coarse rice flour or grits and 2 tablespoons (30 ml) quinoa flour.

- For Orange Muffins, replace the milk or water with 1 cup (250 ml) orange juice and add ½ teaspoon (2 ml) orange flavoring.

- For Cinnamon Raisin Muffins, add ½ teaspoon (2 ml) ground cinnamon to the dry ingredients. Add ½ cup (125 ml) raisins to the batter just before spooning into the muffin tins.

- For Festive Spice Muffins, add ½ teaspoon (2 ml) ground cinnamon, ¼ teaspoon (1 ml) ground mace, ¼ teaspoon (1 ml) ground nutmeg, ¼ teaspoon (1 ml) ground all-spice, and ¼ teaspoon (1 ml) ground ginger to the dry ingredients.

- For Asian Spice Muffins, add ½ teaspoon (2 ml) ground cinnamon, ½ teaspoon (2 ml) ground cardamom, ¼ teaspoon (1 ml) ground nutmeg, ¼ teaspoon (1 ml) ground cloves, ¼ teaspoon (1 ml) ground ginger to the dry ingredients.

- For Fruit Juice Muffins, replace part or all of the water with fruit juice. Depending on the juice used, the muffins may have an unusual tint.

- For Marmalade Muffins, omit the sugar. Combine the water and oil with ½ cup (125 ml) orange marmalade.

- **For Dried Fruit Muffins**, add ½ cup (125 ml) raisins, chopped dates, or chopped dried apricots to the batter just before spooning into the muffin tins.

- **For Crunchy Seed or Nut Muffins**, stir ¼ cup (60 ml) toasted sesame or sunflower seeds or ½ cup (125 ml) chopped walnuts, pecans, almonds, or cashews into the batter. Roasting the seeds or nuts first will give them a deeper, richer flavor. (See page 353.)

- **For Lemon Poppy Seed Muffins**, add ¼ cup (60 ml) poppy seeds to the dry ingredients, and add 1 teaspoon (5 ml) lemon flavoring when whisking in the milk or water.

- **For Zany Muffins**, add any combination of the choices listed above.

- **For Chocolate Muffins**, increase the sugar to ¾ cup (185 ml) and add 3 tablespoons (45 ml) unsweetened cocoa powder to the dry ingredients. These are almost cupcakes!

- **For Onion-Herb Muffins**, reduce the sugar to 2 teaspoons (10 ml), add 1 teaspoon (5 ml) dried thyme and 1 teaspoon (5 ml) dried rosemary to the dry ingredients. Stir ½ cup (125 ml) finely chopped onions into the batter just before spooning into the muffin tins.

- **For Dilly Muffins**, add 2 teaspoons (10 ml) dried dill weed to the dry ingredients.

- **For Quick Bread**, oil a metal 9 x 5-inch (23 x 13-cm) loaf pan. Use any of the variations listed above. Pour into the prepared pan and bake on the center rack of a preheated 350°F (180°C) oven for 60 to 70 minutes, or until a cake tester (or toothpick) inserted in the center tests clean.

Tips: If you choose not to use baking cups to line the muffin tin, be sure to liberally oil the tin. Baking cups are strongly recommended, however. They will not only make cleanup a breeze, they will help keep the muffins soft, tender, and moist.

- Adding ingredients, such as seeds, nuts, raisins, or more sweetener, will increase the amount of batter. As a result, you may need to prepare an additional muffin cup or two to accommodate the larger quantity.

SUNNY SEED BREAD

Yields 1 loaf (12 slices)

This loaf is delicious for breakfast, snacks, or sandwiches. It's not too sweet, which makes it quite versatile, and every bite packs a delightful crunch.

2 cups	Jo's Gluten-Free All-Purpose Flour Mix, p. 182	500 ml
1 tablespoon	baking powder	15 ml
1 teaspoon	xanthan gum or guar gum	5 ml
½ teaspoon	salt	2 ml
⅓ cup	sunflower seeds	85 ml
2 tablespoons	sesame or pumpkin seeds	30 ml
2 tablespoons	sesame tahini or other seed butter (see page 354)	30 ml
1 cup	water	250 ml
⅓ cup	organic canola or safflower oil	85 ml
⅓ cup	pure maple syrup	85 ml
1 teaspoon	apple cider vinegar or fresh lemon juice	5 ml

Preheat the oven to 350°F (180°C). Oil a metal 8½ x 4¼ x 3⅛-inch (22 x 11 x 8-cm) loaf pan and set aside.

Combine the flour mix, baking powder, xanthan gum, and salt in a large bowl. Stir with a dry wire whisk. Then stir in the sunflower and sesame or pumpkin seeds.

Place the seed butter in a separate bowl. Gradually whisk in the water until smooth and milky. Whisk in the oil, maple syrup, and vinegar or lemon juice, and beat until well combined. Pour into the dry ingredients and stir just until combined. Spoon into the prepared pan and smooth out the top with a spatula.

Bake for 60–70 minutes or until a cake test inserted in the center comes out clean. Let cool in the pan on a rack for 10 minutes. Remove from the pan and let cool completely on a rack before slicing or storing.

VARIATIONS: Try poppy seeds or flaxseeds in addition to, or in place of, the sesame or pumpkin seeds.

• Use 1 cup (250 ml) nondairy milk or light coconut milk in place of the seed butter and water.

PER SLICE: 216 calories:, protein: 3 g, fat: 11 g, carbohydrate: 26 g, dietary fiber: 1.5 g, calcium: 92 mg, iron: 1.1 mg, magnesium: 23 mg, sodium: 206 mg, zinc: 0.9 mg, folate: 22 mcg, riboflavin: 0 mg, vitamin C: 0 mg, vitamin E: 1.5 mg, omega-3 fatty acids: 0.6 g.

% CALORIES FROM: protein 6%,   fat 46%,   carbohydrate 48%

Scones or Biscuits

This versatile recipe can be used to make either scones, a type of Scottish quick bread, or baking powder biscuits. Both are immensely popular with those who miss breads. These tend to dry out quickly; however, they remain soft for a few days if stored in a sealed container with a wedge of apple, which adds moisture to the air. Alternatively, you may put a somewhat dried out scone into the microwave for 10 seconds, or warm it briefly in the oven to revive it.

2¾ cups	Jo's Gluten-Free All-Purpose Flour Mix, p. 182	685 ml
¼ cup	sugar	60 ml
2 teaspoons	baking powder	10 ml
½ teaspoon	xanthan gum or guar gum	2 ml
¼ teaspoon	salt	1 ml
⅓ cup	organic canola or coconut oil	85 ml
½ cup	water	125 ml
¼ cup	pure maple syrup	60 ml
2 tablespoons	unsweetened applesauce	30 ml
1 tablespoon	vanilla flavoring	15 ml
⅓ cup	currants or raisins	85 ml

Preheat the oven to 400°F (205°C). Line a baking sheet with parchment paper, or lightly oil the baking sheet, and set it aside.

Combine the flour mix, sugar, baking powder, xanthan gum, and salt in a large bowl. Using a fork, stir in the oil, then work it in with your fingers until the mixture resembles fine crumbs. In a separate bowl, combine the water, maple syrup, applesauce, and vanilla flavoring. Stir into the dry ingredients and mix until evenly combined. Add the currants or raisins and knead in the bowl for about 30 seconds until evenly distributed.

Place the dough on the prepared baking sheet and pat it into an 8-inch (20-cm) circle. Cut it into 12 equal wedges and carefully separate them so they have room to expand. If the knife becomes sticky, rinse it off. Bake for 20–25 minutes or until the edges are slightly golden. Remove from the oven and place the baking sheet on a wire rack to cool for 5 minutes. Then transfer the scones to the wire rack to finish cooling. The scones are best served warm.

VARIATIONS:

- For less sweet biscuits or scones replace the ¼ cup (60 ml) maple syrup with an additional ¼ cup (60 ml) water.

- FOR BAKING POWDER BISCUITS, omit the vanilla and currants. Roll out or pat the dough on a flat surface between two sheets of waxed paper. Cut into 2-inch (5-cm) rounds using a biscuit cutter or inverted glass, or cut into triangles. Bake for 12–18 minutes.

- FOR CRANBERRY SCONES, replace currants with ⅓ cup (85 ml) sweetened dried cranberries.

PER SCONE OR BISCUIT: calories: 225, protein: 2 g, fat: 7 g, carbohydrate: 37 g, dietary fiber: 1.5 g, calcium: 60 mg, iron: 1 mg, magnesium: 22 mg, sodium: 135 mg, zinc: 0.7 mg, folate: 25 mcg, riboflavin: 0 mg, vitamin C: 0 mg, vitamin E: 1.4 mg, omega-3 fatty acids: 0.6 g.

% CALORIES FROM: protein 5%,   fat 28%,   carbohydrate 67%

Great Gluten-Free Pizza Crust

Yields one 10-inch (25-cm) or one 12-inch (30-cm) crust

This crust holds together well and tastes delicious, plus it provides protein and other nutrients. It's so much quicker and tastier than yeasted, wheat-based pizza crusts that even friends and family who are able to eat gluten will be clamoring for the recipe. For toppings, see our Pizza Party! recipe on page 312.

10-inch (25-cm) regular crust or 12-inch (30-cm) thin crust:

1½ cups	Jo's Gluten-Free All-Purpose Flour Mix, p. 182	375 ml
¼ cup	quinoa flour	60 ml
¼ cup	chickpea flour	60 ml
1 teaspoon	xanthan gum or guar gum	5 ml
½ teaspoon	baking powder	2 ml
½ teaspoon	salt	2 ml
3 tablespoons	olive oil	45 ml
½ cup	water	125 ml

12-inch (30-cm) regular crust or 10-inch (25-cm) thick crust:

1¾ cups	Jo's Gluten-Free All-Purpose Flour Mix, p. 182	435 ml
¼ cup	quinoa flour	60 ml
¼ cup	chickpea flour	60 ml
1 teaspoon	xanthan gum or guar gum	5 ml
½ teaspoon	baking powder	2 ml
½ teaspoon	salt	2 ml
¼ cup	olive oil	60 ml
⅔ cup	water	170 ml

Preheat the oven to 425°F (220°C). Liberally oil one 10-inch (25-cm) or one 12-inch (30-cm) pizza pan, and set aside.

Combine the flour mix, quinoa and chickpea flours, xanthan or guar gum, baking powder, and salt in a large bowl. Stir with a dry wire whisk until evenly mixed. Stir in the oil using a fork, then work it in with your fingers. Pour in the water and stir until all the liquid has been absorbed. The dough will be slightly sticky. Form into a ball.

Place the ball in the center of the prepared pan, and pat and press it into a 10-inch (25-cm) or 12-inch (30-cm) circle, about ¼-inch (0.5-cm) thick, except at the edges, which

---

Per quarter: calories: 347, protein: 5.5 g, fat: 12 g, carbohydrate: 50 g,
dietary fiber: 3.5 g, calcium: 50 mg, iron: 1.8 mg, magnesium: 59 mg,
sodium: 364 mg, zinc: 1.1 mg, folate: 69 mcg, riboflavin: 0.1 mg,
vitamin C: 0 mg, vitamin E: 1.8 mg, omega-3 fatty acids: 0.1 g.

% Calories from: protein 7%, fat 33%, carbohydrate 60%

should be about ½-inch (1-cm) thick to contain the sauce and toppings. Be sure to patch any tears. Bake 10 minutes. Cool. Fill with your desired sauce and toppings. Then bake 25–30 minutes or until the edges are golden brown.

RICEBREAD OR CORNBREAD SQUARES

Yields 9–12 servings

Try these versatile squares at breakfast with fruit spread, or partnered with a vegetarian chili and garden-fresh salad for dinner.

1½ cups	brown or white rice flour (coarse or fine) or yellow cornmeal	375 ml
½ cup	Jo's Gluten-Free All-Purpose Flour Mix, p. 182	125 ml
1 tablespoon	baking powder	15 ml
½ teaspoon	salt	2 ml
½ teaspoon	xanthan gum or guar gum	2 ml
1 cup	water	250 ml
½ cup	pure maple syrup	125 ml
½ cup	organic canola oil or melted coconut oil	125 ml

Preheat the oven to 350°F (180°C). Oil an 8-inch (20-cm) square metal baking pan and set aside.

Combine the rice flour or cornmeal, flour mix, baking powder, salt, and xanthan gum in a large bowl. Stir with a dry wire whisk until evenly mixed. In a separate bowl, stir together the water, maple syrup, and oil. Pour into the flour mixture, beating quickly with a wire whisk until well combined and nearly lump free. Pour into the prepared pan, using a rubber spatula to scrape out the bowl. Bake on the center rack of the oven for 45–50 minutes or until a cake tester (or toothpick) inserted into the center tests clean.

Place the pan on a cooling rack and let cool completely in the pan before cutting. May be stored a day or two at room temperature, but will keep best if refrigerated after that.

TIP: To give a "cornbread" yellow appearance to Ricebread Squares, add ¼ teaspoon (1 ml) turmeric to the dry ingredients.

PER SQUARE (⅑ RECIPE): calories: 282, protein: 2.5 g, fat: 13 g, carbohydrate: 38 g, dietary fiber: 1.5 g, calcium: 97 mg, iron: 0.9 mg, magnesium: 37 mg, sodium: 268 mg, zinc: 1.5 mg, folate: 10 mcg, riboflavin: 0 mg, vitamin C: 0 mg, vitamin E: 3.2 mg, omega-3 fatty acids: 1.2 g.

% CALORIES FROM: protein 3%,   fat 43%,   carbohydrate 54%

Gluten-Free Chapatis

Chapatis are round, flat, unleavened bread common in West Asia, particularly India. They also are popular in Eastern Africa, especially among the Swahili people and in Swahili-speaking countries. The Malay and Indian populations of South Africa also eat chapatis. Serve them with dips, Indian-style dal, stews, or African-style curry dishes. You can also gently fold them in half like a soft-shell taco and fill them with seasoned beans, or use each chapati like a thick slice of bread to make a sandwich.

2 cups	Jo's Gluten-Free All-Purpose Flour Mix, p. 182	500 ml
1 teaspoon	baking powder	5 ml
1 teaspoon	salt	5 ml
½ teaspoon	sugar	2 ml
¼ teaspoon	xanthan gum or guar gum	1 ml
2 tablespoons	coconut oil, softened	30 ml
¾–1 cup	warm water	185 ml to 250 ml

Combine the flour mix, baking powder, salt, sugar, and xanthan gum in a large bowl. Stir with a dry wire whisk until evenly mixed. Cut in the coconut oil using a pastry blender, fork, or two knives. Finish working it in with your hands. Add the warm water, starting with ¾ cup (185 ml), and mix well using a fork and then your hands. Continue to add water as needed until a soft, cohesive dough is formed. If the dough is a little dry, add a few tablespoons of extra water; if it is sticky, add a little extra flour mix.

Transfer the dough to a floured surface and knead for 5 minutes. Return the dough to the bowl, cover with plastic wrap or a towel, and allow to rest for 30 minutes.

Heat a nonstick griddle or skillet over medium heat. Meanwhile, divide the dough into 6 or 8 equal pieces. Work with one piece at a time, and cover the remainder so they do not dry out. Form the piece into a ball and place it between two sheets of waxed paper. Using a rolling pin on a flat surface, roll it into a round disk about ⅛-inch (0.3-cm) thick and about 6–8 inches (15–20 cm) in diameter. (Lightly wetting the flat surface will keep the bottom sheet of waxed paper from slipping.) Carefully peel off the top sheet of waxed paper, and flip the chapati over so it is resting in the open palm of

---

PER CHAPATI (⅙ RECIPE): calories: 128, protein: 1.5 g, fat: 5 g, carbohydrate: 19 g, dietary fiber: 1 g, calcium: 51 mg, iron: 0.6 mg, magnesium: 14 mg, sodium: 473 mg, zinc: 0.3 mg, folate: 18 mcg, riboflavin: 0 mg, vitamin C: 0 mg, vitamin E: 0.1 mg, omega-3 fatty acids: 0 g.

% CALORIES FROM: protein 4%,   fat 36%,   carbohydrate 60%

your hand and the remaining sheet of waxed paper is now on top. Carefully remove the remaining sheet of waxed paper and gently flip the chapati onto the hot griddle or into the hot skillet.

Bake one chapati at a time until lightly puffed, the surface has a few bubbles, and the bottom has a few brown flecks, about 1 or 2 minutes. Bake the second side briefly, just until lightly browned, about 1 minute. Keep the cooked chapatis wrapped in a clean tea towel until serving time. This will keep them warm, soft, and pliable.

CHICKPEA CREPES

Yields 7–8 small crepes

Use these savory crepes to complement any grain or vegetable dish, or stuff them with your favorite fillings and roll them up like tortillas.

1 cup	chickpea flour	250 ml
¼ teaspoon	garlic powder (optional)	1 ml
¼ teaspoon	turmeric	1 ml
¼ teaspoon	salt	1 ml
1 cup	water	250 ml
	Oil, as needed	

Toast the flour in a dry skillet over medium heat. Stir constantly until it turns a shade darker, emits a nutty aroma, and no longer tastes raw, about 5 minutes. Transfer to a medium bowl and stir in the garlic powder, if using, turmeric, and salt. Gradually whisk in the water, beating vigorously to avoid lumps.

Oil a small, heavy skillet (nonstick works best) and heat over medium-high heat. Drop a scant ¼ cup (60 ml) of the batter onto the hot skillet and immediately rotate it to spread the batter evenly and make a thin round. Cook until the crepe begins to brown on the bottom. Carefully turn it over and cook the other side. Repeat until all the batter is used up, re-oiling the pan between each crepe.

Stack the crepes on a plate or clean tea towel after they are cooked. Cover them with a clean tea towel to keep them warm until serving time.

PER CREPE (¹/7 RECIPE, without oil): calories: 49, protein: 3 g, fat: 1 g, carbohydrate: 8 g, dietary fiber: 1.5 g, calcium: 7 mg, iron: 0.7 mg, magnesium: 22 mg, sodium: 92 mg, zinc: 0.4 mg, folate: 57 mcg, riboflavin: 0 mg, vitamin C: 0 mg, vitamin E: 0 mg, omega-3 fatty acids: 0 g.

% CALORIES FROM: protein 23%,   fat 16%,   carbohydrate 61%

Pumpkin Spice Bread

Yields 10–12 slices

This delicious specialty bread is ideal for a crisp fall morning and is the perfect balance of sweet and spice. The heavenly aroma will make your whole house smell wonderful!

¾ cup	canned pumpkin	185 ml
½ cup	pure maple syrup	125 ml
½ cup	brown sugar	125 ml
⅓ cup	organic canola or safflower oil	85 ml
¼ cup	unsweetened applesauce	60 ml
1½ cups	Jo's Gluten-Free All-Purpose Flour Mix, p. 182	375 ml
¼ cup	quinoa flour	60 ml
1½ teaspoons	baking powder	7 ml
1½ teaspoons	baking soda	7 ml
1 teaspoon	ground cinnamon	5 ml
1 teaspoon	xanthan gum or guar gum	5 ml
½ teaspoon	salt	2 ml
½ teaspoon	ground allspice	2 ml
¼ teaspoon each	ground ginger, nutmeg, cloves	1 ml each
½ cup	chopped pecans (optional)	125 ml
½ cup	raisins (optional)	125 ml

Preheat the oven to 350°F (180°C). Oil an 8½ x 4¼ x 3⅛-inch (22 x 11 x 8-cm) loaf pan. Combine the pumpkin, maple syrup, brown sugar, oil, and applesauce in large bowl. Beat with an electric mixer on low until very smooth, about 1 minute.

Combine in a separate bowl, the flour mix, quinoa flour, baking powder, baking soda, cinnamon, xanthan gum, salt, allspice, ginger, nutmeg, and cloves. Stir with a dry wire whisk until evenly combined. Gradually beat into the pumpkin mixture in three additions at low speed. Stir in the optional nuts and raisins, if using.

Transfer the batter to the prepared pan and smooth out the top with a spatula. Bake for 60–70 minutes or until a tester inserted in the center comes out clean.

Cool the pan on a wire rack for 10 minutes. Remove the bread from the pan and cool upside down on a wire rack for about 20 minutes. Turn upright and cool completely before slicing. May be stored a day or two at room temperature, but will keep best if refrigerated after that. This bread freezes well.

PER SLICE (¹/10 RECIPE): calories: 252, protein: 2 g, fat: 8 g, carbohydrate: 43 g, dietary fiber: 2 g, calcium: 70 mg, iron: 1.3 mg, magnesium: 29 mg, sodium: 375 mg, zinc: 1.1 mg, folate: 20 mcg, riboflavin: 0 mg, vitamin C: 1 mg, vitamin E: 2.1 mg, omega-3 fatty acids: 0.7 g.

% CALORIES FROM: protein 3%,   fat 29%,   carbohydrate 68%

Banana Bread

Moist and flavorful banana bread makes a tasty breakfast or nutritious snack.

¾ cup	brown sugar, packed	185 ml
¼ cup	organic canola or safflower oil	60 ml
1 teaspoon	vanilla flavoring	5 ml
1¾ cups	Jo's Gluten-Free All-Purpose Flour Mix, p. 182	435 ml
2 teaspoons	baking powder	10 ml
1¼ teaspoons	ground cinnamon	6 ml
1 teaspoon	xanthan gum or guar gum	5 ml
½ teaspoon	salt	2 ml
1½ cups	mashed ripe bananas (about 3 medium)	375 ml
½ cup	sunflower seeds or chopped pecans or walnuts (optional)	125 ml
½ cup	raisins (optional)	125 ml)

Preheat the oven to 350°F (180°C). Oil an 8½ x 4¼ x 3⅛-inch (22 x 11 x 8-cm) loaf pan.

Cream together the brown sugar, oil, and vanilla flavoring in a large bowl. In a separate bowl, combine the flour mix, baking powder, cinnamon, xanthan gum, and salt, stirring with a dry wire whisk until evenly combined. Add to the wet ingredients in three additions, alternating with the mashed bananas and ending with the flour mix. Stir in the seeds and raisins, if using. The batter will be somewhat soft. Transfer to the prepared pan.

Bake 60–70 minutes, or until a tester inserted in the center comes out clean. Cool in the pan on a wire rack for 10 minutes. Remove from the pan and cool upside down on a wire rack for 20–30 minutes. Turn upright and cool completely before slicing. May be stored a day or two at room temperature, but it will keep best if refrigerated after that. This bread freezes well.

PER SLICE: calories: 197, protein: 1.5 g, fat: 5 g, carbohydrate: 36 g, dietary fiber: 1.5 g, calcium: 60 mg, iron: 0.8 mg, magnesium: 24 mg, sodium: 172 mg, zinc: 0.3 mg, folate: 21 mcg, riboflavin: 0 mg, vitamin C: 3 mg, vitamin E: 1.2 mg, omega-3 fatty acids: 0.5 g.

% CALORIES FROM: protein 3%,   fat 24%,   carbohydrate 73%

PERFECTION PIE CRUST

Yields ONE OR TWO 9-inch (23-cm) CRUSTS
(about 8–10 OR 16–20 SERVINGS)

This recipe is super easy to make and the dough is very forgiving. The taste is delicious and texture is light, crispy, and flaky. It's certain to be a big hit and a great match with all your sweet and savory pies.

ONE CRUST:

1 cup	Jo's Gluten-Free All-Purpose Flour Mix, p. 182	250 ml
2 tablespoons	quinoa flour	30 ml
½ teaspoon	xanthan gum or guar gum	2 ml
½ teaspoon	salt	2 ml
6 tablespoons	vegetable shortening or coconut oil	90 ml
3–4 tablespoons	cold water	45–60 ml

TWO CRUSTS:

2 cups	Jo's Gluten-Free All-Purpose Flour Mix, p. 182	500 ml
¼ cup	quinoa flour	60 ml
1 teaspoon	xanthan gum or guar gum	5 ml
¼ teaspoon	salt	1 ml
¾ cup	vegetable shortening or coconut oil	185 ml
⅓–½ cup	cold water	85–125 ml

Combine the flour mix, quinoa flour, xanthan gum, and salt in a large bowl. Using a pastry cutter, cut in the shortening until particles are the size of small peas. Sprinkle 3 tablespoons of the water over the flour mixture. Toss and stir with a fork until it starts to cling and a ball can be formed. If the dough appears too dry, add a bit more cold water as needed (one tablespoon at a time), mixing well after each addition. If the dough is too sticky, sprinkle a bit more flour mix over it.

Turn the dough out of the bowl onto a lightly floured surface and gently knead six to ten times to form a ball. If making two crusts, divide the dough into two equal pieces. Roll out each crust between two sheets of waxed paper to the desired size and thickness. Remove the top piece of waxed paper and gently flip over the dough. Carefully place it into the pie pan, with the waxed paper facing up. Use the waxed paper to help with pressing the dough gently against the sides and bottom of the pie pan. Carefully

---

PER SERVING (⅛ SINGLE CRUST): calories: 159, protein: 1.5 g, fat: 10 g, carbohydrate: 15 g, dietary fiber: 1 g, calcium: 4 mg, iron: 0.4 mg, magnesium: 15 mg, sodium: 148 mg, zinc: 0.3 mg, folate: 14 mcg, riboflavin: 0 mg, vitamin C: 0 mg, vitamin E: 0.2 mg, omega-3 fatty acids: 0.3 g.

% CALORIES FROM: protein 3%,   fat 58%,   carbohydrate 39%

remove the waxed paper. Fill with your favorite filling and cover with the second crust (if using). If using a top crust, vent it and trim the edges. Flute the edges and bake according to your favorite pie recipe directions.

For a prebaked shell (to use with cooked puddings and other fillings that do not require further baking), prick the bottom and sides with a fork, and bake at 400°F (205°C) for about 20 minutes. Cool completely before filling.

AMISH PAT-IN-THE-PAN PIE CRUST

Yields one 9- or 10-inch (23- or 25-cm) crust
(about 8–10 servings)

This amazing crust is exceptionally rich and flaky—perfect for all your sweet or savory pies. Try it with our Creamy Quiche, page 328.

2 cups	Jo's Gluten-Free All-Purpose Flour Mix, p. 182	500 ml
2 teaspoons	sugar	10 ml
1 teaspoon	salt	5 ml
1 teaspoon	xanthan gum or guar gum	5 ml
6 tablespoons	coconut oil	90 ml
⅓ cup	water	85 ml
2 tablespoons	olive oil	30 ml

Combine the flour mix, sugar, salt, and xanthan gum in a 9-inch (23-cm) or 10-inch (25-cm) pie plate. Add the coconut oil, water, and olive oil to the flour mixture and stir together with a fork. Finish by using your fingers. Pat and press the crust into the bottom of the pie plate and up the sides. Prick the bottom and sides all over with the tines of a fork and flute the edges.

Fill with your favorite filling and bake as directed in the recipe. For a prebaked shell (to use with cooked puddings and other fillings that do not require further baking), prick the bottom and sides with a fork, and bake at 400°F (205°C) for about 25 minutes. Cool completely before filling.

PER SERVING (⅛ RECIPE): calories: 255, protein: 2 g, fat: 14 g, carbohydrate: 28 g, dietary fiber: 1.5 g, calcium: 8 mg, iron: 0.7 mg, magnesium: 21 mg, sodium: 295 mg, zinc: 0.4 mg, folate: 27 mcg, riboflavin: 0 mg, vitamin C: 0 mg, vitamin E: 0.65 mg, omega-3 fatty acids: 0 g.

% CALORIES FROM: protein 3%,   fat 52%,   carbohydrate 45%

CHOCOLATE SHEET CAKE

This moist, light cake is perfect for any party, holiday, or special gathering. Serve it plain or topped with your favorite frosting or frosting alternative (see page 181).

2¾ cups	Jo's Gluten-Free All-Purpose Flour Mix, p. 182	685 ml
⅔ cup	unsweetened cocoa powder	170 ml
¼ cup	quinoa flour	60 ml
2 teaspoons	baking soda	10 ml
1¼ teaspoons	xanthan gum or guar gum	6 ml
2 cups	sugar	500 ml
2 cups	water	500 ml
⅔ cup	organic canola or safflower oil	170 ml
2 teaspoons	apple cider vinegar or fresh lemon juice	10 ml
2 teaspoons	vanilla flavoring	10 ml

Preheat the oven to 350°F (180°C). Oil a 9 x 13-inch (23 x 33-cm) baking pan and set aside. Combine the flour mix, cocoa powder, quinoa flour, baking soda, and xanthan gum in a large bowl. Stir with a dry wire whisk to mix. In a separate large bowl, combine the sugar, water, oil, vinegar or lemon juice, and vanilla flavoring. Using an electric mixer, gradually beat in the flour mixture in three additions, beating well after each addition. Immediately pour into the prepared baking pan. Bake on the center rack of the oven for about 45 minutes, or until a cake tester (or toothpick) inserted in the center tests clean. Cool completely before frosting.

PER SERVING: calories: 382, protein: 3 g, fat: 14 g, carbohydrate: 63 g, dietary fiber: 3 g, calcium: 15 mg, iron: 1.5 mg, magnesium: 49 mg, sodium: 217 mg, zinc: 0.8 mg, folate: 27 mcg, riboflavin: 0 mg, vitamin C: 0 mg, vitamin E: 3.0 mg, omega-3 fatty acids: 1.2g.

% CALORIES FROM: protein 3%,   fat 32%,   carbohydrate 65%

CONTAINS: Chocolate

Chocolate Snack Cake

This cake is light and divinely chocolaty! Plus, its smaller size makes it ideal for snacking.

1¼ cups	Jo's Gluten-Free All-Purpose Flour Mix, p. 182	310 ml
½ cup	unsweetened cocoa powder	125 ml
1 teaspoon	baking soda	5 ml
¾ teaspoon	xanthan gum or guar gum	4 ml
½ teaspoon	salt	2 ml
½ cup	organic canola oil	125 ml
1 cup	brown sugar	250 ml
2 teaspoons	vanilla flavoring	10 ml
¼ cup	unsweetened applesauce	60 ml
¼ cup	pure maple syrup	60 ml
¼ cup	fortified nondairy milk or water	60 ml

Preheat the oven to 350°F (180°C). Generously oil a 9-inch (23-cm) round or 8-inch (20-cm) square metal cake pan. Set aside.

Combine the flour mix, cocoa powder, baking soda, xanthan gum, and salt in a large bowl. Stir with a dry wire whisk until well combined. In a separate large bowl, using an electric mixer, cream together the oil, brown sugar, and vanilla flavoring. Beat in the applesauce and maple syrup. Then stir in the milk or water or use the mixer on low. Gradually add the flour mixture in three additions, beating well after each addition. Pour into the prepared pan and bake for 30 minutes or until a cake tester (or toothpick) inserted in the center tests clean.

Per serving (¹⁄12 cake): calories: 239, protein: 1.5 g, fat: 10 g, carbohydrate: 37 g, dietary fiber: 2 g, calcium: 34 mg, iron: 1.2 mg, magnesium: 33 mg, sodium: 214 mg, zinc: 0.7 mg, folate: 13 mcg, riboflavin: 0 mg, vitamin C: 0 mg, vitamin E: 2.1 mg, omega-3 fatty acids: 0.9 g.

% Calories from: protein 3%, fat 37%, carbohydrate 60%

CONTAINS: Chocolate

Glazed Lemon Pound Cake

This satisfying cake makes a wonderful dessert or special breakfast. Serve it with your favorite herbal tea and watch your cares melt away.

Cake:

⅓ cup	coconut oil	85 ml
1 cup	sugar	250 ml
2 tablespoons	unsweetened applesauce	30 ml
2 teaspoons	lemon zest (grated lemon peel)	10 ml
2¼ cups	Jo's Gluten-Free All-Purpose Flour Mix, p. 182	560 ml
¼ cup	quinoa flour	60 ml
1 teaspoon	xanthan gum or guar gum	5 ml
1 teaspoon	baking powder	5 ml
½ teaspoon	baking soda	2 ml
¼ teaspoon	salt	1 ml
½ cup	water	125 ml
¼ cup	fresh lemon juice	60 ml
1 teaspoon	lemon extract or flavoring	5 ml

Lemon Glaze:

2 tablespoons	sugar	30 ml
2 tablespoons	fresh lemon juice	30 ml

Preheat the oven to 350°F (180°C). Generously oil an 8½ x 4¼ x 3⅛-inch (22 x 11 x 8-cm) loaf pan and set aside.

Using an electric mixer and a large bowl, cream together the coconut oil and sugar on medium speed until light and fluffy. Mix in the applesauce on low speed until blended. Add the lemon zest.

In a medium bowl, whisk together the flour mix, quinoa flour, xanthan gum, baking powder, baking soda, and salt. In a small bowl or measuring cup, combine the water, lemon juice, and lemon extract. On medium speed, beat the dry ingredients into the oil and sugar mixture, alternating with the lemon water, beginning and ending with the dry ingredients. Mix just until combined. Spoon the batter into the prepared pan. The batter will be thick and somewhat elastic.

Bake on the center rack of the oven until the top is golden brown and a cake tester (or toothpick) inserted into center comes out clean, about 60 minutes. Cool the cake in the pan for 5 minutes, then remove from pan and cool on a rack.

For the glaze, combine the sugar and lemon juice in a small saucepan. Bring to a boil and boil for 1 minute. Remove from the heat and let cool. Drizzle over the pound cake while the glaze and cake are still warm. Place a sheet of waxed paper under the cake before drizzling on the glaze to make cleanup easier.

VARIATIONS:

- For Glazed Lemon-Poppy Seed Pound Cake, beat ¼ cup (60 ml) poppy seeds into the batter before spooning it into the pan.

- For Glazed Lemon-Sesame Seed Pound Cake, beat ¼ cup (60 ml) sesame seeds into the batter before spooning it into the pan.

- For Glazed Orange Pound Cake, replace the lemon zest with an equal amount of orange zest, replace the lemon juice with an equal amount of fresh orange juice, and replace the lemon extract or flavoring with orange extract or flavoring. This version may be combined with either of the seed variations above.

PER SLICE: calories: 275, protein: 2.5 g, fat: 8 g, carbohydrate: 48 g, dietary fiber: 1.5 g, calcium: 33 mg, iron: 0.8 mg, magnesium: 26 mg, sodium: 166 mg, zinc: 0.5 mg, folate: 27 mcg, riboflavin: 0 mg, vitamin C: 3 mg, vitamin E: 0.4 mg, omega-3 fatty acids: 0 g.

% CALORIES FROM: protein 3%,   fat 27%,   carbohydrate 70%

CONTAINS: * Citrus (lemon)

Basic White Cake

*Light, fluffy, and moist, this divine cake is ideal for every special occasion.
Spread your favorite filling between the layers and frost the top and sides.
We've had great success with a fruit spread filling and vanilla icing all around.*

Two Layers:

6 tablespoons	coconut oil	90 ml
1½ cups	sugar	375 ml
¼ cup	unsweetened applesauce	60 ml
1½ tablespoons	grated lemon zest	22 ml
2¾ cups	Jo's Gluten-Free All-Purpose Flour Mix, p. 182	685 ml
¼ cup	quinoa flour	60 ml
1¼ teaspoons	xanthan gum or guar gum	6 ml
1½ teaspoons	baking powder	7 ml
¾ teaspoon	baking soda	4 ml
¼ teaspoon	salt	1 ml
1 cup + 2 tablespoons	water	280 ml
1½ tablespoons	fresh lemon juice	22 ml
1½ teaspoons	vanilla flavoring	7 ml

Three Layers:

9 tablespoons	coconut oil	135 ml
2¼ cups	sugar	560 ml
6 tablespoons	unsweetened applesauce	90 ml
2 tablespoons	grated lemon zest	30 ml
4½ cups	Jo's Gluten-Free All-Purpose Flour Mix, p. 182	1125 ml
⅓ cup	quinoa flour	85 ml
2 teaspoons	xanthan gum or guar gum	10 ml
2¼ teaspoons	baking powder	11 ml
1 teaspoon	baking soda	5 ml
Heaping ¼ teaspoon	salt	1+ ml
1⅔ cups	water	420 ml
2½ tablespoons	fresh lemon juice	37 ml
2½ teaspoons	vanilla flavoring	12 ml

Preheat the oven to 350°F (180°C). Generously oil two or three 9-inch (23-cm) non-stick round cake pans. Line the cake pans with parchment paper. (Use the pan to trace a circle on the parchment paper and then cut it to fit the bottom of the pan.) Set aside.

Using an electric mixer and a large bowl, blend together the coconut oil and sugar on medium speed until light and fluffy. Mix in the applesauce on low speed until blended. Add the grated lemon zest.

In a medium bowl, whisk together the flour mix, quinoa flour, xanthan gum, baking powder, baking soda, and salt. In another medium bowl, combine the water, lemon juice, and vanilla flavoring. On low speed, beat the dry ingredients into the oil and sugar mixture, alternating with the lemon water, beginning and ending with the dry ingredients. Mix until just combined. The batter will be thick and somewhat elastic. Spoon the batter into the prepared pans and smooth the tops.

Bake for 20 to 25 minutes or until the tops are golden brown and a cake tester (or toothpick) inserted into centers comes out clean. Cool the cakes in the pans for 5 minutes, then remove from the pans and cool on racks.

PER SLICE (two layers, 1/10 of cake): calories: 348, protein: 3 g, fat: 9 g, carbohydrate: 63 g, dietary fiber: 2 g, calcium: 47 mg, iron: 1 mg, magnesium: 31 mg, sodium: 219 mg, zinc: 0.6 mg, folate: 32 mcg, riboflavin: 0 mg, vitamin C: 2 mg, vitamin E: 0.4 mg, omega-3 fatty acids: 0 g.

% CALORIES FROM: protein 3%,   fat 24%,   carbohydrate 73%

CONTAINS: * CITRUS (lemon)

Ultra-Fudge Brownies

These are the ultimate fudge brownies. No one will believe they are made without eggs, butter, dairy products, soy, or gluten-containing flours.

1 cup	sugar	250 ml
½ cup	organic canola or safflower oil	125 ml
½ cup	pure maple syrup	125 ml
⅓ cup	unsweetened applesauce	85 ml
1 teaspoon	vanilla flavoring	5 ml
1 cup	Jo's Gluten-Free All-Purpose Flour Mix, p. 182	250 ml
½ cup	unsweetened cocoa powder	125 ml
2 teaspoons	baking powder	10 ml
½ teaspoon	xanthan gum or guar gum	2 ml
¼ teaspoon	salt	1 ml
¼–½ cup	chopped walnuts (optional)	60–125 ml

Preheat the oven to 350°F (180°C). Oil an 8-inch (20-cm) square metal baking pan and set aside.

Combine the sugar, oil, maple syrup, applesauce, and vanilla flavoring in a large bowl. Mix well.

In separate bowl, combine the flour mix, cocoa powder, baking powder, xanthan gum, and salt. Stir with a dry wire whisk until evenly combined. Gradually add to the oil mixture in three additions. Stir until well blended after each addition. Stir in the optional chopped nuts.

Spread the batter evenly into the prepared pan. Shake the pan so the batter reaches all corners of the pan equally. Bake on the center rack of the oven for 40 to 45 minutes or until a cake tester (or toothpick) inserted in the center tests clean. Place the pan on a rack and let the brownies cool completely before cutting into squares.

VARIATION: FOR DECADENT DOUBLE-FUDGE BROWNIES, stir ¼–½ cup (125 ml) dairy-free chocolate chips into the batter before pouring into the prepared pan.

TIP: The texture of these brownies is even better a day or two after baking. If you cannot wait that long, be sure to let them cool completely before cutting, as this will prevent them from being gummy or falling apart.

PER BROWNIE: calories: 179, protein: 1 g, fat: 8 g, carbohydrate: 28 g, dietary fiber: 1.5 g, calcium: 46 mg, iron: 0.7 mg, magnesium: 20 mg, sodium: 136 mg, zinc: 0.7 mg, folate: 8 mcg, riboflavin: 0 mg, vitamin C: 0 mg, vitamin E: 1.5 mg, omega-3 fatty acids: 0.6 g.

% CALORIES FROM: protein 2%, fat 37%, carbohydrate 61%

CONTAINS: * Chocolate

BLUEBERRY BUCKLE

This makes a delicious, moist coffeecake or dessert.

CAKE:

¼ cup	coconut oil	60 ml
¾ cup	sugar	185 ml
2 tablespoons	unsweetened applesauce	30 ml
1¾ cups	Jo's Gluten-Free All-Purpose Flour Mix, p. 182	435 ml
¼ cup	quinoa flour	60 ml
2 teaspoons	baking powder	10 ml
1 teaspoon	xanthan gum or guar gum	5 ml
½ teaspoon	salt	2 ml
½ cup	fortified plain or vanilla nondairy milk, light coconut milk, or water	125 ml
2 cups	unthawed frozen blueberries	500 ml

TOPPING:

½ cup	sugar	125 ml
⅓ cup	Jo's Gluten-Free All-Purpose Flour Mix, p. 182	85 ml
3 tablespoons	coconut oil	45 ml
½ teaspoon	cinnamon	2 ml

Generously oil a 9-inch (23-cm) square or round pan and preheat the oven to 375°F (190°C). Combine ¼ cup (60 ml) coconut oil, sugar, and applesauce in a large bowl. In a medium bowl, combine the flour mix, quinoa flour, baking powder, xanthan gum, and salt. Add half of the flour mixture to the oil mixture and beat to incorporate; then beat in the milk. Beat in the rest of the flour mixture; mix just until combined. Fold in the blueberries, and then spoon into the prepared pan.

Combine the topping ingredients in a medium bowl, mixing with a fork until it is evenly blended and forms crumbles. Sprinkle on top of the blueberry cake mixture and bake for 60 minutes or until the top is beginning to brown and a cake tester (or toothpick) comes out clean. Cool on a rack before serving.

PER SERVING: calories: 195, protein: 1.5 g, fat: 5 g, carbohydrate: 35 g, dietary fiber: 2 g, calcium: 65 mg, iron: 0.7 mg, magnesium: 20 mg, sodium: 185 mg, zinc: 0.4 mg, folate: 19 mcg, riboflavin: 0 mg, vitamin C: 1 mg, vitamin E: 0.6 mg, omega-3 fatty acids: 0 g.

% CALORIES FROM: protein 3%,   fat 25%,   carbohydrate 72%

CHOCOLATE CHIPPERS

Yields 24–30 cookies

These magnificent chocolate chip cookies are exceptionally chocolaty. Cool the cookies completely before storing or eating, unless you prefer your chocolate chips gooey.

1½ cups	Jo's Gluten-Free All-Purpose Flour Mix, p. 182	375 ml
½ teaspoon	baking soda	2 ml
½ teaspoon	xanthan gum or guar gum	2 ml
¼ teaspoon	salt	1 ml
¾ cup	brown sugar	185 ml
⅓ cup	sugar	85 ml
¼ cup	organic canola or safflower oil	60 ml
2 tablespoons	unsweetened applesauce	30 ml
2 teaspoons	vanilla flavoring	10 ml
1½ cups	dairy-free chocolate chips	375 ml

Preheat the oven to 350°F (180°C). Line two baking sheets with parchment paper, and set aside.

Whisk together the flour mix, baking soda, xanthan gum, and salt in a medium bowl. In a separate large bowl, cream together the sugars, oil, applesauce, and vanilla flavoring using an electric mixer. Beat until light and fluffy. On low speed, gradually beat in the flour mixture in two or three additions. The dough will be very stiff and sticky. This is the way it's supposed to be.

Stir in the chocolate chips, using your hands if necessary. Drop by tablespoons onto the prepared baking sheets. The cookies will spread, so leave a good inch (2.5 cm) or two between them. Bake on the center rack, one sheet at a time, for 12–15 minutes or until the cookies are lightly browned. Let stand on the cookie sheet for a full 5 minutes. Then, using a metal spatula, transfer to a rack to cool completely.

VARIATIONS:

• For Crunchy Chocolate Chippers, reduce the amount of chocolate chips to 1 cup (250 ml) and add ½ cup (125 ml) of coarsely chopped sunflower seeds, pumpkin seeds, pecans, or walnuts.

PER COOKIE (1/24 recipe): calories: 111, protein: 0.5 g, fat: 4 g, carbohydrate: 19 g, dietary fiber: 0.5 g, calcium: 9 mg, iron: 0.3 mg, magnesium: 7 mg, sodium: 55 mg, zinc: 0.1 mg, folate: 7 mcg, riboflavin: 0 mg, vitamin C: 0 mg, vitamin E: 0.5 mg, omega-3 fatty acids: 0.2 g.

% CALORIES FROM: protein 3%,   fat 29%,   carbohydrate 68%

CONTAINS: * Chocolate

- For Cake-style Chocolate Chippers, beat 2 tablespoons (30 ml) of water into the sugar and applesauce mixture prior to beating in the flour mixture.

- For Chocolate-Free Chippers, omit the chocolate chips and add 1 cup (250 ml) raisins or other chopped dried fruit of your choice.

DIVINE MACAROONS

Yields about 16–18 small macaroons

Did you consider that without eggs and wheat, confections such as macaroons would be a thing of the past? This recipe brings good news to macaroon lovers!
Stored in a tin, these cookies retain their moist, chewy, texture for a week. Parchment paper is reusable; though not essential, it allows the bottom surface of the cookies to cook evenly and keeps them from sticking to the pan.

2½ cups	unsweetened shredded coconut	625 ml
½ cup	Jo's Gluten-Free All-Purpose Flour Mix, p. 182	125 ml
½ teaspoon	xanthan gum or guar gum	2 ml
¼ teaspoon	salt	1 ml
½ cup	water	125 ml
¼ cup	brown rice syrup	60 ml
¼ cup	pure maple syrup	60 ml
1 teaspoon	almond, orange, lemon, coconut, or vanilla flavoring	5 ml

Preheat the oven to 325°F (165°C). Line a baking sheet with parchment paper. Combine the coconut, flour mix, xanthan gum, and salt in a large bowl. In a separate bowl, combine the water, syrups, and flavoring of your choice. Pour into the dry ingredients and stir until evenly blended.

Using moistened fingers, form into 1½-inch (4-cm) balls, pressing the mixture together firmly. Place on the prepared baking sheet and bake on the center rack of the oven until golden brown, about 30–35 minutes.

Per macaroon: calories: 138, protein: 1.5 g, fat: 9 g, carbohydrate: 13 g, dietary fiber: 3 g, calcium: 8 mg, iron: 0.6 mg, magnesium: 16 mg, sodium: 43 mg, zinc: 0.6 mg, folate: 5 mcg, riboflavin: 0 mg, vitamin C: 0 mg, vitamin E: 0 mg, omega-3 fatty acids: 0 g.

% Calories from: protein 5%, fat 59%, carbohydrate 36%

CHOCOLATE CRINKLES

The tops of these cookies "crinkle" or crack when baked, creating an attractive contrast between the dark chocolate cookie and the white confectioners' sugar on top. With a deep chocolate flavor reminiscent of brownies, they are as delicious as they are attractive. The cookies will firm up as they cool, so be careful not to overbake them or they will become too hard.

1¼ cups	Jo's Gluten-Free All-Purpose Flour Mix, p. 182	310 ml
¼ cup	unsweetened cocoa powder	60 ml
3 tablespoons	quinoa flour	45 ml
1 tablespoon	chickpea flour	15 ml
1 teaspoon	baking powder	5 ml
¼ teaspoon	salt	1 ml
¼ cup	coconut oil	60 ml
1 cup	sugar	250 ml
1 teaspoon	vanilla flavoring	5 ml
2 tablespoons	unsweetened applesauce	30 ml
1 tablespoon	cold water	15 ml
¼ cup	confectioners' sugar	60 ml

Preheat the oven to 325°F (165°C). Line two or three baking sheets with parchment paper and set aside.

Combine the flour mix, cocoa powder, quinoa flour, chickpea flour, baking powder, and salt in a medium bowl. In a large bowl, using an electric mixer, beat the coconut oil, sugar, and vanilla flavoring until light and fluffy, about 3 minutes. Beat in the applesauce and water.

Gradually beat in the flour mixture in three additions until uniform. The dough will be stiff and able to be formed into balls. With your palms, roll the dough into 1-inch (2.5-cm) balls, then roll in confectioners' sugar. Arrange the balls on the prepared baking sheets, 2 inches (5 cm) apart. Bake on the center rack of the oven, one sheet at a time, for 16–18 minutes. Do not overbake! Let the cookies cool 5 minutes on the baking sheets, then transfer to wire racks to finish cooling.

PER COOKIE: calories: 61, protein: 0.5 g, fat: 2 g, carbohydrate: 11 g, dietary fiber: 0.5 g, calcium: 9 mg, iron: 0.2 mg, magnesium: 8 mg, sodium: 28 mg, zinc: 0.1 mg, folate: 5 mcg, riboflavin: 0 mg, vitamin C: 0 mg, vitamin E: 0.1 mg, omega-3 fatty acids: 0 g.

% CALORIES FROM: protein 3%, fat 25%, carbohydrate 72%

CONTAINS: * Chocolate

CRISPY MAPLE 'NILLA WAFERS

These delectable, wafer-thin cookies are a delightful treat. For special occasions, just before baking sprinkle the tops lightly with colored sugar or chocolate or multicolored jimmies (press them in gently), or press in coconut, chocolate chips, carob chips, pumpkin seeds, raisins, currants, dried cranberries, chopped dates, chopped figs, or other favorite cookie decorations.

1½ cups	Jo's Gluten-Free All-Purpose Flour Mix, p. 182	375 ml
½ teaspoon	baking powder	2 ml
½ teaspoon	xanthan gum or guar gum	2 ml
⅛ teaspoon	salt	0.5 ml
¼ cup	pure maple syrup	60 ml
3 tablespoons	organic canola or safflower oil	45 ml
1 tablespoon	vanilla flavoring	15 ml

Preheat the oven to 350°F (180°C). Line two baking sheets with parchment paper. Combine the flour mix, baking powder, xanthan gum, and salt in a large bowl. In a separate small bowl, whisk together the maple syrup, oil, and vanilla flavoring. Pour into the dry ingredients, and stir well.

Form into balls, each about the size of a walnut, rolling them between the palms of your hands. Place the balls an inch (2.5 cm) or two (5 cm) apart on the baking sheets. Press each ball into a thin disk using the bottom of a large, heavy jar or drinking glass. (Be sure the bottom is perfectly flat or it will leave an imprint in the cookies.) To lift the glass from the cookie, turn it slightly before lifting. The dough should be very thin, about ¼ inch (0.5 cm) or a little less.

Bake on the center rack, one sheet at a time, for about 12 minutes or until the edges and bottoms are golden brown. Remove from the oven, place the baking sheet on a rack, and cool cookies completely before storing.

PER WAFER: calories: 70, protein: 0.5 g, fat: 2 g, carbohydrate: 11 g,
dietary fiber: 0.5 g, calcium: 12 mg, iron: 0.3 mg, magnesium: 7 mg, sodium: 29 mg, zinc: 0.3 mg,
folate: 8 mcg, riboflavin: 0 mg, vitamin C: 0 mg, vitamin E: 0.5 mg, omega-3 fatty acids: 0.2 g.

% CALORIES FROM: protein 6%,   fat 30%,   carbohydrate 64%

HEAVENLY DATE SQUARES

These luscious squares have a delectable layer of date butter sandwiched between a thick, melt-in-your-mouth shortbread crust. One bite and your taste buds will be in heaven!

FILLING:

1½ cups	chopped pitted dates, packed	375 ml
¾ cup	water	185 ml
¼ teaspoon	salt	1 ml

CRUST:

3 cups	Jo's Gluten-Free All-Purpose Flour Mix, p. 182	750 ml
⅔ cup	sugar	170 ml
1½ teaspoons	xanthan gum or guar gum	7 ml
¾ teaspoon	ground cinnamon	4 ml
½ teaspoon	baking powder	2 ml
½ teaspoon	baking soda	2 ml
¼ teaspoon	salt	1 ml
¼ cup	organic canola or safflower oil	60 ml
¼ cup	coconut oil	60 ml

Preheat the oven to 350°F (180°C). For the filling, combine the dates, water, and salt in a medium saucepan. Bring to a boil, reduce the heat, cover, and simmer until the dates are very soft, about 15 minutes, stirring once or twice. Remove from the heat and set aside to cool.

For the crust, combine the flour, sugar, xanthan gum, cinnamon, baking powder, baking soda, and salt in a large bowl. Stir together with a dry wire whisk. Stir in the oils with a fork, then finish by working them in with your hands until well combined.

Press half of the crust mixture into the bottom of an ungreased 8 x 8-inch (20 x 20-cm) metal pan. The dough will be crumbly, so press it firmly into the pan. Carefully spread the date mixture evenly over the crust, spreading it out with the back of a large spoon. Crumble the remaining crust mixture evenly over the date mixture to form a top crust.

PER SQUARE: calories: 237, protein: 2 g, fat: 7 g, carbohydrate: 41 g, dietary fiber: 2.5 g, calcium: 20 mg, iron: 0.7 mg, magnesium: 21 mg, sodium: 129 mg, zinc: 0.4 mg, folate: 22 mcg, riboflavin: 0 mg, vitamin C: 0 mg, vitamin E: 0.9 mg, omega-3 fatty acids: 0.3 g.

% CALORIES FROM: protein 3%,   fat 28%,   carbohydrate 69%

Pat it down firmly but gently. Bake until the top is lightly browned, about 50 minutes. Cool. Cut into squares while warm. The crust will be very crumbly when hot. As the squares cool, the crust will become firmer.

APRICOT SQUARES

Yields 24 SQUARES

These scrumptious treats are light and crumbly, perfect as a midday snack with a cup of lemon tea. Dried apricots are not only delicious, they're also nutritious, packed with vitamins A and C, iron, potassium, and fiber. But don't fret if you don't have any on hand; try different dried fruits for variation.

¾ cup	coconut oil	185 ml
1 cup	brown sugar, firmly packed	250 ml
2¾ cups	Jo's Gluten-Free All-Purpose Flour Mix, p. 182	685 ml
¼ cup	quinoa flour	60 ml
2 teaspoons	ground cinnamon	10 ml
1¼ teaspoons	xanthan gum or guar gum	6 ml
1 teaspoon	vanilla flavoring	5 ml
1 cup	chopped dried apricots	250 ml
1 cup	chopped sunflower seeds, pumpkin seeds, or nuts	250 ml

Preheat the oven to 350°F (180°C). Oil a 9 x 13-inch (23 x 33-cm) baking pan. In a large bowl, using an electric mixer, cream the coconut oil with the brown sugar until light and fluffy. Beat in the flour mix, quinoa flour, cinnamon, xanthan gum, and vanilla flavoring. The mixture will resemble coarse crumbs. Stir in the apricots and seeds.

Pat firmly into the prepared pan. Bake until the top is golden, about 40–45 minutes. Cool completely in the pan. Cut into 2-inch (5-cm) squares.

PER SQUARE: calories: 208, protein: 2 g, fat: 10 g, carbohydrate: 28 g, dietary fiber: 2 g, calcium: 20 mg, iron: 1.0 mg, magnesium: 22 mg, sodium: 6 mg, zinc: 0.5 mg, folate: 26 mcg, riboflavin: 0 mg, vitamin C: 1 mg, vitamin E: 2.9 mg, omega-3 fatty acids: 0 g.

% CALORIES FROM: protein 5%,   fat 42%,   carbohydrate 53%

PEACH KUCHEN

Kuchen (pronounced KOO-kin) is derived from an Old German word for "cake." With its origins in Germany in the 1800s, kuchen is typically some sort of dough with a filling, fruit being the most popular. While kuchen has taken on many forms over the years, the kuchen recipe in a particular family is, of course, the "right" one—and it's often kept a secret! This gluten-free version features peaches with a touch of cinnamon-sugar. It's easy to prepare and is simply delicious. Serve with your favorite nondairy frozen dessert for an extra-special treat.

1¾ cups	Jo's Gluten-Free All-Purpose Flour Mix, p. 182	435 ml
¼ cup	quinoa flour	60 ml
1 teaspoon	xanthan gum or guar gum	5 ml
½ teaspoon	salt	2 ml
¼ teaspoon	baking powder	1 ml
¼ cup	sugar	60 ml
6 tablespoons	coconut oil	90 ml
12	peeled peach halves (fresh or canned in juice, drained)	12
1 teaspoon	ground cinnamon	5 ml

Preheat the oven to 375°F (190°C). Oil an 8 x 8-inch (20 x 20-cm) baking pan and set aside.

Combine the flour mix, quinoa flour, xanthan gum, salt, baking powder, and 2 tablespoons (30 ml) of the sugar in a large bowl. Stir with a dry wire whisk until evenly mixed. Cut in the coconut oil with a pastry blender, fork, or two knives, and then work it in with your fingers until the mixture is crumbly. Pat an even layer of this mixture over the bottom and halfway up the sides of the prepared pan.

Arrange the peaches over the pastry, cut side down. Stir together the remaining 2 tablespoons (30 ml) of sugar and the cinnamon and sprinkle over the peaches. Bake 55–60 minutes. Serve warm or cold.

PER SERVING: calories: 260, protein: 3 g, fat: 10 g, carbohydrate: 41 g, dietary fiber: 3 g, calcium: 22 mg, iron: 1 mg, magnesium: 31 mg, sodium: 148 mg, zinc: 0.6 mg, folate: 26 mcg, riboflavin: 0 mg, vitamin C: 3 mg, vitamin E: 1.8 mg, omega-3 fatty acids: 0 g.

% CALORIES FROM: protein 4%,   fat 34%,   carbohydrate 62%

Great Seasonings and Spice Mixes

S ome of us prefer the natural, unseasoned flavors of vegetables, beans, and gluten-free grains. Others are far happier with the added zing imparted by herbs and spices; otherwise, meals can seem boring or bland. Unfortunately, many commercial seasonings and seasoning mixes can trigger reactions, due to the presence of ingredients such as wheat and soy or chemicals such as MSG. MSG is present, for example, in Accent, Zest, hydrolyzed vegetable protein (HVP), hydrolyzed plant protein, (HPP), packaged soup mixes, and in some packaged foods that show "flavoring" on the ingredient list.

Fortunately, most herbs and many spices are hypoallergenic. As any gourmet chef will tell you, a sprig of rosemary, several leaves of basil, or a small arc of thyme make attractive garnishes and can add delicious flavor to a simple meal. Herbs, which are the leaves of plants that grow at temperate latitudes, can be used either fresh or dried. (Note that one teaspoon of a dried herb can be used to replace one tablespoon of a fresh herb.) Spices are parts of plants that normally grow in the tropics; occasionally they trigger reactions in certain individuals. Cinnamon is from the bark of a plant; anise, caraway, mustard, and nutmeg are seeds. Allspice is a "berry"; before it is ground it looks like a large peppercorn. Chili, other peppers, and paprika are in the same botanical family as potatoes and tomato, the nightshade family.

Sometimes tiny amounts of an herb or spice may be used to give a delicate nuance of flavor. For optimal flavor, buy herbs and spices in small amounts and replenish your supply every six months. Both herbs and spices can be affected by heat and light, so your best bet is to store them a little distance away from the stove and in a dark cupboard or in opaque containers.

Seasoning mixes provide richness and depth; they can transform the simplest meal into haute cuisine. Yet it's not always easy to find the right balance of flavors for our cooking needs. This is why we developed this section. You can mix these seasoning blends, store them in labeled jars or sealed bags, and use them in recipes from this book or in recipes you have created. We also provide tips and ideas for adding superb flavor to all of your meals. You can say no to foods that cause a reaction, but with a little help and imagination, say yes to outstanding flavor!

Tips for Storing Herbs and Spices

- Store herb containers in a dark, cool, dry place up to six months.
- Because heat diminishes spice flavors, avoid displaying seasonings on open racks above or near stovetops or ovens.
- Store seldom-used seasonings in the freezer to maintain freshness.

Fancy Rice and Grains

Perk up the flavor of brown, basmati, or white rice, or other favorite grains, with your choice of additions. Keep in mind that most seasonings work best when combined with similarly flavored seasonings—sweet with sweet and savory with savory. Curry powder is the exception, as it unifies and complements both sweet and savory seasonings.

*Add one or more of the following to taste **prior** to cooking:*

- chopped onions
- crushed or chopped garlic
- chopped shallots
- diced celery
- finely chopped kale or collard greens
- minced sun-dried tomatoes
- minced jalapeño or other hot peppers
- raisins, currants, or other chopped dried fruit
- shredded or finely chopped carrots

*Add a pinch or two to taste of one or more of the following spices or herbs **prior** to cooking:*

- crushed red chili peppers
- curry powder
- dried basil, dill weed, oregano, tarragon, thyme, or rosemary
- grated fresh gingerroot
- ground coriander
- ground ginger, cinnamon, or allspice
- paprika
- whole cloves
- whole or ground cumin
- whole or ground fennel seed, caraway, or aniseed

*Add one or more of the following to taste **after** cooking:*

- chopped fresh herbs (such as parsley, cilantro, basil, dill weed, or mint)
- fresh lemon or lime juice
- lemon, lime, or orange zest
- minced bell pepper
- organic flaxseed oil or garlic-chili flaxseed oil
- peeled and finely chopped apple
- toasted seeds or nuts
- vinegar (balsamic, white wine, umeboshi, or rice vinegar)
- whole poppy seeds

GOMASIO

Yields ½ cup (125 ml)

Sesame seeds, common to Asian and Middle Eastern cuisines, may be the earliest known condiment with its use dating back to 1600 B.C. "Open sesame," the well-known phrase from the Arabian Nights, reflects a feature of the sesame seed pod, which bursts open when it reaches maturity. Sesame seeds and sea vegetables (such as kelp, dulse, and nori) are rich in minerals and may be found at natural food stores. Sprinkled over vegetables, soups, or on cooked grains and beans, gomasio deepens the overall flavor of a dish.

½ cup	hulled sesame seeds	80 g
½ teaspoon	salt	3 g
¼ teaspoon	kelp, dulse, or nori powder	0.5 g

Dry-roast the sesame seeds in a skillet over medium heat for 5 to 7 minutes, stirring frequently until the seeds can be crushed between your thumb and finger. Transfer to a mortar or food grinder. Add the salt and sea vegetable powder. Using the pestle and grinding in a circular motion, or using the pulse action of the grinder, grind the seeds until most of them (about three-quarters of them) are crushed and coated with their own oil. Store in a sealed jar in the refrigerator for several weeks.

NOTE: To grind this amount of seeds all at once, you will need a mortar that has a 2-inch deep bowl and a 3½-inch wide mouth. If your mortar is smaller, crush the seeds in batches. Alternatively, use a small electric grinder.

PER TEASPOON (4 G): calories: 20, protein: 0.91 g, fat: 2 g, carbohydrate: 0.3 g, dietary fiber: 0.5 g, calcium: 5 mg, iron: 0.3 mg, magnesium: 12 mg, sodium: 50 mg, zinc: 0.3 mg, folate: 4 mcg, riboflavin: 0 mg, vitamin B12: 0 mcg, vitamin C: 0 mg, vitamin E: 0.1 mg, omega-3 fatty acids: 0 g

% CALORIES FROM: protein 7%, fat 77%, carbohydrate 6%

GARAM MASALA

In India, "garam" means hot or spicy, and "masala" means mixture or blend. This blend of sweet spices is warming, rather than hot, and is used to flavor rice or bean dishes and desserts. As it consists of ground seeds (coriander and cumin), it provides minerals such as iron.

4 teaspoons	ground coriander	7 g
2 teaspoons	ground cumin	4 g
1 teaspoon	pepper	2 g
1 teaspoon	ground cloves	2 g
1 teaspoon	ground cinnamon	2 g

Place the ingredients in a small jar, close the lid tightly, and shake well to combine thoroughly.

PER TEASPOON (3 G): calories: 9, protein: 0.30.5 g, fat: 00.5 g, carbohydrate: 2 g, dietary fiber: 1 g, calcium: 23 mg, iron: 1 mg, magnesium: 8 mg, sodium: 3 mg, zinc: 0.1 mg, folate: 0.51 mcg, riboflavin: 0 mg, vitamin B12: 0 mcg, vitamin C: 0.81 mg, vitamin E: 0 mg, omega-3 fatty acids: 0 g

% CALORIES FROM: protein 12%, fat 33%, carbohydrate 55%

KICKAPOO SPICE BLEND

Use this mix whenever you want to kick up the flavor of your food several notches. It's spicy, so add it gradually.

2½ tablespoons	paprika	16 g
2 tablespoons	salt	36 g
2 tablespoons	garlic powder	17 g
1 tablespoon	pepper	6 g
1 tablespoon	onion powder	6 g
1 tablespoon	cayenne	5 g
1 tablespoon	dried oregano	4 g
1 tablespoon	dried thyme	4 g

Place the ingredients in a small jar, close the lid tightly, and shake well to combine thoroughly.

PER TEASPOON (3 G): calories: 5, protein: 0 g, fat: 0 g, carbohydrate: 1 g, dietary fiber: 0.5 g, calcium: 8 mg, iron: 0.4 mg, magnesium: 3 mg, sodium: 405 mg, zinc: 0.1 mg, folate: 2 mcg, riboflavin: 0 mg, vitamin B12: 0 mcg, vitamin C: 1 mg, vitamin E: 0 mg, omega-3 fatty acids: 0 g.

% CALORIES FROM: protein 14%, fat 17%, carbohydrate 69%

CREOLE SPICE BLEND

Yields about ½ cup (40 grams)

Add a blast of the Bayou to your favorites soups, stews, and sauces. Filé powder is made from the ground, dried leaves of the sassafras tree. Its woodsy flavor is reminiscent of root beer. Filé powder is integral to Creole cuisine and is used to thicken and flavor gumbos and other Creole dishes. This spice mixture is best stirred into a dish after it has finished cooking, because too much heat can make filé tough and stringy. Look for filé powder in the spice or gourmet section of your supermarket.

2 tablespoons	paprika	13 g
2 tablespoons	dried basil	8 g
2 tablespoons	dried thyme	8 g
1 tablespoon	cayenne	5 g
1 tablespoon	filé powder (dried sassafras leaves)	2 g
1½ teaspoons	chili powder	4 g

Place the ingredients in a small jar, close the lid tightly, and shake well to combine thoroughly.

PER TEASPOON (2 G): calories: 5, protein: 0.5 g, fat: 0 g, carbohydrate: 1 g, dietary fiber: 0.5 g, calcium: 16 mg, iron: 0.8 mg, magnesium: 4 mg, sodium: 2 mg, zinc: 0.1 mg, folate: 3 mcg, riboflavin: 0 mg, vitamin B12: 0 mcg, vitamin C: 1 mg, vitamin E: 0 mg, omega-3 fatty acids: 0 g

% CALORIES FROM: protein 13%, fat 25%, carbohydrate 62%

FIVE-ALARM CHILI POWDER

This chili powder is more intense and pungent than packaged brands, so you might need to use a little less than usual.

6 tablespoons	paprika	36 g
2 tablespoons	turmeric	12 g
1 tablespoon	crushed red chili peppers	4 g
1 teaspoon	ground cumin	2 g
1 teaspoon	dried oregano	1.5 g
½ teaspoon	cayenne	0.9 g
½ teaspoon	garlic powder	1.4 g
½ teaspoon	salt	3 g
¼ teaspoon	ground cloves	0.5 g

Combine all the ingredients in a food processor or blender and grind into a fine powder. Alternatively, grind the chili peppers into a fine powder and combine them in a jar with the remaining ingredients. Seal tightly and shake well until evenly blended.

PER TEASPOON (2 G): calories: 7, protein: 0 g, fat: 0 g, carbohydrate: 1 g, dietary fiber: 0.5 g, calcium: 5 mg, iron: 0.4 mg, magnesium: 0 mg, sodium: 39 mg, zinc: 0 mg, folate: 0 mcg, riboflavin: 0 mg, vitamin B12: 0 mcg, vitamin C: 0 mg, vitamin E: 0 mg, omega-3 fatty acids: 0 g.

% CALORIES FROM: protein 14%, fat 24%, carbohydrate 62%

ALL-PURPOSE HERB BLEND

Yields ¼ cup (14 g)

Add this tasty herbal mix to soups, salads, dressings, grains, and vegetables.

1 tablespoon	dried thyme	4.2 g
1 tablespoon	dried oregano	4.5 g
2 teaspoons	rubbed sage	1.4 g
1 teaspoon	dried rosemary	1.2 g
1 teaspoon	dried marjoram	0.6 g
1 teaspoon	dried basil	1.4 g
1 teaspoon	dried parsley flakes	0.3 g

Place the ingredients in a small jar, close the lid tightly, and shake well to combine thoroughly.

PER TEASPOON (1.1 G): calories: 3, protein: 0 g, fat: 0.1 g, carbohydrate: 1 g, dietary fiber: 0.5 g, calcium: 19 mg, iron: 0.8 mg, magnesium: 3 mg, sodium: 0 mg, zinc: 0.1 mg, folate: 3 mcg, riboflavin: 0 mg, vitamin B12: 0 mcg, vitamin C: 1 mg, vitamin E: 0 mg, omega-3 fatty acids: 0 g.

% CALORIES FROM: protein 11%,   fat 22%,   carbohydrate 67%

ITALIAN SEASONING

Yields about ¾ cup ground, 1 cup unground (60 g)

Punch up the flavor of your tomato sauce, Italian dressing, and other Italian specialties with this simple herbal blend. If you prefer a powder, just buzz everything in a food processor or blender until finely ground.

¼ cup	dried basil	16.8 g
¼ cup	dried parsley	3.6 g
2 tablespoons	dried oregano	9 g
2 tablespoons	dried minced onions	7 g
2 tablespoons	dried minced garlic	16.8 g
1 tablespoon	dried thyme	4.2 g
1 teaspoon	pepper	2 g
¼ teaspoon	dried sage	0.2 g

Place the ingredients in a small jar, close the lid tightly, and shake well to combine thoroughly.

PER TEASPOON (1.3 G): calories: 4, protein: 0 g, fat: 0 g, carbohydrate: 1 g, dietary fiber: 0.5 g, calcium: 15 mg, iron: 0.5 mg, magnesium: 3 mg, sodium: 1 mg, zinc: 0 mg, folate: 0 mcg, riboflavin: 0 mg, vitamin B12: 0 mcg, vitamin C: 1 mg, vitamin E: 0 mg, omega-3 fatty acids: 0 g.

% CALORIES FROM: protein 15%,   fat 9%,   carbohydrate 76%

ETHIOPIAN SPICE MIX
(Berbere)

Yields about ¼ cup (27 g)

This snappy mix will turn up the heat and flavor of any soup, stew, or bean dish. Start with a small amount and add more gradually as you see fit. Berbere is a hot pepper seasoning essential for many Ethiopian dishes. You can buy it at some African and Middle Eastern stores, but it's easy to make your own at home.

2 tablespoons	paprika	12 g
1½ tablespoons	cayenne	8.1 g
1 teaspoon	dried basil	1.4 g
½ teaspoon	ground ginger	0.9 g
¼ teaspoon	pepper	0.5 g
¼ teaspoon	ground allspice	0.5 g
¼ teaspoon	ground cardamom	0.5 g
¼ teaspoon	ground cinnamon	0.5 g
¼ teaspoon	ground cumin	0.5 g
¼ teaspoon	ground fenugreek	1 g
¼ teaspoon	ground nutmeg	0.6 g
¼ teaspoon	turmeric	0.5 g
⅛ teaspoon	ground cloves	0.25 g
OPTIONAL		
1 tablespoon	onion powder	6 g
1 teaspoon	garlic powder	1.4 g

Place the ingredients in a small jar, close the lid tightly, and shake well to combine thoroughly.

PER TEASPOON (1.9 G): calories: 7, protein: 0 g, fat: 0 g, carbohydrate: 1 g, dietary fiber: 0.5 g, calcium: 6 mg, iron: 0.3 mg, magnesium: 1 mg, sodium: 1 mg, zinc: 0 mg, folate: 1 mcg, riboflavin: 0 mg, vitamin B12: 0 mcg, vitamin C: 1 mg, vitamin E: 0 mg, omega-3 fatty acids: 0 g.

% CALORIES FROM: protein 14%, fat 28%, carbohydrate 58%

SWEET AND HOT MIX

This aromatic blend combines sweet and hot Indian spices. It adds spark and tang to tomato and potato dishes, and is especially delicious as a soup or vegetable seasoning. It is very hot, however, so use with caution.

1 tablespoon	cayenne	5.4 g
1 tablespoon	ground cumin	6 g
1 tablespoon	ground coriander	6 g
½ tablespoon	ground fenugreek	6 g
1 teaspoon	ground cardamom	2 g
1 teaspoon	ground cinnamon	2 g
1 teaspoon	ground nutmeg	2.2 g
1 teaspoon	ground cloves	2 g
¼ teaspoon	ground turmeric	0.5 g
¼ teaspoon	salt	1.5 g
¼ teaspoon	pepper	0.5 g

P lace the ingredients in a small jar, close the lid tightly, and shake well to combine thoroughly.

PER TEASPOON (2.2 G): calories: 8, protein: 0 g, fat: 0 g, carbohydrate: 1 g, dietary fiber: 1 g, calcium: 10 mg, iron: 0.3 mg, magnesium: 1 mg, sodium: 40` mg, zinc: 0 mg, folate: 0 mcg, riboflavin: 0 mg, vitamin B12: 0 mcg, vitamin C: 0 mg, vitamin E: 0 mg, omega-3 fatty acids: 0 g.

% CALORIES FROM: protein 15%,   fat 31%,   carbohydrate 54%

Banner Breakfasts

*I*n this section we present a range of breakfast ideas from cold cereal to hot porridge, to quick shakes and power-packed smoothies. If you broaden your breakfast horizons to include ideas from other cultures, you'll find that some people even enjoy a steaming bowl of lentil soup to start their day! Here are a few more suggestions to keep your morning meals interesting:

- Cream of buckwheat
- Cream of rice
- Crispy rice cereal
- Corn flakes
- Rice flakes
- Gluten-free mixed grain flakes
- Gluten-free mixed grain hot cereal
- Rice cake or corn cake with seed or nut butter and fruit spread
- Puffed rice, millet, corn, or amaranth
- Gluten-free muffins, biscuits, or quick bread, pages 184–189 and 194–195
- Gluten-Free Chapatis, page 192
- Chickpea Crepes, page 193, or corn tortillas stuffed with refried beans, beans and rice, beans or rice and salad greens with dressing, or leftover chili or stew
- Veggie Rice Roll, page 325
- Simple Nori Rolls, page 322
- Green Grits, page 232
- Leftover pizza wedge, page 312

SAVORY, SMOOTH, AND SWEET SPREADS

Finding a suitable breakfast spread for gluten-free bread, biscuits, or toast can seem challenging, especially if you are dairy allergic or simply don't want cholesterol-laden butter or the trans-fatty acids found in many margarines. Here are some flavorful alternatives that provide plenty of nutritional pluses. A thin layer each of sesame tahini or pumpkin seed butter and blackstrap molasses is not only great on morning toast, but also increases your intake of iron and other trace minerals. Almond butter is a tasty source of calcium. Cashew butter and pumpkin seed butter provide zinc. Also, glance through the Dips and Spreads section of this book (pages 239–254); many people appreciate the protein boost of hummus or another bean dip as part of their breakfast or for a mid-morning snack. Here are some super spreads that provide plenty of nutrition and wonderfully satisfying flavor:

- Butters made from sunflower seeds, sesame seeds, or pumpkin seeds, page 354

- Mashed avocado

- Chickpea miso, thinly spread

- Mustard, plain or seasoned, thinly spread

- Fruit jams, spreads, butters, and conserves

- Rice syrup, thinly spread

- Spicy North African Spread, page 247

- Golden Yam Spread, page 248

224

MARVELOUS MORNING MUESLI

Yields 2 cups (500 ml)

This creamy, nourishing breakfast can be prepared with ease the night before, and leftovers make a delicious evening snack. It also is great to take on camping trips or overnight stays when mixed ahead and stored in spill-proof containers.

¾ cup	rolled brown rice flakes and/or rolled quinoa flakes (see note below)	185 ml
2 tablespoons	raisins, currants, dried cherries, or dried cranberries	30 ml
2 tablespoons	seeds or chopped walnuts, almonds, or other nuts (optional)	30 ml
¼ teaspoon	ground cinnamon	1 ml
1 cup	fortified nondairy milk or fruit juice	250 ml
1	apple, grated or finely chopped (peeling is optional)	1

Combine the flakes, raisins, optional seeds, cinnamon, milk, and apple in a medium bowl. Cover and refrigerate overnight. Alternatively, the apple may be stirred in just before serving. Serve with additional nondairy milk or juice, if desired.

VARIATION: Instead of apple, use berries, peaches, mango, banana, or whatever fresh fruit is in season.

• Rolled brown rice flakes and quinoa flakes are comparable to rolled oats and can be used similarly. If you cannot find them in your local natural food store, they can be purchased from the following companies:

In the United States:

• Enjoy Life Foods, www.enjoylifefoods.com, 1-888-50-ENJOY or 773-889-5070

• Gold Mine Natural Food Company, www.goldminenaturalfood.com, 1-800-475-3663

In Canada:

• Grainworks, www.grainworks.com, 1-800-563-3756

PER CUP (250 ML): calories: 245, protein: 3.5 g, fat: 2 g, carbohydrate: 55 g, dietary fiber: 3.5 g, calcium: 170 mg, iron: 0.9 mg, magnesium: 50 mg, sodium: 48 mg, zinc: 0.7 mg, folate: 9 mcg, riboflavin: 0.1 mg, vitamin C: 4 mg, vitamin E: 2.5 mg, omega-3 fatty acids: 0 g.

% CALORIES FROM: protein 5%, fat 8%, carbohydrate 87%

BASIC WHOLE GRAIN CEREAL
(stovetop method)

YIELDS 5 CUPS (1.25 L)

This is a great way to begin the adventure of using whole, gluten-free grains in a satisfying and delicious breakfast. Leftovers can be refrigerated and used as a warm cereal or a nourishing, soothing snack or cold pudding for several days. Begin with this basic recipe, using one-third cup each of brown rice, millet, and quinoa, to make a total of one cup of grain. Short-grain rice will make a creamier cereal than long-grain rice. For a unique flavor, use buckwheat instead of quinoa. Amaranth is sticky; it's best not to use more than one-quarter cup of it in your mix. You might like to try basmati rice or cornmeal. This recipe and the one that follows it are from The New Becoming Vegetarian, *by Vesanto Melina and Brenda Davis.*

1 cup	uncooked grain (see Tips)	250 ml
4 cups	water	1 L
¼–½ teaspoon	salt	1–2 ml
½ cup	dried fruit	125 ml
½ cup	fortified nondairy milk	125 ml

Place the grain, water, and salt to taste in the top of a double boiler or a heavy saucepan and bring to a boil. If using a double boiler, place the top pan above the boiling water and allow the grain to simmer for 1–3 hours. If the saucepan is directly over on the heat, lower the heat and simmer for 1–3 hours, checking occasionally so it does not boil dry. The longer the porridge cooks, the creamier it will become. If necessary, add a little extra water.

Add dried fruit and milk and cook another 30 minutes. If desired, serve with fresh fruit and/or Jiffy Fruit Sauce, page 235, and/or additional nondairy milk.

VARIATIONS: Experiment to find your favorite combinations. Each grain contributes its own unique flavor, texture, and nutritional benefits. Amaranth, quinoa, millet, wild rice, and buckwheat are high in protein and iron. Wild rice provides extra zinc; quinoa is high in calcium and vitamin E.

• For the dried fruit, try raisins, cranberries, or cherries, or chopped apricots, prunes, apples, figs, or dates.

PER CUP (250 ML): calories: 193, protein: 4.5 g, fat: 2 g, carbohydrate: 41 g, dietary fiber: 3 g, calcium: 50 mg, iron: 2.1 mg, magnesium: 63 mg, sodium: 22 mg, zinc: 0.9 mg, folate: 20 mcg, riboflavin: 0.1 mg, vitamin C: 1 mg, vitamin E: 1.2 mg, omega-3 fatty acids: 0 g.

% CALORIES FROM: protein 9%, fat 8%, carbohydrate 83%

- If you omit the dried fruit, leftovers can be used as an accompaniment to savory dishes.

TIPS: To speed up cooking, the grain may be soaked in half the water (2 cups) overnight. Do not drain prior to cooking as this will wash away the water soluble vitamins and minerals. Just transfer the grain and soaking water to the saucepan, add the remaining 2 cups of water and the salt, and proceed as directed.

- To cut the cooking time in half, place the grain and water in the top of a double boiler or other saucepan to soak overnight. In the morning, simply add salt and continue with the cooking process as directed. Pre-soaking not only reduces the cooking time, it also increases mineral availability. Made with faster-cooking grains (such as millet and quinoa), the cereal is ready in 30 minutes; with short-grain brown rice, it is ready in 45 minutes. Wild rice and buckwheat will take longer.

HOT CINNAMON APPLE TOPPING

Yields about 2 cups (500 ml)

This chunky sauce made with fresh apples is a tempting topping for pancakes, French toast, or hot porridge. It's also delicious on nondairy frozen dessert and has a gentle, mellow sweetness that is not overpowering.

2	Granny Smith apples, peeled, cored, and cut into 12 equal slices per apple	2
1⅓ cups	frozen apple juice concentrate	335 ml
¼ cup	raisins or chopped dates	60 ml
1 tablespoon	fresh or frozen lemon juice	15 ml
½ teaspoon	ground cinnamon	2 ml

Place all the ingredients in a medium saucepan and bring to a boil. Reduce the heat to medium-low and simmer, stirring occasionally, until the apples are soft but not mushy. Serve hot or warm.

PER ½ CUP (125 ML): calories: 219, protein: 1 g, fat: 0 g, carbohydrate: 56 g, dietary fiber: 2.5 g, calcium: 31 mg, iron: 1.3 mg, magnesium: 22 mg, sodium: 25 mg, zinc: 0.2 mg, folate: 1.8 mcg, riboflavin: 0.1 mg, vitamin C: 8 mg, vitamin E: 0.1 mg, omega-3 fatty acids: 0 g.
% CALORIES FROM: protein 1%,   fat 2%,   carbohydrate 97%

SLOW-COOKER WHOLE GRAIN CEREAL
(Crock-Pot method)

Yields 5 (1.25 L) or 10 cups (2.5 L)

A Crock-Pot is ideal for cooking whole grains for breakfast. It simmers the cereal gently while you sleep through the night; then it's hot and ready when you wake up. This slow method allows even more of the grain's natural sweetness to develop and makes the minerals in it more available. Refrigerate any leftovers for the next day's breakfast, or serve it later in the day, warm or cold, as a creamy pudding for a snack or dessert. The cereal will thicken as it cools, so you may want to add more liquid.

5 CUPS (1.25 L)

1 cup	uncooked grain (see variations)	250 ml
4 cups	water	1 L
½ teaspoon	salt	2 ml
½ cup	dried fruit	125 ml
½ cup	fortified nondairy milk	125 ml

OPTIONAL INGREDIENTS

¼ cup	seeds or chopped nuts	60 ml
¼ cup	shredded dried coconut	60 ml
1 teaspoon	vanilla flavoring	5 ml
1 tablespoon	pure maple syrup	15 ml
½ teaspoon	ground cinnamon	2 ml

10 CUPS (2.5 L)

2 cups	uncooked grain (see variations, facing page)	500 ml
8 cups	water	2 L
1 teaspoon	salt	5 ml
1 cup	dried fruit	250 ml
1 cup	fortified nondairy milk	250 ml

OPTIONAL INGREDIENTS

½ cup	seeds or chopped nuts	125 ml
½ cup	shredded dried coconut	125 ml
2 teaspoons	vanilla flavoring	10 ml
2 tablespoons	pure maple syrup	30 ml
1 teaspoon	ground cinnamon	5 ml

P lace the grain in a sieve and rinse well. Combine the grain, water, and salt to taste in a large slow cooker (Crock-Pot) and cook on low heat until most of the water has been absorbed, about 8 hours or overnight. Then add the dried fruit, milk, and any optional ingredients, and cook for 30 minutes more or longer. If the mixture is too thick, add more water or milk. Serve hot or cold for breakfast with fresh fruit or Jiffy Fruit Sauce, page 235, and nondairy milk.

VARIATIONS:

- Create combinations that are uniquely yours. Equal amounts of brown rice, millet, and quinoa make a pleasant mixture. Include cornmeal, buckwheat groats, basmati rice, or a few tablespoons of amaranth or wild rice in your grain mix. Amaranth, quinoa, millet, wild rice, and buckwheat are excellent sources of protein and iron. Wild rice provides extra zinc; quinoa is high in calcium and vitamin E.

- For the dried fruit, experiment with raisins, cranberries, cherries, or chopped apricots, prunes, apples, figs, or dates.

- Add some or all of the optional ingredients listed.

- For the seeds and nuts, choose among whole or ground flaxseeds; sesame, pumpkin, or sunflower seeds; or chopped almonds, walnuts, cashews, or hazelnuts.

PER CUP (250 ML), without optional ingredients: calories: 188, protein: 4.5 g, fat: 2 g, carbohydrate: 40 g, dietary fiber: 3.5 g, calcium: 48 mg, iron: 1.8 mg, magnesium: 69 mg, sodium: 21 mg, zinc: 0.9 mg, folate: 18 mcg, riboflavin: 0.1 mg, vitamin C: 1 mg, vitamin E: 1.1 mg, omega-3 fatty acids: 0 g.

% CALORIES FROM: protein 9%,   fat 8%,   carbohydrate 83%

CREAMY GOLDEN PORRIDGE

Yields about 3 cups (750 ml)

The Aztecs believed amaranth had special properties that would give them amazing strength. Because of this, it became one of the main foods of the Aztec royalty. This tasty, protein-rich cereal is a power-packed way to start your morning. Leftovers can be stored in the refrigerator and reheated. A double boiler works great for this recipe, but a regular saucepan will work fine, too, if you keep a close eye on the porridge and stir it often. Just add a little extra water to the leftover porridge to keep it moist and creamy.

¼ cup	amaranth flour	60 ml
¼ cup	millet flour	60 ml
¼ cup	coarse brown rice flour or rice grits, or yellow cornmeal or corn grits	60 ml
Pinch	of salt	Pinch
¼ cup	sesame tahini or other seed butter (see page 354)	60 ml
3 cups	water	750 ml

Combine the flours, salt, and seed butter in the top of a double boiler or in a large pot with a heavy bottom. Gradually stir in the water. Bring to a boil. Reduce the heat to low, stirring almost constantly with a wire whisk to prevent the mixture from lumping, burning, or sticking. Simmer 20–25 minutes or until thick and creamy. (If not using a double boiler, continue stirring frequently.) Add more water, if necessary. Serve hot, with nondairy milk and sweetener.

VARIATION: For an outstanding combination, replace the amaranth flour with toasted amaranth bran flour and add millet flour and cornmeal. Toasted amaranth bran flour is available from Nu-World Amaranth at www.nuworldfoods.com.

NOTE: To make flours from whole grains, see page 159.

PER CUP (250 ML): calories: 248, protein: 7 g, fat: 12 g, carbohydrate: 29 g, dietary fiber: 4 g, calcium: 54 mg, iron: 2.3 mg, magnesium: 80 mg, sodium: 17 mg, zinc: 1.8 mg, folate: 37 mcg, riboflavin: 0.1 mg, vitamin C: 1.3 mg, vitamin E: 0.7 mg, omega-3 fatty acids: 0.1 g.

% CALORIES FROM: protein 11%,   fat 43%,   carbohydrate 46%

WHEAT-FREE MINI-PANCAKES

Yields about 18 small pancakes

Did you think you couldn't have scrumptious pancakes without a trace of wheat or gluten? Well, here they are! A trick to good pancakes is to preheat the skillet so a drop of water dances across the surface. Oil the skillet well so the pancakes don't stick. This recipe is from Raising Vegetarian Children, *by Jo Stepaniak and Vesanto Melina.*

½ cup	brown rice flour	125 ml
½ cup	chickpea flour	125 ml
1½ teaspoons	baking powder	7 ml
½ cup	fresh blueberries (optional)	125 ml
¾ cup	fortified nondairy milk	185 ml
1 tablespoon	soft coconut oil or organic canola or safflower oil (plus extra as needed for cooking)	15 ml

Combine the flours, baking powder, and blueberries (if using) in a medium bowl. In small bowl or measuring cup, mix the milk and oil, then pour into the flour mixture and stir to combine.

Oil a large, heavy skillet or griddle and place over medium-high heat. When hot, spoon in the batter using about 1 tablespoon to make each 2-inch pancake. Cook the pancakes until lightly browned and bubbles pop through the top, about 2 minutes per side, turning once carefully. To prevent sticking, oil the griddle well between batches. Serve warm with maple syrup, Hot Cinnamon Apple Topping, page 227, or In-A-Jiffy Breakfast Pudding or Fruit Sauce, page 235.

PER PANCAKE: calories: 37, protein: 1 g, fat: 1 g, carbohydrate: 6 g, dietary fiber: 0.5 g, calcium: 37 mg, iron: 0.3 mg, magnesium: 9 mg, sodium: 46 mg, zinc: 0.2 mg, folate: 12 mcg, riboflavin: 0 mg, vitamin C: 0 mg, vitamin E: 0.2 mg, omega-3 fatty acids: 0 g.

% CALORIES FROM: protein 10%,   fat 27%,   carbohydrate 63%

Breakfast Grits

Yields 4 servings (4 cups/1000 ml)

This Southern breakfast staple is a great soluble-fiber alternative to cooked cereals that contain gluten. Serve it on its own or sprinkled with toasted pumpkin or sunflower seeds.

4½ cups	water	1125 ml
1 cup	brown rice grits (see box) or corn grits (polenta)	250 ml
½ teaspoon	salt	2 ml

Place the water, grits, and salt in a heavy saucepan and bring to a boil, stirring often. Reduce the heat to a simmer. Cover and cook over low heat for 15–20 minutes, stirring occasionally. When the grits have thickened, remove from the heat and let stand covered a few minutes to thicken more. The longer the grits stand, the thicker they will get. Serve hot, with nondairy milk or light coconut milk, brown sugar, maple syrup, olive or coconut oil or dairy-free margarine, toasted seeds or nuts, Jiffy Fruit Sauce, page 235, or your favorite jam.

Variation:

For Scrambled Grits, chill the fully cooked recipe of Breakfast Grits or any plain leftovers in the refrigerator for at least eight hours or overnight or longer. The grits will become very firm. When you are ready to prepare the Scrambled Grits, mince or shred your favorite vegetables (carrots, onions, shallots, garlic, scallions, broccoli, kale) and sauté them in olive oil. Then add the cold grits.

Alternatively, steam the vegetables until tender or use leftover cooked vegetables. If using steamed or leftover vegetables, heat a small amount of olive oil in a skillet. When hot, add the cooked vegetables and cold grits. Season with salt and pepper

---

Per cup (250 ml): calories: 150, protein: 3 g, fat: g, carbohydrate: 32 g, dietary fiber: 2 g, calcium: 15 mg, iron: 0.8 mg, magnesium: 64 mg, sodium: 302 mg, zinc: 0.9 mg, folate: 8 mcg, riboflavin: 0 mg, vitamin C: 0 mg, vitamin E: 0.3 mg, omega-3 fatty acids: 0 g.

% Calories from: protein 8%,   fat 6%,   carbohydrate 86%

and your favorite fresh or dried herbs, spices, hot sauce, chili powder, or curry powder, if you like. Add cooked beans for a heartier meal (red kidney beans are especially attractive in this dish). Cook and stir over medium-high heat until hot and lightly browned. A nonstick skillet will work best.

TIP: Scrambled Grits make a satisfying breakfast, lunch, or light supper, especially with the addition of beans and a variety of vegetables. For more of a yellow egg color, add a tiny pinch of turmeric.

Brown rice grits is coarsely ground brown rice that is about the same texture as corn grits (which also is known as *polenta*). There are packaged brands of rice cereal designed for this purpose (such as Bob's Red Mill's Creamy Brown Rice Farina and Arrowhead Mills' Rice & Shine), but many are too fine to make good grits. You can grind your own rice grits by whirling raw brown rice in a dry blender until it is very finely cracked. Cooking times may vary depending on how finely or coarsely the grits are ground.

RICE AND RAISIN PUDDING

This nutritious but not-too-sweet pudding is made with arborio rice, a short-grain Italian rice with a high starch content. It is traditionally used for making risotto, because its starch gives this classic Italian dish its characteristic creaminess. For the same reason, arborio rice is ideal for making lusciously creamy rice pudding. Do not rinse arborio rice before using it, as this will wash away the essential starch. Serve this pudding warm or chilled for breakfast, dessert, or snacktime.

3½ cups	fortified vanilla nondairy milk	875 ml
½ cup	arborio rice	125 ml
¼ cup	raisins, packed	60 ml
¼ cup	pure maple syrup	60 ml
Pinch	of salt	Pinch
	Ground cinnamon (optional)	

Combine the milk, rice, raisins, maple syrup, and salt in a medium saucepan and bring to a boil. Reduce the heat and simmer gently, stirring often, until the rice is tender and the liquid is thickened and creamy, about 45 minutes. Garnish with a sprinkle of cinnamon, if desired.

VARIATION: For an even richer, creamier pudding, use coconut milk (light or regular) in place of some or all of the nondairy milk. Add 1 teaspoon of vanilla flavoring if using only coconut milk.

TIP: The pudding will continue to thicken as it cools. For an even creamier pudding, increase the milk to 4 cups and extend the cooking time to 1 hour.

PER CUP (250 ML): calories: 391, protein: 4.5 g, fat: 2 g, carbohydrate: 88 g, dietary fiber: 1 g, calcium: 388 mg, iron: 0.9 mg, magnesium: 8 mg, sodium: 161 mg, zinc: 1.2 mg, folate: 0.4 mcg, riboflavin: 0 mg, vitamin C: 0 mg, vitamin E: 4.8 mg, omega-3 fatty acids: 0 g.

% CALORIES FROM: protein 4%, fat 6%, carbohydrate 90%

In-A-Jiffy Breakfast Pudding or Fruit Sauce

Yields 2 cups (500 ml)

Fruit sauces are a refreshing change from sugary syrups and provide vitamin C and protective phytochemicals. This simple combination contains no added sugar and requires no cooking. Dried fruit provides additional sweetness. This recipe is thick and delicious enough to be served on its own as a pudding, but it also makes a tasty topping for hot porridge or for Wheat-Free Mini-Pancakes, page 231. This recipe is from The New Becoming Vegetarian, *by Vesanto Melina and Brenda Davis.*

1	medium banana	1
1	medium orange, peeled and seeded	1
1–2 tablespoons	raisins, dried cherries, dried cranberries, or chopped dried apricots (optional)	15–30 ml
1½ cups	fresh or frozen berries or sliced fruit (see tips below)	375 ml

Place the banana, orange, optional dried fruit, and half (¾ cup/185 ml) of the berries or sliced fruit in a blender and purée until smooth. Pour into a medium bowl. Stir in the remaining half of the berries or sliced fruit.

Tips:

- One to two tablespoons (15–30 ml) of orange juice concentrate may be used in place of the orange.

- For the berries or fruit, try blueberries, raspberries, or peeled, sliced kiwi fruit. Feel free to experiment and invent your own blend using your favorite fruits.

Per ½ cup (125 ml): calories: 146, protein: 2 g, fat: 1 g, carbohydrate: 37 g, dietary fiber: 6 g, calcium: 36 mg, iron: 0.4 mg, magnesium: 29 mg, sodium: 7 mg, zinc: 0.3 mg, folate: 38 mcg, riboflavin: 0.1 mg, vitamin C: 54 mg, vitamin E: 1.4 mg, omega-3 fatty acids: 0.1 g.

% Calories from: protein 5%,   fat 4%,   carbohydrate 91%

CONTAINS: * Citrus (orange)

QUICK CHOCOLATE SHAKE

Yields 1 ¼ cup (310 ml)

This creamy shake is an excellent source of calcium and vitamins B$_{12}$ and D when made with fortified nondairy milk. It also provides instant energy.

1	banana, fresh or frozen (see tips below)	1
2 teaspoons	unsweetened cocoa powder	10 ml
¾ cup	fortified nondairy milk (plain, vanilla, or chocolate)	185 ml

Peel the banana, break it into chunks, and place it in a blender along with the cocoa and milk. Process until smooth.

TIPS:

• Select ripe bananas for freezing, as they are much sweeter than bananas that are barely ripe and have a less starchy aftertaste.

• To prepare bananas for freezing, peel them and leave whole or break them into chunks. Then place them in plastic bags or airtight containers and freeze.

• A squeeze of fresh lemon juice sprinkled on the bananas will keep them from turning brown.

• Frozen bananas last several weeks, depending on how ripe they were when frozen and the temperature of your freezer.

PER RECIPE: calories: 208, protein: 2.5 g, fat: 2 g, carbohydrate: 50 g, dietary fiber: 5 g, calcium: 230 mg, iron: 0.9 mg, magnesium: 18 mg, sodium: 68 mg, zinc: 0.2 mg, folate: 1 mcg, riboflavin: 0 mg, vitamin C: 9 mg, vitamin E: 3 mg, omega-3 fatty acids: 0 g.

% CALORIES FROM: protein 4%,   fat 8%,   carbohydrate 88%

CONTAINS: * Chocolate

FANTASTIC FRUIT SMOOTHIE

Yields 2 cups (500 ml)

For delicious combinations, try apple juice with blueberries, raspberries, or mango. Made with apple juice and blueberries, this smoothie provides 2 mg of vitamin E and plenty of phytochemicals. With orange juice and strawberries, it's rich in vitamin C. For a calcium boost, use calcium-fortified juice. For increased thickness, use frozen fruit. If using room temperature fruits, those who prefer a colder drink can add a few ice cubes before blending (this will also make the smoothie thicker).

1	banana, fresh or frozen (see tips, facing page	
1 cup	berries or sliced fruit	250 ml
1 cup	fruit juice	250 ml

Peel the banana, break it into chunks, and place in a blender along with the fruit and juice. Process until smooth.

PER CUP (250 ML): calories: 134, protein: 2 g, fat: 0.6 g, carbohydrate: 33 g, dietary fiber: 3.5 g, calcium: 190 mg, iron: 0.5 mg, magnesium: 25 mg, sodium: 1.4 mg, zinc: 0.2 mg, folate: 56 mcg, riboflavin: 0.1 mg, vitamin C: 106 mg, vitamin E: 0.3 mg, omega-3 fatty acids: 0.1 g.

% CALORIES FROM: protein 6%,   fat 4%,   carbohydrate 90%

*Nutritional analysis done using strawberries and calcium-fortified orange juice.

PINK CADILLAC SMOOTHIE

Yields 2 cups (500 ml)

This refreshing smoothie provides a wonderful boost of vitamin C. For added calcium, use calcium-fortified orange juice instead of fresh squeezed. For a thicker smoothie, freeze the mango or strawberries overnight.

1 cup	cubed mango	250 ml
1 cup	strawberries, red raspberries, pitted fresh cherries, pitted plums, pitted nectarines or peaches, or other fruit of your choice	250 ml
1 cup	calcium-fortified or fresh orange juice (about 3 oranges)	250 ml

Place all the ingredients in a blender and process until smooth.

PER CUP (250 ML): calories: 134, protein: 1.5 g, fat: 1 g, carbohydrate: 33 g, dietary fiber: 3.5 g, calcium: 170 mg, iron: 0.4 mg, magnesium: 16 mg, sodium: 10 mg, zinc: 0.1 mg, folate: 46 mcg, riboflavin: 0.1 mg, vitamin C: 109 mg, vitamin E: 1.1 mg, omega-3 fatty acids: 0.1 g.

% CALORIES FROM: protein 4%,   fat 3%,   carbohydrate 93% CONTAINS: * Citrus (orange)

*Nutritional analysis done using strawberries and calcium-fortified orange juice.

POWERHOUSE SMOOTHIE

This delicious "meal in a glass" can improve the day's nutrient intake for toddlers and adults alike, providing calories, fiber, minerals, vitamins, and omega-3 fatty acids. It's fun for children and parents or caregivers to make together as a shared activity. Vanilla-flavored nondairy milk will provide the sweetest taste. This recipe is from Becoming Vegan, *by Brenda Davis and Vesanto Melina.*

1 cup	calcium-fortified orange juice	250 ml
1 cup	fortified nondairy milk	250 ml
1½	frozen bananas, peeled and frozen (see tips, page 236)	1½
1 cup	frozen strawberries, blueberries, raspberries, or mango pieces	250 ml
1–2 tablespoons	ground flaxseeds, or 1–2 teaspoons (5 to 10 ml) flaxseed oil	15–30 ml
¼–½	avocado, peeled (optional)	¼–½
1–2 tablespoons	seed or nut butter, such as sesame tahini, pumpkin seed butter, sunflower seed butter, or cashew or almond butter (optional)	15–30 ml

Combine the juice, nondairy milk, banana, berries, flaxseeds, optional avocado, and optional seed or nut butter in a blender. Process until very smooth and creamy with no lumps.

VARIATIONS: Be creative in your additions. People have even found this smoothie to be a good way to get a little cooked carrot into children who are picky eaters!

• FOR CHOCOLATE POWERHOUSE SMOOTHIE, replace the orange juice with fortified chocolate or carob nondairy milk.

PER SERVING: calories: 240, protein: 3 g, fat: 3 g, carbohydrate: 55 g, dietary fiber: 5 g, calcium: 327 mg, iron: 1.2 mg, magnesium: 48 mg, sodium: 57 mg, zinc: 0.3 mg, folate: 50 mcg, riboflavin: 0.1 mg, vitamin C: 78 mg, vitamin E: 2.5 mg, omega-3 fatty acids: 1 g

% Calories from: protein 5%,   fat 11%,   carbohydrate 84%

CONTAINS: * Citrus (orange)

PER SERVING WITH ½ AVOCADO and 2 tablespoons sesame tahini: calories: 410, protein: 7 g, fat: 19 g, carbohydrate: 62 g, dietary fiber: 8 g, calcium: 354 mg, iron: 2.4 mg, magnesium: 82 mg, sodium: 67 mg, zinc: 1.2 mg, folate: 95 mcg, riboflavin: 0.2 mg, vitamin C: 82 mg, vitamin E: 3.9 mg, omega-3 fatty acids: 1.1 g.

% Calories from: protein 6%,   fat 38%,   carbohydrate 56%

CONTAINS: * Citrus (orange)

Dips and Spreads

SPREADS AND SANDWICHES FOR BROWN BAG LUNCHES, QUICK MEALS, AND SNACKS

For those with food allergies, it might be difficult to imagine what to toast for breakfast, pack for lunch, or prepare for a quick meal, especially in a culture that is so dependent on bread and sandwiches made from gluten-containing flour, yeast, dairy products, and eggs. Fortunately, there are many options—it simply takes a little imagination. Here are ideas for gluten-free alternatives for bread, toast, sandwiches, and wraps, including flavorful fillings and condiments.

THE "BREADS"

- Biscuits, pages 188–189
- Chickpea Crepes, page 193
- Commercial gluten-free breads (see Resources, page 363–367)
- Corn cakes
- Corn tortillas
- Gluten-Free Chapatis, pages 192–193
- Lettuce "bread" or wraps (whole lettuce leaves, washed and patted dry)
- Papadums, page 356
- Rice cakes (also good toasted)
- Ricebread or Cornbread Squares, page 191, with sweet spreads, or seed or nut butters
- Rice paper wraps
- Sunny Seed Bread, page 187
- Kale, collard, or cabbage wraps (whole kale, collard, or cabbage leaves steamed or boiled until tender, patted dry, and filled with a savory grain filling, as in a cabbage roll), served warm or chilled

THE CONDIMENTS

- Avocado Mayonnaise, page 289
- Barbecue sauce
- Beannaise, page 288
- Chickpea miso
- Creamy Tarragon Dressing, page 289
- Hot sauce
- Ketchup
- Lemon-Seed Salad Dressing, page 290
- Mashed avocado
- Mustard, plain or seasoned
- Pepperoncini
- Pickles or pickle relish

PROTEIN-RICH FILLINGS

- Bean salad
- Brown Rice Patties, page 315
- Colorful Chili Dip, page 251
- Creative Grain Spread, page 253
- Hot or cold cooked bean burgers
- Hummus, page 242
- Italian Chickpea Spread, page 252
- Monster Mash Roll-Up, page 254
- Red Bean Hummus, page 244
- Savory Spinach Spread, page
- Seed or nut butters
- Spicy North African Spread, page 247
- Tangy White Bean Spread, page 243

EVEN MORE FILLINGS TO CHEW ON

- Baby arugula
- Cooked greens, such as kale or collards (well drained or squeezed dry)
- Grated or thinly sliced raw vegetables
- Grilled vegetables
- Leftover casseroles
- Leftover thick stew or chili
- Lightly steamed vegetables
- Raw spinach
- Roasted vegetables
- Salad greens
- Sauerkraut
- Seasoned potatoes

WINNING FILLING COMBOS

- Bean burgers; dill pickle slices; tomato slices; mustard; vegan mayo
- Brown Rice Patty, warmed or cold, page 315; red onion slice; tomato or ketchup; relish; mustard; sprouts
- Creative Grain Spread, page 253; alfalfa sprouts; Beannaise, page 288
- Grilled or broiled portobello mushroom; barbecue sauce
- Hummus or Red Bean Hummus, pages 242 and 244; sprouts; chopped olives
- Mashed avocado; slices of raw or roasted red bell pepper; baby arugula
- Mashed beans; lettuce; red onion slice; barbeque sauce
- Mashed beans; lettuce; tomato; scallions; Avocado Mayonnaise, page 289
- Monster Mash Roll-Up, page 254; cucumber slices
- Raw spinach; thinly sliced mushrooms, raw or sautéed; red onion slice; dressing
- Salad greens; chopped raw veggies; dressing
- Seed or nut butter; jam or rice syrup
- Seed or nut butter; sliced banana
- Seed or nut butter; thinly sliced strawberries or orange sections
- Seed or nut butter; grated carrot; sliced cucumber; red onion slice
- Seed or nut butter; raisins or other chopped dried fruit
- Seed or nut butter; steamed broccoli florets; balsamic vinegar
- Seed or nut butter; lettuce or sprouts

SANDWICHES WITH AN INTERNATIONAL FLAIR:

- Black Bean Tostadas, pages 310–311
- Falafels (in Gluten-Free Chapatis, pages 192–193, or corn tortillas)
- Nori Rolls, pages 322–323, or from a deli or Japanese restaurant
- Pizza wedge, pages 312–313
- Roll-Ups, page 254
- Time-Saving Tacos, page 313
- Veggie Rice Roll, page 325

MAKING DELICIOUS NUT-FREE SPREADS

Many spreads, especially those that are bean- or grain-based, call for nut or seed butters to add richness, body, and flavor. But what can you do if you are allergic to nuts or seeds? Create a delicious spread by blending beans or grains or a mixture of both. Then add one or more of the following, in amounts to suit your taste:

NOTE: If you cannot have citrus, feel free to substitute wine vinegar (red, white, or balsamic) in any of the following recipes. You can also try rice vinegar or umeboshi plum vinegar. Just cut back on any added salt if you use umeboshi vinegar, as it is very salty. If you cannot have vinegar, feel free to substitute fresh lemon, lime, or even orange juice.

- avocado, puréed or mashed
- barbecue sauce
- chopped olives or olive tapenade
- cooked and puréed green peas
- cooked beets or broccoli or other cooked vegetables, puréed with a small amount of water
- grated raw carrots
- ketchup
- marinated artichoke hearts, minced or puréed

- mashed potatoes
- olive or flaxseed oil
- prepared mustard
- puréed cooked carrots, sweet potatoes, or winter squash
- roasted red peppers (skin and seeds removed), puréed
- sun-dried tomatoes packed in oil, minced or puréed
- tomato paste

Hummus

This traditional Middle Eastern chickpea dip is a staple for lunches and snacks. It makes a delicious dinner when served with Gluten-Free Chapatis, pages 192–193, instead of pita bread, rice-stuffed grape leaves, sliced fresh tomatoes, and a tossed salad. You may use a blender to make this and other bean spreads if you have one with a strong motor.

3½ cups	drained cooked or canned chickpeas, reserve liquid	875 ml
½–¾ cup	fresh lemon juice, or ¼–½ cup (60–125 ml) balsamic or red wine vinegar	125–185 ml
⅓ cup	sesame tahini or other seed butter (see page 176), or 3 tablespoons (45 ml) extra-virgin olive oil	85 ml
2 tablespoons	extra-virgin olive oil	30 ml
¼–½ teaspoon	crushed garlic	1–2 ml
	Salt	
1 teaspoon	paprika	5 ml
2 tablespoons	minced fresh parsley or cilantro (optional)	30 ml

Blend the chickpeas in a food processor with a little of the lemon juice or vinegar—just enough to make a smooth, thick paste. Add the remainder of the lemon juice or vinegar to taste along with the seed butter, oil, garlic, and salt to taste, and process or blend until smooth. If necessary, add a little of the cooking liquid to achieve a smooth, creamy consistency. To serve, transfer the hummus to a serving platter and sprinkle with the paprika and optional parsley or cilantro. Spread on bread or use as a dip.

Variations:

• Garnish with hot paprika or cayenne pepper instead of mild paprika.

• Add 1–1½ teaspoons (5–7 ml) ground cumin during processing.

Per ½ cup (125 ml): calories: 190, protein: 7.5 g, fat: 10 g, carbohydrate: 21 g, dietary fiber: 5.5 g, calcium: 47 mg, iron: 2.4 mg, magnesium: 41 mg, sodium: 8 mg, zinc: 1.4 mg, folate: 122 mcg, riboflavin: 0.1 mg, vitamin C: 9 mg, vitamin E: 0.8 mg, omega-3 fatty acids: 0.1 g.

% Calories from: protein 15%, fat 43%, carbohydrate 42%

Tangy White Bean Spread

Yields about 2 cups (500 ml)

Fresh herbs are the secret ingredient in this special spread. If you can't get fresh basil or cilantro, or if they aren't your favorites, you can use fresh dill weed or even parsley, in a pinch.

2 cups	drained cooked or canned white beans (one 16-ounce/450-gram can)	500 ml
1–2 tablespoons	fresh lemon juice or white wine vinegar	15–30 ml
1½ tablespoons	extra-virgin olive oil	22 ml
1 tablespoon	sesame tahini or other seed butter (see page 176) or additional olive oil	15 ml
¾ teaspoon	salt	4 ml
½ teaspoon	crushed garlic	2 ml
Large pinch	cayenne	Large pinch
¼–½ cup	fresh basil or cilantro	60–125 ml

Combine the beans, lemon juice, olive oil, tahini, salt, garlic, and cayenne in a food processor. Blend into a smooth paste. Pulse in the basil or cilantro until it is coarsely chopped and evenly distributed.

PER ½ CUP (125 ML): calories: 197, protein: 9.5 g, fat: 8 g, carbohydrate: 24 g, dietary fiber: 6 g, calcium: 92 mg, iron: 3.6 mg, magnesium: 63 mg, sodium: 654 mg, zinc: 1.4 mg, folate: 79 mcg, riboflavin: 0.1 mg, vitamin C: 3 mg, vitamin E: 1.0 mg, omega-3 fatty acids: 0.1 g.

% CALORIES FROM: protein 19%, fat 34%, carbohydrate 47%

Red Bean Hummus

Who said hummus must only be made with chickpeas? Here is a delectable twist on the old favorite. It provides an excellent balance between protein, fat, and carbohydrate.

1¾ cups	drained cooked or canned pinto beans (one 15-ounce/425 g can)	435 ml
1 tablespoon	red wine vinegar	15 ml
1 tablespoon	balsamic vinegar or chickpea miso	15 ml
1 tablespoon	extra-virgin olive oil	15 ml
½ teaspoon	salt	2 ml
¼ teaspoon	ground cumin	1 ml
¼ teaspoon	crushed garlic	1 ml
¼ cup	water, more or less as needed	60 ml
2–4 tablespoons	sesame tahini or other seed butter (see page 176)	30–60 ml
½ teaspoon	bottled hot pepper sauce	2 ml
¼–½ cup	sliced scallions or chopped fresh cilantro	60–125 ml

Combine the beans, vinegars, olive oil, salt, cumin, and garlic in a food processor. Add just enough water as necessary to facilitate processing. Process several minutes until completely smooth, stopping to scrape down the sides of the work bowl as needed. Add the tahini and blend into a smooth paste. Pulse in the scallions or cilantro until coarsely chopped and evenly distributed.

VARIATION: Those who are avoiding vinegar can replace the two vinegars with 2 tablespoons fresh lemon juice, or more or less to taste.

PER ½ CUP (125 ML): calories: 162, protein: 7.5 g, fat: 6 g, carbohydrate: 22 g, dietary fiber: 7 g, calcium: 50 mg, iron: 2.4 mg, magnesium: 49 mg, sodium: 312 mg, zinc: 1.2 mg, folate: 136 mcg, riboflavin: 0.1 mg, vitamin C: 3 mg, vitamin E: 1 mg, omega-3 fatty acids: 0.1 g.

% CALORIES FROM: protein 18%,   fat 32%,   carbohydrate 50%

CONTAINS: * FERMENTED foods (VINEGAR)

Green Bean Pâté

Rich in protein, fiber, minerals, and unsaturated (healthy) fats, this classic "meaty" spread is wonderful served on a bed of lettuce garnished with tomatoes, or as a spread for brown rice crackers. Refrigerate leftovers in a covered container for a satisfying snack the next day.

1 tablespoon	extra-virgin olive oil	15 ml
1	large onion, diced	1
2 cups	steamed green beans, cooled and coarsely chopped	500 ml
1¾ cups	drained cooked or canned white beans (one 15-ounce/425 g can)	435 ml
1 cup	raw sunflower seeds or pumpkin seeds, or chopped pecans or walnuts	250 ml
Pinch	of ground allspice	Pinch
	Salt and pepper	

Heat the oil in a skillet over medium-high heat. Add the onion and sauté until dark brown and caramelized, about 30 minutes. Reduce the heat as necessary to keep the onion from burning. If the onion sticks to the pan, add a little water.

Combine the onion, green beans, white beans, and seeds in a food processor, and process into a smooth paste. Season with allspice, salt, and pepper to taste. Chill thoroughly before serving.

Per ¼ cup (60 ml): calories: 182, protein: 7.7 g, fat: 10 g, carbohydrate: 18 g, dietary fiber: 5.5 g, calcium: 65 mg, iron: 2.5 mg, magnesium: 55 mg, sodium: 116 mg, zinc: 1.5 mg, folate: 84 mcg, riboflavin: 0.1 mg, vitamin C: 5 mg, vitamin E: 8.5 mg, omega-3 fatty acids: 0.1 g.

% Calories from: protein 16%,   fat 47%,   carbohydrate 37%

Lentil "Chopped Liver"

Yields 4 cups (1 L)

This luscious mock liver pâté is simply out of this world. The secret is the slow-cooked, caramelized onions. Serve it on or between lettuce leaves or with rice crackers or Gluten-Free Chapatis, pages 192–183. Your guests won't believe this isn't chopped liver!

1½ cups	dry lentils	375 ml
4 cups	water	1 L
2 tablespoons	extra-virgin olive oil	30 ml
2	large onions, chopped	2
1 cup	raw or toasted pumpkin or sunflower seeds, or chopped walnuts or pecans	250 ml
1 tablespoon	chickpea miso (optional)	15 ml
	Salt and pepper	

Rinse the lentils and place them in a large saucepan. Add the water; bring to a boil, reduce the heat, cover, and simmer for 45 minutes. Remove the cover and continue to simmer, stirring often, until any liquid has cooked off and the lentils are very tender.

Meanwhile, heat the oil in a large skillet. Add the onions and cook over medium-low heat until very dark and caramelized, about 1 hour. Lower the heat as necessary so the onions do not burn.

Place the lentils, onions, seeds, optional miso, and salt and pepper to taste in a food processor and purée into a thick paste. Chill thoroughly before serving.

Per ¼ cup (60 ml): calories: 158 protein: 10 g, fat: 8 g, carbohydrate: 14 g, dietary fiber: 6.5 g, calcium: 20 mg, iron: 3.8 mg, magnesium: 98 mg, sodium: 16 mg, zinc: 1.8 mg, folate: 90 mcg, riboflavin: 0.1 mg, vitamin C: 3 mg, vitamin E: 0.5 mg, omega-3 fatty acids: 0.5 g.

% Calories from: protein 24%, fat 43%, carbohydrate 33%

SPICY NORTH AFRICAN SPREAD

Yields about 1 cup (250 ml)

Here's a spicy spread to enjoy in sandwiches (for example, with gluten-free bread) or on biscuits for a lively breakfast or with soups or salads. The base is tahini, a sesame seed butter. Some brands of tahini are drier or more runny than others. If you find that your butter is too thick, add a tablespoon of vegetable broth or water to thin the spread. The thinned spread also makes a delicious topping for rice or corn pasta or potatoes. If you cannot have sesame, substitute pumpkin or sunflower seed butter.

½ cup	sesame tahini or other seed butter (see page 176)	125 ml
3–4 tablespoons	fresh lemon juice	45–60 ml
3 tablespoons	finely sliced scallions	45 ml
¼ cup	minced fresh cilantro	45 ml
¼–½ teaspoon	crushed garlic	1–2 ml
1½ teaspoons	ground cumin	7 ml
1 teaspoon	paprika	5 ml
1 teaspoon	chickpea miso, or salt to taste	5 ml
¼ teaspoon	chili powder or paste (optional)	1 ml

Combine all the ingredients in a food processor and blend until smooth.

PER ¼ CUP (60 ML): calories: 192, protein: 6 g, fat: 16 g, carbohydrate: 9 g, dietary fiber: 2 g, calcium: 58 mg, iron: 1.9 mg, magnesium: 33 mg, sodium: 69 mg, zinc: 1.5 mg, folate: 37 mcg, riboflavin: 0.1 mg, vitamin C: 9 mg, vitamin E: 0.8 mg, omega-3 fatty acids: 0.1 g.

% CALORIES FROM: protein 11%, fat 71%, carbohydrate 18%

CONTAINS: * CITRUS (LEMON)

GOLDEN YAM SPREAD

Yields 1 ⅓ cups (335 ml)

This practically fat-free spread is packed with the protective antioxidant beta-carotene (a form of vitamin A), plus another golden vitamin, riboflavin. Its deep orange color makes it very attractive served with rice crackers, baked corn chips, or vegetable sticks.

3	small yams, peeled, cut into ½-inch-thick (1 cm) slices	3
2 teaspoons	grated fresh ginger	10 ml
1½ teaspoons	fresh lemon juice or balsamic vinegar	7 ml
1 teaspoon	chickpea miso, or salt to taste	5 ml
½ teaspoon	ground cumin	2 ml
½ teaspoon	crushed garlic	2 ml
¼ teaspoon	ground coriander	1 ml
	Cayenne	
2 tablespoons	chopped fresh cilantro	30 ml

Steam the yam slices until soft and place them in a food processor along with the fresh ginger, lemon juice, miso, cumin, garlic, coriander, and cayenne. Purée until smooth. Add the cilantro and pulse briefly, just until evenly incorporated.

PER ⅓ CUP: calories: 162, protein: 3 g, fat: <1 g, carbohydrate: 37 g, dietary fiber: 3 g, calcium: 39 mg, iron: 17 mg, magnesium: 17 mg, sodium: 91 mg, zinc: 0.5 mg, folate: 18 mcg, riboflavin: 0.2 mg, vitamin C: 27 mg, vitamin E: 0.5 mg, omega-3 fatty acids: 0 g.

% CALORIES FROM: protein 7%,   fat 4%,   carbohydrate 89%

WARM EGGPLANT PESTO

Here's a superb dairy-free pesto that is very simple to prepare. It is equally delicious as a dip or topping served at room temperature, or as a warm sauce over brown rice pasta or your favorite gluten-free grains.

½ cup	water, more or less as needed	125 ml
1	medium onion, diced	1
½ teaspoon	crushed garlic	2 ml
1	large eggplant, peeled	1
1 cup	pecans or raw sunflower or pumpkins seeds	250 ml
½ cup	fresh basil, firmly packed	125 ml
2–4 tablespoons	chickpea miso	30–60 ml
2–3 tablespoons	fresh lemon juice	30–45 ml

Heat the water in a large nonstick skillet. Add the onion and garlic and cook over medium-high heat for 5 minutes. Meanwhile, cut the eggplant into ½-inch (1-cm) cubes. Add to the onion, cover, and reduce the heat to medium. Cook, stirring often, 25–30 minutes or until the eggplant is very soft. If necessary, add a little more water to keep the eggplant from sticking to the pan. When tender, transfer the eggplant mixture to a blender. Add the remaining ingredients and process until completely smooth. The mixture will be thick. Serve immediately, while warm, or at room temperature. Store any leftovers in the refrigerator and reheat to serve.

PER ½ CUP (125 ML): calories: 170, protein: 3.5 g, fat: 13 g, carbohydrate: 11 g, dietary fiber: 3.5 g, calcium: 19 mg, iron: 0.8 mg, magnesium: 37 mg, sodium: 251 mg, zinc: 1.1 mg, folate: 24 mcg, riboflavin: 0.1 mg, vitamin C: 7 mg, vitamin E: 0.6 mg, omega-3 fatty acids: 0 g.

% CALORIES FROM: protein 8%, fat 67%, carbohydrate 25%

CONTAINS: * CITRUS (LEMON) * FERMENTED foods (MISO)

Savory Spinach Spread

Yields about 2½ cups (625 ml)

*Serve this delightfully creamy spread on rice crackers or over hot baked pota-
toes or rice pasta. Easy and quick to prepare, it is rich in protein, calcium, iron,
zinc, and fiber. To save time, thaw the spinach in the microwave or in a pot of
hot water and shred the carrots in the food processor before puréeing the dip.*

1¾ cups	drained cooked or canned white beans (one 15-ounce/425 g can)	435 ml
2 tablespoons	fresh lemon juice or white wine vinegar	30 ml
2 tablespoons	extra-virgin olive oil	30 ml
¾ teaspoon	onion powder	4 ml
½ teaspoon	dried tarragon	2 ml
¼ teaspoon	garlic powder	1 ml
¼ teaspoon	salt	1 ml
1 (10-ounce) box	frozen chopped spinach, thawed	1 (285 g) box
1 cup	shredded carrots (about 1 or 2 carrots)	250 ml
¼ cup	thinly sliced scallions	60 ml

Combine the beans, lemon juice, oil, onion powder, tarragon, garlic powder, and
salt in a food processor and blend until smooth and creamy. Transfer to a
medium bowl. Squeeze the spinach as dry as possible. Stir it into the bean paste along
with carrots and scallions. Mix well. Chill thoroughly before serving.

PER ½ CUP (125 ML): calories: 166, protein: 8 g, fat: 6 g, carbohydrate: 22 g, dietary fiber: 6.5 g,
calcium: 129 mg, iron: 3.7 mg, magnesium: 76 mg, sodium: 319 mg, zinc: 1.2 mg, folate: 123 mcg,
riboflavin: 0.1 mg, vitamin C: 20 mg, vitamin E: 1.5 mg, omega-3 fatty acids: 0.1 g.

% CALORIES FROM: protein 19%,   fat 31%,   carbohydrate 50%

Colorful Chili Dip

Serve this zesty dip with baked corn chips, or roll it in corn tortillas or Gluten-Free Chapatis, pages 192–193, along with your favorite salad fixings. This dip is low in fat yet packed with nutrients. Feel free to experiment with different types of beans, such as black beans, kidney beans, chickpeas, black-eyed peas, or navy beans.

1¾ cups	drained cooked or canned pinto beans (one 15-ounce can/425 g)	435 ml
1	medium scallion, sliced	1
2 tablespoons	balsamic vinegar or fresh lime juice	30 ml
1 teaspoon	chili powder	5 ml
½ teaspoon	ground cumin	2 ml
½ teaspoon	dried oregano	2 ml
Several shakes	of Tabasco or a dash of cayenne	Several shakes
¼ cup	minced red bell peppers	60 ml
¼ cup	minced green bell pepper	60 ml

Combine all the ingredients, except the bell peppers, in a food processor, and blend until smooth and creamy. Transfer to a bowl and stir in the bell peppers. Mix well. Chill thoroughly before serving.

PER ½ CUP (125 ML): calories: 117, protein: 6.5 g, fat: <1 g, carbohydrate: 22 g, dietary fiber: 7 g, calcium: 49 mg, iron: 2.4 mg, magnesium: 45 mg, sodium: 192 mg, zinc: 0.9 mg, folate: 136 mcg, riboflavin: 0.1 mg, vitamin C: 29 mg, vitamin E: 0.9 mg, omega-3 fatty acids: 0.1 g.

% CALORIES FROM: protein 22%,   fat 4%,   carbohydrate 74%

Italian Chickpea Spread

Yields about 1½ cups (375 ml)

Enjoy this delicious spread with rice crackers, corn tortillas, or with Gluten-Free Chapatis, pages 192–193. It's light yet satisfying and an excellent source of iron, zinc, folate, vitamin E, and protein.

1¾ cups	drained cooked or canned chickpeas (one 15-ounce can/425 g)	435 ml
2 tablespoons	extra-virgin olive oil	30 ml
1 tablespoon	water	15 ml
1 tablespoon	balsamic vinegar or fresh lemon juice	15 ml
½ teaspoon	dried basil	2 ml
½ teaspoon	dried oregano	2 ml
¼–½ teaspoon	crushed garlic	1–2 ml
	Salt and pepper	

Combine the chickpeas, oil, water, vinegar, basil, oregano, and garlic in a food processor and blend into a smooth paste, stopping to scrape down sides of work bowl as necessary. Season with salt and pepper to taste. Chill several hours or overnight before serving to allow the flavors to blend.

Variation:

For Italian White Bean Spread, replace the chickpeas with an equal amount of cooked white beans of your choice.

Per ½ cup (125 ml): calories: 226, protein: 8 g, fat: 10 g, carbohydrate: 27 g, dietary fiber: 9 g, calcium: 59 mg, iron: 2.9 mg, magnesium: 56 mg, sodium: 4 mg (without salt), zinc: 1.1 mg, folate: 172 mcg, riboflavin: 0.1 mg, vitamin C: 2 mg, vitamin E: 2.1 mg, omega-3 fatty acids: 0.1 g.

% Calories from: protein 14%, fat 39%, carbohydrate 47%

CREATIVE GRAIN SPREAD

This is an exciting way to use up small amounts of leftovers, although you might enjoy this spread so much you'll want to cook grain specifically for it. Use your imagination to turn whatever you have in the fridge or pantry into a special and original sandwich filling. This recipe can be easily doubled or tripled, if desired.

One-half cup will give you about 10 percent of your day's supply of protein and more than 10 percent of your fiber, beta-carotene, pyridoxine, niacin, copper, magnesium, manganese, phosphorus, selenium, and zinc.

FOUNDATION:

2 cups	cooked grain (rice, quinoa, millet, polenta, etc.)	500 ml
¼–½ cup	seed or nut butter	60 to 125 ml
1	large carrot, shredded	1
	Water, as needed	
	Salt	

SEASONING OPTIONS:

- bottled hot sauce
- cayenne
- crushed garlic
- ginger, freshly grated
- herbs, dried (basil, oregano, dill weed, tarragon, thyme, sage, etc.)
- herbs, minced fresh (parsley, cilantro, basil, dill, oregano, thyme, etc.)
- horseradish
- mustard
- pepper
- pickle relish
- scallions, sliced
- spices (curry powder, garam masala, cumin, ginger, coriander, paprika, etc.)
- tomato paste, ketchup, or minced, oil-packed, sun-dried tomatoes
- vinegar (white or red wine, balsamic, rice, umeboshi)

Place all the foundation ingredients in a food processor fitted with a metal blade. Process until the grain is coarsely chopped but not puréed. Add about 1 tablespoon (15 ml) of water, if needed, to facilitate processing. The mixture should be very thick, not runny. Season with the options of your choice.

PER ½ CUP (125 ML): calories: 206, protein: 5 g, fat: 9 g, carbohydrate: 28 g, dietary fiber: 3 g, calcium: 36 mg, iron: 1.3 mg, magnesium: 60 mg, sodium: 13 mg, zinc: 1.3 mg, folate: 21 mcg, riboflavin: 0 mg, vitamin C: 2 mg, vitamin E: 0.8 mg, omega-3 fatty acids: 0.1 g.

% CALORIES FROM: protein 10%, fat 37%, carbohydrate 53%

MONSTER MASH ROLL-UP

Yields about 2 cups (500 ml)

Here is a creative bean spread that offers endless ideas for fillings for rice paper roll-ups, taco shells, and Gluten-Free Chapatis, pages 192–193. It also allows you to explore beans that perhaps you've never tried before: adzuki, black turtle, mung beans, pintos, white beans (navy, cannellini), and black-eyed peas.

| 2 cups | drained cooked or canned beans (one 16-ounce can/450 g) | (500 ml) |

OPTIONAL ADDITIONS:

- Avocado Mayonnaise, page 289
- barbeque sauce
- Beannaise, page 288
- capers
- carrots, minced or shredded
- citrus juice (lemon, lime, or orange)
- garlic
- herbs, fresh or dried
- horseradish
- ketchup
- miso, chickpea
- mustard
- oil (olive or flaxseed)
- onion
- pickles (chopped or relish)
- salt and pepper
- seed butter (see page 176) or nut butter
- spices
- sun-dried tomatoes
- tomato paste
- Ume-Roasted Seeds or Nuts, page 353
- vegetables, cooked
- vegetables, raw (minced or grated)
- vinegar (red or white wine, balsamic, rice, umeboshi)

Place the beans in a food processor fitted with a metal blade and process until ground. Add the optional ingredients of your choice, adding a small amount of water, if needed, to facilitate processing. Taste, adjust seasonings, and add more optional ingredients as necessary to achieve the flavor and texture you desire.

SOME IDEAS TO GET YOU STARTED:

- adzuki beans with sesame tahini and umeboshi vinegar
- black beans with Avocado Mayonnaise, page 289, chopped onions, pickle relish, chili powder, and salt
- black beans with sesame tahini, orange juice, Tabasco, chopped fresh cilantro, and salt
- kidney beans (coarsely mashed), with Ume-Roasted Seeds or Nuts, page 353, olive oil, balsamic vinegar, thinly sliced scallions, and chopped fresh cilantro or parsley
- pinto beans with sun-dried tomatoes, fresh lemon juice fresh or dried basil, garlic, salt, and cayenne
- red beans with ketchup, balsamic vinegar, garlic, fresh or dried basil, cayenne, and salt
- white beans with Avocado Mayonnaise, page 289, drained white horseradish, salt, and pepper
- white beans with olive oil, mustard, garlic, salt, and pepper
- white beans, cooked carrots, dried thyme, dried or prepared mustard, salt, and pepper

Salads and Dressings

$\mathcal{E}$veryone knows that salads are good for us. Fresh vegetables contain more vitamins and minerals per calorie than any other food. They provide a wealth of antioxidants and protective phytochemicals that safeguard us from disease. However, healthful salads may be a challenge for those with food allergies and sensitivities—especially the dressings, which often contain soy oil, dairy products, eggs, or even fish (such as the anchovies in Caesar dressing). But don't let food intolerances doom your diet to bland or repetitive salads. In this section you will find a bounty of salad and dressing recipes free of dairy, gluten, soy, and animal products.

Fast food restaurants and uninspired family patterns have set abysmally low standards for salad appeal, with the norm consisting mostly of iceberg lettuce, a few wedges of tomato, and a boring packaged or bottled dressing. Prepare for a new vision of what "salad" means. We have taken salads way above and beyond boring. In this section you will discover succulent blends of fresh, colorful, flavorful vegetables, along with scrumptious dressings—all free of common allergens. The colors and flavors are sure to delight you! To boost nutrition, make every day a salad day; use one of the salads here or your own creation as a main dish or a generous side dish.

To encourage your intake of essential fatty acids, which may be lacking in people with food allergies (and in those without allergies), we include a few dressing recipes that call for flaxseed oil (pages 291, 293, and 296). It's the best plant source of omega-3 fatty acids, a class of fats that the body needs to control inflammation in the body tissues and help prevent chronic disease.

Feel free to interchange ingredients in these recipes, or to experiment with your own substitutions.

Fresh Spring Salad

What a pleasing lunch or side salad! It's superb in spring and summer when there is an abundance of fresh vegetables and herbs, and it's equally delightful year round.

1 head	romaine lettuce, or 2 heads Bibb lettuce	1 head
2	ripe tomatoes	2
1	cucumber, peeled and seeded	1
1	green bell pepper	1
8	red radishes	8
	Minced mild red onions or thinly sliced scallions	
	Minced fresh cilantro, parsley, basil, or dill weed	
3–4 tablespoons	fresh lemon juice	45–60 ml
3 tablespoons	extra-virgin olive oil	45 ml
	Salt and pepper	

Finely chop or dice the lettuce, tomatoes, cucumber, pepper, and radishes, if using. Place them in a large bowl along with the onions and fresh herbs, to taste. Dress with the lemon juice, oil, and salt and pepper to taste just before serving. Toss gently.

Per 2 cups (500 ml): calories: 139, protein: 2.5 g, fat: 11 g, carbohydrate: 10 g, dietary fiber: 3.5 g, calcium:47 mg, iron: 1.5 mg, magnesium: 23 mg, sodium: 55 mg, zinc: 0.4 mg, folate: 142 mcg, riboflavin: 0.1 mg, vitamin C: 68 mg, vitamin E: 2.4 mg, omega-3 fatty acids: 0.2 g.

% Calories from: protein 7%, fat 67%, carbohydrate 26%

Contains: * Citrus (lemon) * Tomato

Baby Greens with Arugula and Avocado

Yields about 8–16 cups (2–4 L)

Young greens are tender and delicious, while arugula and olives add sharpness and bite. Avocado contributes a creamy richness. Together, they make an outstanding salad that is high in healthful monounsaturated fatty acids, iron, and folate.

2 cups	mesclun (mixed baby salad greens)	500 ml
1 head	romaine lettuce, washed, dried, and torn	1 head
1 cup	arugula, washed, dried, and chopped	250 ml
1	tomato, diced	1
1	Hass avocado, peeled and diced	1
15	pitted kalamata olives, chopped	15
¼ cup	extra-virgin olive oil	60 ml
2 tablespoons	balsamic vinegar	30 ml
2 tablespoons	fresh lime or lemon juice	30 ml
½ cup	raw or toasted pumpkin seeds, sunflower seeds, or pignolias (pine nuts)	125 ml

Combine the mesclun, romaine, arugula, tomato, avocado, and olives in a large bowl and toss gently. Drizzle the olive oil, vinegar, and lime or lemon juice over the top and toss until evenly distributed. Sprinkle with the seeds and toss gently once more.

TIP: Hass avocados generally are smaller than most other avocados and have a thick, bumpy skin that turns black when the avocado is ripe. Hass avocados have more oil than other types of avocados, making them tastier and creamier. Although Hass avocados are recommended for this recipe, other types may be substituted if you prefer.

PER ⅛ RECIPE: calories: 183, protein: 3.5 g, fat: 17 g, carbohydrate: 7 g, dietary fiber: 2.5 g, calcium: 33 mg, iron: 2.2 mg, magnesium: 64 mg, sodium: 128 mg, zinc: 0.9 mg, folate: 80 mcg, riboflavin: 0.1 mg, vitamin C: 16 mg, vitamin E: 1.9 mg, omega-3 fatty acids: 0.1 g.

% CALORIES FROM: protein 8%,   fat 78%,   carbohydrate 14%

CONTAINS: * Citrus (lemon) * Fermented foods (olives, vinegar) * Tomato

SENSATIONAL SUNSET SALAD

There is something striking about this salad, with its wide range of greens, speckled with a spray of purple. It's the perfect salad for a warm summer evening, although it can be enjoyed year-round. It is rich in the antioxidant vitamins A, C, and E, and folate.

3 tablespoons	fresh lime or lemon juice	45 ml
2 tablespoons	extra-virgin olive oil	30 ml
2 tablespoons	apple cider vinegar	30 ml
2 tablespoons	pure maple syrup	30 ml
Pinch	of salt	Pinch
Dash	of Tabasco (optional)	Dash
8 cups	chopped mixed lettuces	2000 ml
2 cups	finely shredded or minced purple cabbage	500 ml
1 cup	finely chopped fresh cilantro or parsley	250 ml
2	Hass avocados, peeled and diced	2

Combine the lime or lemon juice, olive oil, vinegar, maple syrup, salt, and optional Tabasco in a large salad bowl. Whisk until well combined. Add the remaining ingredients in the order given, and toss gently until evenly mixed. Serve at once.

PER 2 CUPS (500 ML): calories: 190, protein: 3 g, fat: 15 g, carbohydrate: 14 g, dietary fiber: 5.5 g, calcium: 70 mg, iron: 2 mg, magnesium: 51 mg, sodium: 60 mg, zinc: 1 mg, folate: 136 mcg, riboflavin: 0.2 mg, vitamin C: 35 mg, vitamin E: 2.8 mg, omega-3 fatty acids: 0.2 g.

% CALORIES FROM: protein 6%,   fat 67%,   carbohydrate 27%

CONTAINS: * CITRUS (LEMON OR LIME) * FERMENTED foods (VINEGAR)

Winter Delight Salad

The sweet taste of orange juice balances the sharp and bitter flavors of the greens. One serving of these dark leafy greens supplies enough vitamin K to get you through today and most of the week!

⅓ cup	extra-virgin olive oil	85 ml
¼ cup	orange juice	60 ml
2 tablespoons	balsamic vinegar	30 ml
1 tablespoon	dried mint	15 ml
½–1 teaspoon	salt	2–5 ml
¼ teaspoon	cayenne	1 ml
4 cups	chopped romaine lettuce	1000 ml
4 cups	chopped Swiss chard	1000 ml
2 cups	finely chopped kale	500 ml
2 cups	chopped spinach	500 ml

Combine the olive oil, orange juice, vinegar, mint, salt, and cayenne in a large salad bowl. Whisk until well combined. Add the remaining ingredients in the order given, tossing gently after each addition so that the dressing is evenly distributed. Serve at once.

PER 2 CUPS (500 ML): calories: 144, protein: 2 g, fat: 13 g, carbohydrate: 6 g, dietary fiber: 2 g, calcium: 73 mg, iron: 1.8 mg, magnesium: 40 mg, sodium: 268 mg, zinc: 0.3 mg, folate: 85 mcg, riboflavin: 0.1 mg, vitamin C: 51 mg, vitamin E: 2.6 mg, omega-3 fatty acids: 0.2 g.

% CALORIES FROM: protein 6%,   fat 77%,   carbohydrate 17%

CONTAINS: * CITRUS (ORANGE) * FERMENTED foods (VINEGAR)

BUILD YOUR BONES SALAD

Yields without broccoli, 6 cups (1.5 L);
with broccoli, 7 cups (1.75 L)

To prepare kale for use in a salad, first place each leaf on a cutting board, fold the leaf in half lengthwise, and remove the stem, using a knife. Then slice the leafy portion matchstick thin. A two-cup (500-ml) portion of this salad, with a little Lemon-Seed Salad Dressing (page 290), provides about as much calcium as one-half cup (125 ml) of cow's milk or fortified soymilk. As a bonus, the calcium present in these greens is about twice as well absorbed as that in milk. Vitamins A and K, which help maintain lifelong bone health, and folate, a vitamin needed for cell division, also are present in substantial amounts.

2 cups	kale or collards, stems removed and thinly sliced	500 ml
2 cups	chopped napa cabbage (Chinese cabbage)	500 ml
2 cups	torn romaine lettuce	500 ml
1 cup	small broccoli florets (optional)	250 ml
½ cup	grated carrot	125 ml

Toss together all the ingredients in a large bowl until well combined. Serve with Lemon-Seed Dressing, page 290, or any other dressing you prefer.

PER 2 CUPS (500 ML): calories: 42, protein: 3 g, fat: 0.5 g, carbohydrate: 8 g, dietary fiber: 2.5 g, calcium: 128 mg, iron: 1.6 mg, magnesium: 29 mg, sodium: 59 mg, zinc: 0.4 mg, folate: 97 mcg, riboflavin: 0.1 mg, vitamin C: 85 mg, vitamin E: 0.7 mg, omega-3 fatty acids: 0.1 g.

% CALORIES FROM: protein 24%,   fat 9%,   carbohydrate 67%

VEGGIE RAINBOW PLATTER

Serve a platter filled with colorful, cut up vegetables

- to encourage your family to eat their veggies when they come in from school or work;

- as an attractive way to serve any of these foods at mealtimes;

- as a low-cal, healthful snack while watching TV;

- as an artistic accompaniment to festive meals;

- as a great way to get vitamins, antioxidants, phytochemicals, and fiber.

Here's a list of veggies you can serve raw, on their own, or with one of the dressings on pages 290–296 or spreads on pages 239–254 to use as a dip.

- asparagus tips
- broccoli florets
- carrot sticks
- cauliflower florets
- celery sticks
- cherry tomatoes
- cucumber discs
- green onion strips
- green peas in pods

- jicama sticks
- mushrooms, whole or sliced
- parsnip sticks
- red, yellow, orange, and green pepper strips
- snow pea pods
- turnip strips
- yam strips
- zucchini strips or coins

PER CUP (250 ML) of mix: calories: 45, protein: 2 g, fat: 0.2 g, carbohydrate: 10 g, dietary fiber: 3 g, calcium: 27 mg, iron: 0.8 mg, magnesium: 20 mg, sodium: 20 mg, zinc: 0.4 mg, folate: 43 mcg, riboflavin: 0.1 mg, vitamin C: 38 mg, vitamin E: 0.4 mg, omega-3 fatty acids: 0 g.

% CALORIES FROM: protein 16%,   fat 4%,   carbohydrate 80%

Confetti Coleslaw

A blend of fresh flavors and bright colors combine to make this coleslaw stand out from the ordinary. It's a delicious accompaniment to spicy chili or any bean dish or soup, and it's always a potluck favorite.

2 cups	thinly sliced or shredded red cabbage	500 ml
½ cup	thinly sliced or shredded green cabbage	125 ml
1	large carrot, shredded	1
1	red or yellow bell pepper, finely diced	1
½	small red onion, thinly sliced	½
3 tablespoons	extra-virgin olive oil	45 ml
2 tablespoons	red or white wine vinegar	30 ml
1 teaspoon	sugar or other sweetener of your choice	5 ml
½ teaspoon	prepared yellow mustard	2 ml
	Salt and pepper	

Combine the cabbage, carrot, pepper, and onion in a large bowl and toss well. Whisk together the remaining ingredients and pour over the vegetables. Toss to thoroughly combine. Chill for at least 1 hour before serving.

VARIATION: For Creamy Coleslaw, use ½ cup (125 ml) Beannaise, page 288, or more to taste, instead of the oil.

PER CUP (250 ML): calories: 130, protein: 1 g, fat: 11 g, carbohydrate: 8 g, dietary fiber: 2 g, calcium: 32 mg, iron: 0.5 mg, magnesium: 13 mg, sodium: 59 mg, zinc: 0.2 mg, folate: 22 mcg, riboflavin: 0 mg, vitamin C: 82 mg, vitamin E: 2 mg, omega-3 fatty acids: 0.1 g.

% CALORIES FROM: protein 4%,   fat 71%,   carbohydrate 25%

CONTAINS: * FERMENTED foods (MUSTARD; VINEGAR)

Apricot Slaw

Here's a coleslaw with a special twist. It's also rich in vitamin E and omega-3 fatty acids (from the canola oil). We recommend organic canola oil (so you'll be certain that it's not genetically modified), which is rich in omega-3s. If possible, let the salad rest an hour or so before serving so the flavors have a chance to marry.

1 (6 cups)	medium cabbage, shredded	1500 ml
2	large carrots, grated	2
½ cup	finely chopped dried apricots	125 ml
⅓ cup	organic canola or safflower oil	85 ml
1 tablespoon	pure maple syrup	15 ml
3 tablespoons	white wine vinegar or fresh lemon juice	45 ml
⅛–¼ teaspoon	ground nutmeg	pinch–1 ml
½–1 teaspoon	celery seeds (optional)	2–5 ml
	Salt	

Combine the cabbage, carrots, and apricots in a large bowl. In a separate small bowl, whisk together the oil, maple syrup, vinegar, and nutmeg until emulsified. Pour over the cabbage and toss to mix. Sprinkle with the optional celery seeds and season with salt to taste. Toss again until evenly combined.

PER CUP (250 ML): calories: 157, protein: 1.5 g, fat: 11 g, carbohydrate: 15 g, dietary fiber: 2.6 g, calcium: 42 mg, iron: 1 mg, magnesium: 13 mg, sodium: 41 mg, zinc: 0.3 mg, folate: 29 mcg, riboflavin: 0 mg, vitamin C: 23 mg, vitamin E: 2.4 mg, omega-3 fatty acids: 1 g.

% CALORIES FROM: protein 4%,   fat 61%,   carbohydrate 36%

TUNISIAN NEW POTATO SALAD

Requiring just a few familiar ingredients, this unique and tangy vinaigrette potato salad is sure to be a hit with your family and friends.

1 pound	new potatoes	450 g
¼ cup	fresh lemon juice	60 ml
¼ cup	extra-virgin olive oil	60 ml
1 teaspoon	ground cumin	5 ml
½ teaspoon	paprika	2 ml
Pinch	of cayenne	Pinch
	Salt	

B oil the potatoes in salted water until tender. Cut in half, if small, or quarters, if large. Dress with the lemon juice, oil, cumin, paprika, cayenne, and salt to taste. Toss gently. Serve warm or thoroughly chilled.

PER CUP (250 ML): calories: 223, protein: 2.5 g, fat: 14 g, carbohydrate: 22 g, dietary fiber: 3 g, calcium: 21 mg, iron: 1.4 mg, magnesium: 28 mg, sodium: 48 mg, zinc: 0.4 mg, folate: 34 mcg, riboflavin: 0 mg, vitamin C: 26 mg, vitamin E: 1.8 mg, omega-3 fatty acids: 0.1 g.

% CALORIES FROM: protein 5%,   fat 56%,   carbohydrate 39%

CONTAINS: * CITRUS (LEMON) * POTATO

MEXICAN POTATO SALAD

This colorful and delightfully different potato salad is low in fat but high in flavor and very easy to prepare.

1 pound	red potatoes, cut into bite-size chunks	450 g
1 tablespoon	extra-virgin olive oil	15 ml
1	small onion, diced	1
1 teaspoon	crushed garlic	5 ml
1 (15- or 16-ounce) can	yellow corn, drained	1 (425–450 g) can
1	large ripe tomato, diced	1
1 cup	chopped fresh cilantro	250 ml
½ cup	vegetable broth	125 ml
2 tablespoons	fresh lime juice	30 ml
	Salt	
	Pepper	
	Cayenne	

S team the potatoes until tender, and transfer them to a large bowl. While the potatoes are steaming, heat the oil in a medium skillet. When hot, add the onion and garlic and sauté until the onion is tender, about 10 minutes. Add to the potatoes along with the corn, tomato, and cilantro. Pour the vegetable broth and lime juice over the salad and toss gently to combine. Season with salt, pepper, and cayenne to taste, and gently toss again until the seasonings are evenly distributed. Serve warm or thoroughly chilled.

PER CUP (250 ML): calories: 200, protein: 4.5 g, fat: 4 g, carbohydrate: 41 g, dietary fiber: 4.5 g, calcium: 22 mg, iron: 1.3 mg, magnesium: 28 mg, sodium: 333 mg, zinc: 0.5 mg, folate: 62 mcg, riboflavin: 0.1 mg, vitamin C: 26 mg, vitamin E: 1.0 mg, omega-3 fatty acids: 0 g.

% CALORIES FROM: protein 8%, fat 18%, carbohydrate 74%

CONTAINS: * CITRUS (LIME) * CORN * POTATO * TOMATO

CHILLED NOODLES IN A SPICY SAUCE

Yields about 4 cups (1 L)

Enticing, enchanting, and irresistible!

½ cup	sesame tahini or other seed butter (see page 176), or crunchy or smooth almond butter	125 ml
2 tablespoons	balsamic vinegar	30 ml
2 tablespoons	toasted sesame oil or extra-virgin olive oil	30 ml
1 tablespoon	fresh lemon juice or umeboshi vinegar	15 ml
2 teaspoons	grated fresh ginger, or ½ teaspoon (2 ml) ground ginger	10 ml
1 teaspoon	pure maple syrup or brown rice syrup	5 ml
½ teaspoon	crushed garlic	2 ml
	Cayenne, chipotle pepper, or Tabasco	
	Salt	
	Water, as needed	
12 ounces	brown rice spaghetti or corn spaghetti	340 g

OPTIONAL ADDITIONS AND GARNISHES:

- Chopped fresh cilantro or parsley
- Grated carrots
- Grated or very thinly sliced cabbage (napa, green, or red)
- Minced jalapeño pepper
- Red, yellow, orange, or green bell peppers, cut into matchsticks
- Sliced or diced water chestnuts or jicama
- Thinly sliced scallions
- Toasted sesame seeds, pumpkin seeds, sunflower seeds, or slivered almonds

Combine the tahini, vinegar, oil, lemon juice, ginger, syrup, garlic, and cayenne pepper and salt to taste in a large bowl. Stir vigorously until smooth and well combined. Gradually whisk in enough water, about 1 cup (250 ml), to make a pourable sauce.

Boil the noodles in salted water until just tender. Drain well. Rinse well under cold water, then drain again. Add to the bowl with the sauce and any optional additions of your choice and toss until evenly coated. Adjust salt seasoning, if necessary. Chill thoroughly before serving. The noodles will absorb any excess sauce as they chill. Garnish with scallions, cilantro, and/or toasted seeds or almonds, if desired.

PER ½ CUP (125 ML): calories: 281, protein: 9 g, fat: 13 g, carbohydrate: 34 g, dietary fiber: 3 g, calcium: 39 mg, iron: 2.8 mg, magnesium: 61 mg, sodium: 88 mg, zinc: 2 mg, folate: 15 mcg, riboflavin: 0.1 mg, vitamin C: 2 mg, vitamin E: 0.6 mg, omega-3 fatty acids: 0.1 g.

% CALORIES FROM: protein 13%, fat 40%, carbohydrate 47%

CONTAINS: * FERMENTED foods (VINEGAR)

WARM NOODLES WITH A SEED SAUCE AND SNOW PEAS

Almost everyone agrees this noodle salad is irresistible. Although it is best served warm or at room temperature, chilled leftovers make an awesome packed lunch or picnic meal, It's rich in thiamin, iron, zinc, and protein and will give you energy through the afternoon. Toasted sesame oil has a lovely flavor and aroma. For economy you may use a combination of regular sesame oil and the toasted oil. If you cannot have sesame, substitute olive oil.

1 pound	brown rice noodles or corn noodles (linguini, fettuccine, or spaghetti)	450 g
3 tablespoons	toasted sesame oil or extra-virgin olive oil	45 ml
½ pound	snow peas, trimmed	225 g
½ cup	sesame tahini or other seed butter (see page 176)	125 ml
2 tablespoons	balsamic vinegar or fresh lime juice	30 ml
1 teaspoon	crushed garlic	5 ml
1 teaspoon	sweetener of your choice	5 ml
	Salt	
	Cayenne	
¼ cup	water, more or less as needed	60 ml
1	English cucumber, diced or cut into half-moons	1
2	scallions, thinly sliced	1

Cook the noodles in boiling, salted water until tender. Drain in a colander, refresh under cold running water, and drain again. Transfer to a large bowl and toss with the sesame or olive oil (this will help keep the noodles from sticking together). While the noodles cook, blanch the snow peas in boiling water for 1 minute. Drain, cool, and cut into thirds or quarters. Set aside.

In a medium bowl, cream together the tahini, vinegar, garlic, sweetener, salt, and cayenne to taste. Beating with a fork, add just enough water to make a thick but pourable sauce. Pour over the cooked noodles, add the reserved snow peas, cucumber, and scallions, and toss gently but thoroughly. Adjust seasonings, if necessary. Serve warm or at room temperature.

PER CUP (250 ML): calories: 289, protein: 9.5 g, fat: 12 g, carbohydrate: 37 g, dietary fiber: 4 g, calcium: 49 mg, iron: 3.3 mg, magnesium: 69 mg, sodium: 88 mg, zinc: 2 mg, folate: 25 mcg, riboflavin: 0.1 mg, vitamin C: 15 mg, vitamin E: 0.5 mg, omega-3 fatty acids: 0.1 g.

% CALORIES FROM: protein 13%,   fat 37%,   carbohydrate 50%

WARM BROWN RICE AND BRUSSELS SPROUTS SALAD

Yields about 6 cups (1.5 L)

The natural sweetness of the rice and the bright, lively seasonings perfectly complement the mildly astringent sprouts, drawing out their tastiest qualities. What's more, this combination is rich in the minerals copper, iron, magnesium, manganese, selenium, and zinc.

2¼ cups	water	560 ml
1 cup	brown rice (or a blend of various brown and wild rices)	250 ml
1 pound	fresh brussels sprouts	450 g
2–3 tablespoons	fresh lemon juice or red wine vinegar	30–45 ml
2 tablespoons	toasted sesame oil	30 ml
1 tablespoon	hot pepper sesame oil (see tip below)	15 ml
1 tablespoon	balsamic vinegar	15 ml
1 teaspoon	grated fresh ginger	5 ml
	Garlic powder	
	Salt	
2	roasted or fresh red bell peppers, diced or cut into matchsticks	2
½ cup	lightly toasted sunflower or pumpkin seeds, pignolia nuts, or slivered almonds (optional)	125 ml

Combine the water and rice in a very large pot. Bring to a boil, cover, reduce the heat, and simmer on low for 25 minutes. Meanwhile, trim and wash the brussels sprouts, and cut them lengthwise in half, if small, or in quarters, if large. Distribute the brussels sprouts evenly over the top of the rice, cover, and continue to cook 20–25 minutes longer or until the water is absorbed and the rice and brussels sprouts are tender. Remove from the heat and let rest, covered, 10 minutes.

Season with the lemon juice, sesame oils, balsamic vinegar, fresh ginger, and garlic powder and salt to taste. Toss gently. Serve warm, garnished with the red peppers and optional seeds.

TIP: The hot sesame oil adds a pleasant bite to this dish. If you prefer no heat, use an additional tablespoon (15 ml) of toasted sesame oil instead.

PER CUP (250 ML): calories: 221, protein: 5.5 g, fat: 8 g, carbohydrate: 34 g, dietary fiber: 5 g, calcium: 45 mg, iron: 1.7 mg, magnesium: 67 mg, sodium: 51 mg, zinc: 1 mg, folate: 62 mcg, riboflavin: 0.1 mg, vitamin C: 142 mg, vitamin E: 1.4 mg, omega-3 fatty acids: 0.1 g.

% CALORIES FROM: protein 10%,   fat 31%,   carbohydrate 59%

CONTAINS: * FERMENTED foods (vinegar) * SESAME

CURRIED RICE AND FRUIT SALAD WITH APRICOT DRESSING

Apricot preserves make a light and flavorful foundation for the salad dressing, while the unique combination of fruits and seasonings creates an exotic and delightful taste sensation.

4 cups	water	1 L
2 cups	white basmati rice	500 ml
2 tablespoons	organic canola or safflower oil	30 ml
1 tablespoon	curry powder	15 ml
1 tablespoon	grated fresh ginger	15 ml
1 teaspoon	salt	5 ml
½ teaspoon	crushed garlic	2 ml
2	crisp apples (such as Granny Smith), diced (peeling is optional)	2
1½ cups	well-drained crushed pineapple packed in juice	375 ml
1	ripe banana, sliced	1
½ cup	chopped fresh cilantro	125 ml
⅓ cup	unsweetened shredded coconut	85 ml
1 tablespoon	dried mint	15 ml
½ cup	fruit-sweetened apricot preserves	125 ml
2 tablespoons	fresh lemon juice	30 ml
	Chipotle chili powder or cayenne (optional)	

Combine the water, rice, 1 tablespoon (15 ml) of the oil, curry powder, fresh ginger, salt, and garlic in a large saucepan and bring to a boil. Reduce the heat to low, cover, and simmer until the rice is tender and the water is absorbed, about 15 minutes. Fluff with a fork and allow to cool.

In a large bowl, combine the cooled rice, apples, pineapple, banana, cilantro, coconut, and mint. In a separate small bowl, combine the preserves, lemon juice, and remaining 1 tablespoon (15 ml) of oil. Stir or whisk until well combined and pour over the salad. Season with chili powder or cayenne to taste. Adjust salt seasoning, if necessary. Serve immediately.

PER CUP (250 ML): calories: 240, protein: 3 g, fat: 5 g, carbohydrate: 49 g, dietary fiber: 2.5 g, calcium: 16 mg, iron: 0.6 mg, magnesium: 16 mg, sodium: 218 mg, zinc: 0.2 mg, folate: 7 mcg, riboflavin: 0 mg, vitamin C: 7 mg, vitamin E: 0.7 mg, omega-3 fatty acids: 0.3 g.

% CALORIES FROM: protein 5%,   fat 18%,   carbohydrate 77%

CONTAINS: * CITRUS (LEMON)

Rice, Zucchini, and Corn Salad

Yields about 7½ cups (1.875 L)

Here is a nourishing, whole-grain salad that will satisfy the hungriest of appetites.

3 cups	cooked brown rice, or a mixture of brown and wild rice	750 ml
1 pound	small zucchinis, cut in half lengthwise and sliced into half moons	450 g
2 cups	cooked whole corn kernels (fresh, frozen, or drained canned)	500 ml
¼ cup	thinly sliced scallions	60 ml
¼ cup	extra-virgin olive oil	60 ml
3 tablespoons	fresh lemon juice	45 ml
2 teaspoons	Dijon mustard	10 ml
2 teaspoons	dill weed	10 ml
	Salt	

Combine the rice, zucchini, corn, and scallions in a large bowl. In a separate bowl, whisk together the oil, lemon juice, mustard, dill weed, and salt to taste. Pour over the rice and vegetables and toss well. Adjust seasoning, if necessary. Serve warm or thoroughly chilled.

Per cup (250 ml): calories: 208, protein: 4.5 g, fat: 9 g, carbohydrate: 31 g, dietary fiber: 3.5 g, calcium: 28 mg, iron: 1.1 mg, magnesium: 62 mg, sodium: 63 mg, zinc: 0.9 mg, folate: 33 mcg, riboflavin: 0.1 mg, vitamin C: 11 mg, vitamin E: 1.6 mg, omega-3 fatty acids: 0.1 g.

% Calories from: protein 8%, fat 36%, carbohydrate 56%

CONTAINS: * Citrus (lemon) * Corn * Fermented foods (mustard)

MEDITERRANEAN DILLED VEGETABLE AND RICE SALAD

Yields about 10 cups (2.5 L)

Kalamata olives and dill weed add a lot of flavor to this salad, so a light dressing suits it quite well. To turn this dish into a delicious main course, serve it on a bed of mixed salad greens.

3 cups	cooked white or basmati rice	750 ml
3	ripe tomatoes, diced	3
1	medium zucchini, diced	1
1	red bell pepper, diced	1
1 cup	frozen peas, cooked according to package directions and drained	250 ml
⅔ cup	chopped kalamata olives	170 ml
¼ cup	diced red onions	60 ml
3 tablespoons	fresh lemon juice	45 ml
2 tablespoons	extra-virgin olive oil	30 ml
1 tablespoon	dried dill weed	15 ml
	Salt and pepper	

Combine all the ingredients in a large bowl and toss gently. Serve at once.

PER CUP (250 ML): calories: 136, protein: 3 g, fat: 4 g, carbohydrate: 22 g, dietary fiber: 2 g, calcium: 25 mg, iron: 1.8 mg, magnesium: 23 mg, sodium: 115 mg, zinc: 0.5 mg, folate: 54 mcg, riboflavin: 0.1 mg, vitamin C: 37 mg, vitamin E: 1.0 mg, omega-3 fatty acids: 0.1 g.

% CALORIES FROM: protein 8%, fat 27%, carbohydrate 65%

CONTAINS: * CITRUS (LEMON) * FERMENTED foods (olives) * TOMATO

Tri-Color Quinoa-Corn Salad

Quinoa turns this tasty salad into a satisfying meal, with a good balance of protein, healthful fats, and carbohydrate, plus the minerals iron, zinc, and magnesium. The multitude of colors from the vegetables makes it especially appetizing.

2 cups	water	500 ml
1 cup	quinoa, rinsed well and drained	250 ml
½ teaspoon	salt	2 ml
2 cups	cooked corn kernels (fresh, frozen, or drained canned)	500 ml
1	red bell pepper, cut into small dice	1
½ cup	thinly sliced scallions	125 ml
3–4 tablespoons	extra-virgin olive oil	45–60 ml
3 tablespoons	fresh lemon juice	45 ml
2 teaspoons	Dijon mustard	10 ml
	Salt and pepper	

Place the water in a heavy pot and bring to a boil over high heat. Stir in the quinoa and salt, cover, and reduce the heat to low. Cook for 15 minutes. Remove from the heat and let rest, covered, for 5 minutes. Fluff with a fork and transfer to a large bowl. Stir in the corn, bell pepper, and scallions.

In a small bowl, whisk together the oil, lemon juice, and mustard. Pour over the quinoa and vegetables and toss gently. Season with salt and pepper to taste. Serve warm or thoroughly chilled.

VARIATION: Replace the olive oil with flaxseed oil or a mixture of half olive oil and half flaxseed oil.

PER CUP (250 ML): calories: 221, protein: 5.5 g, fat: 9 g, carbohydrate: 33 g, dietary fiber: 3.5 g, calcium: 32 mg, iron: 3.1 mg, magnesium: 75 mg, sodium: 275 mg, zinc: 1.3 mg, folate: 42 mcg, riboflavin: 0.2 mg, vitamin C: 44 mg, vitamin E: 2.4 mg, omega-3 fatty acids: 0.1 g.

% CALORIES FROM: protein 10%, fat 34%, carbohydrate 56%

CONTAINS: * Citrus (lemon) * Corn * Fermented foods (mustard)

Quinoa Tabouli

Yields about 10 cups (2.5 L)

Quinoa makes an ideal substitute for bulgur and combines well with the traditional Middle Eastern flavors of this time-honored salad.

1½ cups	quinoa, rinsed well and drained	375 ml
3 cups	water	750 ml
2 cups	coarsely chopped fresh parsley	500 ml
2 cups	cherry tomatoes, cut in half	500 ml
1	English cucumber, peeled and diced	1
⅔ cup	sliced scallions or chives	170 ml
¼ cup	fresh lemon juice	60 ml
3 tablespoons	extra-virgin olive oil	45 ml
4 teaspoons	dried mint	20 ml
	Salt and pepper	

Place the quinoa in a medium saucepan over medium heat and toast it until the grains are dry, fragrant, and turn a shade darker, about 5 minutes. Add the water and bring to a boil. Cover, reduce the heat to low, and simmer 12–15 minutes or until all the water is absorbed and the grain is tender. Remove from the heat and let stand, covered, 5 minutes.

Fluff the quinoa with a fork and transfer it to a large bowl. Let it cool, fluffing it occasionally with a fork. When cool, add the parsley, tomatoes, cucumber, scallions, lemon juice, oil, mint, and salt and pepper to taste. Toss gently until evenly mixed. Adjust seasonings, if necessary. Serve at once or thoroughly chilled.

VARIATIONS: Instead of cherry tomatoes, substitute 2 large ripe tomatoes, diced.

- To turn this salad into a more substantial main dish, add one or more of the following:
  * 1–1¾ cups (250–435 ml) drained cooked or canned chickpeas
  * 1 cup (250 ml) halved and thinly sliced red radishes
  * 1 cup (250 ml) diced carrots

PER CUP (250 ML): calories: 151, protein: 4.5 g, fat: 6 g, carbohydrate: 22 g, dietary fiber: 3 g, calcium: 47 mg, iron: 3.6 mg, magnesium: 70 mg, sodium: 35 mg, zinc: 1.1 mg, folate: 45 mcg, riboflavin: 0.1 mg, vitamin C: 26 mg, vitamin E: 2.1 mg, omega-3 fatty acids: 0.1 g.

% CALORIES FROM: protein 11%,   fat 34%,   carbohydrate 55%

CONTAINS: * CITRUS (LEMON) * TOMATO

Citrus Fruit and Grain Salad

Yields about 7 cups (1.75 L)

Tart and juicy, this scrumptious salad uses fresh fruit and pantry staples to create the centerpiece of a meal.

4 cups	cooked whole grains (brown rice, wild rice, quinoa, or a combination)	1 L
2	navel oranges, peeled and chopped	2
½ cup	minced fresh parsley	125 ml
⅓ cup	raisins	85 ml
¼ cup	extra-virgin olive oil	60 ml
3 tablespoons	fresh lemon juice	45 ml
1 tablespoon	wine vinegar (red, white, or balsamic)	15 ml
2 teaspoons	Dijon mustard	10 ml
	Salt and pepper	

Combine the cooked grains, oranges, parsley, and raisins in a large bowl. In a small bowl, whisk together the oil, lemon juice, vinegar, and mustard. Pour over the grain and fruit and toss well. Season with salt and pepper and toss again. Serve chilled.

PER CUP (250 ML)*: calories: 224, protein: 4 g, fat: 9 g, carbohydrate: 33 g, dietary fiber: 3 g, calcium: 36 mg, iron: 1.6 mg, magnesium: 53 mg, sodium: 65 mg, zinc: 1 mg, folate: 35 mcg, riboflavin: 0.1 mg, vitamin C: 32 mg, vitamin E: 1.8 mg, omega-3 fatty acids: 0.1 g.

% CALORIES FROM: protein 7%,   fat 35%,   carbohydrate 57%

*Nutritional analysis done using a combination of brown rice, wild rice, and quinoa.

CONTAINS: * Citrus (lemon; orange)
* Fermented foods (mustard; vinegar)

Yellow Rice and Black Bean Salad

Yields about 7½ cups (1.875 L)

This hearty, colorful salad blends a variety of tangy flavors to create a memorable main dish. Turmeric, a potent anticancer agent, gives the rice a golden hue. The optional addition of chipotle chili powder adds a bit of smoky heat that perfectly complements the other seasonings.

3 cups	water	750 ml
1 teaspoon	salt	5 ml
1 teaspoon	crushed garlic	5 ml
¼ teaspoon	turmeric	1 ml
1½ cups	white basmati rice	375 ml
1¾ cups	drained cooked or canned black beans (one 15- or 16-ounce/425–450 g can)	435 ml
1	red or green bell pepper, diced	1
1	ripe tomato, diced	1
½ cup	chopped fresh cilantro	125 ml
¼ cup	sliced scallions	60 ml
3 tablespoons	fresh lime or lemon juice	45 ml
2 tablespoons	extra-virgin olive oil	30 ml
1 tablespoon	red wine vinegar	15 ml
	Salt and pepper	
	Chipotle chili powder (optional)	

Place the water, salt, garlic, and turmeric in a large pot and bring to a boil. Stir in the rice, reduce the heat to low, cover tightly, and simmer until the rice is tender and the water is absorbed, about 15 minutes. Remove from the heat, fluff with a fork, and set aside to cool.

Combine the cooled rice, beans, bell pepper, tomato, cilantro, and scallions in a large bowl and toss gently. In a separate small bowl, combine the lime juice, oil, and vinegar. Pour over the beans and toss to combine. Season with salt, pepper, and the optional chipotle chili powder to taste.

Per cup (250 ml): calories: 242, protein: 7 g, fat: 5 g, carbohydrate: 44 g, dietary fiber: 5 g, calcium: 24 mg, iron: 1.4 mg, magnesium: 34 mg, sodium: 436 mg, zinc: 0.5 mg, folate: 70 mcg, riboflavin: 0.1 mg, vitamin C: 38 mg, vitamin E: 0.8 mg, omega-3 fatty acids: 0.1 g.

% Calories from: protein 12%, fat 17%, carbohydrate 71%

CONTAINS: * Citrus (lime or lemon)
* Fermented foods (vinegar) * Tomato

Salads and Dressings 275

Ruby Wild Rice Salad

Yields about 8½ cups (2.125 L)

This salad fits the bill for holiday gatherings and other special occasions, as well as everyday feasts. It is made with dried cranberries, which look like glistening rubies. Radishes and seeds add crunch.

4 cups	cooked wild rice (about 1¾ cups/435 ml dry)	1000 ml
1¼ cups	diced daikon (Japanese radish) or other radishes	310 ml
1 cup	sunflower or pumpkin seeds, lightly pan toasted (see page 353)	250 ml
1 cup	sweetened dried cranberries	250 ml
1	orange, yellow, or red bell pepper, diced	1
½ cup	sliced scallions	125 ml
⅓ cup	orange juice	85 ml
2 tablespoons	balsamic vinegar	30 ml
2 tablespoons	extra-virgin olive oil	30 ml
1 teaspoon	Dijon mustard	5 ml
	Salt and pepper	

Combine the cooked wild rice, daikon, seeds, cranberries, bell pepper, and scallions in a large bowl. Toss to mix. In a separate small bowl, whisk together the orange juice, vinegar, oil, and mustard until well combined. Pour over the salad and toss gently until evenly distributed. Season with salt and pepper to taste. Chill or serve at once.

TIP: See page 168 for instructions on cooking wild rice, and page 132 for its nutritional attributes.

PER CUP (250 ML): calories: 258, protein: 6.5 g, fat: 11 g, carbohydrate: 36 g, dietary fiber: 4.5 g, calcium: 25 mg, iron: 1.4 mg, magnesium: 51 mg, sodium: 92 mg, zinc: 1.9 mg, folate: 69 mcg, riboflavin: 0.1 mg, vitamin C: 36 mg, vitamin E: 8.35 mg, omega-3 fatty acids: 0.1 g.

% CALORIES FROM: protein 10%, fat 38%, carbohydrate 53%

CONTAINS: * CITRUS (ORANGE)
* FERMENTED foods (MUSTARD; VINEGAR)

Tasty Taco Salad

This dish makes a wonderful addition to any picnic or barbecue. Make sure to add the tortilla chips just before serving to keep them crisp. Their crunchiness is a pleasant foil for the tender vegetables and beans.

1¾ cups	drained cooked or canned pinto beans (one 15-ounce/425 g can)	435 ml
1¾ cups	drained cooked or canned black beans (one 15-ounce/425 g can)	435 ml
1½ cups	fresh, thawed frozen, or drained canned corn	375 ml
1	ripe tomato, diced	1
1	green bell pepper, diced	1
½ cup	chopped fresh cilantro or parsley (or a mix of each)	125 ml
¼ cup	diced red onion	60 ml
2 tablespoons	extra-virgin olive oil	30 ml
2 tablespoons	ketchup	30 ml
2 tablespoons	fresh lime juice	30 ml
1 tablespoon	white wine vinegar	15 ml
2 teaspoons	sugar or other sweetener of your choice	10 ml
1 teaspoon	chili powder	5 ml
½ teaspoon	ground cumin	2 ml
½ teaspoon	crushed garlic	2 ml
	Salt and pepper	
	Tabasco or other bottled hot pepper sauce	
	Shredded lettuce or mixed salad greens	
	Baked tortilla chips, for garnish	

Combine the beans, corn, tomato, bell pepper, cilantro, and onion in a large bowl. In a separate small bowl, whisk together the oil, ketchup, lime juice, vinegar, sugar, chili powder, cumin, garlic, and salt, pepper, and Tabasco to taste. Pour over the salad, toss gently, and let rest in the refrigerator 30 to 60 minutes to allow the flavors to blend.

To serve, make a bed of lettuce on a serving platter or individual salad plates. Mound the salad on top and garnish with the tortilla chips just before serving.

PER CUP (250 ML): calories: 194, protein: 8 g, fat: 5 g, carbohydrate: 32 g, dietary fiber: 8 g, calcium: 54 mg, iron: 2.2 mg, magnesium: 57 mg, sodium: 367 mg, zinc: 1.1 mg, folate: 112 mcg, riboflavin: 0.1 mg, vitamin C: 23 mg, vitamin E: 1.4 mg, omega-3 fatty acids: 0.2 g.

% CALORIES FROM: protein 16%, fat 22%, carbohydrate 62%

CONTAINS: * CITRUS (LIME) * CORN * TOMATO
* FERMENTED foods (KETCHUP; VINEGAR)

Marinated Vegetable, Bean, and Olive Salad

This crunchy vegetable salad is very easy to prepare, but it needs to marinate for several hours for its full flavor to develop.

2 cups	bite-size cauliflower florets (about 1/2 pound/225 g)	500 ml
1 cup	cut green beans (in 1-inch/2.5 cm lengths)	250 ml
1	medium carrot, diced	1
1¾ cups	drained cooked or canned red kidney beans (one 15- or 16-ounce/425–450 g can)	435 ml
1 (14-ounce) can	water-packed artichoke hearts, drained	1 (397 ml) can
1	green or red bell pepper, diced	1
20	pitted kalamata olives	20
¼ cup	diced red onion	60 ml
	Salt and pepper	
¼ cup	red wine vinegar	60 ml
½ teaspoon	crushed garlic	2 ml
1 teaspoon	dried oregano	5 ml
½ teaspoon	dried basil	2 ml
3 tablespoons	extra-virgin olive oil	45 ml

Blanch or steam the cauliflower, green beans, and carrot until tender-crisp. Refresh under cold water to stop the cooking and drain well. Transfer to a large bowl and add the kidney beans, artichoke hearts, bell pepper, olives, onion, and salt and pepper to taste.

In a separate small bowl, whisk together the vinegar, garlic, oregano, and basil. Beat in the oil until well blended. Pour over the vegetables and kidney beans and toss gently. Cover and refrigerate a minimum of 4 hours or overnight, tossing occasionally. Adjust seasonings before serving, if necessary.

PER CUP (250 ML): calories: 167, protein: 6 g, fat: 8 g, carbohydrate: 19 g, dietary fiber: 5.5 g, calcium: 39 mg, iron: 1.3 mg, magnesium: 29 mg, sodium: 680 mg, zinc: 0.5 mg, folate: 53 mcg, riboflavin: 0.1 mg, vitamin C: 35 mg, vitamin E: 1.0 mg, omega-3 fatty acids: 0.1 g.

% CALORIES FROM: protein 14%,   fat 42%,   carbohydrate 44%

CONTAINS: * Fermented foods (olives; vinegar)

COLORFUL FRENCH LENTIL SALAD WITH KALAMATA OLIVES

Yields 6–8 servings (about 7 cups/1.75 L of bean salad, not including the mixed greens)

Sharp, tangy kalamata olives perfectly complement the earthy flavor of lentils. French lentils, which are a small variety, are best for this salad as they are firm and hold their shape well. If starting with uncooked lentils, use 1½ cups (375 ml) of dry lentils to get 3 cups (750 ml) of cooked lentils.

3 cups	drained cooked or canned French lentils (two 15- or 16-ounce/425–450 g cans)	750 ml
3	bell peppers (1 green, 1 red, 1 yellow or orange), diced	3
½ cup	sliced kalamata olives	125 ml
½ cup	chopped fresh cilantro or parsley	125 ml
2 teaspoons	dried mint, crumbled	10 ml
⅓ cup	fresh lemon juice	85 ml
3 tablespoons	extra-virgin olive oil	45 ml
2 tablespoons	white wine vinegar	30 ml
1 teaspoon	Dijon mustard	5 ml
½ teaspoon	crushed garlic	2 ml
	Salt and pepper	
12 cups	mixed salad greens (about ½ pound/225 g)	3000 ml

Combine the lentils, bell peppers, olives, cilantro, and mint in a large bowl, and toss gently. In a separate small bowl, whisk together the lemon juice, oil, vinegar, mustard, garlic, and salt and pepper to taste until well combined. Pour over the lentils and toss gently. Adjust seasonings if necessary. To serve, line individual salad plates or a large serving platter with the salad greens and spoon the lentil mixture on top.

TIP: For instructions on how to cook French lentils, see page 164.

PER 2 CUPS (500 ML): calories: 132, protein: 6 g, fat: 5 g, carbohydrate: 16 g, dietary fiber: 6 g, calcium: 39 mg, iron: 2.8 mg, magnesium: 31 mg, sodium: 236 mg, zinc: 0.9 mg, folate: 142 mcg, riboflavin: 0.1 mg, vitamin C: 54 mg, vitamin E: 1.2 mg, omega-3 fatty acids: 0.1 g.

% CALORIES FROM: protein 18%,   fat 35%,   carbohydrate 47%

CONTAINS: * Citrus (lemon)
* Fermented foods (mustard; olives; vinegar)

Dilled White Bean and Tomato Salad

Yields about 5 cups (1.25 L)

This salad is especially delightful when fresh dill weed and summer tomatoes are in season. It's an excellent source of protein, folate, and minerals.

3 cups	drained cooked or canned chickpeas (two 15- or 16-ounce/425–450 g cans)	750 ml
1	small (or ½ large) red onion, halved and thinly sliced	1
2 tablespoons	fresh lemon juice	30 ml
2 tablespoons	white wine vinegar	30 ml
3 tablespoons	chopped fresh dill weed, or 1 tablespoon (15 ml) dried dill weed	45 ml
1 teaspoon	salt	5 ml
¼ teaspoon	pepper	1 ml
3 tablespoons	extra-virgin olive oil	45 ml
1	large ripe tomato, chopped	1

Combine the beans and onion in a large bowl and toss gently. In a separate small bowl, whisk together the lemon juice, vinegar, dill weed, salt, and pepper. Vigorously whisk in the oil until well blended. Pour over the beans and toss gently. Add the tomato just before serving, tossing gently until evenly incorporated.

Per cup (250 ml): calories: 252, protein: 9 g, fat: 11 g, carbohydrate: 30 g, dietary fiber: 8 g, calcium: 55 mg, iron: 3 mg, magnesium: 53 mg, sodium: 477 mg, zinc: 1.6 mg, folate: 179 mcg, riboflavin: 0.1 mg, vitamin C: 9 mg, vitamin E: 1.6 mg, omega-3 fatty acids: 0.1 g.

% Calories from: protein 14%, fat 39%, carbohydrate 47%

CONTAINS: * Citrus (lemon)
* Fermented foods (vinegar) * Tomato

CHICKPEA SALAD
WITH TOMATOES AND OLIVES

Yields about 8 cups (2 L)

This versatile salad can be a main course when served over a bed of tender salad greens, or it can be an accompaniment. Sharp-tasting greens, such as arugula, mizuna, watercress, and frizee, complement this dish nicely, so be sure to add some to your salad mix.

4 cups	drained cooked or canned chickpeas (two 15- or 16-ounce/425–450 g cans)	1000 ml
3	large ripe tomatoes, diced	3
½	medium onion, finely diced (about ¾ cup/185 ml)	½
¼ cup	chopped fresh mint, or 1 tablespoon (15 ml) dried mint	60 ml
2 tablespoons	fresh lemon juice	30 ml
2 tablespoons	white wine vinegar	30 ml
1 teaspoon	Dijon mustard	5 ml
¼–½ teaspoon	crushed garlic	1–2 ml
2 tablespoons	extra-virgin olive oil	30 ml
½ cup	sliced kalamata olives	125 ml
	Salt and pepper	

Combine the chickpeas, tomatoes, onion, and mint in a large bowl. In a separate small bowl, whisk together the lemon juice, vinegar, mustard, and garlic. Slowly whisk in the oil until well blended. Pour over the chickpeas and toss gently. Add the olives and toss again. Season with salt and pepper to taste. Let the salad rest in the refrigerator 30 minutes before serving to allow the flavors to blend.

PER CUP (250 ML): calories: 204, protein: 7 g, fat: 6 g, carbohydrate: 32 g, dietary fiber: 6.5 g, calcium: 58 mg, iron: 2.6 mg, magnesium: 45 mg, sodium: 475 mg, zinc: 1.4 mg, folate: 95 mcg, riboflavin: 0.1 mg, vitamin C: 20 mg, vitamin E: 1.2 mg, omega-3 fatty acids: 0.1 g.

% CALORIES FROM: protein 13%, fat 26%, carbohydrate 61%

CONTAINS: * Citrus (lemon)
* Fermented foods (mustard; olives; vinegar) * Tomato

Salad of Chickpeas, Tomato, and Seeds

Yields about 2½ cups (625 ml)

This delightful salad is a fine example of how simple ingredients often create the most memorable dishes. It is rich in protein, B vitamins (thiamin, riboflavin, niacin, folate, pyridoxine), iron, and zinc.

1¾ cups	drained cooked or canned chickpeas (one 15- or 16-ounce/425–450 g can)	435 ml
1	medium tomato, chopped	1
¼ cup	sunflower or pumpkin seeds, lightly pan toasted (see page 353)	60 ml
¼ cup	raisins	60 ml
¼ cup	chopped fresh cilantro or parsley	60 ml
2 tablespoons	fresh lemon juice	30 ml
1 tablespoon	extra-virgin olive oil	15 ml
	Salt and pepper	

Combine all the ingredients in a large bowl. Toss gently until well mixed. Adjust seasonings, if necessary. Serve at once to prevent the herbs from wilting and the tomato from weeping.

Variation: For a version that provides a day's supply of omega-3 fatty acids and then some (4.2 grams), use walnuts instead of seeds and replace the olive oil with 1 tablespoon flaxseed oil.

Per cup (250 ml): calories: 289, protein: 11 g, fat: 11 g, carbohydrate: 40 g, dietary fiber: 9 g, calcium: 66 mg, iron: 3.7 mg, magnesium: 67 mg, sodium: 14 mg, zinc: 2 mg, folate: 196 mcg, riboflavin: 0.1 mg, vitamin C: 18 mg, vitamin E: 5.7 mg, omega-3 fatty acids: 0.1 g.

% Calories from: protein 15%, fat 33%, carbohydrate 52%

CONTAINS: * Citrus (lemon) * Tomato

WHITE BEAN SALAD WITH CARROTS AND SUN-DRIED TOMATOES

Yields about 4½ cups (1.125 L)

Colorful and crunchy, this salad packs a jolt of flavor in every bite. It's also loaded with fiber, calcium, and iron, so eat up!

3 cups	drained cooked or canned white beans (two 15- or 16-ounce/425–450 g cans)	750 ml
6	sun-dried, oil-packed tomatoes, chopped	6
2	medium carrots, thinly sliced	2
2 tablespoons	red wine vinegar	30 ml
2 tablespoons	chopped fresh parsley	30 ml
1 tablespoon	drained capers	15 ml
1	large shallot, minced	1
½ teaspoon	crushed garlic	2 ml
½ teaspoon	Dijon mustard	2 ml
¼ teaspoon	salt	1 ml
¼ teaspoon	pepper	1 ml
3 tablespoons	extra-virgin olive oil	45 ml

Combine the beans, sun-dried tomatoes, and carrots in a large bowl and toss gently. In a separate small bowl, whisk together the vinegar, parsley, capers, shallot, garlic, mustard, salt, and pepper.

Vigorously whisk in the oil until well blended. Pour over the beans and toss gently to mix. Adjust seasonings, if necessary.

PER CUP (250 ML): calories: 319, protein: 13.5 g, fat: 11 g, carbohydrate: 44 g, dietary fiber: 10 g, calcium: 145 mg, iron: 5.8 mg, magnesium: 98 mg, sodium: 233 mg, zinc: 2.1 mg, folate: 121 mcg, riboflavin: 0.1 mg, vitamin C: 9 mg, vitamin E: 1.7 mg, omega-3 fatty acids: 0.1 g.

% CALORIES FROM: protein 17%, fat 29%, carbohydrate 54%

CONTAINS: * Fermented foods (CAPERS; MUSTARD; VINEGAR) * Tomato

Herbed Green and White Bean Salad with Tomatoes

Yields about 6 cups (1.5 L)

Tender-crisp green beans provide a crunchy snap in this heavenly combination of beans, tomatoes, and herbs. This salad makes a delicious accompaniment to simple rice, grain, or pasta dishes.

2½ cups	cut fresh or frozen green beans (cut in 1½-inch/3.5 cm lengths)	625 ml
1½ pounds	ripe tomatoes, diced (about 4 medium)	680 g
1¾ cups	drained cooked or canned white beans (one 15- or 16-ounce/425–450 g can)	435 ml
2 tablespoons	extra-virgin olive oil	30 ml
1 tablespoon	balsamic vinegar	15 ml
½ teaspoon	crushed garlic	2 ml
½ cup	chopped fresh basil, or 2 tablespoons (30 ml) dried basil	125 ml
¼ cup	chopped fresh mint, or 1 tablespoon (15 ml) dried mint	60 ml
	Salt and pepper	

Blanch or steam the green beans until tender-crisp. Refresh under cold water to stop the cooking and drain well. Place in a large bowl along with the tomatoes, white beans, oil, vinegar, and garlic, and toss gently. Add the herbs and salt and pepper to taste and toss again gently. Serve at once or thoroughly chilled, if using dried herbs. If using fresh herbs, serve within 1 hour.

PER CUP (250 ML): calories: 160, protein: 7.5 g, fat: 5 g, carbohydrate: 23 g, dietary fiber: 6.5 g, calcium: 100 mg, iron: 3.8 mg, magnesium: 62 mg, sodium: 44 mg, zinc: 1 mg, folate: 92 mcg, riboflavin: 0.2 mg, vitamin C: 44 mg, vitamin E: 1.8 mg, omega-3 fatty acids: 0.1 g.

% CALORIES FROM: protein 17%,   fat 28%,   carbohydrate 54%

CONTAINS: * FERMENTED foods (VINEGAR) * TOMATO

Chick-A-Dee Pea Salad

Yields about 2 cups (500 ml)

For an attractive luncheon, scoop this salad onto lettuce-lined plates, garnish it with a little paprika, and surround it with fresh tomato wedges. It's also delicious spread on crisp brown rice crackers or rice cakes. It has an excellent balance of protein, fat and carbohydrate.

1¾ cups	drained cooked or canned chickpeas (one 15- or 16-ounce/425–450 g can)	435 ml
½ cup	finely diced celery	125 ml
2 tablespoons	fresh lemon juice	30 ml
1 tablespoon	extra-virgin olive oil	15 ml
1	thinly sliced scallion, or grated onion to taste	1
2 tablespoons	minced fresh parsley (optional)	30 ml
2 teaspoons	well-drained pickle relish or chopped pickles	10 ml
2 teaspoons	brown mustard	10 ml
¼ teaspoon	paprika	1 ml
	Salt and pepper	

Chop the chickpeas in a food processor or mash them well with a potato masher or fork. Stir in the remaining ingredients and mix thoroughly. Chill before serving. Adjust seasonings, if necessary.

PER CUP (250 ML): calories: 323, protein: 13.5 g, fat: 11 g, carbohydrate: 45 g, dietary fiber: 12 g, calcium: 101 mg, iron: 4.8 mg, magnesium: 77 mg, sodium: 224 mg, zinc: 2.3 mg, folate: 268 mcg, riboflavin: 0.1 mg, vitamin C: 18 mg, vitamin E: 1.6 mg, omega-3 fatty acids: 0.1 g.

% CALORIES FROM: PROTEIN 16%,   FAT 30%,   CARBOHYDRATE 54%

CONTAINS: * Citrus (lemon)
* Fermented foods (mustard; pickles)

PINEAPPLE BLACK BEAN SALAD

Yields about 5 cups (1.25 L)

This exotic salad combines sweet pineapple, fragrant spices, and tart lime to produce the wonderful taste of the tropics.

3 cups	drained cooked or canned black beans (two 15- or 16-ounce/425–450 g cans)	750 ml
1	red or green bell pepper, diced	1
1 cup	drained crushed pineapple, packed in juice	250 ml
2	scallions, thinly sliced	2
½ teaspoon	ground allspice	2 ml
1 teaspoon	dried mint	5 ml
	Chipotle chili powder	
	Salt and pepper	
¼ cup	fresh lime juice	60 ml
2 tablespoons	orange juice	30 ml
2 tablespoons	extra-virgin olive oil	30 ml
¼–½ teaspoon	crushed garlic	1–2 ml

Combine the beans, bell pepper, pineapple, scallions, allspice, mint, and chili powder, salt, and pepper to taste in a large bowl. In a separate small bowl, whisk together the lime juice, orange juice, oil, and garlic until well combined. Pour over the bean mixture and toss gently until evenly distributed. Adjust seasonings, if necessary. Serve at once or store in the refrigerator and bring to room temperature before serving.

PER CUP (250 ML): calories: 233, protein: 10 g, fat: 6 g, carbohydrate: 36 g, dietary fiber: 10 g, calcium: 47 mg, iron: 2.6 mg, magnesium: 85 mg, sodium: 279 mg, zinc: 1.3 mg, folate: 169 mcg, riboflavin 0.1 mg, vitamin C: 34 mg, vitamin E: 1.0 mg, omega-3 fatty acids: 0.2 g.

% CALORIES FROM: protein 16%, fat 24%, carbohydrate 60%

CONTAINS: * CITRUS (LIME; ORANGE)

SOUTHERN-STYLE BLACK-EYED PEA AND CORN SALAD

Yields about 8 cups (2 L)

This colorful salad melds a variety of exciting flavors. It holds up well on a buffet table and makes a delightful contribution to any picnic spread.

2 cups	cooked white or brown rice	500 ml
2 cups	fresh, thawed frozen, or drained canned corn	500 ml
1¾ cups	drained cooked or canned black-eyed peas (one 15-ounce/425 g can)	435 ml
1	red bell pepper, finely diced	1
1	green bell pepper, finely diced	1
½ cup	sliced scallions	125 ml
½ cup	chopped fresh cilantro	125 ml
¼ cup	chopped green olives	60 ml
2 tablespoons	fresh lemon juice	30 ml
2 tablespoons	extra-virgin olive oil	30 ml
1 tablespoon	white wine vinegar	15 ml
	Salt and pepper	
	Tomato wedges, for garnish (optional)	

Combine the rice, corn, beans, bell peppers, scallions, cilantro, and olives in a large bowl. Add the lemon juice, oil, and vinegar, and toss gently to mix. Season with salt and pepper to taste and gently toss again. Serve at once or thoroughly chilled. Garnish with the optional tomato wedges just before serving.

PER CUP (250 ML): calories: 172, protein: 5 g, fat: 5 g, carbohydrate: 29 g, dietary fiber: 3.5 g, calcium: 28 mg, iron: 1.5 mg, magnesium: 31 mg, sodium: 218 mg, zinc: 0.8 mg, folate: 74 mcg, riboflavin: 0.1 mg, vitamin C: 36 mg, vitamin E: 0.9 mg, omega-3 fatty acids: 0.1 g.

% CALORIES FROM: protein 12%,   fat 24%,   carbohydrate 65%

CONTAINS: * Citrus (lemon) * Corn
* Fermented foods (olives; vinegar)

BEANNAISE

At last, a vegan mayonnaise that is moderately low in fat, healthful, delicious, and soy free! It also is far less expensive than store-bought vegan mayonnaise, yet it rivals the taste and versatility. Best of all, you just can't get any fresher than homemade. Use this creamy spread anywhere you would use mayonnaise—on sandwiches, in potato and pasta salads, or as a starting point for other sauces and dressings. You'll find endless ways to enjoy it, and every time you do you'll add a touch of luscious flavor, healthful dietary fiber, and a wonderful protein boost, too!

1¾ cups	drained cooked or canned white beans (one 15- or 16-ounce/425–450 g can)	435 ml
2 tablespoons	fresh lemon juice	30 ml
1 tablespoon	white wine vinegar or additional fresh lemon juice	15 ml
½ teaspoon	salt	2 ml
¼ teaspoon	dry mustard	1 ml
⅓ cup	extra-virgin olive oil	85 ml
⅓ cup	organic canola or safflower oil (or a blend of both)	85 ml

Place the beans, lemon juice, vinegar, salt, and dry mustard in a blender (for the smoothest dressing) or food processor fitted with a metal blade. Process until very creamy. With the appliance running, drizzle in the oils in a slow, steady stream through the cap opening in the lid. Continue processing until well blended and completely smooth, stopping to scrape down the sides of the container as needed. Chill thoroughly before using. Keeps about 7 days in the refrigerator. May be frozen.

PER 2 TABLESPOONS (30 ML): calories: 104, protein: 2 g, fat: 8 g, carbohydrate: 6 g, dietary fiber: 1 g, calcium: 19 mg, iron: 0.8 mg, magnesium: 13 mg, sodium: 66 mg, zinc: 0.3 mg, folate: 17 mcg, riboflavin: 0 mg, vitamin C: 1 mg, vitamin E: 1.4 mg, omega-3 fatty acids: 0.4 g.

% CALORIES FROM: protein 7%,   fat 71%,   carbohydrate 22%

CONTAINS: * CITRUS (LEMON)

AVOCADO MAYONNAISE

Yields about 2 cups (500 ml)

Keeps well for up to two days in the refrigerator.

2	large Hass avocados, mashed	2
2–5 tablespoons	extra-virgin olive oil	30–75 ml
2–5 tablespoons	apple cider vinegar or fresh lemon or lime juice	30–75 ml
2 tablespoons	orange juice	30 ml
2–3 teaspoons	pure maple syrup	10–15 ml
¼–½ teaspoon	crushed garlic	1–2 ml
¼–½ teaspoon	salt	1–2 ml

Combine all the ingredients in a food processor or blender and process until smooth. Start with the smaller amounts of oil and vinegar and add more only if needed to achieve a thick, rich, and creamy mayonnaise-like consistency.

PER 2 TABLESPOONS (30 ML): calories: 62, protein: 0.5 g, fat: 6 g, carbohydrate: 3 g, dietary fiber: 1 g, calcium: 5 mg, iron: 0.3 mg, magnesium: 9 mg, sodium: 40 mg, zinc: 0.2 mg, folate: 15 mcg, riboflavin: 0 mg, vitamin C: 3 mg, vitamin E: 0.5 mg, omega-3 fatty acids: 0 g.

% CALORIES FROM: protein 3%, fat 76%, carbohydrate 21%

CONTAINS: * CITRUS (ORANGE)

CREAMY TARRAGON DRESSING

Yields about 1 cup (250 ml)

Beyond topping salads, this dressing makes a lively sauce for potatoes, beans, and grains, as well as a luscious dip for raw veggies.

½ cup	water	125 ml
⅓ cup	sesame tahini or other seed butter (see page 176)	85 ml
¼ cup	umeboshi plum vinegar	60 ml
2 teaspoons	dried tarragon	10 ml

Combine all the ingredients in a small bowl and whisk vigorously until well blended and smooth. If a thinner sauce is needed, whisk in a small amount of additional water, about 1–2 teaspoons (5-10 ml) at a time, until the desired consistency is achieved.

PER 2 TABLESPOONS (30 ML): calories: 61, protein: 2 g, fat: 5 g, carbohydrate: 2 g, dietary fiber: 0.5 g, calcium: 20 mg, iron: 0.6 mg, magnesium: 10 mg, sodium: 4 mg, zinc: 0.5 mg, folate: 10 mcg, riboflavin: 0 mg, vitamin C: 0 mg, vitamin E: 0.2 mg, omega-3 fatty acids: 0 g.

% CALORIES FROM: protein 11%, fat 74%, carbohydrate 15%

CONTAINS: * FERMENTED foods (VINEGAR)

LEMON-SEED SALAD DRESSING

Yields 1 ⅓ cups (335 ml)

This dressing is sure to become a favorite on baked potatoes, salads, steamed broccoli, and other vegetables. You may prefer to replace half of the seed butter with flaxseed oil to add omega-3 fatty acids. With a little less water, it makes a terrific dip.

½ cup	sesame tahini or other seed butter (see page 176)	125 ml
¼ cup	fresh lemon juice	60 ml
1 teaspoon	Dijon or yellow mustard	5 ml
¼ teaspoon	crushed garlic	1 ml
1–2 tablespoons	balsamic vinegar	15–30 ml
½ cup	water	125 ml
	Pepper or cayenne	

Combine the tahini or other seed butter, lemon juice, mustard, garlic, and vinegar in a blender and process until smooth. Add the water and pepper or cayenne to taste and process until well blended. Alternatively, combine the tahini, lemon juice, mustard, garlic, and vinegar in a medium bowl. Gradually and vigorously whisk in the water, beating until smooth and creamy. Season with pepper or cayenne to taste. Will keep for several weeks in the refrigerator.

PER 2 TABLESPOONS (30 ML): calories: 70, protein: 2 g, fat: 6 g, carbohydrate: 3 g, dietary fiber: 0.5 g, calcium: 18 mg, iron: 0.5 mg, magnesium: 11 mg, sodium: 17 mg, zinc: 0.5 mg, folate: 12 mcg, riboflavin: 0 mg, vitamin C: 3 mg, vitamin E: 0.3 mg, omega-3 fatty acids: 0.1 g.

% CALORIES FROM: protein 11%, fat 72%, carbohydrate 17%

CONTAINS: * CITRUS (LEMON) * FERMENTED foods (MUSTARD; VINEGAR)

TOMATO AND SEED BUTTER DRESSING

Yields about 2 cups (500 ml)

Enjoy this luscious, creamy dressing on your favorite salad greens or as a sauce for steamed veggies, rice, potatoes, or pasta. Made with flaxseed oil, this dressing provides about two-thirds of your daily supply omega-3 fatty acids.

2	ripe tomatoes (about 9 ounces/250 g)	
½ cup	fresh lemon juice	125 ml
¼ cup	extra-virgin olive oil or flaxseed oil	60 ml
¼ cup	sesame tahini or other seed butter (see page 176)	60 ml
½–1 teaspoon	salt	2–5 ml
1 teaspoon	ground cumin	5 ml

Place all the ingredients in a blender and process until completely smooth. Best if used within 24 hours.

VARIATION: FOR HERBED TOMATO AND SEED BUTTER DRESSING, omit the cumin and add 1 teaspoon (5 ml) dried basil, 1 teaspoon (5 ml) dried dill weed, and ½ teaspoon (2 ml) dried oregano.

PER 2 TABLESPOONS (30 ML): calories: 61, protein: 1 g, fat: 6 g, carbohydrate: 2 g, dietary fiber: 0.5 g, calcium: 8 mg, iron: 0.3 mg, magnesium: 7 mg, sodium: 76 mg, zinc: 0.2 mg, folate: 8 mcg, riboflavin: 0 mg, vitamin C: 8 mg, vitamin E: 0.6 mg, omega-3 fatty acids: 1.3 g.

% CALORIES FROM: protein 6%,   fat 78%,   carbohydrate 16%

CONTAINS: * CITRUS (LEMON) * TOMATO

GINGER-MISO DRESSING

Yields about 1¼ cups (310 ml)

Enliven any salad or grain dish with this tangy, flavorful dressing.

1 cup	water	250 ml
6 tablespoons	sesame tahini or other seed butter (see page 176)	90 ml
3–4 tablespoons	fresh lemon juice	45–60 ml
3 tablespoons	chickpea miso	45 ml
2 teaspoons	grated fresh ginger	10 ml

Combine all the ingredients in a blender and process until completely smooth.

PER 2 TABLESPOONS (30 ML): calories: 81, protein: 2.5 g, fat: 6 g, carbohydrate: 5 g, dietary fiber: 0.5 g, calcium: 17 mg, iron: 0.5 mg, magnesium: 12 mg, sodium: 181 mg, zinc: 0.5 mg, folate: 12 mcg, riboflavin: 0 mg, vitamin C: 3 mg, vitamin E: 0.3 mg, omega-3 fatty acids: 0.1 g.

% CALORIES FROM: protein 12%,   fat 64%,   carbohydrate 24%

CONTAINS: * CITRUS (LEMON) * FERMENTED FOODS (MISO)

CAESAR'S BEST DRESSING

Yields 2 cups (500 ml)

The olives give this creamy dressing bite, while the nori replaces the anchovies typically used in Caesar dressings. It has a very rich flavor, so a little goes a long way. In addition to the traditional romaine lettuce used in Caesar salads, it's delicious on potatoes or even grated cabbage and carrots for a very special coleslaw. Depending on the dryness of the beans, this may be the consistency of a dip or spread, so thin with a little more water, if desired. For a dressing that is high in omega-3 fatty acids, choose the flaxseed oil variation that follows.

1¾ cups	drained cooked or canned white beans (one 15-ounce/425 g can)	435 ml
12	pitted green olives	12
3–4 tablespoons	water, or more if needed	45–60 ml
2 tablespoons	toasted nori flakes, or 1 toasted nori sheet, crumbled	30 ml
2 tablespoons	fresh lemon juice	30 ml
1 tablespoon	white wine vinegar	15 ml
1 tablespoon	Dijon mustard	15 ml
1 teaspoon	crushed garlic	5 ml
1 teaspoon	pepper	5 ml
½ teaspoon	salt	2 ml
½ cup	extra-virgin olive oil	125 ml

Place the beans, olives, water, nori, lemon juice, vinegar, mustard, garlic, pepper, and salt in a food processor or blender, and process until completely smooth. With the processor or blender running, slowly drizzle in the oil through the cap opening in the lid. Serve at once or thoroughly chilled. Add more water if a thinner consistency is desired.

TIP: Nori is a sweet and delicate tasting sea vegetable. Its color is a lustrous, rich purple-black. Toasting nori makes it sweeter. If buying flakes, look for green nori flakes or "sushi nori," which have been pre-toasted. If using a sheet of nori, you may carefully toast it whole over a gas flame, or crumble and dry roast it in a skillet until it turns bright green.

VARIATIONS: FOR CAESAR'S FLAXSEED DRESSING, replace the olive oil with flaxseed oil and increase the lemon juice to ¼ cup (60 ml).

PER 2 TABLESPOONS (30 ML): calories: 97, protein: 2 g, fat: 8 g, carbohydrate: 6 g, dietary fiber: 1.5 g, calcium: 27 mg, iron: 1 mg, magnesium: 17 mg, sodium: 175 mg, zinc: 0.3 mg, folate: 22 mcg, riboflavin: 0 mg, vitamin C: 1 mg, vitamin E: 1 mg, omega-3 fatty acids: 0.1 g.

% CALORIES FROM: protein 9%,   fat 23%,   carbohydrate 68%

CONTAINS: * CITRUS (LEMON)
* FERMENTED foods (MUSTARD; olives; VINEGAR)

- For Caesar's Reduced-Fat Dressing, increase the water to ⅓ cup (85 ml) and reduce the olive oil to 2 to 3 tablespoons (30 to 45 ml).

- For Caesar's Tasty Dip, use well-drained beans and omit the water. If desired, add a little water to create the desired thickness. This may be too thick to process in a blender, so use a food processor instead.

BEETS-ALL SALAD DRESSING

Yields 2½ cups (625 ml)

You are bound to love this colorful, bright, nutritious dressing. If you omit the second half-cup (125 ml) of water, it also makes a great dip for veggies. Here's a tip to simplify peeling beets. First, steam or boil the beet until it is tender (a fork will slide in easily). Quickly cool it by placing it in cold water. The skin will slip off easily in your hand. If you prefer, drained canned beets may be used as an alternative to fresh. If using flaxseed oil, you may want to increase the lemon juice to ⅓ cup (85 ml).

1 cup	water	250 ml
½ cup	raw sunflower seeds	125 ml
1½ teaspoons	fresh oregano, or ½ teaspoon (2 ml) dried	7 ml
1½ teaspoons	fresh thyme, or ½ teaspoon (2 ml) dried	7 ml
1½ teaspoons	fresh basil, or ½ teaspoon (2 ml) dried	7 ml
3 tablespoons	fresh lemon juice	45 ml
2 tablespoons	chickpea miso	30 ml
1 tablespoon	balsamic vinegar	15 ml
¼ cup	extra-virgin olive oil or flaxseed oil	60 ml
1	boiled, peeled beet, chopped (about ¾–1 cup/185–250 ml)	1

Combine ½ cup (125 ml) of the water and the sunflower seeds in a blender and process until smooth, stopping to scrape down the sides of blender as necessary. Add the herbs, lemon juice, miso, and vinegar and blend again. Then add the oil and beet and blend until completely smooth. Blend in the remaining ½ cup water. More water may be added if the dressing is too thick.

PER 2 TABLESPOONS (30 ML): calories: 52, protein: 1 g, fat: 5 g, carbohydrate: 2 g, dietary fiber: 0.5 g, calcium: 8 mg, iron: 0.3 mg, magnesium: 15 mg, sodium: 67 mg, zinc: 0.3 mg, folate: 14 mcg, riboflavin: 0 mg, vitamin C: 1 mg, vitamin E: 2 mg, omega-3 fatty acids: 0 g (1.5 g made with flaxseed oil).

% CALORIES FROM: protein 8%,   fat 78%,   carbohydrate 14%

CONTAINS: * Citrus (lemon)
* Fermented foods (miso; vinegar)

Asian Dressing

Rice vinegar is a delicate vinegar with about half the acidity of other vinegars. The combination of rice vinegar and rice syrup with toasted sesame oil and the five spices in the Chinese seasoning—cinnamon, fennel, anise, star anise, and pepper—makes an intriguing blend. Chinese 5-spice seasoning is available in the spice section of most supermarkets and gourmet food stores, as well as Asian markets.

¼ cup	brown rice vinegar	60 ml
1 tablespoon	water	15 ml
1 tablespoon	organic canola oil	15 ml
1 teaspoon	grated fresh ginger	5 ml
½ teaspoon	crushed garlic	2 ml
¼ teaspoon	toasted sesame oil	1 ml
⅛ teaspoon	Chinese 5-spice seasoning	1 pinch

Combine all the ingredients in a jar with a tight fitting lid. Vigorously shake the jar until the dressing is well blended and emulsified.

PER 2 TABLESPOONS (30 ML): calories: 58, protein: 0 g, fat: 3 g, carbohydrate: 8 g, dietary fiber: 0 g, calcium: 2 mg, iron: 0 mg, magnesium: 0 mg, sodium: 2 mg, zinc: 0 mg, folate: 0 mcg, riboflavin: 0 mg, vitamin C: 0 mg, vitamin E: 0.6 mg, omega-3 fatty acids: 0.3 g.

% CALORIES FROM: protein 0%,   fat 44%,   carbohydrate 56%

CONTAINS: * FERMENTED foods (VINEGAR) * SESAME

Sesame-Citrus Vinaigrette

Yields about 1⅔ cups (420 ml)

Sweet, tart, and tantalizing, this is splendid on both vegetable and fruit salads.

1 cup	orange juice	250 ml
⅓ cup	brown rice vinegar	85 ml
¼ cup	toasted sesame oil	60 ml
2 tablespoons	balsamic vinegar	30 ml
	Salt	

Combine the orange juice, brown rice vinegar, sesame oil, and balsamic vinegar in a medium bowl and whisk vigorously until well blended. Season with salt to taste.

Per 2 tablespoons (30 ml): calories: 44, protein: <1 g, fat: 4 g, carbohydrate: 2 g, dietary fiber: 0 g, calcium: 3 mg, iron: 0 mg, magnesium: 2 mg, sodium: 12 mg, zinc: 0 mg, folate: 5 mcg, riboflavin: 0 mg, vitamin C: 9 mg, vitamin E: 0.2 mg, omega-3 fatty acids: 0 g.

% Calories from: protein 1%, fat 79%, carbohydrate 20%

CONTAINS: * Citrus (orange) * Fermented foods (vinegar) * Sesame

Maple-Mustard Dressing

Yields about 1¼ cups (310 ml)

Add sass to baby greens, zing to grain salads, and liveliness to humdrum slaw.

¾ cup	organic canola or safflower oil	185 ml
3 tablespoons	Dijon mustard	45 ml
3 tablespoons	apple cider vinegar	45 ml
1½–2 tablespoons	pure maple syrup	22–30 ml
	Salt	

Combine the oil, mustard, vinegar, and maple syrup in a small bowl, and whisk vigorously until well combined. Season with salt to taste. Whisk again before serving.

Variation: For a version that is higher in omega-3 fatty acids, replace the canola oil with flaxseed oil and replace the vinegar with 5 tablespoons (75 ml) of fresh lemon juice.

Per 2 tablespoons (30 ml): calories: 163, protein: 0.5 g, fat: 17 g, carbohydrate: 3 g, dietary fiber: 0 g, calcium: 9 mg, iron: 0.2 mg, magnesium: 1 mg, sodium: 129 mg, zinc: 0.2 mg, folate: 0 mcg, riboflavin: 0 mg, vitamin C: 0 mg, vitamin E: 4 mg, omega-3 fatty acids: 1.6 g (5 g when made with flaxseed oil).

% Calories from: protein 1%, fat 92%, carbohydrate 7%

CONTAINS: * Fermented foods (mustard; vinegar)

FRENCH DIJON DRESSING

Yields 1 1/2 cups (375 ml)

This lively dressing will perk up even the plainest salad. It's great on steamed broccoli and other vegetables too. Made with flaxseed oil, a serving provides an outstanding way to meet your recommended intake of omega-3 fatty acids for the day.

3 tablespoons	minced onions	45 ml
3 tablespoons	sugar	45 ml
2 teaspoons	crushed garlic	10 ml
3/4 teaspoon	salt	4 ml
3/4 cup	fresh lemon juice	185 ml
1 1/2 tablespoons	Dijon mustard	22 ml
1/4 teaspoon	paprika	1 ml
1/4 cup	water	60 ml
1/2 cup	organic canola, safflower, or flaxseed oil	125 ml

Combine the onions, sugar, garlic, and salt in a food processor or blender and pulse briefly to combine. Add the lemon juice, mustard, and paprika, and process for 1 minute. While the machine is running, add the water through the cap opening, then slowly drizzle in the oil and continue processing until thickened. Store in the refrigerator. Will keep for about 7 days.

VARIATION: For a tasty version that is high in omega-3 fatty acids, replace the canola oil with flaxseed oil. If you would like to make it thicker and creamier, add 2 table-spoons of ground flaxseeds.

Store flaxseed oil in the freezer or refrigerator. With prolonged exposure to air, a "fishy" aroma will develop, as is the case with fish. In both situations, this is due to the oxidation of omega-3 fatty acids. To prevent this, purchase flaxseed oil in small packages and use it up within a few weeks after opening.

PER 2 TABLESPOONS (30 ML): calories: 103, protein: 0.5 g, fat: 10 g, carbohydrate: 5 g, dietary fiber: 0 g, calcium: 6 mg, iron: 0.1 mg, magnesium: 2 mg, sodium: 193 mg, zinc: 0.1 mg, folate: 3 mcg, riboflavin: 0 mg, vitamin C: 7 mg, vitamin E: 2 mg, omega-3 fatty acids: 0.9 g (5 g when made with flaxseed oil).

% CALORIES FROM: protein 1%, fat 80%, carbohydrate 19%

CONTAINS: * CITRUS (LEMON) * FERMENTED foods (MUSTARD)

Satisfying Soups

*N*othing satisfies like soup. Think of a creamy, warm bisque on a cold winter day, or a light, refreshing gazpacho on a hot summer night. Yet if you have food intolerances, you may have concluded that soup is often out of the question. In their long list of ingredients, recipes contain many potential allergens such as dairy products, fish stock, or wheat noodles. Canned and packaged soups contain additives that are not always obvious at first glance. The soups in this section are free of such troublesome ingredients; they have been created especially for people with food sensitivities. These soups are perfect as a light lunch with rice crackers or with a quick bread from the baking section (pages 179 through 212). Not only are they ideal as a healthy starter for supper, they can also serve as a main dish, especially if you add some extra vegetables and beans. Try a thick, hearty soup as a topper for rice noodles or cooked grains, or puréed as a sauce or dip. Our soups are chock-full of good nutrition but contain no traces of dairy, gluten, soy, or meat products. We recommend these soups for you and your family or for when you cook for a crowd. They are easy to make, and all (except the gazpacho) freeze well.

Because most soups have water and vegetables as their base, which take up a lot of volume in your stomach (but contain relatively few calories), soups are the perfect way to help you lose weight, if that is your goal. Soups that contain beans, peas, and lentils are particularly helpful because these high-protein foods are tremendously effective at leveling out your blood sugar, giving you staying power between meals. Other good choices, if you would like to lose weight, are our soups with less than two hundred calories per serving, as starters for your meal.

For those who would like to gain weight, choose soups with a higher calorie level, eat more, and consider boosting the calorie density (or "calories per bite") by stirring in additional puréed vegetables, beans, or seed or nut butters that have been thinned with a little warm water or vegetable stock.

VEGETABLE STOCK

This simple stock can be made frequently and stored fresh, or it can be made in larger quantities and frozen. It's the perfect base for your homemade soups, sauces, and gravies, bringing a rich fullness and depth to the flavor. Stock also can be made from commercial powders and cubes; however, check ingredients for yeast, dairy derivatives, starches, and hydrogenated fats.

6 cups	water	1.5 L
2	medium carrots, peeled and coarsely chopped	2
2	stalks celery, sliced	2
1	large onion, diced	1
1 bulb	fennel, thinly sliced (optional)	1 bulb
½ cup	fresh parsley (leaves and stems)	125 ml
1 teaspoon	crushed garlic	5 ml
½ teaspoon	dried rosemary, basil, or thyme	2 ml
10	whole peppercorns, coarsely crushed	10
3	bay leaves	3

Place all the ingredients in a large soup pot and bring to a boil. Reduce the heat and simmer uncovered for 30 minutes. Strain through a colander, sieve, or cheesecloth. Discard the vegetables and allow the stock to cool before storing or freezing.

VARIATIONS:

• A large, sliced leek may be used in place of or in addition to the onion.

• For even faster preparation, this stock may be cooked in a pressure cooker for 10 minutes instead of simmering on the stovetop.

• Feel free to add any leftover vegetables or peelings you have on hand, but avoid using members of the cabbage family (such as broccoli, cauliflower, kale, and brussels sprouts), as their taste and odor are too strong and will overpower the stock.

Lentil and Rice Soup

Simple ingredients blend to make a hearty lentil soup that is out of this world. It's high in protein, healthful complex carbohydrates, fiber, iron, zinc, and B vitamins. The combination will give you staying power.

8 cups	water or vegetable stock	2 L
1 cup	dried lentils, rinsed and drained	250 ml
½ cup	brown rice, rinsed and drained	125 ml
1	large onion, chopped	1
¼ cup	extra-virgin olive oil	60 ml
	Salt and pepper	

Combine the water, lentils, and rice in a large soup pot and bring to a boil. Reduce the heat, cover, and simmer 1½ –2 hours, stirring occasionally, until the lentils are very tender and the soup is thick. Add a little extra water during cooking, if necessary.

Meanwhile, sauté the onion in the olive oil for 30–60 minutes or until very tender and brown, adjusting the heat as necessary so the onion doesn't burn. Add the onion and oil to the soup, season with salt and pepper, and simmer 10–15 minutes longer.

Per 2 cups (500 ml): calories: 388, protein: 16 g, fat: 15 g, carbohydrate: 49 g, dietary fiber: 16 g, calcium: 46 mg, iron: 4.8 mg, magnesium: 93 mg, sodium: 60 mg, zinc: 2.4 mg, folate: 217 mcg, riboflavin: 0.2 mg, vitamin C: 5 mg, vitamin E: 2.1 mg, omega-3 fatty acids: 0.2 g.

% Calories from: protein 16%,   fat 35%,   carbohydrate 49%

CREAM OF CAULIFLOWER AND LIMA BEAN SOUP

Yields about 2 quarts (2 L)

This is a creamy, blended soup with a portion of the whole lima beans added for extra texture. Because of the cauliflower, just one serving of this soup supplies your entire requirement for vitamin C. We recommend using Fordhook lima beans, which are large, sweet, and meaty. If you have access to fresh Fordhook limas, use one pound (454 g) instead of the frozen limas and cook them in boiling water until tender.

1 (16-ounce)	package frozen Fordhook lima beans	454 g
1 tablespoon	extra-virgin olive oil	15 ml
1½ cups	chopped onions	375 ml
2 teaspoons	whole caraway seeds	10 ml
	or 1½ teaspoons (7 ml) ground caraway seeds	
1 teaspoon	crushed garlic	5 ml
1	medium cauliflower, cut into small florets	1
5 cups	vegetable stock or water	1.25 L
	Salt and pepper	
	Chopped fresh cilantro or parsley for garnish (optional)	

Cook the lima beans according to the package directions. Drain and divide in half. Heat the oil in a large pot over medium high heat. Add the onions, caraway seeds, and garlic and cook, stirring often, 10–15 minutes or until the onions are soft. Add the cauliflower and stock or water and bring to a boil. Reduce the heat, cover, and simmer until the cauliflower is very tender, about 10–12 minutes.

In a blender, purée the soup in batches along with half the lima beans. Return the blended soup to the soup pot and stir in the remaining whole lima beans. Season with salt and pepper to taste. Warm over medium-low heat until the beans are heated through and the soup is hot. Garnish with the optional chopped cilantro or parsley.

PER 2 CUPS (500 ML): calories: 258, protein: 12.5 g, fat: 5 g, carbohydrate: 43 g, dietary fiber: 13.5 g, calcium: 106 mg, iron: 3.0 mg, magnesium: 73 mg, sodium: 725 mg, zinc: 1.1 mg, folate: 120 mcg, riboflavin: 0.2 mg, vitamin C: 87 mg, vitamin E: 1.1 mg, omega-3 fatty acids: 0.2 g.

% CALORIES FROM: protein 19%,   fat 17%,   carbohydrate 64%

WHITE BEAN AND CABBAGE SOUP

Yields about 12 cups (3 L)

This delectable recipe uses simple ingredients to create a warming and satisfying soup.

2 tablespoons	extra-virgin olive oil	30 ml
1	large onion, chopped	1
1 teaspoon	crushed garlic	5 ml
8 cups	water	2 L
3 cups	drained cooked white beans or two (15-ounce/425-g) cans	750 ml
1	small head green cabbage, finely chopped	1
½ pound	winter squash or pumpkin, peeled and chopped	225 g
1 teaspoon	dried thyme	5 ml
	Salt and pepper	

Heat the oil in a large soup pot. Add the onion and sauté until it begins to brown. Add the garlic and sauté for 1 minute. Add the remaining ingredients and bring to a boil. Reduce the heat, cover, and simmer, stirring occasionally, for 1 hour.

PER 2 CUPS (500 ML): calories: 243, protein: 10.5 g, fat: 5 g, carbohydrate: 40 g, dietary fiber: 15 g, calcium: 166 mg, iron: 3.9 mg, magnesium: 84 mg, sodium: 284 mg, zinc: 1.2 mg, folate: 135 mcg, riboflavin: 0.1 mg, vitamin C: 76 mg, vitamin E: 1.3 mg, omega-3 fatty acids: 0.2 g.

% CALORIES FROM: protein 17%, fat 19%, carbohydrate 64%

QUICK BROCCOLI BISQUE

Yields about 9 cups (2.25 L)

This quick and satisfying soup is creamy but not heavy. It is a super-rich source of fiber, calcium, iron, and zinc, yet is virtually fat free, because its creaminess is derived from blended beans rather than dairy products.

8 cups	chopped fresh broccoli florets (about 2 bunches)	2 L
7 cups	vegetable stock or water	1.75 L
2 cups	chopped celery	500 ml
1	large onion, chopped	1 l
2 teaspoons	dried basil	10 ml
1 teaspoon	crushed garlic	5 ml
3 cups	drained cooked white beans or two (15- or 16-ounce/425–450-g) cans Salt and pepper	750 ml

Combine the broccoli, vegetable stock or water, celery, onion, basil, and garlic in a large pot and bring to a boil. Reduce the heat, cover, and simmer until the vegetables are tender, about 15 minutes. Combine about one-third of the soup mixture with one-half of the beans (1½ cups/375 ml) in a blender and process until completely smooth. Transfer to a bowl. Blend half of the remaining soup mixture with the remaining beans and process until completely smooth. Return the blended mixtures to the pot, season with salt and pepper to taste, and simmer an additional 10 minutes or until hot.

PER 2 CUPS (500 ML): calories: 276, protein: 17 g, fat: 2 g, carbohydrate: 51 g, dietary fiber: 19.5 g, calcium: 222 mg, iron: 5.6 mg, magnesium: 125 mg, sodium: 1116 mg, zinc: 2.0 mg, folate: 276 mcg, riboflavin: 0.3 mg, vitamin C: 124 mg, vitamin E: 3.0 mg, omega-3 fatty acids: 0.3 g.

% CALORIES FROM: protein 23%, fat 7%, carbohydrate 70%

CREAMY CARROT BISQUE WITH EXOTIC SPICES

Yields about 7 cups (1.75 L)

Although there are no dairy products in this exotically flavored soup, the texture is incredibly creamy. In addition to the beta-carotene, which gives the soup its vivid color, it is rich in essential though less well-known minerals: chromium, copper, magnesium, manganese, molybdenum, phosphorus, and potassium.

2 tablespoons	olive oil	30 ml
1 large	onion, coarsely chopped	1 large
1 pound	carrots, trimmed, scraped, and sliced	454 g
1 large	potato, peeled and coarsely chopped	1 large
½ teaspoon	ground cardamom	2 ml
½ teaspoon	ground cinnamon	2 ml
¼ teaspoon	ground ginger	1 ml
¼ teaspoon	ground nutmeg	1 ml
	Salt and cayenne	
7 cups	hot vegetable stock or water	1.75 L

Heat the oil in a large soup pot. Add the onion and sauté for 5 minutes. Stir in the carrots and potato and stir until coated with the oil. Add the cardamom, cinnamon, ginger, nutmeg, salt, and cayenne and sauté for 10 minutes. Pour in the hot stock or water and bring to a boil. Reduce the heat, cover, and simmer until the vegetables are very tender, about 30 minutes. Purée in batches in a blender until smooth. Serve hot.

PER 2 CUPS (500 ML): calories: 286, protein: 5 g, fat: 8 g, carbohydrate: 51 g, dietary fiber: 8 g, calcium: 66 mg, iron: 2.2 mg, magnesium: 65 mg, sodium: 252 mg, zinc: 1 mg, folate: 39 mcg, riboflavin: 0.1 mg, vitamin C: 33 mg, vitamin E: 1.7 mg, omega-3 fatty acids: 0.1 g.

% CALORIES FROM: protein 7%,   fat 25%,   carbohydrate 68%

CONTAINS: * POTATO

Purée of Parsnips and Leeks

Yields 1½ quarts (1.5 L)

The delicate sweet taste of parsnips gets zapped with the oniony flavor of leeks and the peppery bite of ginger in this light and creamy soup.

1 tablespoon	extra-virgin olive oil	15 ml
1 cup	sliced leeks (see tip below)	250 ml
1 tablespoon	grated fresh ginger or 1 teaspoon (5 ml) ground ginger	15 ml
4 cups	vegetable stock or water	1 L
1½ pounds	parsnips, peeled and coarsely chopped	
1 cup	hot plain nondairy milk or water	250 ml
	Salt	
	Paprika, for garnish	

Heat the oil in a large pot. Add the leeks and sauté for 5 minutes. Add the ginger and cook for 1 minute, stirring constantly. Add the stock and parsnips and bring to a boil. Reduce the heat, cover, and simmer, stirring occasionally, for 25–30 minutes or until the parsnips are very tender.

Purée the soup in batches in a blender until smooth. Return the blended soup to the soup pot and stir in the hot milk or water. Warm the soup, stirring almost constantly, until it is just heated through, about 5 minutes. Season with salt to taste. Garnish each serving with a light dusting of paprika.

Tip: Rinse leeks thoroughly to remove the sandy grit and dirt. The easiest way to do this is to lay the leek on a cutting board horizontally in front of you, with the root in one hand and your knife in the other. Then make a horizontal cut from the bulb to the green end, lengthwise. Separate the leaves gently so the inner sections of the leek are exposed and rinse well under running water. Alternatively, slice the leek, separate the slices into rings, place in a colander, and rinse well under running water. Use only the white bulb and tender, light green section of the leek.

Per 2 cups (500 ml)*: calories: 273, protein: 3.5 g, fat: 6 g, carbohydrate: 54 g, dietary fiber: 11.5 g, calcium: 200 mg, iron: 2.0 mg, magnesium: 75 mg, sodium: 123 mg, zinc: 1.4 mg, folate: 171 mcg, riboflavin: 0.1 mg, vitamin C: 42 mg, vitamin E: 4.5 mg, omega-3 fatty acids: 0.1 g.

% Calories from: protein 5%, fat 19%, carbohydrate 76%

*Nutritional analysis done using B_{12} fortified rice milk.

304   Food Allergy Survival Guide

SPICY EGGPLANT SOUP

Yields 6 servings (about 12 cups/3 L)

Having allergies doesn't mean that your meals must be bland or dull. The spiciness of this aromatic soup can be adjusted by increasing or decreasing the amounts of ginger and pepper.

7 cups	vegetable stock or water	1.75 L
1 tablespoon	olive oil (optional)	15 ml
2 medium	potatoes, diced	2 medium
1 medium	eggplant, cubed	1 medium
2 medium	carrots, diced	2 medium
1 medium	onion, diced	1 medium
2 tablespoons	grated fresh ginger	30 ml
1 teaspoon	crushed garlic	5 ml
1 cup	chopped fresh or canned tomatoes	250 ml
½ cup	chopped fresh cilantro	125 ml
1 teaspoon	ground cumin	5 ml
½ teaspoon	pepper	2 ml
	Salt	

Heat the oil or 2 tablespoons (30 ml) of the stock in a large soup pot. Add the potatoes, eggplant, carrots, onion, ginger, and garlic, and sauté 3–5 minutes over medium heat or until soft. Add more oil or stock as needed to prevent the vegetables from sticking or burning. Stir in the remaining stock, tomatoes, cilantro, cumin, pepper, and salt to taste. Bring to a boil, reduce the heat, and simmer 20–30 minutes or until the potatoes are very tender. Adjust seasoning, if needed.

PER 2 CUPS (500 ML): calories: 199, protein: 6 g, fat: 1 g, carbohydrate: 45 g, dietary fiber: 8 g, calcium: 71 mg, iron: 2.5 mg, magnesium: 67 mg, sodium: 107 mg, zinc: 1 mg, folate: 57 mcg, riboflavin: 0.2 mg, vitamin C: 52 mg, vitamin E: 0.7 mg, omega-3 fatty acids: 0 g.

% Calories from: protein 11%,   fat 4%,   carbohydrate 85%

CONTAINS: * POTATO * TOMATO

CHUNKY GAZPACHO

Yields about 8 cups (2 L)

A food processor will make fast work of this traditional Spanish dish. Serve it cold on a hot summer day or any time of the year. It's super-low in calories yet rich in fiber and vitamin C. It's the salad you eat with a spoon!

2 cups	chopped fresh or canned crushed tomatoes	500 ml
1 cup	chopped English cucumbers	250 ml
2–4 tablespoons	extra-virgin olive oil	30–60 ml
3 tablespoons	fresh lemon juice	45 ml
3 tablespoons	red wine vinegar	45 ml
½–1 teaspoon	chopped jalapeño peppers	2–5 ml
½ teaspoon	crushed garlic	2 ml
½ teaspoon	salt	2 ml
2 cups	chopped tomatoes	500 ml
1	red bell pepper, finely diced	1
⅔ cup	chopped English cucumbers	170 ml
½ cup	chopped fresh cilantro or parsley	125 ml
¼ cup	chopped red onions	60 ml

Combine the 2 cups (500 ml) chopped fresh or canned tomatoes, 1 cup (250 ml) chopped cucumbers, oil, lemon juice, vinegar, jalapeño peppers, garlic, and salt in a blender and process until smooth. Pour into a large bowl and stir in the remaining ingredients. Chill thoroughly before serving.

PER 2 CUPS (500 ML): calories: 125, protein: 2.5 g, fat: 8 g, carbohydrate: 14 g, dietary fiber: 3.5 g, calcium: 28 mg, iron: 1.3 mg, magnesium: 33 mg, sodium: 313 mg, zinc: 0.3 mg, folate: 48 mcg, riboflavin: 0.1 mg, vitamin C: 113 mg, vitamin E: 2.0 mg, omega-3 fatty acids: 0.1 g.

% CALORIES FROM: protein 7%,   fat 52%,   carbohydrate 41%

CONTAINS: * Citrus (lemon) * Fermented foods (vinegar)
* Tomato

Main Dishes

*E*ntrées are often the most challenging part of meals for those of us with food allergies and intolerances. To begin, the situation may seem especially daunting. We can no longer have foods that we once enjoyed. The main dishes we tolerate may be few and far between, and once we find ones we like, we must then prepare the same items over and over, week after week. With these challenges in mind, we have created a collection of main dishes that are hearty, satisfying, bursting with flavor, and are completely free of the components that give food allergy sufferers the most trouble.

In your exploration of foods that will be health supportive for your body, give these main dishes a try, even ones that appear unusual at first. You're sure to find some that will become long-term favorites. Not sure what to serve with these dishes? Read through the section on side dishes (pages 341–350). Serve a soup (pages 297–306) or a salad (pages 255–296). Check out our meal plans on pages 141–145 to get some nutritionally balanced, delicious combinations. Despite food sensitivities, you'll discover that you can be wonderfully well nourished!

CHILI EXPRESS

This quick chili is good with mashed potatoes, polenta, rice, millet, or quinoa. If there are any leftovers, enjoy it as a salad or as a filling for Gluten-Free Chapatis, pages 192–193, or corn tortillas. A serving provides you with calcium, iron, zinc, magnesium, potassium, folate, and plenty of protein.

TWO SERVINGS

1 tablespoon	olive oil	15 ml
1	onion, chopped	1
1	red bell pepper, diced	1
1	large carrot, diced	1
½ teaspoon	crushed garlic	2 ml
1¾ cups	diced tomatoes, with juice	435 ml
1	large green chili, seeded and sliced into thin rings	1
1¾ cups	drained cooked or canned red kidney beans	435 ml
	Salt, pepper, cumin, chili powder, cayenne to taste	

FOUR SERVINGS

2 tablespoons	olive oil	30 ml
2	onions, chopped	2
2	red bell peppers, diced	2
2	large carrots, diced	2
1 teaspoon	crushed garlic	5 ml
3½ cups	diced tomatoes, with juice	875 ml
2	large green chilies, seeded and sliced into thin rings	2
3½ cups	drained cooked or canned red kidney beans	875 ml
	Salt, pepper, cumin, chili powder, cayenne to taste	

Heat the oil in a medium saucepan. When hot, add the onion, cover, and cook for 5 minutes. Add the red bell pepper, carrot, and garlic. Stir, then cover and cook for 10 minutes. Stir in the tomatoes and chili and continue to cook, uncovered, until the carrot is tender, about 10–15 minutes. Add the kidney beans and cook until they are heated through, about 3–5 minutes. Season with salt, pepper, cumin, chili powder, and/or cayenne to taste. Serve hot.

PER SERVING: calories: 351, protein: 17 g, fat: 8 g, carbohydrate: 57 g, dietary fiber: 15.5 g, calcium: 109 mg, iron: 6.8 mg, magnesium: 111 mg, sodium: 218 mg, zinc: 2.2 mg, folate: 247 mcg, riboflavin: 0.2 mg, vitamin C: 185 mg, vitamin E: 2.4 mg, omega-3 fatty acids: 0.3 g.

% CALORIES FROM: protein 18%, fat 20%, carbohydrate 62%

CONTAINS: * TOMATO

TIP: If you prefer a thicker sauce for your chili, stir in several tablespoons of tomato paste until the desired consistency is obtained.

SLOPPY JOES

Yields about 2 cups (500 ml)

This quick staple is a bean-based version of Sloppy Joes that both kids and grownups adore. Serve it over rice, polenta, mashed potatoes, or gluten-free noodles.

1 tablespoon	olive oil	15 ml
1	medium onion, diced	1
1¾ cups	drained cooked or canned pinto beans, black beans, or French lentils	435 ml
½ cup	ketchup	125 ml
1 tablespoon	balsamic vinegar	15 ml
1 teaspoon	prepared yellow mustard	5 ml
1 teaspoon	sugar	5 ml
	Salt and pepper to taste	

Heat the oil in a medium saucepan. When hot, add the onion and sauté until it is tender and lightly browned, about 10 minutes. Coarsely chop the beans, either by hand or by pulsing them briefly in a food processor. Add the chopped beans, ketchup, vinegar, mustard, and sugar to the onion and mix well. Reduce the heat to medium and simmer uncovered for 10 minutes, stirring often. Season with salt and pepper to taste. Spoon the hot mixture over rice, polenta, mashed potatoes, or gluten-free noodles. Serve at once.

PER CUP (250 ML): calories: 340, protein: 12 g, fat: 9 g, carbohydrate: 56 g, dietary fiber: 12 g, calcium: 119 mg, iron: 3.8 mg, magnesium: 76 mg, sodium: 1438 mg, zinc: 1.8 mg, folate: 146 mcg, riboflavin: 0.2 mg, vitamin C: 14 mg, vitamin E: 4 mg, omega-3 fatty acids: 0.5 g.

% CALORIES FROM: protein 13%, fat 23%, carbohydrate 64%

CONTAINS: * Fermented foods (ketchup; mustard; vinegar) * Tomato

BLACK BEAN TOSTADAS

Enjoy this south-of-the-border specialty with plenty of your favorite toppings.

1¾ cups	drained cooked black beans or one (15-ounce/425-g) can	435 ml
1 tablespoon	balsamic vinegar or fresh lime juice	15 ml
2 teaspoons	chili powder	10 ml
1 teaspoon	garlic powder	5 ml
½ teaspoon	ground cumin	2 ml
½ teaspoon	dried oregano	2 ml
	Salt	
	Tabasco	
8	corn tortillas or Gluten-Free Chapatis, pages 192–193	8
1 tablespoon	extra-virgin olive oil	15 ml
½ cup	finely chopped onions	125 ml

TOPPING OPTIONS (SELECT ONE OR MORE):

1–2 cups	shredded lettuce	250–500 ml
2	ripe tomatoes, chopped	2
1 small	avocado, cut into chunks	1 small
½ cup	shredded carrot	125 ml
½ cup	prepared salsa	125 ml
½ cup	minced fresh cilantro	125 ml
½ cup	sliced black olives	125 ml
2–4	scallions, sliced	2–4
4–6 tablespoons	Beannaise Dressing, p. 288	60–90 ml
¼ cup	finely chopped red onions	60 ml

Coarsely chop the beans by hand or by pulsing them briefly in a food processor. Combine the chopped beans, vinegar, chili powder, garlic powder, cumin, oregano, and salt and Tabasco to taste. Toss until thoroughly combined.

Per 2 tostadas (without topping): calories: 264, protein: 10 g, fat: 6 g, carbohydrate: 46 g, dietary fiber: 10.5 g, calcium: 126 mg, iron: 2.8 mg, magnesium: 92 mg, sodium: 317 mg, zinc: 1.4 mg, folate: 177 mcg, riboflavin: 0.1 mg, vitamin C: 2 mg, vitamin E: 0.7 mg, omega-3 fatty acids: 0.1 g.

% Calories from: protein 15%,   fat 18%,   carbohydrate 67%

Warm the tortillas or Gluten-Free Chapatis one by one in a dry skillet, then stack them in a clean towel to keep them warm. Heat the oil in the skillet. When hot, add the onions and sauté until tender, about 10–15 minutes. Add the bean mixture to the skillet and sauté until warmed through and just starting to brown, about 5 minutes. Spoon an equal portion of the bean mixture onto each of the reserved tortillas or chapatis. Add your favorite toppings, or place bowls of several different toppings on the table. To eat, gently fold the tortillas or chapatis, and pick them up with your hands.

WEST INDIAN RED BEANS IN COCONUT MILK

Yields 4 servings

This is a speedy version of a traditional West Indian recipe. Serve it with brown rice if you have the time to wait for it to cook, or white basmati rice if you are in a hurry.

3½ cups	drained cooked red kidney beans or two (15- or 16-ounce/425 to 450-g) cans	875 ml
1 (14-ounce) can	light or regular coconut milk	1 (397-ml) can
½ cup	water	125 ml
1	large onion, chopped	1
2	carrots, thinly sliced	2
1 to 2 teaspoons	dried thyme, finely crumbled	5 to 10 ml
½ teaspoon	crushed garlic	2 ml
	Salt and pepper	

Combine the beans, coconut milk, water, onion, carrots, thyme, and garlic in a large pot and simmer until the vegetables are tender, about 15–20 minutes, stirring occasionally. Season with salt and pepper to taste. Serve hot with rice.

PER SERVING: calories: 406, protein: 14.5 g, fat: 22 g, carbohydrate: 43 g, dietary fiber: 10.5 g, calcium: 102 mg, iron: 6.7 mg, magnesium: 125 mg, sodium: 842 mg, zinc: 2.0 mg, folate: 136 mcg, riboflavin: 0.2 mg, vitamin C: 9 mg, vitamin E: 1.4 mg, omega-3 fatty acids: 0.2 g.

% CALORIES FROM: protein 14%, fat 46%, carbohydrate 40%

Pizza Party!

Can pizza still be pizza without the cheese? Of course! There are countless alternatives to cheese that add richness and a lively jolt of flavor. Pizza toppings are limited only by your imagination. Here are just a few ideas.

1 recipe   Great Gluten-Free Pizza Crust, page 190–191

Optional Toppings (choose 1 or more)

- artichoke hearts, canned or marinated
- arugula
- baba ganoush
- basil, fresh
- bean dip
- beans, whole, mashed, or refried
- broccoli, minced or bite-size florets
- capers
- caramelized onions (see tip below)
- carrots, shredded
- corn
- eggplant, grilled or roasted
- garlic, roasted or sliced fresh
- hearts of palm
- hummus
- mochi, plain or savory, cut into small dice (see page 355 and tip on next page)
- mushrooms, thinly sliced
- olives, sliced (black, green, oil cured, stuffed)
- onions (red, white, or yellow), chopped or thinly sliced
- peppers (sweet bell, hot, raw, roasted), sliced, diced, or chopped
- pineapple tidbits
- pizza sauce
- salsa
- scallions, sliced
- shallots, minced
- spinach, raw or well-drained cooked
- tomatoes, chopped sun-dried
- tomatoes, crushed, seasoned with fresh or dried herbs
- tomatoes, fresh Roma, sliced or chopped
- tomato sauce
- veggies, minced raw, drizzled with olive oil
- zucchini, sliced or diced

Prebake the pizza crust for 10 minutes, as directed in the recipe. Cool. Top with a small amount of your favorite options. Don't overload the pizza! It will cook better if the toppings are in a thin layer rather than piled in a large heap. Use no more than 1 cup (250 ml) of pizza sauce or tomato sauce (a little less is even better) to prevent the crust from getting soggy. Mist or drizzle the top with a little olive oil, if you desire. Bake 25–30 minutes or until the edges of the crust are golden brown.

Tips:

- Caramelized onions make a delicious pizza topping. Just slice or dice as much onion as you like. You might want to use a little extra as the onion will "shrink" as it cooks. Heat a small amount of olive oil or organic canola oil in a heavy skillet—use about

1 tablespoon (15 ml) per large onion. When it is hot, add the onion and cook over medium heat, stirring often, until it is a rich brown color and very tender. Watch closely and adjust the heat as necessary so the onion does not burn. The longer it cooks, the lower you will need to adjust the heat. It can take from 20–60 minutes to thoroughly caramelize onions. It's a slow process, but the delicious results are worth the wait.

• If using mochi, wait to add it until about 15 minutes before the pizza has finished baking. This will prevent it from overcooking or burning.

TIME-SAVING TACOS

Yields 4 tacos

For an instant meal, one of the fastest and most nutritionally balanced combinations you can serve is the well-loved taco. Just warm the shells and beans, set out the colorful fillings, and serve.

4	hard corn taco shells, warmed in oven or microwave	4
1 cup	refried beans, warmed in a skillet, vegetable steamer, or microwave	250 ml
1 cup	shredded lettuce	250 ml
1	large ripe tomato, chopped	1
½–1	ripe avocado, mashed or chopped	½–1
½ cup	salsa or taco sauce	125 ml
½ cup	sliced pitted olives (optional)	125 ml

Place each ingredient in serving bowls on the table to allow for individual assembly.

PER TACO: calories: 179, protein: 5.5 g, fat: 8 g, carbohydrate: 24 g, dietary fiber: 6.5 g, calcium: 79 mg, iron: 2.2 mg, magnesium: 32 mg, sodium: 498 mg, zinc: 0.4 mg, folate: 50 mcg, riboflavin: 0.1 mg, vitamin C: 18 mg, vitamin E: 1.4 mg, omega-3 fatty acids: 0.1 g.

% CALORIES FROM: protein 12%, fat 37%, carbohydrate 51%

CONTAINS: * CORN * TOMATO

Mahvelous Millet Loaf

Millet is a highly digestible and very versatile grain. Although it can be made fluffy, much like a pilaf, when it is cooked with abundant water millet becomes soft and tender with a texture similar to polenta. It makes an ideal foundation for a meatless loaf. Because this loaf is made with cooked millet and is not baked, it's much quicker to prepare than other types of dinner loaves.

1 cup	millet	250 ml
2½ cups	water	625 ml
1 cup	finely chopped onions	250 ml
1 cup	finely chopped or shredded carrots	250 ml
1 cup	finely diced celery	250 ml
1¼ teaspoons	salt	6 ml
½ teaspoon	crushed garlic	2 ml
½ teaspoon	dried thyme, well crumbled	2 ml
2 tablespoons	extra-virgin olive oil	30 ml
½–1 cup	raw or toasted pumpkin or sunflower seeds	125–250 ml

Oil a large loaf pan and set aside. Rinse the millet well and place it in a large saucepan along with the water, onions, carrots, celery, salt, garlic, and thyme. Bring to a boil. Cover, reduce the heat to medium-low, and simmer for 30 minutes. Remove from the heat and let stand 10 minutes.

Stir in the oil and seeds and mix well. Spoon into the prepared loaf pan, packing the mixture down firmly. Place on a cooling rack and allow the loaf to rest in the pan at room temperature for 15–30 minutes. The longer it rests, the firmer it will be. Carefully turn the loaf out of the pan onto a cutting board or serving platter. Cut into slices and serve.

PER SLICE: calories: 189, protein: 5.5 g, fat: 9 g, carbohydrate: 24 g, dietary fiber: 3.5 g, calcium: 23 mg, iron: 2.3 mg, magnesium: 81 mg, sodium: 386 mg, zinc: 1.2 mg, folate: 36 mcg, riboflavin: 0.1 mg, vitamin C: 4 mg, vitamin E: 0.8 mg, omega-3 fatty acids: 0.1 g.

% CALORIES FROM: protein 11%,   fat 40%,   carbohydrate 49%

Brown Rice Patties

We recommend short-grain brown rice for these tasty patties, because the almost-round kernels tend to be sticky and cling together, especially when the rice is freshly cooked. The patties can be stored in a container in the freezer, using food wrap to separate them.

2 cups	cooked short-grain brown rice	500 ml
1 cup	finely grated carrots	250 ml
½ cup	finely chopped onion	125 ml
½ cup	chopped fresh parsley or cilantro	125 ml
1 teaspoon	salt	5 ml
½ teaspoon	crushed garlic	2 ml
¼ teaspoon	pepper	1 ml
½ cup	Jo's Gluten-Free All-Purpose Flour Mix, p. 182	125 ml
¼ cup	water, or less, if needed	60 ml
	Vegetable oil, as needed, for frying	

Combine the rice, carrots, onion, parsley, salt, garlic, and pepper in a large bowl. Add the flour mix and toss until it is evenly distributed. Gradually stir in the water, only if needed, using just enough to make the mixture hold together. Form into 12 patties, using about ¼ cup (60 ml) of the mixture for each, pressing firmly with your hands. Pan-fry in hot oil over medium heat until brown on each side, about 5–7 minutes per side, turning once.

TIP: A nonstick pan or heavy, well-seasoned, cast-iron skillet will work best.

PER PATTY: calories: 82, protein: 2 g, fat: 0.5 g*, carbohydrate: 17 g, dietary fiber: 1.5 g, calcium: 15 mg, iron: 0.6 mg, magnesium: 7 mg, sodium: 200 mg, zinc: 0.1 mg, folate: 11 mcg, riboflavin: 0 mg, vitamin C: 5 mg, vitamin E: 0.1 mg, omega-3 fatty acids: 0 g.

% CALORIES FROM: protein 9%, fat 5%*, carbohydrate 86%

*Nutritional analysis done without oil used in frying.

Moroccan Millet

This pilaf is great as a one-dish meal or served with a fresh green salad. Peppers, especially red peppers, are among our best sources of vitamin C and the protective group of phytochemicals known as carotenoids. Millet and chickpeas are good sources of the yellow vitamins riboflavin and folate.

2 tablespoons	coconut or olive oil or organic canola or safflower oil	30 ml
1	large red bell pepper, sliced into strips	1
1	large green bell pepper, sliced into strips	1
1	large onion, sliced into half-moons	1
2 tablespoons	crushed garlic	30 ml
2 teaspoons	paprika	10 ml
½ teaspoon	salt	2 ml
1 teaspoon	ground cumin	5 ml
½ teaspoon	ground cinnamon	2 ml
¼ teaspoon	turmeric	1 ml
¼ teaspoon	ground ginger	1 ml
⅛ teaspoon	cayenne	(1 pinch)
1½ cups	millet	375 ml
3 cups	vegetable stock	750 ml
1¾ cups	drained cooked chickpeas or 1 (15-ounce/425-g) can	435 ml
¼ cup	raisins or chopped dates	60 ml
¼ cup	sunflower seeds, pumpkin seeds, or pine nuts (optional)	60 ml
	Salt and pepper	

Preheat the oven to 450°F (230°C). Place 1 tablespoon (15 ml) of the oil in a large roasting pan. Add the peppers, onion, garlic, paprika, and salt. Toss until everything is evenly coated with the oil and well combined. Place in the oven to roast for 20 minutes, stirring 2 or 3 times during the cooking cycle. Remove the vegetables from the oven and allow them to cool until safe to handle; then chop them coarsely.

Meanwhile, heat the remaining tablespoon (15 ml) of oil in a large saucepan. Add the cumin, cinnamon, turmeric, ginger, and cayenne. Stir over medium-high heat until the spices are uniform in color and well combined, about 30 seconds. Add the millet and stir quickly to coat, about 1 minute. Immediately pour in the vegetable stock and bring

---

PER SERVING: calories: 364, protein: 11 g, fat: 8 g, carbohydrate: 63 g, dietary fiber: 10 g, calcium: 59 mg, iron: 3.8 mg, magnesium: 94 mg, sodium: 233 mg, zinc: 1.8 mg, folate: 141 mcg, riboflavin: 0.2 mg, vitamin C: 80 mg, vitamin E: 0.7 mg, omega-3 fatty acids: 0.1 g.

% CALORIES FROM: protein 12%, fat 20%, carbohydrate 68%

to a boil. Reduce the heat, cover, and cook the millet until all the liquid is absorbed, about 20 minutes.

Place the millet in a large bowl and fluff with a fork. Add the roasted vegetables, chickpeas, raisins, and optional seeds. Season with salt and pepper to taste. Toss gently and serve.

IGOR'S SPECIAL

Yields 2 servings

This is a great last-minute company dish, as it is easily doubled and takes practically no time to prepare.

6 ounces	corn or rice pasta	170 g
2 cups	bite-size broccoli florets (fresh or frozen)	500 ml
1	large ripe tomato (or 2 to 3 ripe Roma tomatoes), chopped	1
¼ cup	chopped red onion or sliced scallions	60 ml
¼ cup	whole pumpkin or sunflower seeds or coarsely chopped walnuts	60 ml
1 tablespoon	fresh lemon juice	15 ml
1 tablespoon	balsamic vinegar	15 ml
1 tablespoon	extra-virgin olive oil	15 ml
¼ teaspoon	crushed garlic	1 ml
¼ teaspoon	curry powder	1 ml
Dash	of cayenne	Dash
Dash	of black pepper	Dash
	Salt or umeboshi vinegar	

Cook the pasta in a large pot of salted boiling water until just barely tender. Do not drain. Remove the pot from the heat and add the broccoli florets. Cover and let the pasta and broccoli sit for 5–8 minutes. Drain, rinse well to remove the salt and starch from the pasta, and drain again. Set aside.

While the pasta and broccoli are sitting, combine the tomato, onion, seeds, lemon juice, vinegar, oil, garlic and seasonings in a large bowl. Add the drained pasta and broccoli and toss gently but thoroughly. Taste and adjust vinegar, salt, or other seasonings, if necessary. Toss again and serve.

PER SERVING: calories: 515, protein: 14 g, fat: 17 g, carbohydrate: 82 g, dietary fiber: 14 g, calcium: 59 mg, iron: 4.6 mg, magnesium: 225 mg, sodium: 113 mg, zinc: 3.2 mg, folate: 101 mcg, riboflavin: 0.3 mg, vitamin C: 89 mg, vitamin E: 3.5 mg, omega-3 fatty acids: 0.2 g.

% CALORIES FROM: protein 10%, fat 29%, carbohydrate 61%

CONTAINS: * CITRUS (LEMON) * FERMENTED foods (VINEGAR) * TOMATO

Hearty Bean Stew

Enjoy old-fashioned beef-stew flavor with a new twist—beans instead of beef!

4 cups	diced potatoes (thin-skinned or peeled)	1 L
4	large carrots, sliced in half lengthwise and cut into 1-inch (2.5 cm) chunks	4
2 cups	vegetable broth or water	500 ml
2 stalks	celery, finely chopped	2 stalks
2	bay leaves	2
1 tablespoon	extra-virgin olive oil	15 ml
1 cup	chopped onions	250 ml
2 cups	sliced mushrooms	500 ml
3 tablespoons	rice flour	30 ml
2 tablespoons	sesame tahini or other seed butter (see page 176)	30 ml
3 tablespoons	chickpea miso	45 ml
½ cup	water	125 ml
2 cups	drained cooked beans of choice or 1 (15- or 16-ounce/425 to 450-g) can	500 ml
	Salt and pepper	

Place the potatoes, carrots, broth, celery, and bay leaves in a large saucepan or pot. Bring to a boil, reduce the heat to medium, cover, and simmer, stirring occasionally, until the vegetables are tender, about 20 minutes.

Meanwhile, place the oil in a large skillet over medium-high heat. Add the onions and sauté for 8 minutes or until almost tender. Add the mushrooms and continue to sauté until tender, about 4–6 minutes longer.

Remove the skillet from the heat and stir in the flour. Mix well. Then stir in the seed butter and mix well. Dissolve the miso in the water, then gradually stir it into the skillet mixture, mixing vigorously until the sauce is smooth. Stir this mixture into the hot cooked vegetables and their liquid and mix well.

Stir in the cooked beans and bring to a boil, stirring almost constantly. Reduce the heat to medium and continue to stir and simmer the stew just until the sauce thickens, about 3–5 minutes. Remove the bay leaves and season with salt and pepper. Ladle into bowls and serve hot.

PER SERVING: calories: 459, protein: 18 g, fat: 9 g, carbohydrate: 79 g, dietary fiber: 15 g, calcium: 141 mg, iron: 5.4 mg, magnesium: 126 mg, sodium: 1267 mg, zinc: 2.4 mg, folate: 159 mcg, riboflavin: 0.3 mg, vitamin C: 37 mg, vitamin E: 1.9 mg, omega-3 fatty acids: 0.2 g.

% CALORIES FROM: protein 16%,   fat 17%,   carbohydrate 67%

CONTAINS: * FERMENTED foods (MISO)

Quinoa Primavera

Because quinoa cooks so quickly, this entrée can be on the table in less than thirty minutes! It's rich in iron, plus the vitamin C that helps us absorb iron. We suggest frozen peas because they are "instant." However, you can certainly use garden fresh peas, and lightly steam them, if you are fortunate enough to have those on hand.

2½ cups	water	625 ml
1 cup	quinoa, rinsed well and drained	250 ml
2 cups	frozen green peas, thawed and drained	500 ml
2 tablespoons	olive oil	30 ml
2	medium carrots, thinly sliced on the diagonal	2
2	medium zucchinis, thinly sliced on the diagonal	2
1	red bell pepper, diced	1
1	green bell pepper, diced	1
2	large leeks, thinly sliced (see tip on page 304)	2 l
1 teaspoon	crushed garlic	5 ml
2 teaspoons	dried dill weed	10 ml
	Salt and pepper	

Place the water in a large saucepan and bring to a boil. Stir in the quinoa, cover, and reduce the heat to low. Simmer 15–18 minutes. Remove from the heat and scatter the peas on top of the grain; do not stir. Replace the lid and let rest for 8 minutes.

While the quinoa rests, add the oil to a large skillet or wok over medium-high heat. When the oil is hot, add the carrots, zucchinis, bell peppers, leeks, and garlic. Stir-fry for about 8 minutes or until the carrots are tender-crisp. Stir in the quinoa and peas along with the dill weed. Toss until thoroughly combined. Heat over medium heat, tossing constantly, until the peas are heated through, about 2 minutes. Season with salt and pepper to taste.

PER SERVING: calories: 335, protein: 11 g, fat: 10 g, carbohydrate: 53 g, dietary fiber: 9 g, calcium: 97 mg, iron: 6.8 mg, magnesium: 136 mg, sodium: 155 mg, zinc: 2.3 mg, folate: 106 mcg, riboflavin: 0.3 mg, vitamin C: 107 mg, vitamin E: 4 mg, omega-3 fatty acids: 0.2 g.

% CALORIES FROM: protein 13%,   fat 26%,   carbohydrate 62%

Chickpea Flour Pizza

Yields 1 pizza (ONE OR TWO SERVINGS)

This unusual dish is a cross between a pizza and a high-protein flatbread. It is simple to prepare and tastes amazing. If you have chickpea flour on hand, it can be on the table in a jiffy. Serve it with sliced tomatoes, a salad, or a vegetable side dish.

½ cup	chickpea flour	125 ml
¼ teaspoon	salt	1 ml
¼ teaspoon	dried oregano, crumbled between your fingers	1 ml
¼ teaspoon	dried basil, crumbled between your fingers	1 ml
¼ teaspoon	garlic powder	1 ml
Generous pinch	of cayenne or pepper	Generous pinch
Pinch	of turmeric	Pinch
½ cup	water	125 ml
1 teaspoon	extra-virgin olive oil	5 ml

Combine the chickpea flour, salt, oregano, basil, garlic powder, cayenne, and turmeric in a medium bowl. Gradually whisk in the water, beating well after each addition until completely smooth. Generously oil a 10-inch skillet (nonstick will work best) or mist it well with nonstick cooking spray, and heat over medium-high heat. Stir the batter and pour it into the pan, scraping all of it out with a rubber spatula. Drizzle the olive oil over the top. Cook until the top is set and the bottom is nicely browned, about 5–7 minutes. Adjust the heat as necessary to prevent over-browning. Carefully turn the dough over and cook the other side until well browned, about 5 minutes. Slide onto a round plate and slice into 8 wedges. Serve hot.

PER PIZZA: calories: 218, protein: 10.5 g, fat: 8 g, carbohydrate: 28 g, dietary fiber: 5 g, calcium: 38 mg, iron: 2.7 mg, magnesium: 81 mg, sodium: 615 mg, zinc: 1.4 mg, folate: 203 mcg, riboflavin: 0.1 mg, vitamin C: 1 mg, vitamin E: 0.6 mg, omega-3 fatty acids: 0.1 g.

% CALORIES FROM: protein 19%, fat 31%, carbohydrate 50%

Spinach and Chickpea Curry

Rich and spicy, this exquisite stew tastes like it has been cooking all day, yet it can be ready and on the table in mere minutes. Serve it with basmati or jasmine rice and a cooling cucumber salad.

1½ tablespoons	olive oil, coconut oil, or organic canola oil	22 ml
1 cup	chopped onions	250 ml
1 teaspoon	crushed garlic	5 ml
2 teaspoons	ground cumin	10 ml
2 teaspoons	ground coriander	10 ml
2 teaspoons	chili powder	10 ml
1 teaspoon	turmeric	5 ml
1 teaspoon	ground cinnamon	5 ml
¼–½ teaspoon	pepper	1–2 ml
⅔ cup	water	170 ml
½ cup	tomato paste	125 ml
2 teaspoons	sugar	10 ml
4–6 cups	coarsely torn fresh spinach, stems removed, lightly packed	1–1.5 L
3 cups	drained cooked chickpeas or 2 (15- or 16-ounce/425 to 450-g) cans Salt	750 ml

Heat the oil in a large skillet or pot. Add the onions and garlic and sauté over medium-high heat until the onions are very tender and brown, about 15 minutes. Reduce the heat to medium and stir in the cumin, coriander, chili powder, turmeric, cinnamon, and pepper. Cook for 30 seconds, stirring constantly.

Add the water, tomato paste, and sugar, and stir until well blended. Stir in the spinach and beans. Cook, stirring almost constantly, until the spinach is wilted and the beans are heated through, about 5 minutes longer. Season with salt to taste. Serve immediately.

PER SERVING: calories: 324, protein: 14 g, fat: 9 g, carbohydrate: 50 g, dietary fiber: 14 g, calcium: 140 mg, iron: 6.2 mg, magnesium: 107 mg, sodium: 309 mg, zinc: 2.5 mg, folate: 286 mcg, riboflavin: 0.2 mg, vitamin C: 28 mg, vitamin E: 3.5 mg, omega-3 fatty acids: 0.1 g.

% CALORIES FROM: protein 17%,   fat 25%,   carbohydrate 58%

CONTAINS: * TOMATO

SIMPLE NORI ROLLS

Yields 24 or 48 pieces

Everyone enjoys making and eating nori rolls, and for this reason we have given the larger batch size for use with a party crowd. Bamboo mats, along with less familiar ingredients in this recipe, are available from Asian markets.

FOR 4 EIGHT-INCH ROLLS / 24 PIECES (6 SLICES PER ROLL):

3 cups	freshly cooked Japanese white sticky rice (sushi rice) or brown rice	750 ml
4 sheets	dry or toasted nori sea vegetable (see tip below)	4

FOR 8 EIGHT-INCH ROLLS / 48 PIECES (6 SLICES PER ROLL):

6 cups	freshly cooked Japanese white sticky rice (sushi rice) or brown rice	1.5 L
8 sheets	dry or toasted nori sea vegetable (see tip below)	8

CHOOSE 3 OR MORE OF THE FOLLOWING FILLINGS:

FOR 4 ROLLS		FOR 8 ROLLS
1 cup (250 ml)	grated carrots	2 cups (500 ml)
¼ cup (60 ml)	drained cooked or canned beans	½ cup (125 ml)
½	avocado, thinly sliced into strips	1 whole
½	red pepper, sliced into thin strips	1 whole
4	long, ¼-inch thick slices cucumber	8
3 tablespoons (45 ml)	steamed spinach	⅓ cup (85 ml)
3 tablespoons (45 ml)	Beannaise, page 288	⅓ cup (85 ml)
2 tablespoons (30 ml)	thinly sliced pickled ginger	¼ cup (60 ml)
2 tablespoons (30 ml)	sesame seed sprinkles or Gomasio, page 215, or toasted and ground pumpkin or sunflower seeds (see page 353)	¼ cup (60 ml)

OPTIONAL GARNISHES:

- Thinly sliced pickled ginger
- Sesame seed sprinkles, Gomasio (see recipe on page 215), or toasted, ground pumpkin or sunflower seeds (see page 353)
- Wasabi horseradish powder mixed with a little water to form a thick paste

Set out all the ingredients in bowls or on small plates on the counter or table, along with a bowl of water. Place a sheet of nori on a bamboo sushi mat (make sure the bamboo "rungs" run horizontally). Place ¾ cup (185 ml) of rice on the nori and spread the rice evenly to the right and left edges, and to the bottom edge closest to you, leaving a 1-inch strip of nori free of rice at the top of the nori sheet (the edge farthest from you). In a thin strip along the bottom edge of the nori, from left to right, layer a portion of the fillings you have selected (carrot, beans, avocado, cucumber, spinach, Beannaise, ginger, and/or sesame seed sprinkles). Dip your finger into the bowl of water and moisten the top edge of nori sheet that is free from rice. This wet edge will be used to "glue" the finished roll. Using both hands and firm pressure, lift the edge of the bamboo mat that is closest to you. Roll until the nori roll is formed into a thick log. Press the edge to seal the roll closed. Repeat to assemble the other rolls.

Place each roll on a cutting board, seam side down. Using a sharp serrated knife, cut each roll into 6 equal pieces. Arrange the nori roll pieces on a platter, along with optional garnishes. Serve umeboshi vinegar in small individual bowls for dipping.

TIP: Although optional, toasting makes nori sweeter. If your nori sheets do not come pretoasted (this should be stated on the package), you can toast them yourself. Just wave each sheet over a flame for a few seconds until it changes to a deep green color. Be careful not to get it too close to the flame or it will burn. The nori will soften and become pliable when the hot rice is spread on it.

PER ROLL: calories: 209, protein: 5 g, fat: 4 g, carbohydrate: 38 g, dietary fiber: 5 g, calcium: 30 mg, iron: 1.1 mg, magnesium: 29 mg, sodium: 191 mg, zinc: 1 mg, folate: 44 mcg, riboflavin: 0.1 mg, vitamin C: 27 mg, vitamin E: 0.9 mg, omega-3 fatty acids: 0 g.

% CALORIES FROM: protein 9%,   fat 18%,   carbohydrate 73%

*Nutritional analysis done using carrot, adzuki beans, avocado, red pepper, and pickled ginger.

BEANS AND GREENS

Yields 4 servings

Serve this as a main dish, as a topping for corn bread, or a delicious filling.

3 cups	drained cooked white beans	750 ml
	or 2 (15- or 16-ounce/425 to 450-g) cans	
1 cup	vegetable stock or water	250 ml
½ teaspoon	crushed garlic	2 ml
4 cups	chopped kale leaves, lightly packed	1 L
1–2 tablespoons	olive oil (optional)	15–30 ml
	Salt and pepper	

Place the beans and stock or water in a large pot. Stir in the garlic. Place the chopped kale on top of the beans and bring to a boil. Cover, reduce the heat, and simmer 20–25 minutes, or until the kale is tender to your liking. Remove from the heat and stir in the olive oil, if using. Season with salt and pepper to taste.

PER SERVING: calories: 229, protein: 16 g, fat: 1 g, carbohydrate: 42 g, dietary fiber: 10 g, calcium: 218 mg, iron: 6.2 mg, magnesium: 108 mg, sodium: 508 mg, zinc: 2.2 mg, folate: 128 mcg, riboflavin: 0.2 mg, vitamin C: 81 mg, vitamin E: 0.8 mg, omega-3 fatty acids: 0.2 g.

% CALORIES FROM: protein 26%,   fat 4%,   carbohydrate 70%

STUFFED GREEN PEPPERS

There's something about stuffed peppers that makes dinner guests feel well cared for and family members feel special. Use your favorite tomato sauce—homemade or store-bought. This recipe will make everyone praise your culinary skills, so don't tell them how easy it is to make!

4	very large green bell peppers	4
1 cup	white basmati rice	250 ml
1 cup	very hot water	250 ml
1 cup	well-seasoned tomato sauce	250 ml
1 cup	drained cooked or canned chickpeas	250 ml
¼ cup	sunflower seeds, pumpkin seeds, pine nuts, walnuts, or corn	60 ml
¼ cup	raisins	60 ml
1 teaspoon	salt	5 ml
½ teaspoon	crushed garlic	2 ml
¼ teaspoon	ground cinnamon	1 ml
¼ teaspoon	ground allspice	1 ml
2 cups	well-seasoned tomato sauce	500 ml
1½ cups	water	375 ml
1 tablespoon	extra-virgin olive oil	15 ml

Select very large green peppers that can stand upright without toppling. Cut off the tops (and reserve them) and carefully hollow out the peppers, removing the seeds and ribs. Rinse well and drain. Combine the rice, hot water, 1 cup (250 ml) tomato sauce, chickpeas, seeds, raisins, salt, garlic, cinnamon, and allspice in a large bowl. Stir until well mixed. Divide equally among the green peppers, taking care not to overstuff them. They should be about two-thirds full.

Combine the 2 cups (500 ml) tomato sauce, 1½ cups (375 ml) water, and oil in a large, deep pot that has room for all four peppers. Trim the pepper flesh from around the reserved tops, cut it into large dice, and add it to the sauce. Stand the peppers upright in the sauce, and bring to a boil. Reduce the heat to a simmer, cover, and cook over medium-low heat until the rice is plump and tender, about 60–70 minutes. To serve, place a pepper upright on each dinner plate and ladle some of the sauce around it.

PER SERVING: calories: 464, protein: 12.5 g, fat: 10 g, carbohydrate: 88 g, dietary fiber: 10 g, calcium: 79 mg, iron: 3.9 mg, magnesium: 84 mg, sodium: 1889 mg, zinc: 1.8 mg, folate: 112 mcg, riboflavin: 0.2 mg, vitamin C: 174 mg, vitamin E: 8.3 mg, omega-3 fatty acids: 0.1 g.

% CALORIES FROM: protein 10%,   fat 17%,   carbohydrate 72%

CONTAINS: * TOMATO

VEGGIE RICE ROLL

Yields 1 roll (multiply as needed)

This is such a fun way to enjoy salad and an easy-to-transport, gluten-free sandwich. When the fillings are prepared and set out, everyone can make their own customized roll. Sauce can be spread inside the roll and also put in small bowls for dipping. You may provide just one sauce—such as barbecue sauce, plum sauce, Last Minute Sauce (page 340), Lemon-Seed Salad Dressing (page 290), Thai Hot-and-Sour Sauce (page 339), or Ginger-Miso Dressing (page 291)—or you may offer several choices.

1 sheet	rice paper (about 8½ inches/21 cm in diameter)	1 sheet
	Warm water in a large bowl (about 14 inches/35 cm in diameter)	
⅓ cup	cooked brown rice	85 ml
1 tablespoon or more	sauce of your choice	15 ml
3 slices	avocado	3 slices
2 tablespoons	grated carrot	30 ml
2 tablespoons	raw or toasted seeds, page 353 (optional)	30 ml
2 tablespoons	drained cooked or canned beans (optional)	30 ml
¼ cup	alfalfa sprouts or chopped lettuce	60 ml
	Fresh basil leaves, mint leaves, or cilantro (optional)	

Dip the rice paper sheet into the water for 5 seconds, then place it on a cutting board. Pat it with a dry cloth to absorb excess water. Place the rice on the center of the paper, then cover it with the sauce, avocado, carrot, optional seeds and beans, sprouts, and optional fresh herbs. Fold the right and left margins of the rice paper toward the center. Then fold up the bottom margin. Fold the top margin down, using a bit of pressure to seal the roll.

PER ROLL: calories: 161, protein: 3.5 g, fat: 4 g, carbohydrate: 28 g, dietary fiber: 3 g, calcium: 21 mg, iron: 1 mg, magnesium: 46 mg, sodium: 136 mg, zinc: 0.7 mg, folate: 21 mcg, riboflavin: 0.1 mg, vitamin C: 5 mg, vitamin E: 0.9 mg, omega-3 fatty acids: 0.1 g.

% CALORIES FROM: protein 8%,   fat 22%,   carbohydrate 70%

BUILDING A MEAL
AROUND BAKED POTATOES

It's easy to build a meal around the simple baked potato just by adding some of the nutritious and flavorful toppings listed below. The oven-baked method gives an aromatic and flavorful baked crust on the potatoes. Be sure to bake plenty to have leftovers for the next day. If you like, you may complete the meal with soup or salad. Cold baked potatoes with nutritious toppings also can make a great packed lunch.

Nutritionally speaking, potatoes have gotten a bad rap, but the truth is that spuds are chock-full of vitamin C, B vitamins, minerals, fiber, and antioxidants. In fact, according to a recent study, russet potatoes made the top-twenty list of the foods richest in antioxidants! You may also wish to use sweet potatoes, which are one of the richest sources of beta-carotene, the plant source of vitamin A. They work equally well with the following cooking methods, are very satisfying, and taste pleasantly sweet.

QUICK OVEN-BAKED METHOD FOR POTATOES

To bake in half an hour or less, cut large potatoes in half or in quarters and place them on a dry baking sheet or directly on the oven rack in a very hot 450–500°F (205–260°C) oven. Pierce whole potatoes three or four times with a fork to let steam escape so they don't burst when cooking. The exact cooking time will depend on the size of the potatoes and potato sections. You can tell the potatoes are done when a knife, fork, or skewer can be easily inserted into the potato.

MICROWAVE METHOD FOR POTATOES

A whole pierced potato may be cooked in a microwave on high for about five minutes, depending on the size of the potato.

SPEEDY PRESSURE COOKER METHOD FOR POTATOES

Potatoes also may be pressure cooked. Cut the potatoes into quarters. Pour the minimum amount of water required for your cooker into the pot. Place the potato pieces on a stainless steel steamer rack and put it into the cooker. Seal the cooker and bring up to high pressure over high heat. Reduce the heat just enough to maintain high pressure and cook for about four minutes. Let the pressure come down naturally or use a quick-release method (see the instruction manual for your cooker).

TOPPINGS

Avocado Mayonnaise (page 289)

Beannaise (page 288)

Beets-all Salad Dressing (page 293)

Caesar's Best Dressing (page 292)

Colorful Chili Dip (page 251)

Creamy Tarragon Dressing (page 289)

Ginger-Miso Dressing (page 291)

Great Gravy (page 338)

Hummus (pages 242 and 244)

Italian Chickpea Spread (page 252)

Lemon-Seed Salad Dressing (page 290)

Lentil "Chopped Liver" (page 246)

Miso White Sauce (page 336)

Savory Chickpea Gravy (page 337)

Savory Spinach Spread (page 250)

Tangy White Bean Spread (page 243)

Thai Hot-and-Sour Sauce (page 339)

Warm Eggplant Pesto (page 249)

Warm Seed Butter and Miso Sauce (page 336)

QUICK AND EASY FLAVOR BOOSTERS

Bottled hot sauce

Cayenne or chipotle chili powder

Chickpea miso, thinned with a little water

Chili powder

Chopped fresh herbs (parsley, cilantro, or basil)

Curry powder

Dulse, nori, or kelp powder or flakes

Extra-virgin olive oil

Finely diced red or green pepper, tomato, or cucumber

Flaxseed oil

Garlic powder

Herb blends

Horseradish

Ketchup

Lemon pepper

Lettuce greens

Margarine, nonhydrogenated

Mashed avocado

Salsa

Salt and freshly cracked pepper

Sauerkraut

Seasoned salt

Shredded carrot or zucchini

Tomato sauce

Vinegar, balsamic or umeboshi

Wasabi paste (Japanese hot horseradish)

Your favorite salad dressing

CREAMY QUICHE

This simple quiche is easily adapted to a number of variations. It contains no eggs, cream, cow's milk, or cheese, yet it's very creamy and rich tasting. Serve it with thick slices of fresh tomato on the side and hot steamed greens for a hearty and memorable meal.

1 recipe	(one crust) Amish Pat-In-The-Pan Pie Crust, page 197	1 recipe
3 cups	drained cooked white beans, or 2 (15- or 16-ounce/425 to 450-g) cans	750 ml
¾ cup	coconut milk, or 1 (5.5-ounce/156-ml) can	185 ml
½ cup	water	125 ml
½ cup	Jo's Gluten-Free All-Purpose Flour Mix, page 182	125 ml
2 teaspoons	chickpea miso plus ¼ teaspoon (1 ml) salt or 1 teaspoon (5 ml) salt	10 ml
¼ teaspoon	grated nutmeg	1 ml
¼ teaspoon	turmeric	1 ml
1 tablespoon	olive, coconut, or organic canola oil	15 ml
1½ cups	finely chopped onions	375 ml

Preheat the oven to 400°F (205°C). Prebake the pie crust 12–15 minutes. Let cool. Reduce the oven temperature to 350°F (180°C). Place the beans, coconut milk, water, flour mix, miso, salt, nutmeg, and turmeric in a blender or food processor and process several minutes until the mixture is completely smooth. Stop the machine frequently to stir the mixture and scrape down the sides of the container with a rubber spatula. Set aside.

Heat the oil in a medium skillet over medium-high heat. When hot, add the onions and sauté until tender and golden, about 12 minutes. Stir into the blended mixture and pour into the prepared pie crust. Bake on the center rack of oven until the top is firm, browned, and slightly puffed, about 1 hour. Let rest 15–20 minutes before slicing.

TIP: The quiche will continue to firm up as it cools and will get very firm when leftovers are chilled in the refrigerator. Because of this, it makes an excellent packed lunch.

PER SERVING: calories: 161, protein: 7.5 g, fat: 4 g, carbohydrate: 24 g, dietary fiber: 5 g, calcium: 74 mg, iron: 2.7 mg, magnesium: 56 mg, sodium: 273 mg, zinc: 1.1 mg, folate: 64 mcg, riboflavin: 0 mg, vitamin C: 2 mg, vitamin E: 0.5 mg, omega-3 fatty acids: 0.1 g.

% CALORIES FROM: protein 18%, fat 22%, carbohydrate 60%

VARIATIONS:

- For Broccoli Quiche, steam 2 cups (500 ml) bite-size broccoli florets until tender-crisp. Then stir them into the blended mixture just before pouring into the pie crust. Bake as directed.

- For Spinach Quiche, cook one 10-ounce (284-ml) package frozen chopped spinach according to package directions. Drain well in a wire mesh strainer, pressing firmly with the back of a wooden spoon, or squeeze it with your hands to express as much liquid as possible. Stir into the blended mixture just before pouring into the pie crust. Bake as directed.

- For Mushroom Quiche, add 2 cups (500 ml) sliced mushrooms to the onions once they are soft, and continue sautéing until the mushrooms are tender and almost all of the liquid has evaporated. Stir into the blended mixture just before pouring into the pie crust. Bake as directed.

- For Squash Quiche, omit nutmeg. Add 2 cups (500 ml) diced zucchini or yellow summer squash to the onions once they are soft, and continue sautéing until squash is tender. Fold into blended mixture along with 2 teaspoons (10 ml) dried basil just before pouring into the pie crust. Bake as directed.

- For Fresh Herb Quiche, omit nutmeg. Stir ¼–½ cup (60–125 ml) chopped fresh herbs into the blended mixture. Good choices include cilantro, basil, parsley, or a mixture. If desired, sauté ½–1 teaspoon (2–5 ml) crushed garlic along with the onions.

- For Dried Herb Quiche, omit nutmeg. Stir 2 teaspoons (10 ml) dried herbs into the blended mixture. Good choices include thyme, basil, oregano, dill weed, sage, rosemary, marjoram, or a blend of two or more. If desired, sauté ½–1 teaspoon (2–5 ml) crushed garlic along with the onions.

- For Scallion or Chive Quiche, omit onions and oil. Stir ½–1 cup (125–250 ml) thinly sliced scallions or chives into the blended mixture just before pouring into the pie crust. Bake as directed. This variation may be used in combination with any of the other variations listed above.

- For Spicy Quiche, add ¼ teaspoon (1 ml) cayenne pepper or chipotle chili powder, several shakes of Tabasco, or ½ teaspoon (2 ml) Thai curry paste to the blended mixture. This variation may be used in combination with any of the other variations listed above.

- For Smoky Quiche, add several drops of liquid hickory smoke (regular or mesquite flavor) to the blended mixture. This variation may be used in combination with any of the other variations listed above.

Mandarin Stir Fry

Yields 3½ cups (875 ml)

The marinade that is used here for chickpeas adds a sweet and gingery taste. If you like plenty of ginger, use the larger amount.

Marinade:

2½ tablespoons	chickpea miso	37 ml
¼ cup	water	60 ml
1 tablespoon	brown rice syrup	15 ml
½–1 tablespoon	grated fresh ginger	7–15 ml

Stir-fry mix:

1¾ cups	drained cooked chickpeas or 1 (15-ounce/425-g) can	435 ml
1–2 tablespoons	olive or sesame oil	15–30 ml
1	medium white, yellow, or red onion, thinly sliced	1
2	medium carrots, sliced diagonally	2
3 cups	broccoli florets and peeled and sliced stems	750 ml
	Salt or umeboshi vinegar	

Combine the marinade ingredients in a medium bowl, mixing well to thoroughly incorporate the miso. Add the chickpeas and mix well until they are covered with the marinade. Allow the mixture to marinate for at least 30 minutes, stirring occasionally.

Heat the oil in a wok or cast-iron skillet over medium-high heat. Add the onion and sauté until it is golden brown, about 2 minutes. Add the carrots and sauté until they are just beginning to soften, about 2 minutes. Add the marinated mixture and broccoli and cook until the broccoli is just tender and everything is warmed through, about 2 minutes more. Season with salt or umeboshi vinegar to taste. Serve over brown rice, gluten-free noodles, quinoa, or millet.

PER CUP (250 ML): calories: 250, protein: 11 g, fat: 7 g, carbohydrate: 38 g, dietary fiber: 10 g, calcium: 93 mg, iron: 3.5 mg, magnesium: 68 mg, sodium: 528 mg, zinc: 2 mg, folate: 197 mcg, riboflavin: 0.2 mg, vitamin C: 62 mg, vitamin E: 2 mg, omega-3 fatty acids: 0.2 g.

% CALORIES FROM: protein 17%, fat 24%, carbohydrate 59%

CONTAINS: * Fermented foods (miso)

PAD-THAI FUSION

This simple and unique version of pad thai incorporates a delicious combination of flavors from Italy, Japan, and Thailand. The result is superb! For an ideal side dish, try a colorful medley of steamed vegetables, such as broccoli florets, diagonally sliced carrots, and water chestnuts.

10–12 ounces	rice fettuccine noodles	283–340 g
¼ cup	tomato paste	60 ml
¼ cup	brown rice vinegar	60 ml
¼ cup	water	60 ml
2 tablespoons	pure maple syrup	30 ml
1–2 tablespoons	toasted sesame oil or extra-virgin olive oil	15–0 ml
1 tablespoon	chickpea miso	15 ml
1–2 teaspoons	hot chili sauce, or ½–1 teaspoon/2–5 ml crushed red pepper flakes	5–0 ml
½ teaspoon	crushed garlic	2 ml
¼ cup	thinly sliced scallions	60 ml
¼ cup	plain roasted seeds or Ume-Roasted Seeds, page 353, Chickpea "Nuts," page 352, or chopped roasted almonds	60 ml

Cook the pasta according to the package directions. Drain well and transfer to a large bowl.

While the pasta is cooking, combine the tomato paste, vinegar, water, maple syrup, oil, miso, chili sauce to taste, and garlic in a small bowl. Stir or whisk to make a smooth sauce. Pour over the cooked pasta and toss until evenly coated. Divide the pasta equally among four pasta bowls or dinner plates. Garnish each serving with 1 tablespoon (15 ml) of the scallions and 1 tablespoon (15 ml) of the roasted seeds or Chickpea "Nuts." Serve at once.

PER SERVING: calories: 387, protein: 5.5 g, fat: 8 g, carbohydrate: 73 g, dietary fiber: 3 g, calcium: 41 mg, iron: 1.5 mg, magnesium: 32 mg, sodium: 419 mg, zinc: 1.7 mg, folate: 30 mcg, riboflavin: 0.1 mg, vitamin C: 9 mg, vitamin E: 5 mg, omega-3 fatty acids: 0.1 g.

% CALORIES FROM: protein 6%,   fat 19%,   carbohydrate 75%

CONTAINS: * Fermented foods (miso; vinegar) * Tomato

SENSATIONAL STUFFED SQUASH

Yields 1 medium stuffed squash (5–6 servings)
or 2 medium stuffed squashes (10–12 servings)

In some families or groups of friends, getting together to cook is one of the best parts of a celebration. Assembling this stuffing and baked squash can be the central activity for a wonderful day spent with the people you love. Serve it with Savory Chickpea Gravy (page 337); if you like, add cranberry sauce as well.

5 TO 6 SERVINGS

1	3-pound (1.36 kg) buttercup squash (see note)	1
1 cup	water	250 ml
½	large onion, chopped	½
¼ cup	white basmati rice, rinsed and drained	60 ml
¼ cup	quinoa, rinsed well and drained	60 ml
¼ cup	toasted sunflower seeds or chopped nuts	60 ml
¼ cup	chopped, oil-packed, sun-dried tomatoes (drained)	60 ml
2 tablespoons	chopped fresh parsley	30 ml
1½ teaspoons	olive oil	7 ml
½ teaspoon	dried basil	2 ml
¼ teaspoon	dried oregano	1 ml
¼ teaspoon	crushed garlic	1 ml
	Salt and pepper	

10 TO 12 SERVINGS

2	3-pound (1.36 kg) buttercup squash (see note)	2
2 cups	water	500 ml
1	large onion, chopped	1
½ cup	white basmati rice, rinsed and drained	125 ml
½ cup	quinoa, rinsed well and drained	125 ml
½ cup	toasted sunflower seeds or chopped nuts	125 ml
½ cup	chopped, oil-packed, sun-dried tomatoes (drained)	125 ml
¼ cup	chopped fresh parsley	60 ml
1 tablespoon	olive oil	15 ml
1 teaspoon	dried basil	5 ml
½ teaspoon	dried oregano	2 ml
½ teaspoon	crushed garlic	2 ml
	Salt and pepper	

reheat the oven to 350°F (180°C). Pierce the top of the squash with sharp knife at a 45-degree angle. Pushing the knife blade away from your body, rotate the blade around top of squash, and remove the cone-shaped top piece. Slice off any fibrous material from the cone and set the top aside. Using a large spoon, scoop out the seeds and all the fibrous pulp from the cavity of the squash and discard. Place the squash and top on a dry baking sheet and bake for 30 minutes. Remove from the oven and set aside to cool for 15 minutes.

While the squash is baking, place the water, onion, rice, and quinoa in a large pot and bring to a boil. Lower the heat to medium, cover, and simmer for 15 minutes. Remove from the heat and let rest, covered, for 10 minutes. Fluff with a fork, and add the remaining ingredients.

Spoon the stuffing into the cavity of the squash until almost full. Put the squash top in place and bake for 50–60 minutes or until a toothpick can be inserted easily into the side of the squash. If there is leftover stuffing, place it in a small pan, sprinkle it with 2–3 tablespoons (45 ml) of water, cover, and heat through for the last 20 minutes of the squash cooking time. Remove the squash from the oven and place on a warm serving platter. Slice into wedges to serve.

NOTE: Although other large winter squashes may be used, we recommend buttercup (also known as "turban squash") for this recipe. Its flat bottom, round shape, beautiful dark green shell, and succulent, deep orange flesh make it an impressive edible showpiece for any special occasion. Buttercup squash also is sweeter, more dense, and less watery than other winter squashes, and its skin is very tender when cooked.

PER SERVING: calories: 263, protein: 6 g, fat: 9 g, carbohydrate: 45 g, dietary fiber: 10 g, calcium: 133 mg, iron: 3.1 mg, magnesium: 112 mg, sodium: 60 mg, zinc: 1.1 mg, folate: 87 mcg, riboflavin: 0.1 mg, vitamin C: 56 mg, vitamin E: 4.6 mg, omega-3 fatty acids: 0.1 g.

% CALORIES FROM: protein 9%,   fat 28%,   carbohydrate 63%

CONTAINS: * TOMATO

Sauces and Gravies

*T*hough your menus may be simple, flavorful sauces can bring your meals to life. There's no end to the different ways you can incorporate these succulent sauces and gravies into your menus. Most recipes provide suggestions, but we encourage you to be creative!

These recipes are lifesavers for those who have multiple food sensitivities and have a difficult time buying sauces at the store because they contain so many ingredients that may cause a reaction. Some sauces, like our Pizza Sauce, are old-time favorites, but others have an ethnic flair and will tickle your taste buds. Try Thai Hot-and-Sour Sauce for an authentic Asian meal, or some Mango Salsa with your next Mexican feast. Our sauces and gravies provide exceptional flavor, but that's not all. Unlike dry seasonings, they actually infuse flavor into otherwise dry or bland foods, changing the overall texture of the dish. Thus you'll find that a simple grain or steamed vegetable can be served time after time, yet with new interest.

One of the secrets to eating healthfully for life is creating meals that taste fabulous. If our food tastes great, we will readily eat it; and if it's good for us, we will feel great too. Eating is one of life's pleasures, and that pleasure is everyone's right, even those with food allergies. Ban the notion that your dishes have to be bland or contain only a few ingredients. Indulge in superb flavor!

Pizza Sauce

This flavorful sauce is great for last-minute pizzas or rice-pasta dishes. It's so quick and easy, you may never resort to jarred sauce again!

1 (8-ounce) can	tomato sauce or 1 (8-ounce/250-ml) jar roasted red peppers, drained	1 (250-ml) can
½ teaspoon	dried oregano	2 ml
½ teaspoon	dried basil	2 ml
½ teaspoon	crushed dried rosemary	2 ml
½ teaspoon	ground fennel	2 ml
¼ teaspoon	garlic powder	1 ml
2 teaspoons	sugar	10 ml
½ teaspoon	salt	2 ml

If using the roasted red peppers, remove any seeds and skin and blend in a food processor or blender until smooth. Combine all the ingredients in a small saucepan and bring to boil over medium heat. Reduce the heat to low and simmer for 15 minutes.

Per ½ cup (125 ml): calories: 57, protein: 2 g, fat: <1 g, carbohydrate: 13 g, dietary fiber: 2 g, calcium: 39 mg, iron: 1.4 mg, magnesium: 24 mg, sodium: 1269 mg, zinc: 0.3 mg, folate: 12 mcg, riboflavin: 0.1 mg, vitamin C: 15 mg, vitamin E: 1.6 mg, omega-3 fatty acids: 0 g.

% Calories from: protein 11%, fat 5%, carbohydrate 84%

CONTAINS: * Tomato

WARM SEED BUTTER AND MISO SAUCE

No cooking is required to make this luscious sauce!

⅔ cup	sesame tahini or other seed butter (see page 176)	170 ml
⅓ cup	chickpea miso	85 ml
2 teaspoons	grated fresh ginger (optional)	10 ml
Large pinch	of cayenne pepper (optional)	Large pinch
1–1½ cups	boiling water, as needed	250–375 ml

Combine the tahini, miso, optional ginger and cayenne, and half the water in a bowl. Mash and beat with a spoon until the mixture forms a smooth paste. Gradually beat in the remaining water, using just enough to form a thick but pourable sauce.

PER ¼ CUP (60 ML): calories: 182, protein: 6 g, fat: 15 g, carbohydrate: 9 g, dietary fiber: 1.6 g, calcium: 38 mg, iron: 1.2 mg, magnesium: 26 mg, sodium: 667 mg, zinc: 1.2 mg, folate: 26 mcg, riboflavin: 0.0 mg, vitamin C: 1.2 mg, vitamin E: 0.6 mg, omega-3 fatty acids: 0.1 g.

% CALORIES FROM: protein 13%, fat 69%, carbohydrate 18%

CONTAINS: * FERMENTED foods (MISO)

MISO WHITE SAUCE

For a warm sauce, simply use warm or hot water. Use only fresh lemon juice, not bottled, as bottled lemon juice will make the sauce taste stale and "off." Using pumpkin seed butter instead of tahini will give the sauce a greenish hue. Using sunflower seed butter will make it an off-white sauce; both are delicious.

⅓ cup	sesame tahini or other seed butter (see page 176)	85 ml
¼ cup	chickpea miso	60 ml
2 tablespoons	fresh lemon juice	30 ml
¾ cup	water, more or less as needed	185 ml

Combine the tahini, miso, and lemon juice in a small bowl, mixing well to make a thick paste. Gradually stir or whisk in the water, beating well after each addition, until smooth, using just enough to achieve the desired consistency.

PER ¼ CUP (60 ML): calories: 118, protein: 4.5 g, fat: 9 g, carbohydrate: 6 g, dietary fiber: 1 g, calcium: 24 mg, iron: 0.8 mg, magnesium: 16 mg, sodium: 599 mg, zinc: 0.8 mg, folate: 16 mcg, riboflavin: 0 mg, vitamin C: 3 mg, vitamin E: 0.4 mg, omega-3 fatty acids: 0.1 g.

% CALORIES FROM: protein 14%, fat 66%, carbohydrate 20%

CONTAINS: * CITRUS (LEMON) * FERMENTED foods (MISO)

SAVORY CHICKPEA GRAVY

Yields 3–3½ cups (875 ml)

This handy sauce is a delicious way to enhance even the simplest meals. Folks who swear they don't like beans will love it. Since it is made with toasted chickpea flour, they'll never know they are eating beans!

3 tablespoons	olive oil	45 ml
1 cup	chickpea flour	250 ml
1 teaspoon	dried sage	5 ml
½ teaspoon	dried thyme, crumbled	2 ml
½ teaspoon	dried rosemary, crumbled	2 ml
¼ teaspoon	pepper	1 ml
3½ cups	hot water	875 ml
1–2 tablespoons	umeboshi plum vinegar	15–30 ml
1 tablespoon	balsamic vinegar	15 ml
	Salt	

Heat the oil in a large saucepan over medium heat. Stir in the flour, sage, thyme, rosemary, and pepper, stirring constantly to form a smooth, thick paste. Cook over medium heat until lightly toasted, about 5–10 minutes or until the flour no longer tastes raw. Remove from the heat. Gradually whisk in the hot water, stirring constantly and mixing carefully to avoid lumps. Add the vinegars and salt to taste. Cook over medium heat, whisking occasionally, until hot and bubbly. Whisk in more water, if needed, to achieve the desired consistency.

VARIATION: To replace some or all of the salt, add chickpea miso, thinned with a little water, to taste.

PER ½ CUP (125 ML): calories: 102, protein: 3 g, fat: 7 g, carbohydrate: 8 g, dietary fiber: 2 g, calcium: 12 mg, iron: 0.8 mg, magnesium: 24 mg, sodium: 34 mg, zinc: 0.4 mg, folate: 58 mcg, riboflavin: 0 mg, vitamin C: 0 mg, vitamin E: 0.7 mg, omega-3 fatty acids: 0.1 g.

% CALORIES FROM: protein 12%,   fat 57%,   carbohydrate 31%

CONTAINS: * FERMENTED foods (vinegar)

GREAT GRAVY

This versatile gravy is terrific on everything from beans to mashed potatoes.

¼ cup	arrowroot, kuzu, or cornstarch	60 ml
1 tablespoon	balsamic vinegar	15ml
1 tablespoon	umeboshi plum vinegar	15 ml
3¼ cups	vegetable stock or water	810 ml
1 teaspoon	garlic powder	5 ml
¼ cup	sesame tahini or other seed butter (see page 176)	60 ml
	Salt	

Combine the arrowroot and vinegars in a medium saucepan. Mix well to make a smooth paste. Gradually whisk in the stock or water and garlic powder. Cook over medium-high heat, stirring constantly with the wire whisk until the gravy thickens and comes to a boil. Remove from the heat and beat in the tahini using the wire whisk. Season with salt to taste. Serve at once.

TIP: This makes a very thick gravy. If you prefer a thinner consistency, gradually whisk in a little more water, about 1 or 2 teaspoons (5 or 10 ml) at a time, until it is the consistency you desire.

PER ½ CUP (125 ML): calories: 81, protein: 2 g, fat: 5 g, carbohydrate: 8 g, dietary fiber: 0.5 g, calcium: 18 mg, iron: 0.6 mg, magnesium: 12 mg, sodium: 34 mg, zinc: 0.5 mg, folate: 10 mcg, riboflavin: 0 mg, vitamin C: 0.5 mg, vitamin E: 0.2 mg, omega-3 fatty acids: 0 g.

% CALORIES FROM: protein 9%,   fat 56%,   carbohydrate 35%

CONTAINS: * Fermented foods (vinegar)

THAI HOT-AND-SOUR SAUCE

Yields about 1⅓ cups (335 ml)

This delectable, spicy sauce is fabulous on tossed green salads, sliced tomatoes, steamed cabbage wedges, stir-fried vegetables and rice, and rice noodles with steamed veggies. You're bound to think of many other uses as well.

⅓ cup	sesame tahini, other seed butter (see page 176), or almond butter	85 ml
⅓ cup	fresh lime juice	85 ml
3 tablespoons	water	45 ml
2 tablespoons	balsamic vinegar	30 ml
2 tablespoons	dark sesame oil or extra-virgin olive oil	30 ml
2 tablespoons	sugar	30 ml
2 teaspoons	dried basil	10 ml
1 teaspoon	dried spearmint	5 ml
1 teaspoon	ground ginger	5 ml
1 teaspoon	crushed garlic	5 ml
¼ teaspoon	crushed hot red pepper flakes	1 ml

Combine all the ingredients in a small bowl and whisk until thick and smooth.

PER ⅓ CUP (85 ML): calories: 219, protein: 4 g, fat: 18 g, carbohydrate: 15 g, dietary fiber: 1.5 g, calcium: 49 mg, iron: 1.4 mg, magnesium: 22 mg, sodium: 11 mg, zinc: 1 mg, folate: 22 mcg, riboflavin: 0 mg, vitamin C: 7 mg, vitamin E: 0.8 mg, omega-3 fatty acids: 0.1 g.

% CALORIES FROM: protein 7%,   fat 68%,   carbohydrate 25%

CONTAINS: * Citrus (lime) * Fermented foods (vinegar)

LAST-MINUTE SAUCE

Serve with lightly steamed vegetables and over pasta, whole grains, or salad.

½ cup	seed or nut butter of your choice	125 ml
¼ cup	balsamic vinegar, or 2 tablespoons chickpea miso thinned with 2 tablespoons water	60 ml
¼ cup	ketchup	60 ml
½ cup	water, as needed	125 ml

Cream together the seed butter, vinegar, and ketchup. When well blended, whisk in just enough water to create a pourable sauce. Store leftovers in the refrigerator for 3–5 days. Thin with additional water before serving, if necessary.

PER ¼ CUP (60 ML)*: calories: 135, protein: 4 g, fat: 11 g, carbohydrate: 9 g, dietary fiber: 1 g, calcium: 34 mg, iron: 1 mg, magnesium: 21 mg, sodium: 129 mg, zinc: 1 mg, folate: 21 mcg, riboflavin: 0 mg, vitamin C: 2 mg, vitamin E: 0.6 mg, omega-3 fatty acids: 0.1 g.

% CALORIES FROM: protein 10%, fat 66%, carbohydrate 24%

*Nutritional analysis done using sesame tahini.

CONTAINS: * FERMENTED foods (ketchup; vinegar) * TOMATO

MANGO SALSA

Use this sensational chutney as a complement to any rice dish.

3 cups	diced fresh tomatoes	750 ml
2 cups	diced fresh mangoes	500 ml
½ cup	finely chopped onion	125 ml
½ cup	chopped fresh cilantro	125 ml
¼ cup	fresh lime juice	60 ml
1–2 teaspoons	seeded and minced jalapeño pepper	10 ml
¼ teaspoon	salt	1 ml
¼ teaspoon	crushed garlic	1 ml

Place all the ingredients in a large bowl and stir until well combined. Best served at once.

PER ¼ CUP (60 ML): calories: 19, protein: 0.5 g, fat: <1 g, carbohydrate: 5 g, dietary fiber: 0.5 g, calcium: 5 mg, iron: 0.2 mg, magnesium: 5 mg, sodium: 33 mg, zinc: 0 mg, folate: 8 mcg, riboflavin: 0 mg, vitamin C: 11 mg, vitamin E: 0.3 mg, omega-3 fatty acids: 0 g.

% CALORIES FROM: protein 7%, fat 6%, carbohydrate 87%

CONTAINS: * CITRUS (lime) * TOMATO

Simple Sides

$\mathcal{V}$ariety, of course, is the spice of life. When it comes to food, variety also is the first rule of good nutrition, and it is what gives meals such appeal. These side dishes were specially designed for people with food allergies and intolerances, with an emphasis on good nutrition and quick and easy preparation. The recipes are wonderful additions to main dishes; they also can stand on their own for a light lunch or be doubled for a main course. The Oven Fries on page 342 make an excellent after-school or evening snack and are much more nutritious than what you'll find at the fast-food outlet. Try them with one of the dips on pages 239–254. We have provided tips and variations to suit different tastes and different food allergies. If any of the recipes contain an ingredient you can't tolerate, try substituting it with something you can.

When planning your meal, remember to alternate colors, flavors, and textures. For example, try pairing tangy Marinated Carrot Sticks, page 348, with a savory rice noodle dish. Or how about a crunchy, mild salad with soft, sweet, Easy Baked Beans, page 349

For more side dish ideas, check out the Main Dishes, Dips and Spreads, Baking Basics, and Salads and Dressings sections. We encourage you to improvise!

OVEN FRIES

These thick, oven-baked French fries are low in fat but resonate with fabulous flavor. Potatoes provide a variety of minerals and are high in vitamin C, even after baking.

2	large russet potatoes	2
1 tablespoon	olive oil (optional)	15 ml
1 teaspoon	paprika	5 ml
	or ½ teaspoon (2 ml) curry or chili powder	
¼ teaspoon	salt	1 ml
Dash each	pepper, garlic powder, turmeric	Dash each

Preheat the oven to 450°F (230°C). Line a large baking sheet with parchment paper (for easy cleanup) and set aside. Scrub the potatoes well and remove any eyes and discolored areas. Peeling is optional.

Cut into wedges or French-fry shapes. Place in a large bowl, sprinkle with the optional oil, and toss to coat evenly. Sprinkle with the seasonings and toss again so all pieces are evenly coated. Arrange in a single layer on the prepared baking sheet. Bake until golden brown and fork tender, about 30 minutes. As oven temperatures vary, check for desired brownness after 20–25 minutes. For more even browning, turn over once midway through the cooking cycle.

VARIATIONS:

- You may prefer to bake your potato wedges without any added oil or seasonings, either on a baking sheet or with the wedges set directly on the oven rack.

- For OVEN-ROASTED PARSNIP FRIES, use 1 pound of parsnips, trimmed, peeled, and cut into French-fry shapes or ¼-inch (5 mm) thick diagonal slices.

CONTAINS: * POTATO

Coconut Rice

This is an utterly scrumptious way to prepare rice. The optional chili paste sparks a bit of heat, though it is mellowed by the coconut milk. Brown rice is rich in B vitamins—a serving of this simple recipe provides about one-third of your thiamin, niacin, pantothenic acid, and pyridoxine for the day, along with copper, iron, magnesium, manganese, phosphorus, selenium, and zinc.

1 cup	white or brown rice, rinsed	250 ml
1 cup	water	250 ml
1 cup	coconut milk	250 ml
½–2 teaspoons	Thai chili paste (optional)	2–10 ml
2 tablespoons	toasted, unsweetened coconut shreds (optional; see tip below)	30 ml
	Salt	

Place the rice, water, coconut milk, and chili paste to taste in a saucepan with a tight-fitting lid. Bring to a boil, cover, and reduce the heat to low. If using white rice, cook for 18–20 minutes; if using brown rice, cook for 40 minutes. Remove from the heat and let rest, covered, 5–10 minutes. Season with salt to taste. Transfer to a serving dish, fluff with a fork, and sprinkle with the optional toasted coconut.

TIP: To toast the coconut, place it in a small saucepan over medium to medium-high heat, stirring constantly until it just begins to brown. This will take just a few minutes, so watch that it doesn't burn.

• For Coconut Rice with Veggies, scatter your favorite vegetables, cut into bite-size pieces, on top of the rice during cooking. Longer-cooking veggies can be added to white rice at the start and after about 20 minutes with brown rice, depending on the vegetables, how thick they are cut, and how tender you like them. Shorter-cooking veggies can be added 5–10 minutes before the rice has finished cooking, or you can add them during the resting time, after the rice is done cooking and has been removed from the heat. This will give them a very light steaming.

PER CUP (250 ML): calories: 564, protein: 10 g, fat: 27 g, carbohydrate: 75 g, dietary fiber: 4.5 g, calcium: 44 mg, iron: 5.1 mg, magnesium: 185 mg, sodium: 25 mg, zinc: 2.5 mg, folate: 34 mcg, riboflavin: 0.1 mg, vitamin C: 1 mg, vitamin E: 1.4 mg, omega-3 fatty acids: 0 g.

% CALORIES FROM: protein 6%,   fat 42%,   carbohydrate 52%

*Nutritional analysis done using long-grain brown rice.

ROSEMARY RED RIBBON RICE

Yields about 3 cups (750 ml)

This rice dish is fragrant, festive, and easy to prepare, making it ideal for every-day meals or for entertaining.

1½ cups	vegetable stock or water	375 ml
½ cup	raisins	125 ml
1 teaspoon	crushed garlic	5 ml
½ teaspoon	salt	2 ml
¼–½ teaspoon	dried rosemary, well crumbled	1–2 ml
1 cup	white basmati rice	250 ml
1	small red bell pepper, sliced into matchsticks	1
½ cup	Chickpea "Nuts," page 352, plain or roasted seeds or Ume-Roasted Seeds, page 353, or coarsely chopped walnuts	125 ml
1 tablespoon	extra-virgin olive oil	15 ml

Combine the stock or water, raisins, garlic, salt, and rosemary in a saucepan and bring to a boil. Stir in the rice, cover, and reduce the heat to low. Cook 18–20 minutes or until almost all the liquid has been absorbed.

Remove from the heat, add the red bell pepper, Chickpea "Nuts" or seeds, and oil, and toss gently with a fork until evenly distributed. Cover and let stand for 5–10 minutes. Fluff and serve.

PER CUP (250 ML): calories: 458, protein: 9.6 g, fat: 8 g, carbohydrate: 89 g, dietary fiber: 5.8 g, calcium: 45 mg, iron: 2.3 mg, magnesium: 27 mg, sodium: 628 mg, zinc: 0.6 mg, folate: 61 mcg, riboflavin: 0.1 mg, vitamin C: 50 mg, vitamin E: 1.3 mg, omega-3 fatty acids: 0.1 g.

% CALORIES FROM: protein 8%, fat 16%, carbohydrate 76%

SUMMER SQUASH AND RED PEPPER MEDLEY

Colorful seasonal vegetables require little cooking and minimal seasoning yet make delicious, eye-appealing fare.

1 tablespoon	extra-virgin olive oil	15 ml
½ teaspoon	crushed garlic	2 ml
2	large zucchinis, cut into thick matchsticks	2
2	large yellow summer squash, cut into thick matchsticks	2
½ cup	finely diced red bell pepper	125 ml
1–2 tablespoons	balsamic vinegar	15–30 ml
	Umeboshi vinegar or salt	

Heat the oil in a large skillet or wok over medium heat. Add the garlic and sauté for 30 seconds. Add the zucchini and squash and sauté for 5 minutes. Stir in the red bell pepper and continue to sauté until all the vegetables are tender, about 5 minutes longer. Sprinkle in the balsamic vinegar and toss until the vegetables are evenly coated. Season with umeboshi vinegar or salt to taste.

PER SERVING: calories: 95, protein: 4 g, fat: 4 g, carbohydrate: 14 g, dietary fiber: 5.5 g, calcium: 61 mg, iron: 1.6 mg, magnesium: 75 mg, sodium: 48 mg, zinc: 0.8 mg, folate: 82 mcg, riboflavin: 0.1 mg, vitamin C: 74 mg, vitamin E: 1.0 mg, omega-3 fatty acids: 0.2 g.

% CALORIES FROM: protein 15%,   fat 34%,   carbohydrate 51%

CONTAINS: * Fermented foods (vinegar)

GREEN GRITS

Broccoli adds flavor, nutrition, and beautiful flecks of green to this delicious recipe. Serve it as a side dish in place of rice or potatoes, or even as a savory breakfast porridge. Do not be tempted to substitute cornmeal or rice flour for the grits, as you will not have good results. Use only the more coarsely ground corn grits, also called polenta, or use rice grits, also known as rice farina.

2 cups	water	500 ml
½ cup	yellow corn grits or rice grits (see tips below)	125 ml
½-1 cup	chopped broccoli	125–250 ml
1 tablespoon	extra-virgin olive oil	15 ml
½ teaspoon	salt	2 ml

Combine the water and broccoli in a heavy-bottomed saucepan and bring to a boil. Reduce the heat to medium and simmer for 5 minutes. Remove from the heat and stir in the grits with a long-handled wooden spoon. Return to a boil. Reduce the heat to low, cover, and cook, stirring occasionally, for about 20 minutes. Stir well. Add the olive oil and salt and mix thoroughly. Serve hot.

TIPS:

• Two good brands of brown rice grits are Bob's Red Mill's Creamy Brown Rice Farina and Arrowhead Mills Rice & Shine cereal. You also can make your own rice grits at home by whirling white or brown rice in a dry blender until it is very finely pelletized.

• If the grits stick to the bottom of your saucepan, use a flame tamer or heat diffuser underneath.

PER SERVING AS A SIDE DISH: calories: 113, protein: 2.5 g, fat: 4 g, carbohydrate: 18 g, dietary fiber: 1 g, calcium: 13 mg, iron: 1.0 mg, magnesium: 10 mg, sodium: 299 mg, zinc: 0.2 mg, folate: 53 mcg, riboflavin: 0.1 mg, vitamin C: 11 mg, vitamin E: 0.8 mg, omega-3 fatty acids: 0 g.

% CALORIES FROM: protein 8%,   fat 30%,   carbohydrate 62%

CRISPY ROASTED KALE

Roasting kale is a great way to get finicky eaters to enjoy healthful greens. The leaves turn out crisp and crunchy, like a dark green chip! Roasted kale is delicious as a side dish, unique appetizer, or snack any time of the day.

1	large bunch of kale (curly leaf or dinosaur/lacinato)
	Olive oil spray
	Salt (optional)

Preheat the oven to 400°F (205°C). Lightly oil one or two large baking sheets or line them with parchment paper (for easy cleanup) and set aside. Rinse the kale well and pat dry. Tear the leaves into large, chip-size pieces and arrange in a single layer on the prepared baking sheets. Discard the kale stems and ribs.

Mist the leaves with olive oil and sprinkle lightly with salt, if desired (the salt may be added prior to baking or after, if you prefer). Bake until crisp but not blackened, about 20 minutes. Watch closely, as the kale can burn quickly and become bitter (or turn into blackened charcoal). Perfectly roasted kale will be crisp like a very thin potato chip and sweet.

VARIATION: For Garlic Roasted Kale, sprinkle the kale lightly with garlic powder after misting it with oil. Proceed as directed.

Marinated Carrot Sticks

Yields 6 to 8 servings as a side dish

Serve marinated carrot sticks as a special appetizer, side dish, or tasty addition to a vegetarian antipasto. They also are great to keep in the fridge for a no-fuss, no-muss snack.

8–10	carrots, cut into sticks about 2½ inches (6.5 cm) long by ½ inch (1 cm) thick	8–10
⅓ cup	red wine vinegar	85 ml
¼ cup	extra-virgin olive oil	60 ml
½ teaspoon	crushed garlic	2 ml
Generous pinch	of salt	Generous pinch

Place about an inch (2.5 cm) of water in a large saucepan and bring to a boil. Add the carrots, cover, and cook for 6–8 minutes over medium heat or until tender-crisp. Drain and transfer to a bowl.

Combine the remaining ingredients in a small bowl or measuring cup and whisk until blended. Pour over the carrots and toss until evenly coated. Cover tightly and refrigerate several hours or overnight, tossing again once or twice. Drain or serve with a slotted spoon. Best if brought to room temperature before serving.

Per serving: calories: 120, protein: 1 g, fat: 9 g, carbohydrate: 8 g, dietary fiber: 2.5 g, calcium: 23 mg, iron: 0.5 mg, magnesium: 12 mg, sodium: 82 mg, zinc: 0.2 mg, folate: 11 mcg, riboflavin: 0.1 mg, vitamin C: 8 mg, vitamin E: 1.7 mg, omega-3 fatty acids: 0.1 g.

% Calories from: protein 3%, fat 70%, carbohydrate 27%

CONTAINS: * Fermented foods (vinegar)

EASY BAKED BEANS

Yields about 4 cups (1 L)

Here is a time-honored classic made simple.

2 tablespoons	olive oil	30 ml
2 large	onions, finely chopped	2 large
2 teaspoons	crushed garlic	10 ml
½ cup	tomato paste	125 ml
2 tablespoons	balsamic vinegar	30 ml
2–4 tablespoons	pure maple syrup	30–60 ml
2 teaspoons	prepared yellow mustard	10 ml
3½ cups	drained cooked or canned navy beans	875 ml
	Salt	

Preheat the oven to 350°F (180°C). Oil a 2-quart casserole dish and set aside. Heat the oil in a skillet. When hot, add the onions and garlic and sauté until the onions are well browned and very tender.

Meanwhile, combine the tomato paste, balsamic vinegar, maple syrup, and mustard in a large bowl. Mix well to form a smooth, thick sauce. Add the beans and mix gently. Stir in the cooked onions, season with salt to taste, and spoon into the prepared casserole dish. Cover tightly and bake for 30 minutes.

VARIATION: Substitute cooked lima beans, Great Northern beans, or pinto beans for the navy beans.

PER CUP (250 ML): calories: 414, protein: 19.5 g, fat: 8 g, carbohydrate: 69 g, dietary fiber: 14.5 g, calcium: 150 mg, iron: 5.3 mg, magnesium: 135 mg, sodium: 1358 mg, zinc: 2.6 mg, folate: 164 mcg, riboflavin: 0.2 mg, vitamin C: 21 mg, vitamin E: 3.4 mg, omega-3 fatty acids: 0.3 g.

% CALORIES FROM: protein 18%,   fat 18%,   carbohydrate 64%

CONTAINS: * FERMENTED foods (MUSTARD; VINEGAR) * TOMATO

GARLICKY GREENS

This is a spectacular way to serve greens. Don't be intimidated by the large quantity of garlic. Thinly sliced cooked garlic is surprisingly mild because very little of its pungent oil is released.

2 tablespoons	olive oil	30 ml
6–8	cloves garlic, very thinly sliced	6–8
8 cups	finely chopped or torn greens (see tip below)	2 L
½ cup	water, more or less as needed	125 ml
	Hot sauce (optional)	
	Fresh lemon juice (optional)	
	Salt and pepper	

Heat the oil in a very large saucepan or pot. When hot, add the garlic and cook, stirring constantly, for 30 seconds. Add the greens, toss to coat with the oil, and stir-fry until slightly wilted, about 2–5 minutes.

Pour in just enough water to cover the bottom of the pan and bring to a boil. Reduce the heat, cover, and steam, stirring occasionally, for 20–30 minutes, or until the greens are tender to your liking. There should be very little liquid left in the saucepan. If there is liquid, uncover and simmer briefly until it cooks off. Add a little more water during cooking, only if necessary. Do not let the greens cook dry or they will scorch.

Stir in the optional hot sauce and lemon juice to taste, if desired. Season with salt and pepper to taste.

TIP: For the greens, choose among collards, kale, mustard greens, turnip greens, beet greens, or a mixture of two or more of these. The first four listed are excellent sources of calcium and all are rich in vitamins A, C, and folate.

PER SERVING: calories: 88, protein: 2 g, fat: 7 g, carbohydrate: 6 g, dietary fiber: 2.5 g, calcium: 113 mg, iron: 0.2 mg, magnesium: 8 mg, sodium: 55 mg, zinc: 0.2 mg, folate: 120 mcg, riboflavin: 0.1 mg, vitamin C: 27 mg, vitamin E: 2.5 mg, omega-3 fatty acids: 0.1 g.

% CALORIES FROM: protein 9%,   fat 67%,   carbohydrate 24%

More Treats and Sweets

*I*n this section you'll find quick and healthful snack ideas along with sweet treats that don't require baking. When you're in the midst of a snack "emergency" or want a simple, fast dessert for family or guests, this is where to turn. Many items, such as the Choco-Currant Cranberry Squares, freeze well. Others can be kept in the refrigerator or in a closed container in a cupboard.

In keeping with the theme that you cannot only survive—but thrive—despite food sensitivities, we've taken simple ingredients and created fabulous and sometimes unusual treats. Some, like Puffy Bars, are sweet and crispy, created especially to quash that craving in a jiffy. Others, like Chickpea "Nuts," will give you a satisfying crunch, jam-packed with protein and minerals. Keep either of these handy in a backpack, glove compartment, or dish on the kitchen counter. In this section you'll even discover a dairy-free, soy-free, Berry Delicious "Ice Cream." You'll surprise guests and the neighborhood children with this healthful and creamy offering.

Like any indulgence, these recipes are meant to round out a healthy diet, not be the center of your diet. Still, have no guilt, because unlike commercial snack foods, our recipes are low in sodium, saturated fat, and simple sugars, and they are free of cholesterol. Because they are made from natural ingredients, they also have more vitamins and minerals than most store-bought treats. Plus, while many store-bought snacks and sweets contain ingredients that cause a reaction for food-sensitive people, our recipes are specially designed for those with allergies and intolerances.

Chickpea "Nuts"

You can use these flavorful "nuts" to replace tree nuts in any recipe you like. They are even higher in protein and iron than tree nuts and make a highly nutritious snack. For use in recipes, you may prefer to prepare the "nuts" plain. For snacking, add the optional spices of your choice.

1¾ cups	cooked or canned chickpeas, rinsed and drained 1 (15-ounce can/425-g) can	435 ml
1 tablespoon	olive oil or organic canola or safflower oil	15 ml

OPTIONAL SPICES (CHOOSE ONE OR MORE):

¼ teaspoon	ground cumin	1 ml
¼ teaspoon	ground coriander	1 ml
¼ teaspoon	ground ginger	1 ml
¼ teaspoon	garlic powder	1 ml
⅛ teaspoon	cayenne pepper	1 pinch

Preheat the oven to 400°F (205°C). Line a baking sheet with parchment paper and set aside. Toss the chickpeas with the oil and any optional spices of your choice. Place on the prepared baking sheet and bake until golden and crunchy, about 30 minutes. The "nuts" will get crunchier as they cool, so be careful not to overbake them.

PER ½ CUP (125 ML): calories: 197, protein: 9 g, fat: 7 g, carbohydrate: 26 g, dietary fiber: 7 g, calcium: 47 mg, iron: 3 mg, magnesium: 46 mg, sodium: 7 mg, zinc: 1.5 mg, folate: 165 mcg, riboflavin: 0.1 mg, vitamin C: 1 mg, vitamin E: 0.9 mg, omega-3 fatty acids: 0.1 g.

% CALORIES FROM: protein 17%, fat 31%, carbohydrate 52%

Ume-Roasted Seeds or Nuts

Ume-roasted seeds or nuts make a delightful, savory garnish for grain, bean, and vegetable dishes and are a nutritious, crunchy addition to salads. If you use seeds or cashew nuts, you'll be getting an excellent source of zinc. Almonds are good sources of calcium. Walnuts are high in omega-3 fatty acids.

| ½ cup | raw seeds or nuts | 125 ml |
| | Umeboshi vinegar | |

Place the seeds or nuts in a heavy skillet over medium-high heat. Toast, stirring almost constantly with a wooden spoon, until they are lightly and evenly browned, make a slight crackling sound, and emit a nutty aroma. Remove from the heat and sprinkle a small amount of umeboshi vinegar over the hot seeds or nuts, using just enough to lightly coat them. Quickly toss the seeds or nuts in the hot skillet to dry them and evenly distribute the vinegar. Transfer the nuts or seeds to a shallow bowl or plate and allow to cool. When completely cool, store them in an airtight container at room temperature.

VARIATION: Add a pinch of chili powder, curry powder, or ground ginger to the seeds or nuts just before or after adding the vinegar.

TIPS:

- Some good choices for seeds and nuts include sunflower, pumpkin, cashews, almonds, walnuts, or pecans.

- Pumpkin seeds will make a popping sound and puff up when they are toasted.

- Ume-roasted seeds can replace tree nuts in any savory dish. Reduce the amount of salt in the recipe as need to offset the saltiness of the umeboshi vinegar.

- Plain roasted seeds (without the vinegar) can be used to replace tree nuts in any sweet recipe that calls for raw or roasted nuts.

CONTAINS: * FERMENTED foods (vinegar)

Homemade Seed Butter

Yields ⅔ cup (170 ml)

It is easy to make your own seed butters at home, and it doesn't take much time. Be sure to buy your raw seeds from a trusted source to ensure no contamination from potential allergens.

1 cup	hulled raw or unseasoned dry-roasted seeds (sunflower, pumpkin, or sesame)	250 ml
1–2 tablespoons	organic canola, sunflower, or olive oil, or a combination of two or more	15–30 ml
	Salt (optional)	

Grind the seeds for several minutes in a food processor. Don't rush the process. The more finely ground the seeds, the smoother the finished butter. Once the seeds are finely ground, add the oil. Start with the smaller amount and add more as necessary. You may need slightly more oil than the amount indicated. The more oil you use, the smoother the butter will become. Add a pinch of salt to taste, if desired. Transfer to a storage container and store in the refrigerator. It will keep for several weeks.

VARIATION: If you are able to have nut butters and want to make your own at home, feel free to substitute an equal amount of raw or plain, dry-roasted nuts for the seeds in the recipe.

TIPS: This recipe can be easily doubled. However, don't overload your food processor or you will not be able to grind the seeds to a fine powder.

• Storing the seed butter in the refrigerator will keep it fresh and also help prevent the oil from separating out. If it does separate out, just stir it back in with a knife until it is well combined.

• Seeds vary from batch to batch depending on the season, where they were grown, and their storage conditions. Some seeds will have more or less oil than others, so the amount of oil needed may vary each time you make seed butter.

• Homemade tahini, made from sesame seeds, and other seed butters will not be smooth and runny like tahini or butters made in a factory; they will have a bit of texture to them. Nevertheless, they will taste delicious and can be used just like any other tahini or seed butter.

PER TABLESPOON (15 ML)*: calories: 81, protein: 3 g, fat: 7 g, carbohydrate: 3 g, dietary fiber: 1.5 g, calcium: 16 mg, iron: 1 mg, magnesium: 48 mg, sodium: 0.4 mg, zinc: 0.7 mg, folate: 31 mcg, riboflavin: 0 mg, vitamin C: 0.2 mg, vitamin E: 6.9 mg, omega-3 fatty acids: 0.1 g.

% CALORIES FROM: protein 14%,   fat 74%,   carbohydrate 12%

*Nutritional analysis done using sesame seeds.

MOCHI

Mochi (pronounced MOH-chee) is a traditional Japanese food and makes a nutritious snack, gourmet appetizer, tasty accompaniment to soups and salads, or a delicious side dish. Made from cooked and pounded, naturally sweet short-grain rice with a high starch content, mochi is both wheat free and gluten free. It comes in flat, hard cakes and must be kept refrigerated. (For long-term storage, mochi may be frozen, but it must be thawed before using, as frozen mochi will be too hard to cut.)

The easiest way to prepare mochi is to cut it into 1½-inch (4 cm) squares (use a sharp, heavy knife), place the squares on a baking sheet about 1 inch (2.5 cm) apart, and bake in a preheated 450°F (230°C) oven for 8–10 minutes. The squares will puff up like small puff pastries. The center will be hollow, the top will be crisp, and the bottom and interior will be chewy and gooey, somewhat like cheese. If you like, you can fill baked mochi pockets with raw or roasted vegetables, your favorite bean dip (see pages 239–254), or seed or nut butter and jelly.

Mochi comes plain (no added seasonings) and in a variety of flavors, from sweet to savory. Some flavors may contain nuts or other foods to which you may be sensitive, so be sure to check the ingredients list on the package. The plain is very bland, but that makes it the most adaptable and the most convenient for those with food intolerances. You can mist the baked plain or savory squares with olive oil and sprinkle them lightly with salt or herbs or garlic powder. Or try topping them with a gravy or dipping them into a sauce. They are especially good with warm Pizza Sauce, page 335, for a quick, nutritious treat. Alternatively, the plain or sweet-flavored mochi squares may be served with fruit, applesauce, or jam, or they can be dipped in pure maple syrup for a sweet snack, dessert, or breakfast.

Mochi squares can be placed on top of casseroles or you can finely dice mochi and scatter the pieces over pizza prior to baking to make a crispy, cheesy topping. Add mochi squares to soups or stews shortly before serving. Cover the pot and warm gently so the mochi can soften and become creamy. You can simmer mochi squares in brothy soups—these are the original Japanese dumplings.

Mochi also can be pan-fried. Just cut the mochi into squares, brush both sides lightly with vegetable oil, and cook in a heavy skillet (nonstick or cast iron will work best) over medium heat until browned and lightly puffed, about 6 minutes per side.

Mochi is a quick, delicious, versatile food that can add fun and pleasure to your meals. Be as creative as you like with it and discover new worlds of culinary enjoyment.

Papadums

Papadums are crispy, paper-thin crackers made with chickpea flour and sometimes spices and are available at East Indian grocery stores. They can be mild or spicy depending on the type and amount of seasonings used. Papadums traditionally are eaten as an appetizer with chutney or as an accompaniment to a curry dinner. However, they nicely complement soups, stews, or salads instead of crackers or bread. They also make a pleasant breakfast replacement for toast. Normally deep fried when served in a restaurant, papadums have no added fat when prepared under a broiler.

To prepare them the no-fat way, preheat the broiler and place the oven rack six inches below the broiler. Place 2 papadums on the rack and broil, watching carefully (papadums can burn quickly). Once the heat begins to blister a papadum, move it around using tongs, until the heat blisters every part of the cracker (about 20–30 seconds). For added richness and flavor, mist one side of each papadum with a little extra-virgin olive oil after it is removed from the oven.

Puffy Bars

Yields about 16 large bars or 32 squares

Sweet and quick, this recipe is a real crowd-pleaser.

8 cups	puffed rice	2 L
1 cup	brown sugar	250 ml
½ cup	pure maple syrup	125 ml
⅓ cup	organic canola or safflower oil	85 ml
¼ cup	unsweetened cocoa	60 ml
1 teaspoon	vanilla flavoring	5 ml

Measure puffed rice into a large bowl. Combine the brown sugar, maple syrup, oil, and cocoa in a medium saucepan and bring to a boil. Boil 1 minute, stirring constantly. Remove from the heat and stir in the vanilla flavoring. Pour over the puffed rice and mix well. Spread into a 9 x 13-inch pan, a jelly roll pan, a baking sheet, or smaller pans to cool. Cut into bars or squares. Store leftovers in an airtight container at room temperature. The bars will keep for about 10 days.

Per bar: calories: 151, protein: 0.5 g, fat: 5 g, carbohydrate: 27 g, dietary fiber: 0.5 g, calcium: 21 mg, iron: 2.8 mg, magnesium: 14 mg, sodium: 7 mg, zinc: 0.6 mg, folate: 1.9 mcg, riboflavin: 0.1 mg, vitamin C: 0 mg, vitamin E: 1.0 mg, omega-3 fatty acids: 0.4 g.

% Calories from: protein 2%,   fat 28%,   carbohydrate 70%

CONTAINS: * Chocolate

CRISPY RICE BARS

These rich, crunchy squares make a delicious dessert or sweet snack.

⅔ cup	brown rice syrup	170 ml
¼ cup	sesame tahini, other seed butter (see page 354), or almond butter	60 ml
½ teaspoon	vanilla flavoring	2 ml
2 cups	crisped rice cereal	500 ml

ADDITIONS (CHOOSE ONE):

½ cup	lightly roasted sunflower seeds, chopped almonds, or chopped walnuts	125 ml
½ cup	currants, raisins, or finely chopped apricots	125 ml
½ cup	nondairy chocolate or carob chips	125 ml

Oil an 8-inch square pan or mist it with nonstick cooking spray and set aside. Place the brown rice syrup and tahini in a small saucepan and warm until the mixture is softened and smooth. Remove from the heat and stir in the vanilla flavoring.

Combine the cereal and the addition of your choice in a large bowl. Pour the warm mixture over the cereal mix and combine carefully using a wooden spoon. Work as quickly as possible (this is especially important if using chocolate or carob chips so they do not melt). Pack the mixture evenly into prepared pan, pressing gently with your fingers. Cover the pan with plastic wrap and chill until firm. Slice into squares and store in an airtight container in the refrigerator. Will keep for about 10 days.

PER SQUARE*: calories: 77, protein: 1 g, fat: 2 g, carbohydrate: 14 g, dietary fiber: 0.5 g, calcium: 10 mg, iron: 0.4 mg, magnesium: 7 mg, sodium: 27 mg, zinc: 0.3 mg, folate: 21 mcg, riboflavin: 0.1 mg, vitamin C: 2 mg, vitamin E: 1 mg, omega-3 fatty acids: 0 g.

% CALORIES FROM: protein 5%, fat 23%, carbohydrate 72%

*Nutritional analysis done using sesame tahini and currants.

Berry Delicious "Ice Cream"

Yields 3–4 servings (3 cups)

This creamy, sweet "ice cream" is sure to be a favorite as it's bursting with real fruit flavor. Put it in fancy sherbet glasses and serve it to your guests for a refreshing summer treat. (This recipe is from The New Becoming Vegetarian *by Vesanto Melina and Brenda Davis, The Book Publishing Company, 2003. In Canada,* Becoming Vegetarian, *Wiley Canada.)*

3	frozen bananas (see tips on page 236)	3
1 cup	fresh or frozen berries (such as raspberries, strawberries, or blueberries)	250 ml
1 cup	fortified vanilla or plain nondairy milk or coconut milk	250 ml
2 tablespoons	frozen juice concentrate (orange, citrus blend, peach, or mango)	30 ml

Place the frozen bananas, berries, milk, and frozen juice concentrate in a blender or food processor. Blend or process on high speed until completely smooth. A sturdy blender is ideal; many food processors work well too. (If your blender struggles to blend this, partially thawing the fruit, especially the strawberries, will help.) Serve immediately in bowls or in cups with a spoon. Top with seeds, nuts, or fresh berries, if desired.

PER CUP (250 ML): calories: 187, protein: 2 g, fat: 1 g, carbohydrate: 45 g, dietary fiber: 5.5 g, calcium: 120 mg*, iron: 0.6 mg, magnesium: 46 mg, sodium: 31 mg, zinc: 0.4 mg, folate: 51 mcg, riboflavin: 0.2 mg, vitamin C: 37 mg, vitamin E: 1.9 mg, omega-3 fatty acids: 0.1 g.

% CALORIES FROM: protein 6%, fat 7%, carbohydrate 89%

*Nutritional analysis done using calcium-fortified nondairy milk.

CHOCO-CURRANT CRANBERRY SQUARES

Yields 21 SQUARES ($3\frac{1}{2}$ CUPS/875 ML MIXTURE)

Here's an ideal combination of dried fruit, chocolate, and cereal that you can stir together in minutes.

½ cup	pure maple syrup	125 ml
¼ cup	sesame tahini, other seed butter (see page 354), or nut butter	60 ml
2½ squares (2.5 ounces)	semisweet baking chocolate	71.2 g
⅔ cup	dried currants or cranberries or a combination	170 ml
1¼ cups	puffed rice cereal	310 ml
1¼ cups	gluten-free flaked cereal	310 ml

Place the maple syrup, tahini, and baking chocolate in the top of double boiler and heat over boiling water until the chocolate is just melted. If you do not have a double boiler, place the pan directly over low heat, watching and stirring frequently to prevent burning. Stir to mix evenly and remove from the heat. Add the currants and cereal and mix until well coated with the chocolate mixture. Press into a lightly oiled 4 x 9-inch (10 x 23-cm) loaf pan, making squares about 1 inch (2.5 cm) high. Place in the refrigerate or freezer for 30 minutes to set. Cut into 21 squares.

PER SQUARE: calories: 75, protein: 1 g, fat: 3 g, carbohydrate: 13 g, dietary fiber: 1 g, calcium: 8 mg, iron: 0.4 mg, magnesium: 5 mg, sodium: 1 mg, zinc: 0.2 mg, folate: 3 mcg, riboflavin: 0 mg, vitamin C: 0 mg, vitamin E: 0.1 mg, omega-3 fatty acids: 0 g.

% CALORIES FROM: protein 6%,   fat 29%,   carbohydrate 65%

CONTAINS: * Chocolate

APRICOT CONFECTIONS

Apricots are an excellent source of vitamin A and potassium, but frankly, who cares when these impressive confections taste simply wonderful!

½ pound	dried unsulfured apricots	225 g
	Hot water, as needed	
½ cup	sunflower or pumpkin seeds or coarsely chopped nuts	125 ml
	Confectioners' sugar	
	About 30 whole seeds or nut halves of choice, to decorate	

Pulse apricots in food processor. Then grind to a smooth paste, adding a very small amount of hot water, one teaspoon (5 ml) at a time, only if necessary. Transfer to a bowl and work in the seeds with your hands. Wet or oil your hands so the paste does not stick. Take small lumps of the paste and roll into marble-size balls. Roll in confectioners' sugar and press a whole seed on top of each. Store leftovers in the refrigerator. Will keep for about 2 weeks.

PER PIECE: calories: 45, protein: 1 g, fat: 1 g, carbohydrate: 8 g, dietary fiber: 1 g, calcium: 6 mg, iron: 0.5 mg, magnesium: 5 mg, sodium: 0 mg, zinc: 0.2 mg, folate: 6.2 mcg, riboflavin: 0 mg, vitamin C: 2 mg, vitamin E: 1.3 mg, omega-3 fatty acids: 0.0 g.

% CALORIES FROM: protein 8%, fat 27%, carbohydrate 65%

STUFFED DATES

This incredibly simple, naturally sweet recipe is satisfying and delicious. It's even elegant enough to serve to dinner guests.

Dates (preferably Medjool)
Seed or nut butter (tahini other seed butter, or almond or cashew butter)
Whole pumpkin seeds or whole blanched almonds or other nut of choice

Carefully slit dates with a sharp knife and remove the pit. Fill slit with about ½ teaspoon (2 ml) seed or nut butter. Then gently press in 1 pumpkin seed.

PER DATE: calories: 47, protein: 1 g, fat: 2 g, carbohydrate: 7 g, dietary fiber: 1 g, calcium: 13 mg, iron: 0.2 mg, magnesium: 15 mg, sodium: 1 mg, zinc: 0.2 mg, folate: 3 mcg, riboflavin: 0 mg, vitamin C: 0 mg, vitamin E: 0.9 mg, omega-3 fatty acids: 0 g.

% CALORIES FROM: protein 7%, fat 40%, carbohydrate 53%

CHOCOLATE TOOTSIES

Yields about 40 tootsies

These rich, fudgey balls or rolls will satisfy your chocolate cravings instantly!

¼ cup	brown rice syrup	60 ml
¼ cup	tahini or other seed butter (see page 354), or almond or cashew butter	60 ml
1½ tablespoons	unsweetened cocoa powder	22 ml
1 tablespoon	organic canola or safflower oil	15 ml
½ teaspoon	vanilla flavoring	2 ml
2	brown rice cakes, finely crushed or 1¼ cups (310 ml) puffed or crisped brown rice cereal	2

Place the rice syrup, tahini, cocoa powder, and oil in a medium saucepan. Warm over low heat, stirring often, until melted and well combined. Remove from the heat and stir in the vanilla flavoring. Using a sturdy wooden spoon, stir in the crushed rice cakes or rice cereal until thoroughly incorporated. Let cool until the mixture can be handled easily. Roll between your hands into marble-size balls or pinky-size rolls. Place each ball or roll as it is formed on a sheet of waxed paper or parchment paper. Store in an airtight container at room temperature. Will keep for about 10 days.

PER TOOTSIE: calories: 20, protein: 0.5 g, fat: 1 g, carbohydrate: 2 g, dietary fiber: <1 g, calcium: 5 mg, iron: 0.1 mg, magnesium: 6 mg, sodium: 0 mg, zinc: 0.1 mg, folate: 1.2 mcg, riboflavin: 0 mg, vitamin C: 0 mg, vitamin E: 0.4 mg, omega-3 fatty acids: 0 g.

% CALORIES FROM: protein 6%,   fat 58%,   carbohydrate 36%

CONTAINS: * Chocolate

INCREDIBLE HOT FUDGE SAUCE

Yields 1 ½ cups (375 ml)

Serve this scrumptious sauce warm as a topping for cakes, desserts, nondairy ice cream or sorbet, or as a dipping sauce for fruit. It's cheering to know that cocoa beans are rich in minerals such as iron, magnesium, and zinc. To learn more about kuzu, arrowroot, and similar items, see Ingredients That May Be New to You, pages 171–178.

½ cup	unsweetened cocoa powder	125 ml
2 tablespoons	kuzu, arrowroot, or cornstarch	30 ml
1¼ cups	fortified vanilla nondairy milk or light coconut milk	310 ml
½ cup	pure maple syrup	125 ml

Combine cocoa powder and kuzu in a small bowl, and stir with a dry wire whisk. Transfer to a small saucepan, and gradually whisk in 1/2 cup (125 ml) of the milk. Slowly whisk in the remaining milk and maple syrup, and mix well. Cook over medium heat, whisking constantly, for 2–3 minutes or until thickened. Store in an air-tight container in the refrigerator. Reheat as needed.

PER ¼ CUP (60 ML): calories: 120, protein: 2 g, fat: 1 g, carbohydrate: 29 g, dietary fiber: 2.5 g, calcium: 90 mg, iron: 1.4 mg, magnesium: 39 mg, sodium: 23 mg, zinc: 1.6 mg, folate: 2 mcg, riboflavin: 0 mg, vitamin C: 0 mg, vitamin E: 0.9 mg, omega-3 fatty acids: 0 g.

% CALORIES FROM: protein 4%, fat 10%, carbohydrate 86%

CONTAINS: * Chocolate

RESOURCES

Here are some resources that will help you find products and information specific to your own needs. Please note that this is an incomplete list; it is a work in progress that will be revised as new products and services become available and existing ones become outdated or discontinued. For the most current and complete listing on resources for food sensitivities, please visit our Web site at www.foodallergysurvivalguide.com and click on the resources link. If you use any of the resources mentioned here or earlier in the text, be sure to mention this book as your source of the information

CONSULTATIONS For individual consultations on food sensitivities, contact the following people:

Vesanto Melina, MS, RD	vesanto@nutrispeak.com	604-882-6782	www.nutrispeak.com
Dina Aronson, MS, RD	nutrawiz@aol.com	781-391-6444	www.nutrawiz.com
Michael Klaper, MD	mklaper@flex.com	808-281-6936	www.drklaper.com
Janice Joneja, PhD, RD	jmjoneja@shaw.ca	250-372-3246	

For consultation services regarding product and recipe development, contact:
Jo Stepaniak: jo@vegsource.com

The products listed here are for informational purposes only. The Book Publishing Company and the authors make no claims or guarantees for the products' effectiveness or use. Product formulations are subject to change at any time. We encourage you to contact the company to find out more detailed information specific to your individual needs.

FOOD AND SUPPLIES

The following companies offer high-quality, nutritious foods:

Aunt Candice Foods. Cookies, brownies, and mixes free of wheat, dairy, gluten, casein, corn, soy, and additives. Web: www.auntcandicefoods.com

Alpsnack. Gluten-, wheat-, egg-, and dairy-free organic snack bar made with hemp nuts, almonds, dried fruits, and other natural ingredients. Phone: 760-743-2211. Web: www.alpsnack.com.

Authentic Foods. Dedicated to gluten-free products, from milling, to blending, to packaging. Baking mixes, flours, pasta, snacks, cereals. Phone: 310-366-7612. Web: www.authenticfoods.com

Birkett Mills. Buckwheat products. Web: www.thebirkettmills.com

Bob's Red Mill. Hypoallergenic baking products, flours, mixes, cereals, entrées, grains, beans, dried fruits, seeds, and spices. Many gluten-free products. Phone: 800-349-2173. Web: www.bobsredmill.com

Dietary Specialties. Gluten-free frozen foods, baking mixes, breads, pastas, snacks, and sweets. Phone: 888-640-2800. Web: www.dietspec.com

Eden Foods. Grains, 100 percent buckwheat noodles, beans, seasonings. Phone: 888 441-EDEN. Web: www.edenfoods.com

Edward & Sons. Organic grocery items such as miso soup, rice snaps, sauces, and candies, many of which are free of gluten and other common allergens. Phone: 805-684-8500. Web: www.edwardandsons.com

El Peto. Manufacturer and distributor of a huge line of gluten-, wheat-, yeast-, corn-, milk-, and egg-free products. Phone: 800-387-4064. Web: www.elpeto.com

Ener-G Foods. Egg and milk substitutes, flours, baked goods, mixes, pasta, cereals, soups, gluten-free items. Phone: 800-331-5222. Web: www.ener-g.com

Enjoy Life Foods. Baked goods, snack bars, and cereals free of gluten, wheat, dairy, casein, eggs, soy, nuts, potato, GMOs, and hydrogenated oil. Prepared in a gluten-free and peanut-free facility. Phone: 888-50-ENJOY. Web: www.enjoylifefoods.com

Gluten Free Mixes. Baking and seasoning mixes, flours, and even cake decorating kits, all gluten free. Phone: 866-225-3432. Web: www.glutenfreemixes.com

Gold Mine Natural Food Company. Hard-to-find gluten-free grains, snacks, condiments, dried fruits, and more, most of which are organic. Phone: 1-800-475-FOOD. Web: www.goldminenaturalfood.com

Grainworks. Quinoa and other organic grains. Phone: 800-563-3756 Web: www.grainworks.com

Kinnikinnick Foods. Gluten-, wheat-, and casein-free breads (some are yeast free), mixes, snacks, baking mixes, desserts, and more. Phone: 877-503-4466. Web: www.kinnikinnick.com

Manitoba Harvest Hemp Food and Oils. (Canada) Organic and GMO-free sources of omega-3 fatty acids Phone: 800-665-HEMP. Web: www.manitobaharvest.com

Mail Order Catalog for Healthy Eating. Dairy substitutes, nutritional yeast, gluten-free grains and pastas, soynut butters. Phone: 800-695-2241. Web: www.healthy-eating.com

Mountain Meadows Food Processing Ltd. (Canada) Delicious pea-based spread produced in a peanut-free and nut-free facility. Phone: 780-961-2470. Web: www.peabutter.ca

Mrs. Leepers. Rice and corn pasta. Phone: 816-502-6000. Web: www.mrsleeperspasta.com

Nalgene. Containers of various sizes with tight-fitting, spill-proof lids, valuable for bringing foods and beverages when traveling. Available online or at outdoor equipment stores. Web: www.nalgene-outdoor.com

Nature's Hilights. Gluten-free, dedicated facility producing wheat-, gluten-, and yeast-free, pizza crusts, frozen entrées, and snacks. Phone: 707-462-6605. Web: www.natures-hilights.com

Natures Path Foods. Organic cereals, including gluten-free products. Phone: 888-808-9505. Web: www.naturespath.com

Nu-World Amaranth. Amaranth-based snacks free of dairy, eggs, wheat, rice, corn, oats, soy, potato, and nuts. Phone: 630-369-6819. Web: www.nuworldfoods.com

Omega Nutrition. Organic flaxseed oil and related products. Phone: 800-661-FLAX (3529). Web: www.omeganutrition.com

Pangea. Foods, snacks, mixes, and sweets that are free of eggs and dairy products. Phone: 800-340-1200. Web: www.pangeaveg.com

Pamela's. Wheat-free baked goods and baking mixes, many of which are also free of gluten, eggs, nuts, and soy. Phone: 650-952-4546. Web: www.pamelasproducts.com

Tinkyada. (Canada) Amazing wheat-free, gluten-free rice pasta in a wide variety of shapes and sizes. Phone: 416-609-0016. Web: www.tinkyada.com

The Soynut Butter Company. Peanut-free soynut butter produced in a 100 percent peanut- and treenut-free facility. Also gluten-free tortilla crumbs and cornflake crumbs. Phone: 800-288-1012. Web: www.soynutbutter.com

Vegan Essentials. Better Than Milk fortified rice beverage and a variety of egg- and dairy-free foods. Phone: 866-88-VEGAN. Web: www.veganessentials.com

Vermont Nut-Free Chocolates. Chocolate confections, absolutely free of nuts. The dark chocolate has no dairy ingredients, although it is produced on the same equipment as the milk chocolate. Phone: 1-888-468-8373. Web: www.vermontnutfree.com.

WholeSoy. Drinks and cultured soy yogurt with probiotics (live active cultures). Phone: 415-495-2870. Web: www.wholesoycom.com

Multivitamin-Mineral Supplements

Generally speaking, a multivitamin-mineral supplement is preferable to single trace-mineral supplements. For example, taking a supplement containing a single trace mineral such as zinc can create nutrient imbalances and cause deficiencies of other minerals such as copper. For the mineral calcium, which we need in larger amounts, the situation is different and single-mineral supplements or combinations that include vitamin D, perhaps with magnesium, are acceptable.

Note that many supplement labels suggest that we take several pills or capsules in order to meet recommended intakes (shown in appendixes A and B). However, if our diet supplies a significant portion of our recommended intake, taking several pills may be unnecessary and wasteful; to be economical, we can take just one pill per day or even every other day. A nutritionist can help determine your individual needs from your diet records and laboratory tests.

The companies listed below provide at least one multivitamin-mineral supplement that is free of animal ingredients and hypoallergenic, and most also offer other products such as prenatal and children's supplements and calcium. Be cautious when choosing your supplement, since many companies offer a wide variety of products, some of which are hypoallergenic and some of which are not. Always ask the company; most have toll-free numbers, Web sites, and email addresses.

Abundant Health. Hypoallergenic supplements and personal care products. Phone: 303-422-3175. Web: www.food-allergy.org/oursister.html

All One. A full line of vegetarian multivitamin-mineral supplements in powdered form (three are dairy free; check for specific allergens, including maltodextrin) and a powdered calcium-magnesium supplement. Phone: 800-235-5727. Web: www.all-one.com

Country Life. A full line of vegetarian, hypoallergenic supplements for children and adults, including an adult chewable multi. Phone: 800-645-5768. Web: www.country-life.com

Freeda Vitamins. A wide variety of vegetarian supplements, including a daily vitamin, that are all free of yeast, gluten, lactose, sugar, and salt. Phone: 800-777-3737. Web: www.freedavitamins.com

Futurebiotics. Multivitamin-mineral supplements with herbs; different formulations available. Phone: 800-FOR-LIFE. Web: www.futurebiotics.com/multi.html

KAL. A full line of supplements including a vegetarian multiple. Read labels carefully as some Kal products contain gelatin and/or maltodextrin. Multi-Active and Vegetarian Multiple are vegetarian and hypoallergenic. Phone: 800-733-4525. Web: www.nutraceutical.com/about/kal.cfm

Kirkman. Specially formulated hypoallergenic line of supplements, many of which are also vegetarian and free of soy, corn, and starch. Phone: 800-245-8282. Web: www.kirkmanlabs.com

Nature's Life. A full vegetarian, hypoallergenic supplement line, including a powdered multi with a rice flour base. Phone: 800-247-6997. Web: www.natlife.com

NuLife. (Ontario, Canada) A wide range of formulations for different age and gender groups; most supplements are hypoallergenic and vegetarian. Phone: 800-668-0066. Web: www.nulifevitamins.com

Nutricology. Adult and children's multiple, specially formulated for the highly sensitive individual. Phone: 800-545-9960. Web: www.nutricology.com

Pangea's VeganLife Multivitamin. Multivitamins-minerals with or without iron, and with extra vitamin B_{12}. Phone: 800-340-1200. Web: www.pangeaveg.com

Prescription 2000. Daily multivitamin/mineral. (Check for specific allergens) Phone: 866-88-VEGAN. Web: www.veganessentials.com

Quest. (UK) A full line of hypoallergenic, vegetarian supplements, including multinutrients and other formulations. Phone: +44(0)121 359 0056. Web: www.questvitamins.co.uk

SISU. (Vancouver, Canada) SISU Multi Expecting; SISU Multi Active. (Note that vitamin E is soy derived.) Phone: 800-663-4163. Web: www.sisuhealth.com

Vegetarian Network Victoria. (Australia) Contact individual companies for hypoallergenic formulations. Web: www.vnv.org.au/Vit&Min.htm

Vegan Society. (U.K.) Provides a way to search for companies (such as Vega Nutritionals) that are registered to use the Vegan Society trademark (designating that a product is absolutely free of animal products and animal allergens). Also provides contact information for individual companies to query about their hypoallergenic formulations. Web: www.vegansociety.com

VegLife. A line of vegetarian, hypoallergenic supplements, with and without iron, and one for children, too (chewable, sweetened with sorbitol). Phone: 800-579-4665. Web: www.nutraceutical.com

Probiotics Supplements

Probiotics are discussed on pages 29–31.

American Health. Chewable, naturally flavored, hypoallergenic probiotic supplements. (Liquid acidophilus contains cow's milk.) Phone: 516-244-2021.

Bluebonnet. Milk-free acidophilus plus FOS, available in powder, chewables, and in vegetable capsules. Phone: 800-580-8866. Web: www.bluebonnetnutrition.com

Country Life. Acidophilus in vegetable capsules. Phone: 800-645-5768. Web: www.country-life.com

Freeda Vitamins. Moredophilus powder (in a soy base), Kala (acidophilus tabs in a soy base). Phone: 800-777-3737. Web: www.freedavitamins.com

Garden of Life. Primal Defense, a blend of probiotics in powder or caplets; Fungal Defense, a probiotic blend plus antifungal. Web: www.gardenoflifeusa.com

Kirkman. Hypoallergenic probiotics including Acidophilus Plus Powder, Pro-Bio Gold (mixed probiotics capsules), Pro-Culture Gold (Lactobacillus rhamnosus), Culturelle with Lactobacillus GG, and others. Phone: 800-245-8282. Web: www.kirkmanlabs.com.

Nature's Answer. Acidophilus and acidophilus plus bifidus, vegetarian, and hypoallergenic. Phone: 800-439-2324. Web: www.naturesanswer.com

Nature's Life. Liquid, milk-free, soy-based acidophilus. Phone: 800-247-6997. Web: www.natlife.com

Nature's Plus. Acidophilus in vegetarian capsules. Phone: 800-525-0200 Web: www.naturesplus.com

New Chapter. Several formulations of mixed probiotics: All-Flora in powder or vegetarian capsules; Bioflora (contains barley) in vegetarian capsules; probiotics mixed with vitamins and minerals. Phone: 800-543-7279. Web: www.newchapter.info

Now Foods. Powdered probiotic (with maltodextrin) and probiotics (acidophilus, bifidus) in vegetarian tabs and capsules. Web: www.nowfoods.com

Nutricology. Specially formulated for those with sensitivities and for those who may not benefit from acidophilus. Products include BifidoLife with L. sporogenes, Gastro Flora, Lactobacillus GG, LactoBlend, SymBiotics with FOS (powder). Phone: 800-545-9960. Web: www.nutricology.com

Quest. (UK) Hypoallergenic and vegetarian Acidophilus Plus. Phone: +44(0)121 359 0056. Web: www.questvitamins.co.uk

Schiff. Hypoallergenic, vegetarian acidophilus tablets. Phone: 800-526-6251. Web: www.schiffvitamins.com

Solaray. Chewable Multidophilus sweetened with sugar alcohols. Phone: 800-579-4665. Web: www.nutraceutical.com.

VegLife: FOS-idophilus. Phone: 800-579-4665. Web: www.nutraceutical.com.

Prebiotics and FOS

Prebiotics are discussed on page 32.

Kal: NutraFlora FOS. Phone: 800-579-4665. Web: www.nutraceutical.com

Now Foods: Inulin Prebiotic FOS and Nutra Flora FOS. Web: www.nowfoods.com

VegLife: Peaceful Prebiotic. Phone: 800-579-4665. Web: www.nutraceutical.com

Calcium Supplements

Multivitamin-mineral supplements provide only a small proportion (typically 5–15 percent) of the recommended intake for calcium. (If they contained more, the pill would be too big to swallow.) Thus an extra calcium supplement may be necessary in addition to the calcium we get from foods and calcium-fortified products. Various calcium compounds have different advantages; however, all are beneficial. Calcium citrate malate is better absorbed than other types of calcium supplements. However, it contains less elemental calcium than some other forms of calcium salts. (Elemental calcium is the portion of the calcium salt that is pure calcium.) For example, calcium carbonate is 40 percent calcium and 60 percent carbonate, while calcium citrate contains only 21 percent calcium. Consequently, we would need to take a greater number of calcium citrate malate tablets than calcium carbonate tablets to get an equal amount of calcium, even though we absorb the mineral more efficiently from calcium citrate malate. Calcium carbonate is absorbed best when taken with food or just after eating, while calcium citrate, lactate, or gluconate are well absorbed anytime.

Omega-3 Fatty Acids Supplements (DHA)

O-Mega-Zen3. Highly unsaturated omega-3 fatty acids in vegetable-based capsules (rather than gelatin capsules). Pangea: 800-340-1200. Web: www.veganstore.com; Vegan Essentials: 866-88-VEGAN. Web: www.veganessentials.com

Books

Abraham, Ellen. *Simple Treats: A wheat-free, dairy-free guide to scrumptious baked goods.* Summertown, TN: Book Publishing Company, 2003.

Barber, Marianne, Maryanne Bartoszek Scott, and Elinor Greenberg. *The Parents Guide to Food Allergies.* New York, NY: Henry Holt and Company, LLC, 2001.

Brostoff, Johnathan and Linda Gamlin. *Food Allergies and Intolerance: A Complete Guide to Their Identification and Treatment.* Rochester, VT: Inner Traditions Intl Ltd., 2000.

Collins, Lisa Cipriano. *Caring for Your Child with Severe Food Allergies: Emotional Support and Practical Advice from a Parent Who's Been There.* New York, NY: John Wiley, 2000.

Emsley, John and Peter Fell. *Was It Something You Ate: Food Intolerance, What Causes It and How to Avoid It.* New York, NY: Oxford University Press, Inc., 1999.

Joneja, Janice Vickerstaff. *Dealing with Food Allergies: A Practical Guide to Detecting Culptrit Foods and Eating a Healthy, Enjoyable Diet.* Boulder: Bull Publishing Co., 2003.

Joneja, Janice Vickerstaff, *Digestion, Diet and Disease: Irritable Bowel Syndrome and Gastrointestinal Function.* Rutgers University Press, 2004.

Koerner, Celide Barnes and Anne Munoz-Furlong. *Food Allergies.* New York, NY: John Wiley and Sons Inc., 1998.

Metcalf, Dean, A. Sampson, Ronald Simon, R.M. Christie, Hugh Sampson. *Food Allergy: Adverse Reactions to Foods and Food Additives.* Blackwell Publishing, 2003.

Wedman-St Louis, Betty. *Living with Food Allergies: A Complete Guide to a Healthy Lifestyle.* Lincolnwood, IL: Contemporary Books, 1999.

Willingham, Theresa. *Food Allergy Field Guide: A Lifestyle Manual for Families.* Littleton, CO: Savory Palate, 2000.

Other Publications

A: The New Lifestyle Magazine for People with Allergies. www.allergymagazine.com

Living Without Magazine. www.livingwithout.com

Software

Food allergy and intolerance software: www.allergyadvisor.com

Table 4.1: Food Diary Form

Date: _____

Time	Food Eaten, Supplements, Medications (be as specific as possible)	Portion Size	Feelings/Symptoms	Notes

APPENDIX A: DIETARY REFERENCE INTAKES FOR VITAMINS*

Life Stage, Age, Gender	Vit A[a] (mcg)	Vit C (mg)	Vit D[b] (mcg)	Vit E (mg)	Vit K (mcg)	Thiamin (mg)	Riboflavin (mg)	Niacin[c] (mg)	Vit B6 (mg)	Folate[d] (mcg)	Vit B12[e] (mcg)	Pantothenic Acid (mg)	Biotin (mcg)	Choline (mg)[g]
INFANTS														
0–6 months	400	40	5	4	2.0	0.2	0.3	2	0.1	65	0.4	1.7	5	125
7–12 months	500	50	5	5	2.5	0.3	0.4	4	0.3	80	0.5	1.8	6	150
CHILDREN														
1–3 years	**300**	**15**	**5**	**6**	**30**	**0.5**	**0.5**	**6**	**0.5**	**150**	**0.9**	**2**	**8**	**200**
4–8 years	**400**	**25**	**5**	**7**	**55**	**0.6**	**0.6**	**8**	**0.6**	**200**	**1.2**	**3**	**12**	**250**
MALES														
9–13 years	**600**	**45**	**5**	**11**	**60**	**0.9**	**0.9**	**12**	**1.0**	**300**	**1.8**	**4**	**20**	**375**
14–18 years	**900**	**75**	**5**	**15**	**75**	**1.2**	**1.3**	**16**	**1.3**	**400**	**2.4**	**5**	**25**	**550**
19–30 years	**900**	**90**	**5**	**15**	**120**	**1.2**	**1.3**	**16**	**1.3**	**400**	**2.4**	**5**	**30**	**550**
31–50 years	**900**	**90**	**5**	**15**	**120**	**1.2**	**1.3**	**16**	**1.3**	**400**	**2.4**	**5**	**30**	**550**
51–70 years	**900**	**90**	**10**	**15**	**120**	**1.2**	**1.3**	**16**	**1.7**	**400**	**2.4[h]**	**5**	**30**	**550**
>70 years	**900**	**90**	**15**	**15**	**120**	**1.2**	**1.3**	**16**	**1.7**	**400**	**2.4[h]**	**5**	**30**	**550**
FEMALES														
9–13 years	**600**	**45**	**5**	**11**	**60**	**0.9**	**0.9**	**12**	**1.0**	**300**	**1.8**	**4**	**20**	**375**
14–18 years	**700**	**65**	**5**	**15**	**75**	**1.0**	**1.0**	**14**	**1.2**	**400[i]**	**2.4**	**5**	**25**	**400**
19–30 years	**700**	**75**	**5**	**15**	**90**	**1.1**	**1.1**	**14**	**1.3**	**400[i]**	**2.4**	**5**	**30**	**425**
31–50 years	**700**	**75**	**5**	**15**	**90**	**1.1**	**1.1**	**14**	**1.3**	**400[i]**	**2.4**	**5**	**30**	**425**
51–70 years	**700**	**75**	**10**	**15**	**90**	**1.1**	**1.1**	**14**	**1.5**	**400**	**2.4[h]**	**5**	**30**	**425**
>70 years	**700**	**75**	**15**	**15**	**90**	**1.1**	**1.1**	**14**	**1.5**	**400**	**2.4[h]**	**5**	**30**	**425**
PREGNANCY														
18 years	**750**	**80**	**5**	**15**	**75**	**1.4**	**1.4**	**18**	**1.9**	**600[j]**	**2.6**	**6**	**30**	**450**
19–30 years	**770**	**85**	**5**	**15**	**90**	**1.4**	**1.4**	**18**	**1.9**	**600[j]**	**2.6**	**6**	**30**	**450**
31–50 years	**770**	**85**	**5**	**15**	**90**	**1.4**	**1.4**	**18**	**1.9**	**600[j]**	**2.6**	**6**	**30**	**450**
LACTATION														
18 years	**1,200**	**115**	**5**	**19**	**75**	**1.4**	**1.6**	**17**	**2.0**	**500**	**2.8**	**7**	**35**	**550**
19–30 years	**1,300**	**120**	**5**	**19**	**90**	**1.4**	**1.6**	**17**	**2.0**	**500**	**2.8**	**7**	**35**	**550**
31–50 years	**1,300**	**120**	**5**	**19**	**90**	**1.4**	**1.6**	**17**	**2.0**	**500**	**2.8**	**7**	**35**	**550**

*Recommended Dietary Allowances (RDAs) are in **bold type** and Adequate Intakes (AIs) are in regular type. Both RDA and AI can be used as goals for individual intake. Source: Food and Nutrition Board, The Institute of Nutrition, National Academies of Sciences. All Dietary Reference Intake reports can be accessed free at www.nap.edu (Search for "Dietary Reference Intakes" and several books will be shown—all can be opened online and read free of charge).

a Vitamin A as retinal activity equivalents (RAEs). 1 RAE = 1 µg retinol; 12 µg beta-carotene, 24 µg other pro-vitamin A carotenoids in foods.

b Vitamin D—1 µg cholecalciferol = 40 IU vitamin D. Note that requirement for vitamin D_2 (which is the non-animal form) may be increased by about 65%.

c Niacin as niacin equivalents (NE). 1 mg of niacin = 60 mg tryptophan; 0-6 months must receive preformed niacin, not NE.

d Folate as dietary folate equivalents (DFE). 1 DFE = 1 µg food folate = 0.6 µg of folic acid from fortified food or supplement consumed with food, or 0.5 µg of supplement consumed on an empty stomach.

e Vitamin B_{12}—10–30 percent of people 50 years and above malabsorb vitamin B_{12}; thus they are advised to meet the RDA using B_{12} fortified foods or supplements.

APPENDIX B: DIETARY REFERENCE INTAKES FOR MINERALS

Life Stage, Age, Gender	Calcium (mg)	Chromium (mcg)	Copper (mcg)	Fluoride (mg)	Iodine (mcg)	Iron (mg)	Magnesium (mg)	Manganese (mg)	Molybdenum (mcg)	Phosphorus (mg)	Selenium (mcg)	Zinc (mg)
INFANTS												
0–6 months	210	0.2	200	0.01	110	0.27	30	0.003	2	100	15	2
7–12 months	270	5.5	220	0.5	130	11	75	0.6	3	275	20	3
CHILDREN												
1–3 years	**500**	**11**	**340**	**0.7**	**90**	**7**	**80**	**1.2**	**17**	**460**	**20**	**3**
4–8 years	**800**	**15**	**440**	**1**	**90**	**10**	**130**	**1.5**	**22**	**500**	**30**	**5**
MALES												
9–13 years	**1,300**	**25**	**700**	**2**	**120**	**8**	**240**	**1.9**	**34**	**1,250**	**40**	**8**
14–18 years	**1,300**	**35**	**890**	**3**	**150**	**11**	**410**	**2.2**	**43**	**1,250**	**55**	**11**
19–30 years	**1,000**	**35**	**900**	**4**	**150**	**8**	**400**	**2.3**	**45**	**700**	**55**	**11**
31–50 years	**1,000**	**35**	**900**	**4**	**150**	**8**	**420**	**2.3**	**45**	**700**	**55**	**11**
51–70 years	**1,200**	**30**	**900**	**4**	**150**	**8**	**420**	**2.3**	**45**	**700**	**55**	**11**
>70 years	**1,200**	**30**	**900**	**4**	**150**	**8**	**420**	**2.3**	**45**	**700**	**55**	**11**
FEMALES												
9–13 years	**1,300**	**21**	**700**	**2**	**120**	**8**	**240**	**1.6**	**34**	**1,250**	**40**	**8**
14–18 years	**1,300**	**24**	**890**	**3**	**150**	**15**	**360**	**1.6**	**43**	**1,250**	**55**	**9**
19–30 years	**1,000**	**25**	**900**	**3**	**150**	**18**	**310**	**1.8**	**45**	**700**	**55**	**8**
31–50 years	**1,000**	**25**	**900**	**3**	**150**	**18**	**320**	**1.8**	**45**	**700**	**55**	**8**
51–70 years	**1,200**	**20**	**900**	**3**	**150**	**8**	**320**	**1.8**	**45**	**700**	**55**	**8**
>70 years	**1,200**	**20**	**900**	**3**	**150**	**8**	**320**	**1.8**	**45**	**700**	**55**	**8**
PREGNANCY												
≤18 years	**1,300**	**29**	**1,000**	**3**	**220**	**27**	**400**	**2.0**	**50**	**1,250**	**60**	**13**
19–30 years	**1,000**	**30**	**1,000**	**3**	**220**	**27**	**350**	**2.0**	**50**	**700**	**60**	**11**
31–50 years	**1,000**	**30**	**1,000**	**3**	**220**	**27**	**360**	**2.0**	**50**	**700**	**60**	**11**
LACTATION												
<18 years	**1,300**	**44**	**1,300**	**3**	**290**	**10**	**360**	**2.6**	**50**	**1,250**	**70**	**14**
19–30 years	**1,000**	**45**	**1,300**	**3**	**290**	**9**	**310**	**2.6**	**50**	**700**	**70**	**12**
31–50 years	**1,000**	**45**	**1,300**	**3**	**290**	**9**	**320**	**2.6**	**50**	**700**	**70**	**12**

*Recommended Dietary Allowances (RDAs) are in **bold** type and Adequate Intakes (AIs) are in regular type. Both RDA and AI can be used as goals for individual intake.

Source: Food and Nutrition Board, The Institute of Nutrition, National Academies of Sciences. All Dietary Reference Intake reports can be accessed free at www.nap.edu (Search for "Dietary Reference Intakes" and several books will be shown—all can be opened online and read free of charge).

INDEX

ABOUT THE AUTHORS

Vesanto Melina is a registered dietitian and coauthor of the nutrition classics *The New Becoming Vegetarian* and *Becoming Vegetarian, Becoming Vegan, Raising Vegetarian Children,* and *Healthy Eating for Life to Prevent and Treat Cancer.* She has taught nutrition at Bastyr University in Seattle, Washington, and the University of British Columbia. She is coauthor of the *American Dietetic Association and Dietitians of Canada's Position on Vegetarian Diets (2003)* and *Manual of Clinical Dietetics, 6th edition, 2000.* From her west coast office Vesanto works with patients and clients all over North America. She is a nutrition consultant to major food manufacturers and various levels of government.

Vesanto has first hand experience with her own allergies and those of family members. From adolescence she was hospitalized with lung conditions that continued for several decades, along with continual sinus problems and headaches, until she removed dairy products from her diet. She had atopic eczema in reaction to wheat and eggs, discovered that her lung and skin reactions were stress-related, and became skilled at stress management. She discovered that certain foods (plants in the nightshade family, such as potatoes) trigger symptoms of osteoarthritis. Her son Chris (Xoph) had colic and allergies as a baby and continues to have allergies to tree nuts, several raw fruits, and seafood; however, he survived all this and turned into a wonderfully tall and strong young man. Her friends and neighbors, including many with sensitivities to gluten and lactose, have appreciated being taste-testers for recipes in this book.

Jo Stepaniak is the author of over a dozen books (including *The Ultimate Uncheese Cookbook, Vegan Vittles, The Vegan Sourcebook,* and *Raising Vegetarian Children*) and hundreds of articles on vegetarian cuisine and compassionate living. She has been a vegetarian for more than forty years and a vegan for over half that time. Her own struggles with allergies served as the inspiration for this book and the successful creation of the recipes found herein. Her husband, Michael, has been a tremendous support throughout the process, providing excellent feedback on recipes. Jo has endured and overcome numerous food sensitivities, so she knows firsthand the challenges and frustrations of living with dietary restrictions. One of her greatest gifts to us, and to you, is the versatile baking mix you will find on page 182. With this, those of you with wheat or gluten sensitivities can have your cake and eat it, too (without fear of adverse reactions.) Jo is based in western Pennsylvania; you can visit her Web site at www.vegsource.com/jo.

Dina Aronson is a Boston, Massachusetts, based dietitian whose specialties include chronic disease prevention, vegetarian and vegan nutrition, and lifestyle management. She is the founder and director of NutraWiz.com, a nutrition consulting company. Dina, a nationally recognized writer and speaker, is a coauthor of *Minerals from Plant Foods: Strategies for Maximizing Nutrition* and an editor for the Vegetarian Resource Group's magazine, *Vegetarian Journal*. Her work has appeared in various publications including *Journal of the American Dietetic Association, Today's Dietitian, VegNews, Natural Health,* and *Body & Soul*. Dina has been interviewed for numerous television and radio programs and publications such as *Reader's Digest* and *The Boston Globe*.

Dina regularly consults with groups and individuals—with and without food sensitivities—who want to improve their health and well-being by moving towards a more whole-foods, plant-based diet. She is a consultant for food and nutrition companies, helping them improve effectiveness via creative marketing and evidence-based information. She also gives lectures to various organizations of nutrition professionals and the general public about nutrition and health. Active in many nutrition organizations, Dina is the nutrition advisor for both the Boston Vegetarian Society and for vegfamily.com. She also was the state representative for the Vegetarian Nutrition Dietetic Practice Group for many years. Dina is the recipient of the American Dietetic Association's Recognized Young Dietitian of the Year Award in 2002.

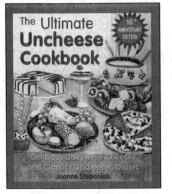

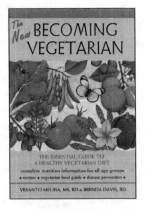
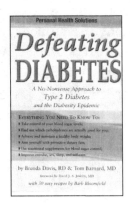